Engaging the Doctrine of Marriage

ENGAGING THE DOCTRINE OF MARRIAGE

*Human Marriage as the Image and Sacrament
of the Marriage of God and Creation*

by
MATTHEW LEVERING

CASCADE Books · Eugene, Oregon

ENGAGING THE DOCTRINE OF MARRIAGE
Human Marriage as the Image and Sacrament of the Marriage of God and Creation

Engaging Doctrine Series

Copyright © 2020 Matthew Levering. All rights reserved. Except for brief quotations in critical publications or reviews, no part of this book may be reproduced in any manner without prior written permission from the publisher. Write: Permissions, Wipf and Stock Publishers, 199 W. 8th Ave., Suite 3, Eugene, OR 97401.

Cascade Books
An Imprint of Wipf and Stock Publishers
199 W. 8th Ave., Suite 3
Eugene, OR 97401

www.wipfandstock.com

PAPERBACK ISBN: 978-1-7252-5193-9
HARDCOVER ISBN: 978-1-7252-5194-6
EBOOK ISBN: 978-1-7252-5195-3

Cataloguing-in-Publication data:

Names: Levering, Matthew, author.

Title: Engaging the doctrine of marriage : human marriage as the image and sacrament of the marriage of god and creation / Matthew Levering.

Description: Eugene, OR: Cascade Books, 2019 | Series: Engaging Doctrine | Includes bibliographical references and index.

Identifiers: ISBN 978-1-7252-5193-9 (paperback) | ISBN 978-1-7252-5194-6 (hardcover) | ISBN 978-1-7252-5195-3 (ebook)

Subjects: LCSH: Marriage—Religious aspects—Christianity. | Marriage—History of Doctrines—Christianity. | Sex—Religious aspects—Christianity.

Classification: BT706 .L20 2020 (paperback) | BT706 (ebook)

Manufactured in the U.S.A. 06/19/20

Contents

Preface: The *Engaging the Doctrine* Series | vii
Acknowledgments | xiii

Introduction
THE ESCHATOLOGICAL MARRIAGE | 1

Chapter 1
GOD AND HIS PEOPLE | 27

Chapter 2
IMAGE OF GOD | 62

Chapter 3
ORIGINAL SIN | 89

Chapter 4
CROSS | 111

Chapter 5
PROCREATION AND MUTUAL LOVE | 138

Chapter 6
SACRAMENT | 185

Chapter 7
SOCIAL JUSTICE | 214

CONCLUSION | 248

Bibliography | 257
Index | 293

Preface
The Engaging the Doctrine Series

Having written four volumes of my *Engaging the Doctrine* series, with more to come (God willing), it seems appropriate to offer a brief explanation of what this coordinated set of books aims to accomplish. Put simply, I am attempting to write something of a "dogmatics." Yet this term, as applied to my *Engaging the Doctrine* series, may need to be kept in scare quotes. The term "dogmatics," of course, conjures up the great achievements of past theologians who organized and presented synthetically the entirety of Christian doctrine.

The fact that I cannot claim to be in their company has always been clear to me but has recently been brought home still more clearly by reading the nineteenth-century Catholic theologian Matthias Joseph Scheeben's introduction to his multi-volume dogmatics. Let me describe it briefly here. Scheeben announces his plan "to give, in a compact, strictly scientific form, a presentation of the entire content of dogmatic theology that is as complete and thorough, clear and synoptic as possible, so as to offer to everyone interested in a solid, rich, and living knowledge of divine truth a resource."[1] Scheeben goes on to say that the pages of his dogmatics will "reproduce as completely as possible the entire doctrinal substance of Catholic dogma in the development given to it by the Church's theology," including issues that "are of particular importance for the Christian life or for the circumstances of our time."[2] In addition to this material content (taking up doctrine speculatively but also in its historical development), Scheeben intends that his dogmatics will formally display "a truly organic arrangement and a strictly scientific development of the doctrinal matter, so that precisely this thorough insight into the connection of the individual doctrines with

---

1. Scheeben, *Handbook of Catholic Dogmatics*, xi.
2. Scheeben, *Handbook of Catholic Dogmatics*, xii.

the key ideas and the highest principles might convey the clear and orderly knowledge of the individual topic."[3]

In addition, while Scheeben wants to show how the Church's doctrines arise from Scripture and Tradition, he does not want to "isolate the individual theses as much as readily occurs with the Scholastic method."[4] Instead of moving from thesis to thesis, he wants to "weave them into a whole in a continuous presentation"; and at the same time he wishes fully to incorporate the Scholastic method's "precision in formulating theses, definitions, and arguments."[5] He seeks to combine "the controversial or polemical task of dogmatics" with the declarative, positive, and speculative tasks.[6] While including "metaphysics and speculation" of the highest order, his dogmatics also aims to be fruitful "for spiritual meditation" and to ensure that "the word of God appears as a word full of spirit and life."[7]

Scheeben has already said a lot in the above, but there is more! In his view, every dogmatics should occupy itself with proving that Scripture and Tradition contain the dogmas of the Church and also with understanding these dogmas "in their nature and correlation, in their cause and effects," and in all the ways that they can be developed.[8] Thus, he separates dogmatics from practical disciplines such as moral theology, ascetic theology, mystical theology, and pastoral theology, and also from historical disciplines such as biblical exegesis, history of doctrine, history of the liturgy, history of the Councils, and history of the saints. The results of the historical disciplines, he argues optimistically, "should serve to prove or to clarify dogmas" and should be informed by the conclusions of dogmatics.[9] He notes that the practical disciplines will partly "be treated in dogmatics itself," given that "God's supernatural activity in the kingdom of grace is so intimately intertwined with man's moral activity that without consideration of the latter it cannot be depicted at all."[10]

Scheeben clearly knew what he was doing in approaching his dogmatics. By contrast, I have stumbled into my more modest and limited task. Even so, in my fashion, I too seek to offer a relatively comprehensive "dogmatics."[11]

3. Scheeben, *Handbook of Catholic Dogmatics*, xii.
4. Scheeben, *Handbook of Catholic Dogmatics*, xiii.
5. Scheeben, *Handbook of Catholic Dogmatics*, xiii.
6. Scheeben, *Handbook of Catholic Dogmatics*, xii.
7. Scheeben, *Handbook of Catholic Dogmatics*, xv.
8. Scheeben, *Handbook of Catholic Dogmatics*, 6.
9. Scheeben, *Handbook of Catholic Dogmatics*, 4–5.
10. Scheeben, *Handbook of Catholic Dogmatics*, 5.
11. Admittedly, many themes touched upon in the volumes of my series receive

PREFACE

The present book, *Engaging the Doctrine of Marriage*, builds upon the three previous volumes of the series: *Engaging the Doctrine of Revelation* (2014), *Engaging the Doctrine of the Holy Spirit* (2016), and *Engaging the Doctrine of Creation* (2017).[12] I envision these dogmatic volumes as an ordered series.

In the first three volumes, my argument broadly runs as follows. The Trinity has revealed himself through the missions of the Son and Spirit, and this divine revelation is faithfully mediated to us through Scripture and Tradition and in a preeminently liturgical context. In the face of diverse controversies, and enriched by liturgical and theological contemplation, the Church enters more deeply into the apostolic deposit of faith and teaches authoritatively on matters that previously had not been fully understood: this is what is meant by "development of doctrine," and under the guidance of the Holy Spirit a rupture—i.e. the Church's rejection of a definitively taught truth of faith—is not possible (volume 1).

At the source of Christian faith is the holy Trinity, three divine Persons who are one God. I suggest that theologians should articulate the mystery of the Trinity by beginning with the Holy Spirit, without neglecting the Father (who will be at the center of my final volume, on eschatology) and the Son (who will be at the center of my volume on the mysteries of Jesus Christ). Debates over the Spirit expose the fundamental fault lines in post-Nicene Trinitarian theology: the inner-Trinitarian *taxis*, the relevance of the analogy from the interior processions of the mind, and the *filioque*. While I hold that the *filioque* is true and is an important part of illuminating the mystery of the Trinity, I do not thereby think that the Orthodox have abandoned Trinitarian faith (by no means!) since the affirmations sought in the formulation of the *filioque* can be affirmed in other ways. The relationship of the Spirit to the incarnate Word and to the one, holy, catholic, and apostolic Church is examined in the same theological movement. After treating pneumatological Christology and ecclesiology (including the life of grace and virtue), I focus upon the unity and holiness of the Church because it seems to me that these two aspects are most contested today, given the *prima facie* evidence that Christians are profoundly divided and that the Church evinces grave moral corruption (volume 2).

Turning to the doctrine of creation, I begin anew with the triune God. I argue first that the freedom of the Trinity to create is not impeded by the eternity of the divine ideas—namely, by the fact that the eternal God knows what he creates in the Word. Nor is the divine simplicity imperiled by God's

---

fuller treatment elsewhere in my writings. Therefore, I do not wish to draw a *sharp* separation between this series and my other published writings.

12. See Levering, *Engaging the Doctrine of Revelation*; Levering, *Engaging the Doctrine of the Holy Spirit*; Levering, *Engaging the Doctrine of Creation*.

free creative act, because even through the divine will to create is free, it is not a different act from the simple, eternal divine Act. After treating the image of God and the innumerable controversies surrounding how to identify it properly, I turn to the vast profusion of creatures over time and space. Given that the human *imago* is central, why should God create dinosaurs, black holes, and the like? I argue that this is what we should expect from the infinite ways in which the Trinity can be participated in finite modes. God loves to express his infinite being through the unfathomable riches of the cosmos. At the same time, the cosmos is not eternal and so all creatures, and the cosmos itself, are subject to decay and deficiencies: the cosmos cannot be mistaken for God. Given the rapid rise in human population, I address the view that the Earth now has too many people. I argue further that evolutionary theory does not render otiose the doctrine of the fall of the first human "images" of God. As I show, there is no need to abandon the doctrines of either creation or fall due to the valuable insights of modern science. Lastly, I suggest that the doctrine of creation should instruct us in our reflection upon why God sent his Son to die upon a cross. Creation is a profoundly relational order, and sin (preeminently original sin) wounds this relational order and establishes humans in a state of injustice in which they owe the punishment of death, a punishment that is intrinsic to turning away from the Life-giver. Christ redeems the world by freely bearing this penalty of death out of supreme love for each and every sinner (volume 3).

The present volume, then, continues the trajectory of the first three volumes by arguing that the purpose of creation is the marriage of God and his people. Creation is properly understood in the light of its goal. Marriage has a crucial signifying role in the economy of creation and redemption. I explore the eschatological marriage of the triune God and his people and also the ways in which Christian sacramental marriage even now "is a great mystery . . . in reference to Christ and the Church" (Eph 5:32).

Like Scheeben, I believe that the central source of Catholic theology is Scripture as mediated in Tradition, with a central role for the Fathers and the medieval schoolmen (above all Thomas Aquinas, for various reasons). As Scheeben did, I also engage a wide range of more recent theologians who have contributed in important ways to dogmatic conversations. In my view, Catholic dogmatics now also needs to include the following elements: a fairly extensive engagement with historical-critical biblical exegesis; ecumenical exchange for the purpose of mutual enrichment and critique; and engagements with the natural sciences and the social sciences where they touch upon doctrinal realities. Appreciation for the insights of the great mystical theologians needs also to be present.

PREFACE

While the unfolding of the volumes should follow a defensible rationale, I consider it appropriate to address related topics without waiting for those topics to appear in the dogmatic order of the volumes. For example, I included in *Engaging the Doctrine of Revelation* a discussion of the Trinitarian missions as the fount of divine revelation. That book also contains discussions of liturgy and ordained priesthood as components of the mediation of divine revelation, although I expect to treat the liturgy and the sacrament of holy order much more fully in later volumes. Likewise, *Engaging the Doctrine of the Holy Spirit* is largely devoted to Trinitarian theology with a focus on the Holy Spirit, but I also explored aspects of Christology, ecclesiology, and the moral life. Again, *Engaging the Doctrine of Creation* treated not only creation, but also central aspects of the doctrine of God, as well as original sin and Christ's cross viewed in light of problems that arise from within the doctrine of creation. The present volume on the doctrine of marriage reengages two issues treated in *Engaging the Doctrine of Creation*: the image of God and original sin, now explored from the angle of marriage.

In each volume, I make clear that the contemporary context plays a role in framing the engagement I undertake. *Engaging the Doctrine of Revelation* responds in part to the resurgence of liberal Catholic theology. *Engaging the Doctrine of the Holy Spirit* responds in part to contemporary anti-Augustinian movements in Trinitarian theology and ecclesiology. *Engaging the Doctrine of Creation* responds in part to the "new atheists" who attack the Christian doctrines of creation and fall; in addition, I have in view the environmental movement. In the present book on the doctrine of marriage, my task consists partly in responding to current misunderstandings or explicit rejections (not least among Catholics) of the requisite elements of Christian marriage.

One final note: in all the *Engaging the Doctrine* volumes, chapters may read like extended surveys of other people's writings. I choose a few particular authors to engage and spend a large amount of space summarizing their work. It may seem that my own voice gets a bit lost. However, there is a method to this approach. In classical dialogues, the opposing viewpoints were presented through the voices of advocates of the distinct positions; and in the work of my teacher Thomas Aquinas, quotations abound. By means of careful selection of texts to explore in each of the chapters, I seek to convey the basic alternatives in the doctrinal debates I am engaging. I strive to develop both the positions I oppose and the positions I support in a manner that avoids the danger of "virtuoso theology"—in which the contribution of a dogmatics is measured by the creativity and rhetorical power of the author. The true theological virtuosos, such as Aquinas, lead us away from such misconceptions by means of ample quotations that instruct us in the sources of our faith and in important ongoing conversations marked by opposing perspectives.

Many thanks to Baker Academic for publishing the first three volumes of this series, and to Cascade for publishing this volume and any other volumes that God enables me to complete.

Acknowledgments

This book arises from gratitude to God for creating marriage in all its dimensions, united by the fact that God creates all things in Christ and for the purpose of everlasting communion. "Great is the Lord and greatly to be praised, in the city of our God!" (Ps 48:1).[1]

Two of my chapters—on the image of God and the Cross—began as the Anthony Jordan Lectures at Newman Theological College in March 2018. What a delight it was to give these lectures and to receive such helpful feedback, not least from NTC's president, Jason West, and dean, Ryan Topping. A version of "Marriage as an Image of the Trinity" appeared in *Ressourcement after Vatican II: Essays in Honor of Joseph Fessio, S.J.*, ed. Nicholas J. Healy, Jr., and Matthew Levering (San Francisco: Ignatius, 2019). Anne Englund Nash's copyediting significantly improved the essay. I have incorporated her edits into the version that appears as chapter 2 of the present book.

Perry Cahall read the entire manuscript and offered numerous suggestions for improvement. I am greatly in his debt. For readers looking for a rich synthetic account of the Catholic Church's understanding of marriage (and sexuality), his book *The Mystery of Marriage* is the book to purchase. My S.T.L. student, Caitlyn Trader, skillfully put together the bibliography. I owe my S.T.D. student Fr. Nick Parker thanks for improving my section on the estimable Catholic philosopher Dietrich von Hildebrand. Many thanks also go to Jason C. Paone, a doctoral candidate in systematic theology at the Catholic University of America. He used the Cascade author's guide to prepare the manuscript for publication, an extensive task, and he also did the index and caught some final typos.

---

1. See Hibbs, "Creation, Gratitude and Virtue," 101–14. See also Bott's point that "[t]he psalmists regard praiseworthiness as a central divine attribute; it belongs to Yahweh's very essence to evoke and receive praise" (Bott, "Praise and Metonymy in the Psalms," 144).

ACKNOWLEDGMENTS

Let me also acknowledge the serendipitous timing of two recent lectures at Mundelein Seminary, one by Helen Alvaré in March and the other by John Cavadini in July. Alvaré's lecture helped me to tie together chapter 7, and Cavadini's lecture did the same for chapter 2. For the privilege of teaching at such a congenial place as Mundelein Seminary, let me especially thank my rector, Fr. John Kartje, and my dean, Fr. Thomas Baima, as well as colleagues such as Dr. Melanie Barrett, Fr. Brendan Lupton, Fr. Emery de Gaál, Dr. Paul Hilliard, Fr. Marek Duran, Fr. Larry Hennessey, and many others who have encouraged my projects. The encouragement that I have received from colleagues at the Seminary has been amplified by Jim and Molly Perry, who graciously endowed the chair that I am privileged to hold. Without their support—and now their friendship as well—much of my work would not have been possible.

Dave Nelson generously read the manuscript and, in addition to encouragement, provided the subtitle. The editor who brought this volume—and, if all goes as planned (God willing), future ones—to Cascade is my longtime friend Michael Thomson. He believed in the value of this volume and in the *Engaging the Doctrine* series as a whole. Even if he hadn't, I would still be in his debt for numerous good Thai lunches over the years. Rodney Clapp shepherded the manuscript through the production process, saving me from some embarrassing errors.

My parents, Ralph and Patty Levering, had a wonderful marriage that lasted over fifty-two years. Sadly, during the writing of this book my beloved mom died at age seventy-three. God be praised for the many graces that she received in her last weeks and months, and for the time she had to surrender herself to God and to say goodbye to more than one hundred friends and family members. I owe deep thanks to my parents for their example and for the love and care they have given to me. I am blessed with an amazing wife, Joy Moretz Levering. Everyone who knows us knows that her love, intelligence, hard work, and gracious attitude are the reason why our family functions. The following words of Sirach apply so well to her: "He will lean on her and will not fall, and he will rely on her and will not be put to shame" (Sir 15:4). I dedicate this book to my most wonderful Joy, praying to Jesus Christ for everlasting blessings upon her and our beloved children.

INTRODUCTION
The Eschatological Marriage

The fundamental purpose of creation—that for which all things were created—is the marriage of God and humankind and, through humankind as microcosm, the marriage of God and the entire cosmos. When Christians today think of marriage, we tend to think in contemporary cultural terms of an intimate partnership that has legal status involving mutual benefits. Our theologies of marriage are often thin doctrinally; we reserve thought about marriage mainly to moral issues. In fact, the doctrine of marriage must center upon the purpose for which God created the whole cosmos, namely, the "mystical marriage"[1] of God and creation. It will then be seen that marriage is not solely about sacramental and moral issues—though it is about these—but also involves and illuminates the doctrines of the Trinity, original sin, and the Cross, as part of illuminating the full mystery of Trinitarian creation, fall, redemption, and deification.

Support in this regard comes from Jewish scholars. Rabbi Jonathan Sacks remarks, "God is a husband and we are his wife."[2] The Jewish biblical scholar Jon D. Levenson says the same, in view of the interpretation of Israel's Scriptures. Regarding "the marriage metaphor of the prophets and the poems of erotic longing in the Song of Songs," he urges that we must learn that God's relationship to his people "is a love simultaneously covenantal and deeply passionate."[3] From a Christian perspective, this will be spelled out in Trinitarian and christological terms, as the whole of creation is guided toward its eschatological consummation. Louis Bouyer comments, "The Church is the Bride, participating by marriage union in all the privileges of her Bridegroom, as being the people of God come to the perfection of the

---

1. Evdokimov, *Orthodoxy*, 102.
2. Sacks, *The Great Partnership*, 172.
3. Levenson, *The Love of God*, 132.

number of the elect ... at the same time as it is mankind (that is, the whole world) brought back to the purity of the primitive design of God for His creation."[4] The plan of God for his creation is the marriage of all of God's people with God in Christ by the Holy Spirit.

Jesus Christ has inaugurated but not yet consummated the marriage of God and creation. This does not mean that human marriage is no longer important. On the contrary, the revelation of the nuptial purpose of creation makes marriages between men and women even more worthy of theological attention. It is necessary to apprehend how Christian marriage and family are—without being superior to consecrated singleness—at the very center of human flourishing. The spiritual writer Heather King, herself unmarried, puts this well: "No matter our age, socioeconomic status, or station, we are called to order our lives to the human family. If we're single, we are called to lay down our lives for other people's children."[5] The eschatological marriage of God and creation does not bypass human families. Christian marriages are signs of the self-surrendering love of Christ. In the sacraments, the Church is directed as Bride toward the Bridegroom who will come in glory at the end of the age. Ideally, as the liturgical theologian Uwe Michael Lang observes, "the whole liturgy is celebrated *obviam Sponso*, facing the Bridegroom. The faithful so anticipate the Lord's Second Coming and can be likened to the virgins in the Gospel parable: 'But at midnight there was a cry, "Behold the bridegroom! Come out to meet him"' (Mt 25:6)."[6]

Given the centrality of the Bridegroom, however, should I have focused first on Jesus Christ rather than on marriage, in the dogmatic order of the present series? After all, according to Scripture, "before the foundation of the world" God "destined us in love to be his sons through Jesus Christ" (Eph 1:4–5); and, moreover, "all things were created through him [Christ] and for him. He is before all things, and in him all things hold together" (Col 1:16–17). He is "the Alpha and the Omega," "the first and the last" (Rev 1:8, 17).[7] As Bonaventure emphasizes, Christ is the goal of God's creative

---

4. Bouyer, *The Meaning of Sacred Scripture*, 198.

5. King, *Ravished*, 80.

6. Lang, *Turning Towards the Lord*, 102, drawing upon Schönborn, *Loving the Church*, 203–6.

7. I am aware that many theologians and biblical scholars today, including many Catholics, allow for *human experience* of the divine but are unable to speak of divine action: see for example Natalie Kertes Weaver's contention that "[w]hen we combine the findings of Scripture scholarship ... we can reasonably conclude that 'revelation' in the Old Testament refers to the Israelites' interpretation of their experience of history as an experience of God working within and directing that history" (Weaver, *Marriage and Family*, 9). Revelation is a properly theocentric concept, even though of course human mediation is always involved.

plan. Speaking in scholastic language about the divine ideas that ground the act of creation and about the *rationes seminales* embedded in creation, Bonaventure concludes that "the highest and noblest perfection cannot exist in this world unless that nature in which the seminal principles are present [the created order], and that nature in which the intellectual principles are present [the soul], and that nature in which the ideal principles are present [God] *are simultaneously brought together in the unity of one person*"—namely, in the incarnate Son, Jesus Christ.[8] If so, it seems that the volume on creation might best be followed by a volume on Christ.

After the present volume, the next two volumes of this series will focus on the doctrines of Israel and Christ. The doctrine of marriage sets the scene by identifying the purpose of creation and the purpose of God's covenantal work in Israel and its Messiah. Erich Przywara remarks that "nuptial love . . . is the fundamental mystery of the Old and New Testaments: from the prophets to the Song of Songs to the gospel of marriage declared by the evangelists from Matthew to John, to the inwardly nuptial theology of the Pauline epistles, and right up to the 'wedding and wedding feast of the Lamb' as the ultimate meaning of Revelation."[9] In inquiring into the goal of creation, it is necessary first and foremost to hear the call to Christ's wedding banquet: "The Spirit and the Bride say, 'Come'" (Rev 22:17).[10] We cannot wait for marriage to appear as a topic within sacramental and moral theology. It should be brought to the front of the line, as the "final cause" of creation and redemption. Thus understood, the doctrine of marriage combines reflection upon the wedding banquet of "Christ the Bridegroom and the Church, his Bride," with a new theological vision of "Christian marriage [as] measured by this highest union."[11]

Not surprisingly, Bonaventure himself appreciates the centrality of the eschatological wedding. Reflecting upon "[t]he steps leading to *sweetness of charity* via the outpouring of the Holy Spirit," he places at the highest point the marriage of God and his people through the Bridegroom Christ.[12] In each step toward the attainment of this goal (through perfect charity), we must "have *firm confidence* in the Groom."[13] We must be inflamed spiritually with desire for union with the Groom (Christ), and through contemplation we should experience God lifting us up to the spiritual "*heights of the*

---

8. Bonaventure, *On the Reduction of the Arts*, 57 (emphasis added).
9. Przywara, *Analogia Entis*, 610.
10. For discussion see Mangina, *Revelation*, 251.
11. Von Balthasar, *The Spirit of Truth*, 343.
12. Bonaventure, *The Triple Way*, 180.
13. Bonaventure, *The Triple Way*, 180.

Groom" so that we can behold interiorly "the *beauty* of the Groom" and rejoice in "the *bounty* of the Groom."[14]

Throughout his reflections, Bonaventure cites the Song of Songs, which for Bonaventure is about Christ's longing for spiritual union with the Church and the Church's longing for spiritual union with Christ. Ultimately, he concludes that we (the bridal Church) must be bound to Christ with "a *bonding strong as cement*, one with the *strength* of the Groom's love."[15] The perfection of our "marriage" with Christ will come from Christ's divine strength, not ours; and yet we will truly be indissolubly bound to Christ, such that we will never renounce our union with him. As John of the Cross makes clear in his hymns (according to Przywara), the purpose of the "chromatic plenitude" of creation is to serve as "an 'image and likeness' of the *one marriage*"—accomplished on the Cross—"in which the totality of creaturely reality is wedded to the 'God who is all in all.'"[16] Here Christian marriage obviously takes on its deepest meaning, but one that is at the same time closely related to the meaning of sacramental marriage.

Thus, to affirm the marriage of God and creation as the very goal of creation, the purpose for which God created the cosmos, does not sideline Christ. On the contrary, Christ is the Bridegroom. Having discussed God's creative work in the previous book of this series, I therefore turn in this book to the purpose of God's creative act: the marriage of God and creation—and so also, more centrally than some previous dogmatics have allowed, the nature and importance of Christian marriage as a sign of the eschatological marriage that Christ has inaugurated.[17]

Christian sacramental marriage bridges creation and redemption. As a created reality, "the good of marriage is intelligible in part precisely as a union of persons sufficiently stable in which to welcome new life and whose acts of bodily communion are *per se aptus* for the generating of new life."[18] When this central element of the created order is forgotten or neglected, as it is by many Catholic theologians today, the result is to compromise both marriage as a created reality *and* marriage as an eschatological sign of the marriage of Christ and the Church. For one thing, as Levenson remarks about biblical Israel and the two lovers in the Song of Songs, "the assumption that there is a significant dichotomy between love for its own sake, on

---

14. Bonaventure, *The Triple Way*, 180.
15. Bonaventure, *The Triple Way*, 181.
16. Przywara, *Analogia Entis*, 611.
17. See also Cloutier, "Composing Love Songs for the Kingdom of God?"
18. Brugger, "Reason's 'Wax Nose,'" 155.

the one hand, and love leading to marriage and children, on the other, is false."[19]

Jesus, Paul, and Human Marriage

Some theologians and biblical scholars today, like the Gnostics, Manichees, and Cathars of old,[20] find in the New Testament a sharp dichotomy between the eschatological marriage of God and humanity, on the one hand, and human marriage, on the other. The former is thought to negate the latter. For example, David Wheeler-Reed holds that in 1 Thessalonians 4 and 1 Corinthians 7, "Paul's advice created a strategy of power that challenged marriage itself"; and Wheeler-Reed also thinks that the Gospels of Matthew and Mark (and perhaps Jesus himself) are "antifamily, antimarriage, antihousehold, and antiprocreation."[21] Given that the kingdom has been inaugurated, all earthly ties have indeed been relativized. But positions such as Wheeler-Reed's, while understandable up to a point, distort the New Testament's testimony. As Brent Waters observes, Jesus "*commends* marriage in prohibiting divorce, insisting that its one-flesh unity embodies a mutual and lifelong fidelity, and his love of children conveys a blessing upon parents. . . . Jesus is calling together the subjects of God's new, universal reign, and familial bonds are condemned only when they prevent, instead of permitting, this more expansive loyalty" to God and his kingdom.[22]

---

19. Levenson, *The Love of God*, 129.

20. See the excellent overview provided by Stoyanov, *The Other God*.

21. Wheeler-Reed, *Regulating Sex in the Roman Empire*, 73, 82. Wheeler-Reed considers that Ephesians and the Pastoral Epistles, all of which he finds to have been written much later, go in the opposite direction. Wheeler-Reed is especially influenced by Dale Martin: see Martin, *Sex and the Single Savior*; Martin, "Familiar Idolatry"; Martin, "Paul Without Passion"; Martin, *New Testament History and Literature*. For a contrary view, see Collins, *What Are Biblical Values?*, 97–98. Collins notes that Jesus "certainly did not reject the institution of marriage for most people," although he goes on to say that in a certain sense at least (and literally at least for some), "Leaving family was the price to be paid for membership in the new community of the kingdom" (*What Are Biblical Values?*, 98, 100).

22. Waters, *The Family*, 9 (emphasis added). See also Bromiley, *God and Marriage*, 38: "Jesus is *for* marriage, not against it. He can be for it, however, only by being against it in the form in which it is attempted by those who do not put the commitment to God first." Commenting on 1 Cor 7, Bromiley adds that Christians must not "absolutize marriage nor anything else that belongs to this passing order," and in this sense "[t]he married, who are tempted to put husband or wife or children first, find greater difficulty in achieving the primary commitment to Christ which lies at the very heart of faith and discipleship" (Bromiley, *God and Marriage*, 59).

Certainly, for Christians awaiting the fullness of the eschatological marriage, marriage and family must not be posited as the ultimate end. Jesus firmly cuts the ground out from under such familial idolatry: "Brother will deliver up brother to death, and the father his child, and children will rise against parents and have them put to death" (Matt 10:21). We sometimes deceive ourselves into thinking that our familial responsibilities stand above all else. In fact, Christians must remember that our primary allegiance is to Christ, keeping in view Christ's words that "whoever does the will of my Father in heaven is my brother, and sister, and mother" (Matt 12:50).

No doubt, then, there is an inevitable tension between the temporal duties and pleasures of family life and bearing witness to the in-breaking of God's new kingdom—but "the tension need not be debilitating" and it should not be exaggerated beyond its real dimensions.[23] The goal of Christians must be nothing less than the eschatological marriage of God and humankind. But along the way, we must be careful not to fall into "false and unfortunate dichotomies."[24] For example, with respect to the "marriage at Cana in Galilee" (John 2:1), the revelation of the inauguration of the kingdom ("the good wine") hardly means that Jesus refused to share in the celebration of the human wedding to which he and his disciples were invited. On the contrary, the eschatological marriage and human marriage (healed and elevated by Jesus) go together, which is why Jesus can say with profound approval, "So they are no longer two but one. What therefore God has joined together, let no man put asunder" (Matt 19:6).[25]

---

23. Waters, *The Family*, 9. Waters also points out that in the first-century context of severe disruption—the context of many of the first hearers of the written Gospels—the tension would be much less. He states, "The teachings against the family are harsh only to an audience that has placed its hope and confidence in a social, economic, and political order derived from stable households" (Waters, *The Family*, 10). Regarding Paul's privileging of singleness, Waters cites Brown, *The Body and Society*, 55–56.

24. Pennington, *The Sermon on the Mount*, 293.

25. For Calum Carmichael, Jesus intends to imply that "marriage is a return to the original androgynous state that God created at the beginning of time" (Carmichael, *Sex and Religion in the Bible*, 9; cf. 102). This argument is not persuasive. Jesus is teaching his disciples about the indissolubility of marriage between a man and a woman. For a similar attempt to get beyond the male-female binary, but from a Greek and Heideggerian philosophical and literary perspective, see Hemming, "Can I Really Count on You?" It seems to me that what Carmichael and Hemming are looking for is simply the unity of men and women as humans. See also the remark of John J. Collins in his *What Are Biblical Values?*, 86: "It has been argued that before the creation of Eve, Adam was undifferentiated, neither male nor female. The argument has a certain logic, but it is undercut by the use of the same word, 'Adam,' for the male *after* the creation of Eve. It is 'the man' (*ha-adam*) who acknowledges Eve as 'flesh of my flesh and bone of my bone' in Genesis 2:23."

INTRODUCTION

The Plan of the Work

The first four chapters of this book lay theological grounding for any Christian understanding of marriage; and the final three chapters explore in more detail the practical and sacramental side of actual Christian marriages. The first chapter explores the "marriage" of God and his people, or Christ and the Church—the consummation of the whole of salvation history. Julie Hanlon Rubio notes that, by comparison to other contemporary understandings of what a wedding should be, "a Catholic wedding has a somewhat different focus, which, if read correctly, yields a theology of marriage built on relationship but rooted in and oriented toward God and community."[26] Emphasizing this distinctive focus, I foreground the marriage of God and creation that stands at the heart of biblical revelation. I don't think that Christian marriage can be understood outside this context.

However, a fundamental question arises at the outset: is the God of Scripture an abuser? Would anyone want to be "married" to the God of Israel, given that, according to Scripture, God treats his bride Israel roughly because of Israel's sins of infidelity? Furthermore, when most people today think of the Bible or the Church, they do not think of an eschatological "marriage." They may think of being redeemed from sin and death, of the liberating power of Christ's teachings, of the need for the grace of the Holy Spirit, and so forth, but not of "marriage."[27] Given this situation, drawing upon Brant Pitre's recent survey, I begin by showing that the biblical story is united by its portrait of a Creator God who wishes to draw his people and the whole creation into a relationship with him so profoundly intimate as to be called marital. Second, I argue that although the biblical narratives use images of marriage drawn from the culture of the ancient Near East and therefore (in the Old Testament) include abusive images—as Gerlinde Baumann and others emphasize—the negative elements are not the heart of the matter.[28] On the contrary, the point is that to be "married" to the true God is to experience a communion of abounding and unending joy, love, and mercy. Given that we are sinners, the analogy must include images of judgment, but the images of superabundant merciful communion stand at

---

26. Rubio, *A Christian Theology of Marriage and Family*, 29.

27. For reflection upon eternal life in terms of the joy of weddings, see McKnight, *The Heaven Promise*, 95–96, 109. For McKnight, admittedly, God resides "[h]igh and lifted up" (*The Heaven Promise*, 109) in his consummated kingdom—an image that does not describe "marital" intimacy.

28. For a similar argument against Baumann, see Levenson, *The Love of God*, chapter 3.

the center of God's merciful plan for giving marriage its full eschatological meaning.

Having established the scriptural and theological centrality of the marriage of God and his people, in chapter 2 I inquire into whether in the marriage of man and woman we find an "image of God" (Gen 1:26–27), as we might expect given the symbolic significance of marriage with regard to our ultimate destiny. If the image of God is found in the marital relationship of the man and the woman, then it seems that single people, including Jesus, would not be in the image of God. (Indeed, even married individuals would not be in the image of God, since they would only be the image of God *as a couple*.) Even so, some theologians, such as Matthias Joseph Scheeben and Pope John Paul II, have taught that the familial conjunction of man, woman, and child provides a valuable image of the Trinity, in its relational difference and fruitfulness. Karl Barth likewise proposes that the man-woman relationship, in its covenant-making relationality, is the "image of God."

In my view, the position of Hans Urs von Balthasar on this topic works best. He argues that the male and female spouses, in their self-surrendering love that is fruitfully generative, give us a rich image of the fruitful generativity and selfless surrender that constitute the Persons of the Trinity. I suggest that even though von Balthasar's understanding of the image requires the complementary insights of Augustinian-Thomistic theologies of the image, nonetheless he is on to something important about how marriage offers an "image of God."[29] In the fruitful self-surrender exemplified by a graced marriage, we perceive the ground for the analogous connection between human marriage and our eschatological sharing in the wondrous depths of the Trinitarian life.

Given that marriage sheds light upon our nuptial communion with God (and upon our nature as created in God's image), chapter 3 pays attention to the fact that marriage is not absent from the act by which the first humans wounded their graced humanity. Does it matter that the first sin was committed by a married couple rather than by an individual human being? Surveying three recent commentaries on Genesis, I identify significant insights but not much attention to the sin of Adam and Eve specifically as a married couple. By contrast, for Ephrem the Syrian, John Chrysostom, and Augustine it greatly matters that the first sinners were a married couple. These Church Fathers perceive that given the purpose of creation—namely the eschatological marriage of God and creation—it makes sense that original sin consist in the fall not merely of individuals but of human solidarity

---

29. Thus I do not agree with the criticisms of the Augustinian doctrine of the *imago* that von Balthasar voices at various places, as for instance in *Truth of God*, 37–43, 85, 161–65.

INTRODUCTION

itself, as found in the intimate communion of the first marriage. Adam and Eve's rebellion against God disrupted their nuptial vocation in more ways than one.

Just as the marital context is important for understanding original sin as the fall of human solidarity, so also the effects of Christ's Cross pertain to marriage. John Piper comments, "Marriage is woven into the wonder of the gospel of the cross of Christ."[30] Of course, a good marriage is not to be equated with the crucifixion of one or both spouses. But today we often minimize the self-sacrificial element required by a good marriage, despite the fact that the New Testament abounds with descriptions of life in Christ that insist upon the necessity of sharing in the Cross. To show how Christian marriage depends upon the Cross of Christ, my fourth chapter turns especially to the writings of Catherine of Siena and Karol Wojtyła (who became Pope John Paul II). These two saints help us to perceive why linking marriage to the redemptive Cross of Christ is not negative toward marriage as though marriage were a cross. Rather, fortified by the spouses cleaving to the Cross of Christ, marriage prepares for and already participates in the eschatological marriage of Christ and his Church. Put simply, as part of the restoration of fallen human solidarity, the spouses must be "configured to Christ's ultimate priestly spousal act of self-donation on Calvary."[31]

The book's final three chapters address practical and sacramental issues that pertain to understanding what Christian marriage is.[32] Chapter

---

30. Piper, *This Momentary Marriage*, 29.

31. Keating, *Remain in Me*, 79. See also the reflections of Wright, "The Christian Spiritual Life and the Family," 189: "The Christian life means treating others as one would like to be treated. It is also a life marked by the capacity for forgiveness. The dynamic pattern of that life is *kenotic*, or self-emptying, as was the life of Jesus. It thus consists of expanding beyond our present, limited capacities for love.... The domestic church is an intimate laboratory in which this *kenotic* pattern can play itself out, if we would but let it. Any parent knows that the advent of a child, even one welcomed with joy, is a stretching, sometimes painful process of growing beyond one's present capacity to love. Love grows as the heart is pried open to welcome a new life. This sort of love is neither generic nor intrinsically self-referential. Rather, parental love, in the majority of people, creates a capacity to care for another in a way that is radically generous, radically new. Sometimes the process feels like 'dying to self' but, if genuinely realized, that dying is in fact a being born into a new, more spacious self, a self whose interest includes, even privileges, another self."

32. Originally, I intended to include one further chapter, on marital indissolubility. That chapter grew into a separate book, *The Indissolubility of Marriage*. In that book, I respond to the approaches to marriage represented well by Bernard Häring's complaints about the formation of *Gaudium et Spes*: see Häring, "Fostering the Nobility of Marriage." Some readers have interpreted the book as a defense of *Amoris Laetitia*. Let me be clear, therefore, that I affirm that *Amoris Laetitia* teaches the doctrine of marital indissolubility and also rightly insists upon the need for compassion toward

5 is about identifying the purposes of marriage, which determine the kind of thing that marriage is or should be. I begin by describing the contrasting paths marked out by Plato and Aristotle. In Plato's *Republic*, Socrates argues that marriage is unnecessary among humans who are truly capable and wise. In his view (although scholars dispute whether Plato intends for us to take him literally), the best class of men and women should avoid marriage. Instead, they should have multiple sexual partners and should rely upon communal child-raising, so that parents will not know their children and vice versa. Socrates opposes marriage partly because it often elevates private family interests over the common good of the city. Aristotle strongly rejects Plato's view and insists upon the goodness of marriage, especially for child-raising.

In light of these two contrasting perspectives, I discuss the "goods" and "ends" of marriage, as set forth by Augustine and John Chrysostom. I then turn to the more recent viewpoints of the Catholic scholars Dietrich von Hildebrand and Cormac Burke. Von Hildebrand proposes to distinguish the "primary meaning" of marriage (mutual love) from its "primary end" (procreation). For his part, Burke argues that procreation and the "good of the spouses" are two equal ends that should not be hierarchically ordered. In response to von Hildebrand and Burke, I contend—in accord with Aristotle and with the earlier Catholic tradition—that marriage has as its *primary* end (which cannot be distinguished from a "primary meaning") the procreation and raising of children. As Donald Wallenfang puts it, "rooted in the intrinsic differences between male and female (and the procreative potential

---

people whose sacramental marriages have failed and who are in a new civil marriage without annulment. But I think that there are formulations and theological arguments in *Amoris Laetitia* that are not adequate to the doctrine of the indissolubility of marriage. Furthermore, the new pastoral strategy regarding Eucharistic communion runs counter to the reality of marital indissolubility, as I show in the book. In favor of the view that knowingly violating the bonds of an indissoluble marriage should not necessarily be an impediment to Eucharistic communion in charity, a view that is mistaken, see also Cantalamessa, *The Gaze of Mercy*, 73. Cantalamessa's arguments are uncharacteristically simplistic. For a representative argument against marital indissolubility, see Lawler, *Marriage and Sacrament*, 75–97, 104–11. See also Lawler's *Marriage and the Catholic Church*, 103–4, where he argues, along surprisingly ultramontanist lines, that there is "a more-than-human power in the Church to dissolve a failed ratified and consummated marriage.... There is a power in that Church [the Catholic Church] that extends to the binding and loosing of sin and to the transformation of bread and wine. That momentous power surely extends also to the reformation of a reformable doctrine the Church itself inaugurated. If a non-consummated marriage between baptized believers, that is, a sacramental marriage which falls under God's law, 'can be dissolved by the Roman Pontiff for a just reason' (Can 1142), a ratified and consummated marriage which falls under the Church's law can also be dissolved by the Roman Pontiff for a similarly just reason."

INTRODUCTION

dependent upon these differences by nature), the basic concept of marriage signifies one man and one woman bound together for life to become husband and wife, father and mother."[33]

In chapter 6, I take up the question of whether marriage truly is a sacrament instituted by Christ and intended to be one of seven sacraments of the Church. The Protestant Reformers rejected the Catholic (and Orthodox) view that marriage is a sacrament in this sense. Recently, Catholic scholars have also begun to call into question marriage's status as a sacrament. As an example of this viewpoint, I examine the Catholic historian Philip Reynolds's claim that in the twelfth century the Church invented the sacrament of marriage. Since a major part of the contemporary debate has to do with the question of doctrinal development, the chapter's second section explores New Testament resources for thinking about doctrinal development, including the question of why Christ does not simply teach everything clearly from the outset. Third, I examine two extended historical-theological arguments in favor of the Church's teaching that marriage is a sacrament, by Edward Schillebeeckx (writing in 1961) and Peter Elliott (writing in 1987). These authors hold that the key elements of marriage's status as a sacrament are already in place in the New Testament, where it is clear that Jesus wills to heal and elevate the created reality of marriage within the supernatural order of grace. Schillebeeckx and Elliott help us to see that the Church's twelfth-century affirmation of marriage as one of the seven sacraments did not simply come out of nowhere but rather represents an authentic development of Christian doctrine.

Having addressed the purposes of marriage and its location within the sacramental mediation of grace, my seventh and final chapter addresses the question of whether Christian marriage is actually good, either for the spouses themselves or for the just ordering of society. After beginning the chapter by examining the pro-marriage emphasis of the African American pastor Christopher Brooks and the social-justice concerns of Ta-Nehisi Coates, I treat a number of scholarly criticisms of Christian marriage. I also examine efforts to do without marriage (or at least without male-female marriage), such as when single women or homosexual couples choose to have a child by means of sperm donation or surrogacy.[34] As a counterpoint

---

33. Wallenfang, *Metaphysics*, 48–49.

34. In my *Aquinas's Eschatological Ethics*, I take up this issue a bit further in discussing chastity. The Evangelical theologian John K. Tarwater has aptly pointed out, "Scripture presents two main purposes of our sexuality, to be united and to generate. Following both creation accounts in Genesis, God enunciates the two purposes. First, he commands the couple to 'Be fruitful and multiply' (Gen 1:28). Second, God says that 'Therefore a man shall leave his father and mother and be joined to his wife, and they

to these critiques of or end-runs around Christian marriage, I survey in some detail the arguments of the *Compendium of the Social Doctrine of the Church*, the sociologist David Popenoe, and the legal scholar Helen Alvaré. I argue that the presence of a father and a mother in the home—the establishment of stable families in which children are raised by their biological parents—is fundamental to the pursuit of social justice and the good of individuals and families. Without this foundation, the ability of persons and societies to participate in the eschatological marriage is deeply wounded, since the wounds caused by injustice impede the blossoming of selfless love, even though the merciful grace of the gospel can overcome these wounds.

These final three chapters are interrelated. The loss of awareness that procreation is the primary end or purpose of male-female marriage has assisted in the disintegration of marriage itself as a common practice. Even in places where divorce rates are relatively low, couples often do without marriage and so do not benefit from the sacrament of marriage healing and elevating their union within the order of grace. Generally, couples in Westernized countries are having few children. Lifetime relationships are rarer. Feelings of loneliness and despair, as well as violence related to family breakdown and to the lack of a father in the home, are more prominently expressed in the culture. Christian faith has spiraled downward in areas where marriage and children are disappearing.[35] There is a relationship between recognizing procreation as the primary "end" of marriage (chapter 5), valuing marriage as a sacrament at least in some sense (chapter 6), and perceiving marriage's powerful contribution to social justice (chapter 7).

Lisa Sowle Cahill contends that "[f]or contemporary Christians, as for most members of modern society, the highest meaning of marriage, and its only really indispensable one, is love."[36] This may be true as a description of

---

shall become one flesh' (Gen 2:24).... In his discussion with the Pharisees concerning divorce, Jesus linked these two creation mandates, procreation and unity" (Tarwater, *Marriage as Covenant*, 104–5).

35. See Eberstadt, *How the West Really Lost God*.

36. Cahill, *Sex, Gender, and Christian Ethics*, 193. See more fully Cahill, *Sex, Gender, and Christian Ethics*, 193–94, quoting Kasper, *Theology of Christian Marriage*, 30. See also the cognate view of marriage offered by Porter, "Contraceptive Use and the Authority of the Church." For the development in marital practice (in Europe) in the medieval period, see Goody, *The Development of the Family and Marriage in Europe*; Herlihy, *Medieval Households*. See also the remarks of d'Avray regarding medieval marriage sermons: "The marriage mysticism of [thirteenth-century] model sermons was of a different kind from the Bernardine [monastic] sort: more matter-of-fact, less high-flown, less about brides and bridegrooms and more about wives and husbands" (*Medieval Marriage Sermons*, 2). For further discussion, see d'Avray, *Medieval Marriage*; d'Avray, *Papacy, Monarchy and Marriage*; Brooke, *Medieval Idea of Marriage*; Parmisano, *The Craft of Love*.

INTRODUCTION

modern Christians, but to suppose that *only* mutual "love" is "indispensable" to—or even necessarily the "highest meaning" of—a Christian marriage is to have forgotten its roots in a self-surrendering fruitfulness that, while profoundly loving, goes well beyond what moderns mean by "love." Marriages that lack mutual love can still be fruitful in all sorts of important ways. This is not to deny, of course, that abuse may and often will require a permanent separation of the couple.

Moreover, there is a strong relationship between understanding the more "practical" dimensions of marriage (chapters 5–7) and understanding marriage's theological role in the economy of salvation, including in our imaging of the triune God's selfless fruitfulness (chapter 2), our distorting of the human *imago* (chapter 3), and the action of Christ's Cross in the healing and perfecting of the spouses (chapter 4). At a still deeper level, there is a relationship between all these dimensions of Christian marriage and the accomplishment of the purpose for which God created: the marriage of God and creation (chapter 1). As Robert Jenson says, "there is one woman and one man in the new one flesh *in that* there is one Israel and one divine bridegroom, one church and one Christ; both unities are aspects of the same mystery."[37] Put simply: unless we understand the marriage of God and creation, we will not understand Christian marriage in its fullness; and, conversely, unless we understand Christian marriage, we will not understand the marriage of God and creation.

---

37. Jenson, *The Triune Story*, 331. As Jenson puts it earlier, "[T]he analogy between the Lord's relation to Israel and conjugal love appears early and often in Israel's Scripture. But now, if the sexual relation of spouses can provide an analogy for the Lord's relation to Israel, the analogy must have some impact also the other way around. And in that direction it will open as a moral opportunity: the sexual relation of spouses can be modeled on the relation of the Lord and Israel" (*Triune Story*, 280). This means that self-surrendering love and the healing power of the Cross will come into play, as will the fact that God's fallen people fell, in Adam and Eve, as a primordial marital communion of persons. Indeed, this relationality belongs to the order of creation. Jenson states, "Our creation as two different kinds of bodies, paired to each other by the paired shape and function of blatant bodily phenomena, is the way God keeps our reality as *communal* beings from being a mere mandate or ideal, and makes it be a fact about the actual things we are" (*The Triune Story*, 281). Or, put more bluntly, "it is as bodies inescapably ordered to each other by vagina and penis that our adaptation to correspondence with the himself communal [i.e. triune] God is made part of what we simply and without choice *are*. . . . There are of course other bonds of mutuality, most of them also in one way or another bodily. But marriage is the only one that creates an actual new bodily unit—the old myth of the creature with two backs who was forcibly divided to make woman and man rested on simple observation. The two bodies envelop and enter each other in a fashion provided for not only by shape but by their function beyond pleasure, the function of this orifice and this member of maintaining God's human creation" (*The Triune Story*, 282).

What about Our Royal Priesthood?

Before proceeding to the chapters, however, let me raise the question of whether the eschatological marriage really is the purpose for which God created human beings. After all, Richard Middleton remarks that when God creates humans in Genesis 1, God himself identifies his purpose: humans are to rule over the earth as God's stewards. Thus Genesis 1:26 states, "Then God said, 'Let us make man in our image, after our likeness; and *let them have dominion* over the fish of the sea, and over the birds of the air, and over the cattle, and over all the earth, and over every creeping thing that creeps upon the earth' [emphasis added]." Middleton notes that the verb for "let them have dominion" or "let them rule" is repeated in Genesis 1:28.[38] For Middleton, as for many scholars, royal rule is the purpose for which God created humans. He explains that "the sort of power or rule that humans are to exercise is generous, loving power. It is power used to nurture, enhance, and empower others, noncoercively, for *their* benefit, not for the self-aggrandizement of the one exercising power."[39] He also emphasizes that all humans are intended to exercise this royal rule, because all humans are God's images. The Orthodox theologian Vladimir Lossky likewise observes, "In the context of the sacerdotal narrative of Genesis, the creation of man 'in the image' of God confers on human beings a dominion over the animals analogous to that which God enjoys over the whole of his creation."[40]

In line with Middleton's perspective, N. T. Wright argues that through "God's supreme act of new creation," all of the ways in which Christians have reigned by wisdom and love in this life will become part of the recreated world.[41] In the new creation, humans will finally fulfill the mandate that God gave from the beginning: to reign over the earth as royal stewards and to spread God's reign. Wright affirms that believers have received "the immense privilege of sharing the intimate life of the triune God himself."[42] But according to him, the key way in which we will share everlastingly in God's life is by reigning. Wright explains that in the coming eschaton, when we receive our resurrected body, "the purpose of this new body will be to rule wisely over God's new world. Forget those images about lounging around playing harps. There will be work to do and we shall relish doing it.

---

38. Middleton, *The Liberating Image*, 51.
39. Middleton, *The Liberating Image*, 295.
40. Lossky, *In the Image and Likeness of God*, 128.
41. Wright, *Surprised by Hope*, 208.
42. Wright, *Surprised by Hope*, 279.

... [T]he biblical view of God's future is of the renewal of the entire cosmos, [and] there will be plenty to be done, entirely new projects to undertake."[43]

Furthermore, in the Gospel of Matthew, shortly after teaching about marriage, Jesus himself promises his disciples that "in the new world, when the Son of man shall sit on his glorious throne, you who have followed me will also sit on twelve thrones, judging the twelve tribes of Israel" (Matt 19:28). This seems clear enough: the eschaton will be primarily about reigning, and not primarily about marital intimacy with God. Additional evidence may seem to come from Jesus' teaching—again about the consummated kingdom of God—that "in the resurrection they neither marry nor are given in marriage, but are like angels in heaven" (Matt 22:30). Marriage, in short, may not really be a fundamental Christian reality at all.

Some scholars have proposed a second option. In their view, God created the human race in order to establish a race of priests who would lead the entire cosmos in its worship of God. Thus, John Walton suggests that "we should think of Genesis 1 in relation to a cosmic temple."[44] In Genesis 1, God creates the cosmos as a temple, and he dwells in its midst on the seventh day. Walton compares Genesis 1's depiction of the seven days of creation with ancient Near Eastern texts about "temple inauguration," including the biblical text of 1 Kings 8.[45] He thinks that Genesis 1 may have functioned liturgically for celebrating God's creation of his cosmic temple and God's enthronement therein.[46] In the cosmic temple, humans (created in God's image) serve as God's "vice regents" or, more specifically, as "priests."[47] Humans recognize God's role as Creator "by our observance of the sabbath" and by means of liturgies by which we celebrate God's place "in the temple that is his church (1 Cor 3:16; 6:19)."[48]

The view that God's purpose in creation was to create priests is found in Ephrem the Syrian's fourth-century *Hymns on Paradise*. Speaking of the Edenic paradise, Ephrem suggests that at his creation, Adam was a priest, but not yet fully so. In Hymn III, Ephrem states that "God did not permit Adam to enter that innermost Tabernacle; this was withheld, so that first he might prove pleasing in his service of that outer Tabernacle."[49] The service of the "outer Tabernacle" consisted in obedience to God's commandment

---

43. Wright, *Surprised by Hope*, 161.
44. Walton, *The Lost World of Genesis One*, 87.
45. Walton, *The Lost World of Genesis One*, 88.
46. He cites Weinfeld's "Sabbath, Temple and the Enthronement of the Lord."
47. Walton, *The Lost World of Genesis One*, 98.
48. Walton, *The Lost World of Genesis One*, 123–24.
49. Ephrem the Syrian, *Hymns on Paradise*, Hymn III.16, p. 96.

not to eat of the fruit of the "tree of the knowledge of good and evil" (Gen 2:17). Ephrem explains that "Adam's keeping of the commandment was to be his censer; then he might enter before the Hidden One into that hidden Tabernacle."[50] But instead Adam (and Eve) disobeyed the commandment. In Hymn XV, Ephrem amplifies his view that God created humans to be priests. He holds that Solomon's temple and its priestly service symbolized and recreated the Edenic condition. In serving God in the Solomonic temple, the priest was supposed to be "robed with knowledge"; and the sanctuary was "a type for Paradise."[51] The Israelite priest was supposed to "put on sanctification," by contrast to the failed priest Adam, who "was stripped of glory."[52] As Ephrem says in Hymn XIII, Jesus Christ is the "High Priest" who by his "death has returned us to our heritage."[53]

Biblically, of course, there need be no opposition between claiming that God created us to be kings and claiming that God created us to be priests. Christ himself is both the messianic Davidic king and the true "high priest" (Heb 2:17).[54] First Peter 2:9 identifies Christians as "a royal priesthood." Revelation 1:6 describes Christians as "a kingdom, priests to his [Christ's] God and Father." Indeed, in its portrait of the crucified and risen Christ entering the liturgical assembly of the blessed, the book of Revelation depicts the blessed singing "a new song" that praises Christ for having "ransomed men for God from every tribe and tongue and people and nation" and for having "made them a kingdom and priests to our God" so that "they shall reign on earth" (Rev 5:9-10). Likewise, those who come to life in the "first resurrection," according to Revelation 20:5-6, "shall be priests of God and of Christ, and they shall reign with him a thousand years."

The book of Revelation is especially important, however, for showing that God created for the purpose of the eschatological marriage. In Revelation, there is no opposition between humans having been created to be royal stewards and priests of God, and humans having been created to be *married to God*. Revelation describes "the holy city, New Jerusalem, prepared as a bride adorned for her husband" (Rev 21:2). An angel calls to the Seer and tells him, "Come I will show you the Bride, the wife of the Lamb" (Rev 21:9).

---

50. Ephrem the Syrian, *Hymns on Paradise*, Hymn III.16, p. 96.
51. Ephrem the Syrian, *Hymns on Paradise*, Hymn XV.7-8, p. 184.
52. Ephrem the Syrian, *Hymns on Paradise*, Hymn XV.8, p. 185.
53. Ephrem the Syrian, *Hymns on Paradise*, Hymn XIII.13, p. 173.

54. See the historical-critical study by Perrin, *Jesus the Priest*. Perrin envisions Jesus' movement as a "counter-temple movement" concerned to bring about a "renewed sacred space," and Perrin argues that Jesus "and his followers self-consciously functioned as proleptic priests within that quest" (*Jesus the Priest*, 8; see also the summaries offered on 280-83). See also Barber, "The New Temple."

The "Bride" is the Church, the New Jerusalem. God and Christ indwell the New Jerusalem so perfectly that the whole city—symbolic of the countless elect people of God—is the perfect temple of God.

I will discuss these points further in the chapters that follow. Let me simply note here that by privileging marriage, I do not intend to detract from believers' royal and priestly roles. Only if our intimacy with God is so profound as to be "marital" can we eschatologically "reign" and consecrate all reality to God. Otherwise, we could not be true sharers in Christ's Sonship or in Christ's royal priesthood. Instead we would have been created simply to stand to the side. It is only if we truly are the "bride" of Christ, intimately united with him and intimately sharing in his communion with the Father in the Spirit, that we can also be priests and kings with him, governing all things in justice and offering them in praise to the Father.

Moreover, the ministry of the ordained priest is inscribed within this eschatological marriage, due to the ordained priest's ability to act sacramentally *in persona Christi*. The Orthodox theologian Dumitru Staniloae says, "The liturgical [ordained] priests do not offer only their own personal sacrifices and prayers but those of the entire community and of all the faithful joined to the sacrifice of Christ. In the priest the unification of all is realized, as in the visible image of Christ, who offers Himself invisibly through the priest as a sacrifice."[55] This beautiful description shows how God's people are enfolded, in their self-offering, within the one priestly self-offering of Christ, the self-offering that brings about the long-desired marital intimacy between God and his (fallen) people. We become the "bride" of "the bridegroom" whose "joy . . . is now full" (John 3:29).

Why Is There No Marriage in Eternal Life, and What about Single People?

Yet, let me pause one more time and ask a further question: why should marriage be so privileged, given that the New Testament and the Church in many ways affirm the superiority of singleness in the Lord? Jana Bennett comments, "A poignant question for theologians should be, What about single people?"[56] Likewise, Albert Hsu remarks, "A truly Christian view of both singleness and marriage will honor both equally without disparaging one or the other."[57] By placing this volume on marriage directly after my volume on creation, have I fallen into the trap of implicitly disparaging singleness?

55. Staniloae, *The Experience of God*, 150.
56. Bennett, *Water Is Thicker Than Blood*, 23.
57. Hsu, *Singles at the Crossroads*, 46–47.

In response, let me reiterate that to participate in the marriage of God and his people, there is no need to enter into a human marriage. The Apostle Paul teaches the value of celibacy: "I wish that all were as I myself am" (1 Cor 7:7). Given that Christians live in the eschatological end-times (the inaugurated kingdom), Paul worries that the daily tasks and responsibilities of married life will focus Christians too firmly on their worldly interests. He counsels, "Are you free from a wife? Do not seek marriage. But if you marry, you do not sin, and if a girl marries she does not sin. Yet those who marry will have worldly troubles, and I would spare you that" (1 Cor 7:27–28). Marriage can indeed focus a couple inward on their own family.[58] My point here is simply that through baptism, confirmation, and the Eucharist, single Christians too are caught up into the eschatological marriage of Christ and his Church. They can therefore exercise a spiritual fatherhood or spiritual "motherhood 'in the order of grace.'"[59]

Bennett observes, "Christians have most often affirmed the high place of *eschatology* in view of vowed nonmarried people over against marriage," whereas Christians "tend to speak of marriage largely in terms of *creation* only."[60] In this book, I aim to "affirm the high place of eschatology" while speaking of marriage "in terms of creation" but *not only* creation. The created order—which is created in grace, in accord with God's plan from "before the foundation of the world" to make us "his sons through Jesus Christ" (Eph 1:4–5)—is created for "marital" union with the triune God. I agree with Paul Evdokimov when he says, "Monastic holiness and married holiness are the two faces of Tabor; the Holy Spirit is the limit of the one and the other. Those who reach the summit by either of these paths 'enter into the peace of God, into the joy of the Lord.'"[61]

---

58. Bennett argues that "[w]e, as members of the Household of God, should not imagine ourselves as separate either from being married or from being single, and we must live as *both*, in our lives as members of Christ's body" (*Water Is Thicker Than Blood*, 128). I agree that Paul teaches that, given the need to focus on the coming of Christ in glory—given that "the form of this world is passing away"—"those who have wives" should "live as though they had none" (1 Cor 7:29, 31). But Paul does not mean this in a literal sense, since he has just stated, for example, that "[t]he husband should give to his wife her conjugal rights, and likewise the wife to her husband" (1 Cor 7:3). I do not see how married people could imagine themselves as not "separate . . . from being single," or how a married person could actually live both as "single" and as "married." After all, married people are in fact married, not single.

59. John Paul II, *Redemptoris Mater*, §45.

60. Bennett, *Water Is Thicker Than Blood*, 128–29 (emphasis added). See also Otten, "Augustine on Marriage, Monasticism, and the Community of the Church."

61. Evdokimov, *The Sacrament of Love*, 73. Evdokimov delivers a rather stringent critique of Augustine and Western theologies of marriage, although he does not appear conversant with medieval (or later) adaptations of Augustine's approach, as for example

INTRODUCTION

Is it a problem, however, that Jesus teaches that in eternal life people "neither marry nor are given in marriage, but are like the angels in heaven" (Matt 22:30)? On the contrary, this is what we should expect. Earthly marriage as a sacrament exists to build us up in the self-surrendering love that already fully characterizes the life of the blessed angels—the life of marriage with God. In the consummated kingdom, all will be intimately bound to all, and all God's people will be present. Precisely because the eschatological marriage will be all-encompassing, sexual intercourse, with its one-to-one exclusivity and procreative power, will not be needed. By God's power and presence, all the delight and pleasure of intimate interpersonal communion will be wondrously amplified, not negated or reduced. Simply put, eternal life will superabundantly fulfill human marriage, through the unimaginable fullness of the "marriage" of Christ and his Church.

In light of this eschatological consummation, Staniloae speaks of the "gradual pneumatization of the couple's bond," through acts of embodied love and service.[62] On earth "the mystery of an ongoing and intensifying

---

Thomas Aquinas's. Evdokimov states, "One can see that the spring itself is muddied. Before preparing a theology from initial Biblical truths, one begins with the Fall and locks everything into the physiological, and it is from the outset that marriage appears unbalanced, marked with the wound of guilt. From this negative and prohibitive aspect, an obsession with the sexual will inevitably spring forth" (*The Sacrament of Love*, 25). But it seems to me that even if the Fathers (West and East) significantly overdid their critique of marital sexual intercourse, they were correct in identifying something distorted in the powerful human sexual drive (even, potentially, as it exists in marriage). Our highly pornographic culture has only confirmed their concerns.

62. Staniloae, *The Sanctifying Mysteries*, 176. Staniloae's teleological vision differs from a historicist teleology that accords no value to natures or the created order. Oliver O'Donovan well describes the latter perspective: "The heart of historicism can be expressed in the thesis that all teleology is historical teleology. The concept of an 'end', it is held, is essentially a concept of development in time. Nothing can have a 'point', unless it is a historical point; there is no point in the regularities of nature as such. What we took to be natural orderings-to-serve and orderings-to-flourish within the regularities of nature are in fact something quite different: they are orderings-to-transformation, and so break out altogether from nature's order. The natural exists only to be superseded: everything within it serves only a supernatural end, the end of history. That may be conceived as the kingdom of heaven; it may be conceived as the communist paradise; or (as especially in liberal historicism) it may be simply an undefined term of self-justifying change, receding infinitely like the horizon as we approach it. But in each case natural order and natural meanings are understood only as moments in the historical process. They are to be dissolved and reconstituted by that process, and their value lies not in any integrity of their own but in being raw material for transformation" (*Resurrection and Moral Order*, 58–59). Liberal moral theology grounds itself in such purely historicist teleology; and O'Donovan's reply is instructive: "We cannot object to the idea that history should be taken seriously. A Christian response to historicism will wish to make precisely the opposite point: when history is made the categorical matrix for all meaning and value, it cannot then be taken seriously *as history*" (*Resurrection*

personal communion" enables the spouses to "experience Christ as the one who appears through the other," as the spouses grow more transparent to Christ.[63] In eternal life this intense intimacy of communion will be shared by the whole Bride with the triune Bridegroom.

Alexander Schmemann remarks that marriage can be a sacrament only if it is "related to the Kingdom which is to come."[64] This means not only that male-female marriage is a sign of the "marriage" of God and creation, but also that if it were not for the marriage of God and creation, male-female marriage would not have the meaning it does. The eschatological reality is the prime analogate. For Schmemann, too, the Virgin Mary's "Yes" is already the inauguration of the eschatological marriage, as the bridal Church comes to be in history.

I seek to follow Schmemann in firmly grounding the royal and priestly status of the human being in the context of the marital purpose of creation. He explains that "man can be truly man—that is, the king of creation, the priest and minister of God's creativity and initiative—only when he does not

---

and Moral Order, 60). As O'Donovan goes on to say, "Creation is the given totality of order which forms the presupposition of historical existence. . . . Because created order is given, because it is secure, we dare to be certain that God will vindicate it in history" (*Resurrection and Moral Order*, 60–61).

63. Staniloae, *The Sanctifying Mysteries*, 177. Staniloae adds, "The wife is the human being who is closest to her husband, and vice versa, and they are thus because they complement and complete one another. In his wife the husband possesses humanity in the highest possible degree of intimacy that can be reached with him, and the same is true of the wife with her husband. They are revealed completely the one to the other within a state of total sincerity; each is to the other as another 'I,' while remaining nevertheless a 'thou' who is necessary to the spouse if he or she is to reveal himself or herself. Each forgets the self, making himself or herself the 'I' of the other. . . . Thus each of the two spouses brings into reality the state for which he or she is yearning and realizes himself or herself as person in reciprocal communion. But this realization only comes about when their bodily love is penetrated by and submerged in a spiritual love" (*The Sanctifying Mysteries*, 178). Staniloae later comments with valuable realism that "prayer is offered on behalf of those who marry so that they may receive the grace of God for many purposes: the grace to be able to control the tendency to exclusively seek the satisfaction of the desires of the flesh, for this degrades each member of the couple to the status of an object of the other's selfish passion; the grace to be able to curb any other type of selfishness or infidelity of one spouse in his or her relations with the other; the grace to strengthen the patient endurance of each when confronted with the limitations of the other; the grace to strengthen the will of each spouse to be of help to the other so that their love in Christ may grow deeper, something that is not possible unless the selfishness of each is brought under control; and finally, the grace of having children, which in itself is identical with the curbing of every kind of selfishness and with the progress of the couple toward the fullness of communion" (*The Sanctifying Mysteries*, 190). By contrast, see the heartbreaking work of Perel, *The State of Affairs*.

64. Schmemann, *For the Life of the World*, 81.

posit himself as the 'owner' of creation and submits himself—in obedience and love—to its nature as the bride of God in *response* and *acceptance*."[65] The point is that human nature, as created in grace, has an eschatological nuptial vocation, which is signified by human marriage but can also be enacted by single persons: we are created in order to give ourselves in love to God, in an intimacy so profound as to be marital.

Joseph Ratzinger adds the cautionary note that God is no mere "partner" on the same level as human creatures. Thus, we can only give ourselves fully to God when we "accept God's [transcendent] otherness and the hiddenness of his will" as the key to the flourishing of our own creaturehood.[66] In accordance with this line of thought, Hans Urs von Balthasar speaks of the Church's graced "feminine receptivity," with Mary as the perfect embodiment of the Church from the first moment of the Incarnation.[67] Behind the priestly and royal status of human beings is the nuptial purpose of God's creation of humans, a purpose revealed most perfectly in Mary's Yes. As Schmemann puts it, in Mary's *fiat* we find "the whole creation, all of humanity, and each one of us recognizing the words that express our ultimate nature and being, our acceptance to be the bride of God, our betrothal to the One who from all eternity loved us."[68]

Commenting on Schmemann's perspective, David L. Schindler suggests that today we often are blind to the nuptial meaning of creation because, given modernity's mechanistic worldview, we tend to reject any "intrinsically liturgical, nuptial, and Marian sense of cosmic-cultural order."[69] Love's receptivity no longer seems of value—if it ever really did—in comparison with obtaining and wielding power. No wonder, then, that the sacrament of marriage often is not well understood. In this regard Schmemann highlights the crowning that takes place in the Orthodox marriage liturgy, a crowning that symbolizes the fact that each family is "a sacrament of and a way to the Kingdom."[70] This is not a romanticizing of marriage but

---

65. Schmemann, *For the Life of the World*, 85.

66. Ratzinger [Benedict XVI], "The Sign of the Woman," 69. See also Schindler, "Liturgy and the Integrity of Cosmic Order," 306 (criticizing the theological perspective of Elizabeth Johnson, C.S.J.): "what is risked in the idea of a partnership that is not innerly qualified by 'handmaidenship' is a slip into a kind of ontological 'pelagianism' that removes the Other-centeredness that lies at the core of, and accords the original and abiding meaning to, the creature's rightful *self-centeredness*."

67. Von Balthasar, "The Marian Mold of the Church," 140.

68. Schmemann, *For the Life of the World*, 86.

69. Schindler, "Liturgy and the Integrity of Cosmic Order," 295. See also Schindler, "Catholic Theology, Gender, and the Future of Western Civilization."

70. Schmemann, *For the Life of the World*, 89.

rather an attempt to show that every marriage derives from, and points to, God's greater purpose, the establishment of God's nuptial kingdom of love.

Here it is necessary to underscore that as "a sacrament of and a way to the Kingdom," Christian marriage involves the Cross of Christ. Schmemann explains that "the way to the Kingdom is the *martyria*—bearing witness to Christ. And this means crucifixion and suffering. A marriage which does not constantly crucify its own selfishness and self-sufficiency, which does not 'die to itself' that it may point beyond itself, is not a Christian marriage."[71] By pointing beyond itself, Christian marriage bears fruit in love unto eternal life. For Schmemann, therefore, the nuptial purpose of creation is not opposed to the truth that Christ is "the one true Priest" and the Church is "the royal priesthood of the redeemed world."[72] To be a priest, whether baptized or ordained, means appreciating "that all things, all nature have their end, their fulfillment in the Kingdom; that all things are to be made new by love."[73] This unimaginably glorious newness in love is what the marriage of God and creation ultimately is.

Is Christian Marriage Outdated?

One final point merits attention before proceeding. Today, the Catholic understanding of marriage has become unpopular and, in many circles, provokes the charge of lack of compassion, unjust discrimination, and self-righteous bigotry. The situation is exacerbated by the fact that many Catholic theologians themselves, having acceded to the cultural norm, argue that scriptural and magisterial teachings on marriage, rooted in male-female complementarity, are essentially meaningless—as though Catholic sexual morality and teaching on marriage could be radically revised without the core of Catholic faith being touched.[74]

An example is a recent book co-authored by the moral theologian James Keenan. He grants that "Catholics are intensely interested in the nature of marriage as the place where faithful love and procreativity concretely

---

71. Schmemann, *For the Life of the World*, 91.

72. Schmemann, *For the Life of the World*, 93.

73. Schmemann, *For the Life of the World*, 93. See also Schmemann, *Introduction to Liturgical Theology*, 29.

74. See for example Farley, *Just Love*; Salzman and Lawler, *The Sexual Person*. The Catholic biblical scholar John J. Collins has advanced this same basic thesis in his chapter on sexuality in his *What Are Biblical Values?* For a much richer analysis, see Collin, *Le mariage Chrétien*. The biblical material has been accurately surveyed by Gagnon, *The Bible and Homosexual Practice*. For a succinct summary of Scripture's consistent perspective on homosexual acts, see Kuby, *The Global Sexual Revolution*, 193–94.

flourish" and that the *Catechism of the Catholic Church* teaches that male-female marriage is the place for genital sexual expression.[75] But in his own constructive discussion of sexuality and the virtues, he leaves marriage almost entirely to the side. Instead, he simply contends that we must "be faithful to the long-standing, particular relationships that we have," and that we must never "abandon our lover."[76] In an extended discussion of sexual relationships, he never mentions marriage between a man and a woman.[77]

Similarly, James Martin has recently published a popular book, *Building a Bridge: How the Catholic Church and the LGBT Community Can Enter into a Relationship of Respect, Compassion, and Sensitivity*. He reports that "LGBT Catholics have told me that they have felt hurt by the institutional church—unwelcomed, excluded, and insulted."[78] The reality that Martin de-

---

75. Harrington and Keenan, *Paul and Virtue Ethics*, 208. Keenan is identified as the "principal writer" for the chapter of the book from which this quotation is drawn (see *Paul and Virtue Ethics*, xiii).

76. Harrington and Keenan, *Paul and Virtue Ethics*, 208.

77. Keenan testified in favor of Massachusetts's early (successful) effort to adopt same-sex marriage. See also the direction of Stephen J. Pope's "The Magisterium's Arguments against 'Same-Sex Marriage'"; and Cahill, "Same-Sex Marriage and Catholicism." Gerard Jacobitz contends, "If sexual orientation is an essential dimension of the human person, if it is not so much *what* a person is but *who* a person is, then it simply cannot be disordered" (Jacobitz, "Seminary, Priesthood, and the Vatican's Homosexual Dilemma," 98). This is to misunderstand the meaning of "disordered" in the technical language of Catholic moral theology. Humans, as body-soul unities, are ordered intrinsically to certain ends as constitutive of human flourishing (whether or not we consciously desire these ends). When we experience desires or commit actions that contradict our intrinsic ordering, these desires or actions are called "disordered." See also Christopher Wolfe's helpful "Homosexuality and the Church." For a representative defense of the moral goodness of homosexual acts in the context of stable same-sex relationships, see Salzman and Lawler, *Sexual Ethics*, chapters 2 and 5. For further discussion, see my chapter on chastity (and the sources cited therein) in my *Aquinas's Eschatological Ethics and the Virtue of Temperance*, and Tushnet, "O Tell Me the Truth About Love," 26–31. From a Protestant perspective aligned with Tushnet's, see Hill, *Washed and Waiting*. By contrast, for a rejection of the Church's teaching on the grounds that the experience (understood in a particular way) of sexually active homosexual persons must be affirmed and celebrated as integral to their identity and well-being, see Gumbleton, "A Call to Listen."

78. Martin, *Building a Bridge*, 16. For a cognate discussion, see Alison, "Following the Still Small Voice." O'Gorman writes, "Many of the women I have met during my lesbian and gay ministry are vulnerable because of the hostility they have experienced from our church and our culture. They are criticized or condemned because all too frequently others see them as engaging in deviant sexual activity. Heterosexuals have often been fixated on this—as though being gay is only about having sex. But it is much deeper than that. . . . [I]t is really all about identity. It is about who I am at my core, the center of my being. It is as deep as questions about who I am as a woman or a man." (O'Gorman and Perkins, *Living True*, 59). I accept that homosexual orientation

scribes is sad: no one should feel excluded from coming to Christ. Yet, Martin knows that the experience of hurt is at least partly due to Scripture and Tradition's rejection of the sexual acts practiced by non-sexually abstinent people who identify as LGBT.[79] In the context of Christian faith, experiences of hurt cannot be overcome by obscuring or denying the nature of marriage and its signification. Martin's call for "respect, compassion, and sensitivity" on all sides is welcome, but Martin's approach in his book—acting as though biblical teaching as mediated by the Church's constant Tradition can simply be bracketed or relativized in discussions among Catholic believers—turns away from what God has revealed about marriage and sexuality in Christ.[80]

To name a final example, in their *Sexual Ethics: A Theological Introduction*, Todd Salzman and Michael Lawler bestow a Catholic theological blessing upon homosexual intercourse, cohabitation, masturbation, contraceptive sex, divorce and remarriage (without annulment), and indeed upon almost everything that the Catholic Church has consistently rejected as incompatible with the vocation of marriage and virtuous human sexuality. Either the Church has never understood its own sacrament, or else, as I think, a strong current of worldly accommodation threatens Catholic marriage today.[81]

---

is often found at the "core" and "center," but homosexual *acts* are not thereby mandated or justified, for reasons I discuss more fully in my book on temperance. For further explorations in "queer" theology, see Cornwall, *Controversies in Queer Theology*; Méndez-Montoya, "Eucharistic Imagination."

79. Arguably, even changing Scripture and Tradition would not solve the problem, which ultimately is rooted in our created sexual bodies that bestow unique privileges upon male-female couples. On this point, see Fastiggi, "Human Equality and Non-discrimination," 9. See also Girgis, Anderson, and George, *What Is Marriage?*, 87: "Whatever the state says . . . no same-sex or group relationship will include organic bodily union, or find its inherent fulfillment in procreation, or *require*, quite apart from the partners' personal preferences, what these two features demand: permanent and exclusive commitment."

80. Martin, *Building a Bridge*, 18. Later in his book, Martin notes that "there are many reasons why almost no gay clergy, and almost no gay and lesbian members of religious orders, are public about their sexuality" (*Building a Bridge*, 42). One reason that Martin does not name, however, is that talking about one's sexuality is not something that people generally do unless they are seeking to act upon their sexual desires. People who have taken a vow of celibacy or who have received the sacrament of marriage do not need to go around talking publicly "about their sexuality" (*Building a Bridge*, 42.), unless perhaps their job involves concretely instructing others in the practice of chastity.

81. David Cloutier pinpoints a fundamental element of the current situation: "The existence of sexual nature is dead; what we have left is sexual energy that we can direct in creative ways. What constitutes good sexual desire is its creativity. It has no inherent purpose other than exploration and intensification of emotions and bodily prowess" (Cloutier, *Love, Reason, and God's Story*, 99). Cloutier is here responding to Grosz,

INTRODUCTION

The Orthodox theologian Vigen Guroian has noted that at the core of this worldly accommodation is a rejection of the teleology found in the created ordering of male and female human persons, a rejection that distorts the sacrament of marriage by removing its necessary "grounding in creation."[82] Guroian recognizes that marriage is a sacrament not merely of human sexual coupling, but specifically of male-female human sexual and personal union: the "male and female are the essential and nonsubstitutable elements of that sacrament."[83]

"Refiguring Lesbian Desire," 278.

82. Guroian, *The Orthodox Reality*, 125. Guroian goes on to explain, "Marriage is a sacrament of love but not just any sort of love. This love union is founded and grounded in God's will, in his creative act of making humankind as male and female so that, through their love for each other and their sexual union, they may be united 'in one flesh'" (Guroian, *The Orthodox Reality*, 129). He notes that when marriage is seen to depend solely on mutual love and consent (with no other criteria), then it becomes formless. As he says, "it is easy to imagine that the sorts of changes in marriage law and tax codes that the supporters of same-sex marriage have won may eventually have to be extended to other same-sex households that are not homosexual. How can the state possibly discriminate—or even ask the questions needed to discriminate—between homosexual and heterosexual couples of the same sex that come to get licensed? How can the state differentiate one love from another? If marriage is no longer defined as strictly between a man and a woman, why shouldn't widows or widowers or brothers or sisters who live together for mutual assistance and economic reasons be granted licenses for domestic partnerships with all the legal benefits and protections now accorded to married couples?" (Guroian, *The Orthodox Reality*, 130). See also the contention of Adriano Oliva, O.P. in his *L'amicizia più grande* that for Thomas Aquinas the essence of marriage does not include the sexual act. Numerous scholars have responded, showing that this claim (which is ludicrous on its face) rests upon profound misunderstandings. See for example Blankenhorn et al., "Aquinas and Homosexuality," and Casanova and Serrano del Pozo, "Being and Operation of Mary's Marriage."

83. Guroian, *The Orthodox Reality*, 132; see also 133–38. Notably, Guroian ties this point to the fact that "Christ is the groom and the church is his bride of the new creation. The referent of the groom is the first man, Adam, and the referent of the bride is the first woman, Eve. The nuptial Adam-Eve humanity of the book of Genesis, the first book of the Bible, is the analogue of the heavenly nuptials of the marriage of the Lamb in the book of Revelation (19:7), the last book of the Bible. The creation of nuptial humanity is an epiphany of the eternal humanity of God precedent to its complete revelation in the incarnation. The creation of nuptial humanity is a prophecy of the church, which itself, through its nuptial union with Christ, fulfills the goal and purpose of creation. Human willing and choosing cannot change marriage's essence or the symbolism that God has ordained for it. Thus in the Orthodox faith there could never be such a thing as same-sex marriage. There is not a same-sex equivalent to bride and groom. To insist that there are such equivalencies and to act on this error not only represents marriage as something it is not but also envisions salvation as something it is not. And because same-sex marriage contradicts the church's understanding of salvation, specifically of marriage as restoration of the divine image in nuptial humanity, it is a grave heresy" (Guroian, *The Orthodox Reality*, 135–36).

There is no need to end this introduction on a depressing note. In Christ, we look forward to the glorious consummation "when there will appear the Spouse of the Lamb, the predestined Church, united to the Lamb in all his glory. That is the time when the entire creation, assembled round the new humanity . . . will be reunited to its creator in the Son, itself son of the Father with Him and in Him, and temple of the Holy Ghost."[84] The failures of the Church over the centuries, failures that sometimes have obscured the proclamation of the gospel but have not miscarried its truth, cannot blind the eyes of faith to the reality of the inaugurated kingdom present even now. "The daughter of the king is decked in her chamber with gold-woven robes; in many-colored robes she is led to the king, with her virgin companions, her escort, in her train. With joy and gladness they are led along as they enter the palace of the king" (Ps 45:13–15).[85]

---

84. Bouyer, *The Seat of Wisdom*, 199.
85. For discussion see Fagerberg, *Consecrating the World*, 83.

Chapter 1

God and His People

As I have emphasized, behind the creation of the cosmos stands God's purpose to accomplish the wondrous marriage of God and his people. Rabbi Joseph B. Soloveitchik tells the story that when he was a boy, his Rabbi told him, "the Almighty waits for mankind to appear and kneel before Him, recognize His kingdom and kingship, and give him the crown. This great event of coronation will occur at some point in the future; we do not know when and how. . . . Then the whole world will find its redemption."[1] This crowning of God as King is not merely a case of inferiors (humans) recognizing their true superior (God). Rather, it will be the consummation of an intense and ages-long romance instigated by God, fulfilling the human person's deepest yearnings for communion with God (and each other). As Soloveitchik puts it, "There is a romance between man and God. Man has an uncontrollable, powerful longing, an invisible craving and desire to unite with God, to be close to Him, to submerge in Him."[2]

But is this desire for intimacy with God actually a good thing for human beings? If the graced purpose of creation is the marriage of God and humankind—and Soloveitchik suggests that such profound intimacy does

---

1. Soloveitchik, *Abraham's Journey*, 109. Describing the coming Messiah, Soloveitchik states that "everything good and fine and noble in man must be passed on to the Messiah. He will have the capacity for *gevurah* and *hesed*. He will be a hero with unlimited power and strength who will defend justice. He will also be a man of unlimited loving-kindness, humble and simple. All these capabilities, capacities, and talents will merge in beautiful harmony in the King Messiah. The Messiah will represent creation at its best" (*Abraham's Journey*, 177).

2. Soloveitchik, *Abraham's Journey*, 22. The same insistence is at the root of de Lubac's *Catholicism*. See my discussion of de Lubac and *Gaudium et Spes* in chapter 4 of my *An Introduction to Vatican II*.

indeed constitute the original purpose, although he does not use the term "marriage"[3]—is the pursuit of this purpose something that humans should desire? In a rather flippant manner, Hans Küng has called into question the desirability of such intimate union with God: "Does a reasonable man today want to become God?"[4] It may be that the lack of desire partly comes about because we know that we are sinners, unworthy of intimate communion with God. Recall the response of the prophet Isaiah to seeing a vision of God (YHWH) enthroned in glory. Far from rejoicing, Isaiah responds in agony: "Woe is me! For I am lost; for I am a man of unclean lips, and I dwell in the midst of a people of unclean lips; for my eyes have seen the King, the LORD of hosts!" (Isa 6:5). It may also be that, as Jon D. Levenson says, we have lost a proper understanding of love: "where love is understood as primarily a sentiment, the dimension of deeds and of the service that the deeds bespeak is lost or radically transformed."[5] Levenson justifiably fears that the sentimental notion of love has resulted in "the perception that all talk of God's love or of loving God is, at base, a treacly thing that appeals only to the emotionally weak," making of religion a mere "crutch."[6]

All this is troubling. Even more troublingly, however, it may appear from Scripture that God has acted like an abusive husband toward his covenantal bride whom he professes to love. Levenson observes, "The severity of the punishments that Hosea's symbolic wife is to endure has understandably attracted the attention of feminist scholars."[7] It may seem that "the

---

3. Soloveitchik holds that after their sin, "Adam and Eve heard the footsteps of the Holy One walking out of the universe. God broke the intimate relationship that was supposed to be realized by Adam. The purpose of the covenant concluded with Abraham was to restore the intimacy that God wanted to prevail between Him and man. At Sinai, the covenant embraced not only one individual but the whole community. The ideal is to extend the covenant even further, to the rest of the world" (Soloveitchik, *Abraham's Journey*, 164–65). For background to the marriage metaphor in Judaism, see Satlow, "Metaphor of Marriage in Early Judaism." Satlow summarizes: "In the Hebrew Bible, the metaphor of God as the husband or lover of Israel or Zion occurs not infrequently.... [Yet] Jews in antiquity by and large ignored, or even subverted, the biblical metaphor that compares the relationship of God to Israel as a husband to wife" ("The Metaphor of Marriage in Early Judaism," 14). Satlow explains this shift in part by pointing out that the metaphor seemingly "gives God the right to take other nations as 'co-wives'" and also that the metaphor "implies a degree of intimacy between God and Israel that is not always compatible with an asexual and transcendent understanding of God" ("The Metaphor of Marriage in Early Judaism," 17; cf. the cruder position of Eilberg-Schwartz, *God's Phallus*). He adds that the shift may also be a response to Christianity's emphasis on the marriage metaphor.

4. Küng, *On Being a Christian*, 442.

5. Levenson, *The Love of God*, 91.

6. Levenson, *The Love of God*, 91.

7. Levenson, *The Love of God*, 99. In particular, Levenson draws attention to

dominant position of men is reinforced by God's role as husband," even if the male citizens of Israel were "expected to identify . . . also with Israel as God's wife."[8] In the prophecy of Jeremiah, God complains bitterly against the spiritual adultery of his people Israel.[9] Indeed, God threatens to pun-

Gerlinde Baumann's work, which I also discuss at length. Levenson emphasizes that the men hearing Hosea's prophecies would have identified not with God but with the wife, symbolic of the whole Israelite nation. He quotes Phyllis Bird, who writes, "It is easy for patriarchal society to see the guilt of the 'fallen woman': Hosea says, 'You (male Israel) are that woman!'" (Bird, "'To Play the Harlot,'" 89, quoted in *The Love of God*, 100). Levenson also quotes Tikva Frymer-Kensky's remark, "Through this imagery, the people of Israel are enabled to feel God's agony. . . . As a result, the image of God as betrayed husband strikes deep into the psyche of the people of Israel and enables them to feel the faithless nature of their actions" (Frymer-Kensky, *In the Wake of the Goddesses*, 147, quoted in *The Love of God*, 101). In accord with my own emphasis in this book, Levenson adds: "The grand finale of Hosea 2 is God's promise to re-betroth his wife whom he divorced, or seemed to divorce, and the prediction of the redeemed cosmos that marriage to her is to inaugurate. The passage thus adds a strong note of expectation, the expectation of nothing less than a transformed world when the Lord and Israel have resumed their intimacy" (*The Love of God*, 104). For the fundamental problem, however, see Collins, *What Are Biblical Values?*, 96: "Neither prophet [neither Hosea nor Ezekiel] is inciting violence against actual women. But the force of the metaphor depends on the credibility of the literal meaning. Readers are expected to agree that this is an appropriate way to deal with an adulterous woman, at least in principle. . . . These metaphorical passages are not representative of the view of women in the Hebrew Bible as a whole, and they were never meant to be prescriptive for the treatment of women. Nonetheless, they provide language that lends itself to supporting abusive views of women."

8. Frishman, "Why Would a Man Want to Be Anyone's Wife?," 44. Bromiley offers some cautions in this regard: not only is it true that "the prophetic understanding of God as the husband of Israel obviously does not conform to the actual situation in normal human marriages," but also "[s]ome prophets do not use the comparison with marriage at all. Even in those who do, it occupies only a relatively small amount of space. Hosea, for whom it has a shattering significance, still uses his lively poetic imagination to describe the people not only as an unfaithful wife but also as silly doves (7:11), a stubborn heifer (4:16), and even a half-baked cake (7:8). For Hosea, Israel is also a luxuriant vine (10:1) and a refractory child (11:1). Ezekiel can also give very realistic depictions of the actual sins and idolatries committed by the people (see 8:7). Jeremiah, too, uses the metaphor of disobedient children (3:14) and an implied comparison with scattered sheep (3:15) in the very same context in which he speaks of the unfaithful wife. God himself appears not only as the faithful husband of unfaithful Israel but also as the good shepherd (Jer. 23:3; Ezek. 34:11), the father (Isa. 64:8), the liberator (Isa. 40), and the mother (Isa. 66:13)" (Bromiley, *God and Marriage*, 33).

9. As will be clear, I read the biblical texts as a canonical unity formed under the inspiration of the Holy Spirit. By contrast, for a historicist view of the biblical texts, see for example Muir, "Accessing Divine Power and Status." See also Troeltsch's "Historical and Dogmatic Method in Theology." Soloveitchik aptly observes, "When we study the Bible, we must be concerned about two things. We must understand the semantics of the word, and we must understand the spiritual message of the Bible. There is an enormous literature of biblical criticism, and the problem with that literature is that it completely misses the spiritual message" (*Abraham's Journey*, 17).

ish Israel in ways that are drawn from the cultural language of powerful husbands threatening unfaithful and powerless wives.[10] At the same time, promising restoration, God assures his people, "I have loved you with an everlasting love; therefore I have continued my faithfulness to you. Again I will build you, and you shall be built, O virgin Israel!" (Jer 31:3–4). God will do this even though the people of Israel broke their covenant with him—a covenant so intimate that, as God says, "I was their husband" (Jer 31:32). Not only *was* God their husband, but God in his "everlasting love" and "faithfulness" still is their husband. God will act to place this relationship on an everlasting foundation.

In Hosea's prophecy, similarly, God warns of a coming tribulation, a dire punishment of his people's spiritual adultery. The prophet describes God threatening his unfaithful "wife" by stripping her naked and having no pity upon her children.[11] Yet, God also promises Israel that "I will betroth you to me for ever; I will betroth you to me in righteousness and in justice, in steadfast love, in mercy. I will betroth you to me in faithfulness; and you shall know the LORD" (Hos 2:19–20).[12]

The Letter to the Hebrews says bluntly, "It is a fearful thing to fall into the hands of the living God" (Heb 10:31). In our fallen condition, few people cross the boundary of death lightly, and perhaps even fewer lightly give over their lives to the will of God. Yet, Thomas Joseph White is correct to affirm that nonetheless "the human person is marked by longings for the infinite. Each human being has a hidden natural desire to see God"; we can be satisfied by nothing less than God.[13] These longings have to do with the

---

10. For critical discussion, see Shields, *Circumscribing the Prostitute*; Moughtin-Mumby, *Sexual and Marital Metaphors*.

11. Peggy L. Day warns against "reconstructing alleged social reality" on the basis of such biblical texts, and specifically she shows that it is a mistake to conclude from texts such as Hosea 2:4–5 that "prostitutes and adulteresses in ancient Israel were stripped naked as a punishment for engaging in these activities" (Day, "Metaphor and Social Reality," 63). See also Day, "Adulterous Jerusalem's Imagined Demise."

12. For a sharp critique of Hosea, see Moughtin-Mumby, *Sexual and Marital Metaphors*, 206–68. In an effort to redeem the prophetic text, Moughtin-Mumby states that "we could argue that it is *Israel* who has taken the initiative to break the relationship with YHWH, leaving him to plead for her return, rather than YHWH who is banishing his passive wife. On this reading, the relationship between YHWH and Israel remains a deeply unhealthy and damaging one, and Israel is left playing the far from ideal role of 'prostitute', underscoring just how problematic is this troubling text even for resistant readers" (*Sexual and Marital Metaphors*, 266). Sadly, the practice of physical abuse of wives by husbands is explicitly permitted (though also limited) by the Qur'ān: see al-Kawtharī, *Al-Arba'īn*, 97–98.

13. White, *The Light of Christ*, 273. See also Kerr, *Immortal Longings*, although White and Kerr differ regarding Henri de Lubac's particular understanding of the

kind of creatures that we are, with the graced call to an intimate dwelling with God that we received from the beginning and to which the whole of Scripture testifies.[14] In his *Confessions*, Augustine perceives that "you [God] have made us for yourself, and our heart is restless until it rests in you."[15]

Yet, what if the God who reveals himself through the prophets is not worthy of our love, because he is terrifyingly abusive? Can we still desire the eschatological marriage of God and his people? In response, this chapter proceeds in two steps. First, I survey the New Testament scholar Brant Pitre's popular book on Jesus as the Bridegroom Messiah who fulfills the marriage covenant promised by God to Israel through the prophets. In this section, I also draw upon Scott Hahn's work on covenant and kinship, since it influences Pitre's perspective. Second, I set forth the concerns of the Old Testament scholar Gerlinde Baumann in order to give full force to the fact that the prophets at times portray God in the role of a dominant male who threatens or implements violence against an unfaithful wife or woman. In the face of this abusive imagery, I suggest a twofold solution.

First, I retrieve the allegorical exegesis of such passages advocated by the Church Fathers (notably, in the present chapter, Jerome). Second, I take note of historical-critical research that shows that in its original historical context this imagery primarily indicated the importance of women for the survival of the people. The people of Israel—including the men—were represented by a woman in the prophetic imagery in part because the very survival of the people depended upon women bearing and raising children. Sadly, the people were represented by the image of an *adulterous* woman (among other images) because in their covenantal relationship to God, the people "are neither a devoted bride nor an obedient son. They are, rather, a people acting like a wife who flagrantly and chronically cheats on her husband, manically pursuing sexual gratification at the expense of covenantal fidelity, or like a son who ungratefully and obstinately refuses to serve his loving, giving father."[16] The Scriptures of Israel portray not a mutually loving marriage between God and his people, but rather an unfaithful people and a faithful God. Levenson comments, "The love, then, between the divine husband and the nation that is his wife is real but only in the past and in the future. . . . The marriage is an ideal recollected from the idyllic past and a

---

natural desire.

14. Mark J. Boda remarks that the entirety of the Old Testament (joined by the New) reveals "God's plan to form a redemptive community" and "God's plan to transform all creation" (Boda, *The Heartbeat of Old Testament Theology*, 8).

15. Augustine, *Confessions*, trans. Chadwick, I.i.1, p. 3. See also Keating, *Deification and Grace*; Hofer, ed., *Divinization*.

16. Levenson, *The Love of God*, 113.

possibility promised for the restored future. It is not the current reality, but reality it surely is and shall be again."[17]

These points are not likely to change Baumann's mind, since the presence of abusive imagery is enough to convince her that Scripture is not inspired by the living God. But I suggest that this approach should suffice to redirect attention to the main point of the prophetic texts, which is—as Pitre says—the everlastingly glorious, entirely unmerited, and supremely fulfilling marriage of God with his people. This marriage is inaugurated, though not yet consummated, by Jesus Christ.

I. Brant Pitre's *Jesus the Bridegroom*

Brant Pitre emphasizes that far from being impersonal or aloof, as we sometimes fear the invisible and immaterial God must be, the God of Israel wishes to draw his people into a relationship so intimate with him as to be comparable only to the most intimate human relationship, marriage.[18] In a brief opening chapter, Pitre argues that "from an ancient Jewish perspective, the God who created the universe is a Bridegroom, and all of human history is a kind of divine love story."[19] What does this have to do with the Torah, which recounts that God gave Moses a law at Mount Sinai? Upon marrying a bride, no bridegroom would simply hand her a set of rules.

Nahum Sarna has pointed out that covenants, in the ancient Near East, carried legal weight and served to confirm the behavior owed by the two parties (typically unequals) to each other.[20] Pitre, indebted to Scott Hahn's *Kinship by Covenant*, adds that "[f]rom a biblical perspective, a 'covenant' was a *sacred family bond* between persons, establishing between them a permanent and sacred relationship."[21] For his part, Hahn focuses attention on the ways in which the covenants involve God, as Father, welcoming his people into a relationship of sonship with him. With good reason, Hahn focuses on the biblical "drama of the development of the covenant relationship between father and son, that is, between God and his people."[22] He points out, among other things, that in Exodus 4:22, God calls Israel his "first-born son," and in Exodus 19:5 God exhorts Israel that if it keeps the covenant

---

17. Levenson, *The Love of God*, 114.
18. Thomas Aquinas describes marriage as the greatest friendship: see Aquinas, *Summa contra gentiles*, Book Three: *Providence*, trans. Bourke, ch. 123, p. 148.
19. Pitre, *Jesus the Bridegroom*, 8.
20. Sarna, *Exploring Exodus*, 134.
21. Pitre, *Jesus the Bridegroom*, 10. See Hahn, *Kinship by Covenant*, 337.
22. Hahn, *Kinship by Covenant*, 338.

(whose stipulations God reveals at Sinai), Israel "shall be my own possession among all peoples." When Israel seals its covenant with God through Moses in Exodus 24, God calls the elders of the people up the mountain to behold him and eat and drink in his presence as his family.[23]

Hahn develops these points for the purposes of a broader account of priesthood in ancient Israel, but what I find important is the "familial shape" that he identifies in each of the covenants found in Scripture.[24] To show the way in which "kinship bonds were extended by covenant to outsiders," Hahn draws upon the work of Old Testament scholars such as Frank Moore Cross and Dennis McCarthy.[25] As Hahn notes, "In a kinship covenant, kinship bonds are extended to bind two parties in a *mutual* relationship based upon a *joint* commitment under divine sanctions."[26] Not all covenants are kinship covenants, but Hahn makes a persuasive case that it is the "familial or relational dimension that integrates and binds together the other dimensions of the covenant that scholars over the past century have identified (i.e., the ethical, cultic, social, juridical, and theological dimensions)."[27] The basic kinds of covenants—kinship, treaty, and grant—can be illumined in Scripture by the relationship of God as Father to his people Israel, whom he covenantally unites to himself as his son.

Pitre takes up Hahn's insight by remarking that at the covenant at Sinai (sealed in Exodus 24), Moses threw sacrificial blood on the altar and on the elders, thereby symbolizing that "the Creator of the world and the twelve tribes of Israel are now in a 'flesh and blood' relationship—that is, they are family," which explains the ensuing covenantal meal in God's presence.[28] By turning to the prophets of Israel, however, Pitre takes things a step further.

---

23. See Hahn, *Kinship by Covenant*, 139–41.

24. Hahn, *Kinship by Covenant*, 172.

25. Hahn, *Kinship by Covenant*, 41. See Cross, "Kinship and Covenant in Ancient Israel"; McCarthy, *Treaty and Covenant*; McCarthy, "Notes on the Love of God in Deuteronomy."

26. Hahn, *Kinship by Covenant*, 37.

27. Hahn, *Kinship by Covenant*, 31. Hahn's proposal is quite complex, and all its elements need not be correct to ground the basic validity of his insight. In terms of the complex details of his proposal, a significant element is his sharp distinction between a "Sinai" covenant (broken by the Golden Calf incident) and a "Deuteronomic" covenant. He argues that "God's initial relationship with Israel at Sinai was a kinship-type covenant, with an emphasis on mutuality and familial relationship," whereas in the post-Golden Calf Deuteronomic covenant "Israel's father-son relationship with God remains intact, but it takes on the character of a master-servant relationship, like that between a suzerain and rebellious vassal" (*Kinship by Covenant*, 32). I see much less disjunction, but I can understand why he arrives at this view.

28. Pitre, *Jesus the Bridegroom*, 11.

He explains, "From the prophets' point of view, what happened at Sinai was not just the giving of a set of laws, but the spiritual wedding of God and Israel," so that God becomes Bridegroom and Israel becomes Bride.[29] Among the prophetic passages that he cites are Jeremiah 2:2, where the Lord recalls Israel's "love as a bride"; and Ezekiel 16:8, where the Lord recalls that "I plighted my troth to you and entered into a covenant with you . . . and you became mine." In Hosea, too, God looks back to the days when he redeemed Israel from Egyptian slavery and Israel answered him as his bride; and God looks forward to restoring and renewing this marital relationship once and for all: "And in that day, says the LORD, you will call me, 'My husband.' . . . And I will betroth you to me for ever" (Hos 2:16, 19).

The point for Pitre is that these prophets present Israel, at the time of the covenant at Sinai (Exodus 24), as God's youthful bride, with God in the role of covenantal Bridegroom. The covenant establishes not simply an adoptive sonship (with Israel becoming the son of the divine Father), although it certainly does establish such a relationship. Even more fundamentally, the covenant establishes a relationship that is so intimate as to be comparable to the love, mutuality, and friendship of a marriage.

How do the laws given to Moses fit in with this portrait? Who would give his wife a set of laws as a wedding gift? Pitre notes that the laws are not mere arbitrary rules; rather, they describe the contours of an intimate relationship. At the core of this relationship is the commandment against idolatry. To be covenantally married to God means to know the one to whom one is married; and Israel is covenantally married to the one Creator God. When Israel worships other gods, therefore, Israel treats them as only God should be treated. Just as the prophets depict God as loving Israel so much as to be Israel's Bridegroom, wishing to draw Israel into perfect intimacy with himself, so also the prophets depict Israel as not simply God's Bride but as God's unfaithful Bride, due preeminently to the sin of idolatry, but also due to Israel's other sins that undermine its relationship with God. The paradigmatic biblical example of Israel's idolatry is its fashioning and worship of a golden calf—symbolic of an Egyptian god. As Pitre points out, what the people do after worshiping the golden calf is part of the problem: they "sat down to eat and drink, and rose up to play" (Exod 32:6). In his commentary on Exodus, Thomas Dozeman notes that the meaning of this verse is that their worship "quickly devolves into ritual chaos, suggesting a sexual orgy."[30] After explaining what the Hebrew words discreetly convey, Dozeman remarks further: "The manufacturing of the golden calf already violated the

---

29. Pitre, *Jesus the Bridegroom*, 11.
30. Dozeman, *Exodus*, 704.

altar laws in 20:22-26. Now the sexual orgy of the people further violates the more specific prohibition against ascending an altar, lest one's nakedness is uncovered (20:26). Exodus 32:25 adds to the chaos of the ritual, describing the people as 'out of control.'"[31]

In pagan worship, temple liturgies and sexual orgies were not uncommonly linked; thus when the Bride of YHWH worships a false god, it is not surprising to find this action linked to sexual acts outside of marriage. The prophets describe this situation in terms of spiritual adultery. Pitre cites a number of prophetic texts to make this point. Examples include Isaiah 1:4, which describes Israel as "estranged" from the Lord, having "forsaken" him; Isaiah 1:21, which describes Israel as "a harlot"; Jeremiah 2:32-33, which compares Israel to a "bride" who has become adulterous; Jeremiah 3:20, in which the Lord complains that "as a faithless wife leaves her husband, so have you been faithless to me, O house of Israel"; and Ezekiel 16:17-18, in which God describes his bride Israel as a "harlot" who took his gifts and made idols out of them. God sums up his charge against Israel in terms of failure to be his faithful bride. Desiring a relationship of profound covenantal intimacy and faithfulness with Israel, God instead is forced to condemn Israel: "Adulterous wife, who receives strangers instead of her husband!" (Ezek 16:32). No wonder that when God wants to symbolize this situation, he commands Hosea to "take to yourself a wife of harlotry" (Hos 1:2) and to "love . . . an adulteress; even as the LORD loves the people of Israel, though they turn to other gods" (Hos 3:1). Hosea obeys the Lord's command, thereby acting out the situation of God and Israel. Beyond mere condemnation, Hosea is preparing for the day when Israel will truly be God's faithful Bride: "in that day, says the LORD, you will call me, 'My husband,' and no longer will you call me, 'My Baal.' . . . I will betroth you to me in faithfulness; and you shall know the LORD" (Hos 2:16, 20). The knowledge will be so intimate as to be comparable to the sexual "knowledge" of husband and wife.

Pitre's book focuses on the coming of the Messiah, as the "Bridegroom God of Israel" whose purpose is to establish the marriage of God and his people once and for all.[32] Pitre is looking ahead, then, to the fulfillment of God's promises. The purpose of God's dealings with his people is to make us sharers in his life, not to intimidate us with rules and punishments. Pitre again cites numerous prophets to indicate the promise of God to renew forever his covenantal marriage with his people. In addition to Hosea 2:16-20, he mentions Isaiah 54, where the Lord promises that he will not permit to endure the breach in the covenantal marriage caused by Israel's sins. Isaiah

31. Dozeman, *Exodus*, 705.
32. Pitre, *Jesus the Bridegroom*, 17.

proclaims, "For your Maker is your husband, the LORD of hosts is his name. . . . For the LORD has called you like a wife forsaken and grieved in spirit, like a wife of youth when she is cast off, says your God. . . . In overflowing wrath for a moment I hid my face from you, but with everlasting love I will have compassion on you" (Isa 54:5–6, 8). It has seemed that God would abandon Israel, because of the punishment of exile caused by sin; but God, as Israel's covenantal husband, will restore his bride to her dignity forever, with "everlasting love." Likewise, Pitre cites Jeremiah 31, where God recalls the "covenant which they [Israel] broke, though I was their husband" and where God promises a new covenant that will forever ensure that Israel obeys God's covenantal law and enjoys the blessings of covenantal marriage: "I will be their God, and they shall be my people" (Jer 31:32–33). Lastly, Pitre cites the promise of God in Ezekiel 16, one of the chapters in which (as noted above) God condemns Israel as a spiritual adulterer. In this chapter, God promises dire punishment, but God concludes with words that foretell the full renewal of the covenantal marriage in perfect mercy: "I will remember my covenant with you [Israel] in the days of your youth, and I will establish with you an everlasting covenant" (Ezek 16:60).

Rightly, then, Pitre speaks of Israel's God as "not a distant deity or an impersonal power, but the Bridegroom who wants his bride to 'know' (Hebrew *yada'*) him intimately, in a spiritual marriage that is not only faithful and fruitful, but 'everlasting' (Hebrew *'olam*)."[33] This restoration of the covenant will redeem Israel not merely juridically, but by truly renewing and perfecting God's people in a profoundly intimate relationship with him. God never ceases to be the Bridegroom, even though his bride—as a sinful people (like all the peoples of the world)—turns away from him. The very purpose of the biblical story of salvation is for God to bring about a marriage of God and humans that is unbreakable and whose intimacy cannot be exaggerated. The goal of human history is for the Bridegroom to take to himself his pure Bride, bringing about the spiritual consummation of the ineffably glorious marriage.

In this regard, Pitre adds that "ancient Jewish interpreters also read the Song of Songs as a symbolic description of the future wedding between the Bridegroom God and his chosen people."[34] Jacob Neusner remarks in

---

33. Pitre, *Jesus the Bridegroom*, 19.

34. Pitre, *Jesus the Bridegroom*, 20. See also Levenson, *The Love of God*, 125–42. Levenson points out that within the larger biblical context, "the question of the identity of the speakers takes on greater urgency than when the book is viewed in isolation. Who, in this larger framework, could these two passionate lovers possibly be? Let us put the question in terms of the rest of the Hebrew Bible: Where in that set of books do we find an intense love in which the lovers are separated much of the time, the male of the

the introduction to his translation of the Song of Songs Rabbah (composed around 500 AD), "The sages who compiled Song of Songs Rabbah read the Song of Songs as a sequence of statements of urgent love between God and Israel, the holy people."[35] The Song of Songs appeared to the Rabbis to be a dialogue between God the Bridegroom and Israel the Bride. Neusner states that "Israel's holy life is metaphorized through the poetry of love and beloved, Lover and Israel."[36] Pitre cites two sayings of Rabbi Akiba (c. 50–135 AD), in which Rabbi Akiba condemns any merely sexual reading of the Song of Songs and, furthermore, argues that the Song of Songs is the holiest of all the texts of Israel's Scriptures. This is because it portrays the very center of all Scripture: the desire of the Bridegroom Creator God for spiritual union with his covenantal people Israel.

Pitre notes some parallels between the Song of Songs and the Torah/Psalms that ancient Jewish interpreters found to be significant. For example, in Song of Songs 1:7 and elsewhere, we find reference to "you whom my soul loves"; this reference led interpreters back to Deuteronomy 6:5, where Moses commands Israel to "love the LORD your God with all your heart, and with all your soul, and with all your might." Lest this connection seems a stretch, Song of Songs 1:4 offers the possibility of a similar connection. It states, "The king has brought me into his chambers. We will exult and rejoice in you." In Psalm 118:24, we are commanded to rejoice in the day the Lord has made. Song of Songs 1:7 also asks the beloved where he pastures his flock; and this query was linked by the interpreters with Psalm 23's presentation of Israel as God's flock: "The LORD is my shepherd" (Ps 23:1). Again, Song of Songs 6:3 states, "I am my beloved's and my beloved is mine; he pastures his flock among the lilies." The interpreters drew a connection to the Lord who is Israel's shepherd and who has promised to be Israel's and to take Israel to himself: "I will take you for my people, and I will be your God"

---

two is not continuously accessible, the identities of the lovers seem to shift in various situations, powerful external forces oppose and threaten the romance, and the consummation of the relationship seems to be continually, maddeningly postponed? Put that way, the question nearly answers itself: the only such romance is that of God and Israel. To be sure, not every detail matches up, and much imaginative interpretation is necessary to sustain the identification. That very process of imaginative interpretation, though, is highly productive theologically and spiritually" (*The Love of God*, 132). Levenson differentiates between allegory and midrash, arguing that the latter is in no way arbitrary. He concludes, "Without the application of the Song of Songs to the Torah, the depth and power of their [God and the people Israel] libidinous passion might never have come to expression. And without the application of the Torah to the Song of Songs, the deeper spiritual import of erotic love would surely have gone unnoticed" (*The Love of God*, 134).

35. Neusner, *Israel's Love Affair with God*, 1.
36. Neusner, *Israel's Love Affair with God*, 3.

(Exod 6:7). For the validity of these connections, Pitre cites the Old Testament scholar Ellen Davis. In her commentary on the Song of Songs, Davis contends that the Song of Songs "is thick with words and images drawn from earlier books. By means of this 'recycled' language, the poet places this love song firmly in the context of God's passionate and trouble relationship with humanity (or, more particularly, with Israel), which is the story the rest of the Bible tells."[37]

Pitre adds that, in fact, the bride in the Song of Songs is described in terms of the Temple, the city of Jerusalem, and the land of Israel. Furthermore, he points out that the Song of Songs "never actually describes the consummation of the marriage."[38] In this regard the attitude of the bride in the Song of Songs, ever losing and seeking her Bridegroom, is summed up by the concluding verse of the Song of Songs: "Make haste, my beloved, and be like a gazelle or a young stag upon the mountain of spices" (Song 8:14). As Pitre notes, Jewish interpreters saw this as descriptive of the day of the restoration of Israel, when the people of Israel would be finally gathered in Jerusalem to offer proper worship. On this day, the Bridegroom will restore Israel by forgiving its sins and consummating the spiritual marriage of God and Israel.

In the above discussion of the marriage of God and Israel, Pitre is preparing for the main chapters of his book, which treat Jesus as the Bridegroom Messiah of Israel. When he turns to this theme, he first directs attention to John 3:28-29, where John the Baptist says, "I am not the Christ, but I have been sent before him. He who has the bride is the bridegroom." In the Gospel of John, as John the Baptist makes clear, Jesus Christ is the bridegroom of Israel, the one who comes to consummate the marriage of

---

37. Davis, *Proverbs, Ecclesiastes, and the Song of Songs*, 231; cited in Pitre, *Jesus the Bridegroom*, 23. See also Levenson, *The Love of God*, 137-38: "When, at the literal level, Moses was anointing the tabernacle and its accoutrements, transferring them from the realm of the profane to that of the sacred, he was enacting, at the midrashic level, the consecration of Israel to God as his bride—a condition that in the rabbinic mind has survived both the tabernacle and the temple that it foreshadowed, and has defined the Jewish people through all their generations. The tabernacle served as the chuppah, the marriage canopy, for the wedding of God and Israel. . . . This is, of course, a theological ideal and not at all an accurate description of the historical facts, as the prophetic and many other biblical and postbiblical texts painfully attest. But it is an ideal with a potent and enduring capacity to inspire behavior, to provoke repentance—and to ignite the love of God among Jews. Within the marital metaphor as these Talmudic rabbis extended and developed it, the Torah, both as narrative and as law, becomes a site of intense erotic passion. Its narrative tells of God's and the Jewish people's falling in love with each other, of his proposing marriage and her accepting the proposal, of the wedding itself and the intimacy and deepening commitment that followed it."

38. Pitre, *Jesus the Bridegroom*, 26.

God and his people. In articulating this point, Pitre is indebted to Jocelyn McWhirter's *The Bridegroom Messiah and the People of God: Marriage in the Fourth Gospel*.[39] Agreeing with Gilberte Baril that the Gospel of John presents Jesus as "the bridegroom of the Messianic nuptials," McWhirter emphasizes that "all Christians should be able to accept and appreciate this [marriage] metaphor since John does not use it to reinforce oppressive gender roles."[40]

Earlier in the Gospel of John, John the Baptist identifies Jesus as the "Lamb of God" (John 1:36). Along these lines, as noted above, the book of Revelation teaches that the consummated Israel, the Bride prepared for her Bridegroom, is "the wife of the Lamb" (Rev 21:9), the wife of Jesus Christ. When the Seer is given a vision of the new creation, he reports the following: "And I saw the holy city, New Jerusalem, coming down out of heaven from God, prepared as a bride adorned for her husband; and I heard a great voice from the throne saying, 'Behold, the dwelling of God is with men. He will dwell with them, and they shall be his people'" (Rev 21:2–3). The great promises of the Old Testament prophecies are echoed here and fulfilled by God.

---

39. McWhirter, *The Bridegroom Messiah*. McWhirter argues that the Gospel of John "alludes to four biblical texts about marriage. One involves similarities between Jesus' encounter with the Samaritan woman in John 4:4–42 and the story about Jacob and Rachel in Gen. 29:1–20. Two others evoke the Song of Songs. Mary of Bethany perfumes the reclining Jesus in a scene reminiscent of Song 1:12, and Mary Magdalene seeks and finds her missing man as does the woman in Song 3:1–4. A fourth allusion is the first to occur in the Gospel narrative. In John 3:29, John the Baptist declares, 'He who has the bride is the bridegroom. The friend of the bridegroom, who stands and hears him, rejoices greatly at the bridegroom's voice. . . .' This saying recalls Jer. 33:10–11: 'In . . . the towns of Judah and the streets of Jerusalem . . . there shall once more be heard the voice of mirth and the voice of gladness, the voice of the bridegroom . . . and the voice of the bride'" (*The Bridegroom Messiah*, 3–4). In McWhirter's view, the author of the Gospel of John "considered Jer. 33:10–11, Gen. 29:1–20, and the Song of Songs appropriate for illustrating the life, death, and resurrection of Jesus because of their messianic significance. According to the conventions of first-century exegesis—conventions based on a belief in the theological unity of Scripture—they can be interpreted as messianic prophecies in light of Ps. 45, which celebrates the wedding of God's anointed king" (*The Bridegroom Messiah*, 4). See also Cambe, "L'influence du Cantique des Cantiques"; Hengel, "The Interpretation of the Wine Miracle at Cana," 101–2; Feuillet, *Le Mystère de l'amour divin dans la théologie johannique*, 231. For approaches similar to McWhirter's—with the drawback, however, of devoting only a few pages to the topic—see Baril, *The Feminine Face of the People of God*, 92–97; Schneiders, *Written That You May Believe*. In her approach to Jesus' messianic status, McWhirter is particularly indebted to Juel's *Messianic Exegesis*.

40. McWhirter, *The Bridegroom Messiah*, 4, 11; Baril, *The Feminine Face of the People of God*, 93.

In a vision near the beginning of the book of Revelation, the Seer identifies Jesus as a "Lamb standing, as though it had been slain" (Rev 5:6). He is worthy of worship, which attests to his divine identity (see Rev 5:13). Thus, Jesus is the divine Bridegroom who accomplishes what God has promised to do for Israel in his covenants and prophecies. Jesus extends the marriage of God and Israel to include the nations in covenantal Israel, now reconfigured around the Messiah.

Is this perspective on the Messianic marriage of God and humanity found solely in the Johannine literature? According to Pitre, the answer is no. The accounts of the Last Supper in the Synoptic Gospels indicate that Jesus intended to inaugurate "the *new wedding covenant* spoken of by the prophets."[41] In all three Synoptic Gospels, Jesus at the Last Supper speaks of the wine as his covenantal blood: his "blood of the covenant" (Matt 26:28; Mark 14:24) or "the new covenant in my blood" (Luke 22:20). In Matthew's and Mark's Last Supper accounts, Jesus makes it clear that his blood will be spilled for the forgiveness of sins; and, indeed, Luke makes this clear as well, even if not necessarily in the Last Supper account. Pitre connects this with Exodus 24, where Moses seals the covenant at Sinai between God and Israel by throwing the sacrificial blood of animals upon the altar and upon the people (as noted above). In addition, Jesus' talk of "the new covenant in my blood" alludes to the covenant promised by Jeremiah 31, where, as Pitre has already pointed out, God refers to himself as Israel's "husband."

Along these lines, the New Testament scholar Joseph Fitzmyer observes in his commentary on Luke 22:20 that "[t]he 'new covenant' is an allusion to Jer 31:31, the promise made by Yahweh of a pact that he would make with 'the house of Israel and the house of Judah.'"[42] Fitzmyer grasps the cultic or sacrificial implications of Jesus' words, but he does not make the connection that the purpose of the sacrificial action (the spilling of Jesus' blood) is to establish once and for all the covenantal marriage of God and humanity. Instead, Pitre draws upon a book published in the 1930s that makes the point that Passover itself was nuptial and therefore Jesus' Passover action is intended to be nuptial as well, with respect to the marital union of God and his people.[43]

In addition to the Synoptics' Last Supper accounts, Pitre has recourse to the parable of the Sons of the Bridechamber, found in Matthew 9, Mark 2, and Luke 5. In Mark 2:19, Jesus responds to the people who question him about why his disciples do not fast: "Can the wedding guests fast while the

---

41. Pitre, *Jesus the Bridegroom*, 49.
42. Fitzmyer, *The Gospel According to Luke*, 1402.
43. See Chavasse, *The Bride of Christ*.

bridegroom is with them? As long as they have the bridegroom with them, they cannot fast." The same point is made in this parable in Matthew and Luke. Jesus adds that "[t]he days will come, when the bridegroom is taken away from them, and then they will fast in that day" (Mark 2:20). This, too, is a clear reference to the future events that will happen to Jesus. Pitre cites the New Testament scholar Adela Yarbro Collins to argue that Jesus intends to make clear that his very presence among his disciples means that there is preparation for an imminent wedding.[44] Pitre also clarifies the meaning of οἱ υἱοὶ τοῦ νυμφῶνος, which the RSV rather misleadingly translates simply as "wedding guests." The literal translation of this phrase is "sons of the bridechamber," an expression that is not found in the Old Testament but that appears in Rabbinic texts. The "sons of the bridechamber" are not simply all invitees to the wedding, but rather they are particular friends of the bridegroom who help to prepare him for the wedding and who attend upon him at the wedding. If the wedding of God and Israel has finally arrived in the Bridegroom Jesus, then it makes sense that Jesus' disciples do not perform the normal fasting required by Jewish law or custom.

Why should we think that Jesus, in describing himself as the "bridegroom," has in view a marriage of God and his people consummated *on his Cross*? As we have seen, Pitre has already suggested that this is the implicit meaning of Jesus' words at the Last Supper about "the new covenant in my blood" (Luke 22:20). Admittedly, examination of the passages in the Old Testament that explicitly foretell a Messiah indicates that (in the words of the New Testament scholar Morna Hooker) "[t]here is no precedent in the Old Testament for referring to any 'messianic' figure as a bridegroom, but the image is used of God (Isa. 54.4-8; 62:5; Ezek. 16.7ff.)."[45] Pitre's point about the Messianic "bridegroom," however, holds firm when the explicitly Messianic passages are canonically combined with the passages that depict the restoration of Israel in terms of God's promise fully to establish the covenantal marriage of God and his people. In claiming for himself the status of the "bridegroom," Jesus in the Synoptic accounts of this parable also points toward his Cross, through his reference to the day when the "bridegroom" will be "taken away" from his disciples. Pitre unpacks the connection of the day of the Cross with the day of the consummation of the marriage between God and his people. Specifically, Pitre states that during the seven-day wedding celebration that was characteristic of Jewish culture at this time, "[o]n the night of consummation, the bridegroom would leave his friends

---

44. See Collins, *Mark*, 198–99.
45. Hooker, *The Gospel According to Saint Mark*, 100.

and family and enter into what was known as the 'bridal chamber' . . . in order to be united to his bride, not to emerge again until morning."[46]

The high point of the seven-day wedding feast, then, was when the bridegroom left his friends; and this is precisely what Jesus says that he will do. Thus, Pitre concurs with the New Testament scholar Craig Keener's remark (about Matthew 9:14–17) that "Jesus is the groom of God's people in the coming messianic banquet. . . . The 'taking' of the bridegroom, of course, is a veiled reference to the impending crucifixion."[47] The bridal chamber of the marriage of God and humanity, therefore, is the Cross, where Jesus spills his "blood of the covenant." By means of this action, Jesus renews and perfects the covenantal marriage of God and his people that was sacrificially sealed at Sinai but to which Israel could not live up. In this action, Jesus takes on the role of Israel's bridegroom, a role that only God can truly have. Pitre cites Joseph Ratzinger on this point: "Jesus identifies himself here as the 'bridegroom' of God's promised marriage with his people and, by doing so, he mysteriously places his own existence, himself, within the mystery of God."[48] As Pitre observes, this is one of Jesus' clearest claims to divinity. Jesus Christ is God come to consummate his marriage with humanity. In making this argument, Pitre includes smaller details such as the crown of thorns (Mark 15:17; Matt 27:29; Luke 22:11) that Jesus wore on the Cross, since a Jewish bridegroom wore "a crown on his wedding day."[49] The fact that on the day of his crucifixion, according to John 19:23, Jesus was dressed in a seamless robe also relates to Jesus' status as Israel's bridegroom. In accord with the covenantal signification of marriage, a Jewish bridegroom dressed like a priest, and the high priest's robe was seamless (see Exodus 28:31–32).

If Israel could not live up to the demands of this marriage—namely the demands of holiness—how can Christ's bride the Church live up to these demands? On the one hand, humanly speaking the members of the Church are sinners and cannot live up to the demands of holiness. But on the other hand, Jesus' sacrificial blood on the Cross accomplishes the forgiveness of sins and provides an ongoing fount of reconciliation for his people. Furthermore, as Pitre remarks, the "blood and water" that come forth from the crucified Jesus' side in John 19:34 has been read as a parallel with the coming forth of Eve from Adam's side; and the Church comes forth from Christ's side when from Christ's side symbolically flow the mysteries of baptism and

---

46. Pitre, *Jesus the Bridegroom*, 90. Regarding the bride-chamber, Pitre directs attention to Psalm 19:4–5 and Tobit 6:15–17.

47. Keener, *A Commentary on the Gospel of Matthew*, 300; cited in Pitre, *Jesus the Bridegroom*, 91–92.

48. Benedict XVI, *Jesus of Nazareth*, 252; cited in Pitre, *Jesus the Bridegroom*, 94.

49. Pitre, *Jesus the Bridegroom*, 103.

the Eucharist. Pitre finds, therefore, that the Church is permanently married to Christ in holiness precisely insofar as Christ is continually giving the Church "supernatural life."[50]

Similarly, although the New Testament scholar Raymond Brown thinks there is likely no connection to the Genesis account of Eve coming forth from Adam's side—and although he considers that baptism and the Eucharist likely are only a secondary symbolic meaning of the text—Brown agrees that the water and blood symbolize supernatural life. In light of John 7:37–39, the water stands for the "living water" that is the Holy Spirit and that is poured out only when Jesus has been "glorified" by shedding his blood on the Cross for the forgiveness of sins.[51] It is evident that for John, as for the Letter to the Ephesians, the Church has its origin and its sustenance in nuptial holiness in Christ the Bridegroom's sacrificial dying for his Bride: "Husbands, love your wives, as Christ loved the church and gave himself up for her, that he might sanctify her" (Eph 5:25–26). In light of Ephesians 5, Pitre concludes that "the day of Jesus' crucifixion is his wedding day"—the prophesied marriage of the divine Bridegroom with his Bride "in an everlasting marriage covenant."[52]

Pitre adds that the wedding, while begun, is not yet complete, since the Bride is not yet fully perfected and the full number of the elect has not yet been gathered. The Cross of the risen and ascended Lord continues to wield its saving power in the world, sanctifying believers. As Pitre says, not only will many persons continue to come to faith while the world endures, but also "those who have come to faith in the Bridegroom and become members of his bride have often 'soiled' their wedding garments through sin and acts of spiritual infidelity."[53] In this light, Pitre points out that the end of the world should be viewed not merely as a cataclysm but as the joyful fullness of the marriage between God and humanity made possible by Christ and his Spirit.

Lest the analogy of marriage seem to break down here—since Christ either consummated it on the Cross or he did not—Pitre notes that in ancient Judaism "one of the duties of the bridegroom was *to prepare a home for his bride*, so that when the wedding was finally consummated he could take her from her own family and bring her to live with him."[54] Pitre has in view John 14:2–3, "In my Father's house are many rooms; if it were not so,

---

50. Pitre, *Jesus the Bridegroom*, 112.
51. See Brown, *The Gospel According to John*, 949–52.
52. Pitre, *Jesus the Bridegroom*, 113.
53. Pitre, *Jesus the Bridegroom*, 115.
54. Pitre, *Jesus the Bridegroom*, 117.

would I have told you that I go to prepare a place for you? And when I go and prepare a place for you, I will come again and will take you to myself." With respect to this passage, his interpretation concurs with that of the New Testament scholar Adeline Fehribach in her book *The Women in the Life of the Bridegroom*.[55]

In Pitre's analysis, then, a tension emerges between the "already" and the "not yet," a tension that characterizes the New Testament's eschatology as a whole. Already, through his Cross and Resurrection, Christ has accomplished the perfect marriage of the divine Bridegroom with his people (Israel reconfigured around the Messiah, now with the Gentiles included). But the marriage of God and humanity, though in this sense accomplished already by Christ, awaits its full accomplishment as, over the course of ongoing history, the full number of the elect is brought in and the members of the Church are sanctified by the power of his Cross and Resurrection. Thus, even though the marriage of God and humanity is accomplished by Christ when he is "glorified" on the Cross (as Pitre says), it is also correct to add—as Pitre does in light of the book of Revelation—that "all of human history is headed toward the wedding supper of the Lamb and the unveiling of the bride of Christ."[56] The Christian understanding of the end of time is not about destruction but rather is about the glorious "'unveiling' (Greek *apokalypsis*) of the bride of Christ. Just as an ancient Jewish bridegroom would lift the veil of his bride on their wedding day, so too at the end of time Jesus will unveil the glory of his bride, the New Jerusalem."[57] Among the characteristics of the Bride are perfect holiness, perfect peace, perfect worship, absence of corruption and death, and the fact that the blessed "shall see his face"—the face of God and the Lamb (Rev 22:4), the face of the Bridegroom who has everlastingly married his beloved people.

Pitre brings his book to a close by displaying the theme of the covenantal marriage of God and humanity as it informs the teaching of the Church Fathers—especially their teaching on the sacraments and the religious life—as well as the teaching of the *Catechism of the Catholic Church* and recent popes. Rather than tracking his discussion of the Fathers, let me simply draw attention to the passages of the *Catechism of the Catholic Church* that Pitre quotes. First, as has been one of the main points of Pitre's book, the *Catechism* states that "[t]he entire Christian life bears the mark of the spousal love of Christ and the Church" (§1617). Second, the *Catechism*

---

55. See Fehribach, *The Women in the Life of the Bridegroom*. More generally, Fehribach's feminist perspective differs from Pitre's.

56. Pitre, *Jesus the Bridegroom*, 121.

57. Pitre, *Jesus the Bridegroom*, 123.

states the following: "The nuptial covenant between God and his people Israel had prepared the way for the new and everlasting covenant in which the Son of God, by becoming incarnate and giving his life, has united to himself in a certain way all mankind saved by him, thus preparing for 'the wedding-feast of the Lamb' [Rev 19:7]" (§1612).[58] Both of these quotations come from the *Catechism*'s section on the sacrament of marriage.

At this stage, however, we must turn again to our original question.[59] In the prophetic books of the Old Testament, it certainly can seem as though God the lover is also God the abuser. Let me now examine why this is so.

II. YHWH THE ABUSIVE MALE?

What are we to make of passages such as the following?

- "The LORD said: Because the daughters of Zion are haughty and walk with outstretched necks, glancing wantonly with their eyes, mincing along as they go, tinkling with their feet; the LORD will smite with a scab the heads of the daughters of Zion, and the LORD will lay bare their secret parts" (Is 3:16–17).

- "Lift up your eyes and see those who come from the north. Where is the flock that was given you, your beautiful flock? What will you say when they set as head over you those whom you yourself have taught to be friends to you? Will not pangs take hold of you, like those of a woman in travail? And if you say in your heart, 'Why have these things come upon me?' it is for the greatness of your iniquity that your skirts are lifted up and you suffer violence" (Jer 13:20–22).

- "Thus says the LORD God, Because your shame was laid bare and your nakedness uncovered in your harlotries with your lovers, and

---

58. The two quotations come from the *Catechism of the Catholic Church*, cited in *Jesus the Bridegroom*, 137.

59. In *Sexual and Marital Metaphors*, Moughtin-Mumby affirms "the inability of the prophetic texts to reverse their own negative sexual and marital metaphorical language," despite their clear attempts to do so and, somewhat more hopefully, "their astonishing tendency to undermine themselves, unravelling their own assumptions and rhetoric, leaving themselves all but impotent" (274–75). In her view, positive meaning emerges from these texts only when the women are viewed as (often strong, resistant, ungeneralizable) individuals, as for example when we recognize that the figure of the prostitute takes "on an astonishing range of different guises in the prophetic text, repeatedly liaising with different literary frames to breed a striking variety of associations, including animal instinct, ruthless entrepreneurship, absurdity, nymphomania, cultic defilement, lust, misunderstanding, the desire for control, and uncontrollability, to name just a few" (*Sexual and Marital Metaphors*, 275–76).

because of all your idols, and because of the blood of your children that you gave to them, therefore, behold, I will gather all your lovers, with whom you took pleasure, all those you loved and all those you loathed; I will gather them against you from every side, and will uncover your nakedness to them, that they may see all your nakedness. And I will judge you as women who break wedlock and shed blood are judged, and bring upon you the blood of wrath and jealousy. And I will give you into the hand of your lovers, and they shall throw down your vaulted chamber and break down your lofty places; they shall strip you of your clothes and take your fair jewels, and leave you naked and bare. ... Because you have not remembered the days of your youth, but have enraged me with all these things; therefore, behold, I will requite your deeds upon your head, says the LORD God" (Ezek 16:36–39, 43).

- "Plead with your mother, plead—for she is not my wife, and I am not her husband—that she put away her harlotry from her face, and her adultery from between her breasts; lest I strip her naked and make her as in the day she was born, and make her like a wilderness, and set her like a parched land, and slay her with thirst" (Hos 2:2–3).

- "Therefore I will take back my grain in its time, and my wine in its season; and I will take away my wool and my flax, which were to cover her nakedness. Now I will uncover her lewdness in the sight of her lovers, and no one shall rescue her out of my hand. And I will put an end to all her mirth, her feasts, her new moons, her sabbaths, and all her appointed feasts. And I will lay waste her vines and her fig trees, of which she said, 'These are my hire, which my lovers have given me.' I will make them a forest, and the beasts of the field shall devour them. And I will punish her for the feast days of the Baals, when she burned incense to them and decked herself with her ring and jewelry, and went after her lovers, and forgot me, says the LORD" (Hos 2:9–13).

- "Behold, I am against you [Nineveh], says the LORD of hosts, and will lift up your skirts over your face; and I will let nations look on your nakedness and kingdoms on your shame. I will throw filth at you and treat you with contempt, and make you a gazingstock" (Nahum 3:5–6).

- "Come down and sit in the dust, O virgin daughter of Babylon; sit on the ground without a throne, O daughter of the Chaldeans! For you shall no more be called tender and delicate. Take the millstones and grind meal, put off your veil, strip off your robe, uncover your legs, pass through the rivers. Your nakedness shall be uncovered, and your shame shall be seen. I will take vengeance, and I will spare no man" (Isa 47:1-3).

With regard especially to Nahum 3 and Isaiah 47, Gerlinde Baumann argues that it is a simple matter: "YHWH appears as the rapist."[60] Drawing on the work of Majella Franzmann, Baumann adds that although "[t]he image of YHWH as rapist can be explained from the context in which the texts originated," nonetheless "[t]his kind of male God-as-rapist image has been handed down for thousands of years without being subjected to any kind of fundamental critique."[61]

Is this claim true? I note that in Jerome's commentary on Nahum 3:5-6, Jerome first emphasizes that Nahum 3 and Ezekiel 16 are using a "metaphor of an adulterous woman" that is not meant to be taken literally.[62] Specifically with respect to Nahum 3:5, where the Lord appears to be describing himself in an act of rape, Jerome hastens to make clear that one would be profoundly misinterpreting the passage if one interpreted it along such lines. On the contrary, says Jerome, in Nahum 3:5 the Lord intends to communicate the following: "although you do not deserve it, I will make you see my virtues, precepts, and words, which you have hidden behind your back. For I commanded that my words should always be moving before your eyes, and should be bound and hanging down."[63] Far from refusing to subject "to any kind of fundamental critique" the "male God-as-rapist image" found in Nahum 3:5-6, Jerome insists sharply that God must not be thought of as a male rapist. For Jerome, the real meaning is that God, as "the true doctor [who] comes from heaven" (namely Christ), will show Nineveh his "virtues, precepts, and words."[64] It may seem that such an interpretation is quite a stretch, but this is precisely the point: Jerome, subjecting the

---

60. Baumann, *Love and Violence*, 195. See also Sanderson, "Nahum," in *The Women's Bible Commentary*, 217-21, at 221: "To involve God in an image of sexual violence is, in a profound way, somehow to justify it and thereby to sanction it for human males who are for any reason angry with a woman." For historical background to Nahum's "presentation of the Judean/Assyrian crisis" and the manner in which Nahum's feminized Nineveh is the object of Yahweh's sexual shaming and abuse, see Chapman, *The Gendered Language of Warfare in the Israelite-Assyrian Encounter*, 103-10.

61. Baumann, *Love and Violence*, 195. Baumann directs attention to Franzmann, "The City as Woman."

62. I am employing an unpublished translation by Sr. Albert-Marie Surmanski, of Jerome's *Commentarium in Naum*, with thanks to Surmanski for the privilege of using her work.

63. Jerome, *Commentarium in Naum*.

64. Jerome, *Commentarium in Naum*.

seeming "God-as-rapist image" to a "fundamental critique," insists upon reading it in an allegorical sense.⁶⁵

Likewise, in his reading of Ezekiel 16, Jerome proposes that the fornicating "Jerusalem" stands for all of us who pass from one sin to the next without repentance. Tropologically, the "brazen harlot" of Ezekiel 16:30 is none other than "every Christian soul that has abandoned the worship of God, indulged in vices and excess, and having pursued a worldly life, has not done well even in that respect, but has both lost the wealth of religion and has not received the riches of the world."⁶⁶ Interpreting Ezekiel 16:38-40, where God promises to gather Jerusalem's "lovers" and allow them to see her naked, strip her bare, and destroy her by stoning and the sword, Jerome first postulates that the literal sense must *not* be understood as signifying a real woman, nor can the metaphor be limited to adultery. Rather, this is a "metaphor of an adulterous and homicidal woman, who not only fornicated against her own husband, but also killed her children."⁶⁷ The metaphor has in view the Babylonian exile, as well as the future destruction of the (second) Temple. In the metaphor, says Jerome, the killing of children stands for rejecting "good thoughts" given by God and instead choosing to "[turn] away unto evil works."⁶⁸ Moreover, lest we get the wrong idea even about this metaphor, Jerome develops a tropological reading which makes clear that Ezekiel 16 is not about women but rather is about "every soul" who has

---

65. By contrast, see the remarks of J. Cheryl Exum: "In describing God's treatment of his wayward wife, the prophets rely upon a rhetorical strategy that encourages the audience to identify and sympathize with a male-identified deity. This is the privileged point of view, the 'I' that condemns the 'you,' the other, whose view is not represented. . . . When readers privilege the deity, which most readers of the Bible still do, they are forced into accepting this position, for to resist would be tantamount to challenging divine authority. This is the position taken almost without exception by biblical commentators, who, until recently, have been almost without exception male. Typically these commentators either ignore the difficulties posed by this divine sexual abuse or reinscribe the gender ideology of the biblical texts; usually they do both in their ceaseless efforts to justify God" (Exum, *Plotted, Shot, and Painted*, 114-15). She cites Wolff, *Hosea*, 34, 38, 44; Andersen and Freedman, *Hosea*, 248-49. Exum goes on to argue, "The contributors to *The Women's Bible Commentary* show the difference reading as a woman makes. The authors of the entries on the prophetic books all wrestle with the implications of biblical violence against women and struggle to find ways of dealing with it. . . . What distinguishes their work from that of their male counterparts is their recognition of divine sexual violence as a problem and their honesty about it. One looks in vain in the standard commentaries for responses like these to the violence against women in the prophetic corpus" (*Plotted, Shot, and Painted*, 117-18, referring to *The Women's Bible Commentary*).

66. Jerome, *Commentary on Ezekiel*, 175.
67. Jerome, *Commentary on Ezekiel*, 177.
68. Jerome, *Commentary on Ezekiel*, 179.

received a gift from God but who chooses instead to worship "demons and contrary powers."[69] Jerome insists upon not attributing to God any violating action toward any woman.

Along similar lines, Mark Sheridan has observed that John Chrysostom is constantly concerned that readers of the Old Testament will read literalistically and assume that the portrayals of God's anger, threats, and abusive actions toward men and women are meant to describe the character of God or what is permissible for God.[70] Chrysostom fears that believers will imagine that God is bodily, that God commits (or desires to commit) acts of brutality, and/or that God has human passions such as anger. According to Chrysostom, God only allows vivid and potentially deeply misleading metaphors to be used about himself in Scripture because God wants to get through to dull readers and to alert them to seek for a *spiritual* meaning. It is this deeper spiritual meaning, and no other, that must be gleaned from metaphors that otherwise would demean God.

For Baumann, the difficulty is not answered by these positions, since Baumann's concern is why God permitted abusive metaphors to be used in Scripture even if they were always meant to signify allegorically.[71] In Hosea, she finds that "a parallel is drawn between land and 'woman/wife' in order to denounce the 'whorish' behavior of both. Divine punishment of 'woman'

69. Jerome, *Commentary on Ezekiel*, 178. For a contrasting approach, see Dempsey, "The 'Whore' of Ezekiel 16." Dempsey recognizes that "imagery and metaphors relating to women are used to communicate to Ezekiel's audience and to the text's (re)readers an ethical message: God will not tolerate injustice" ("The 'Whore' of Ezekiel 16," 72), but she emphasizes that "Yhwh in his anger said and did some despicable things to Jerusalem as her husband. Although Yhwh is willing to forgive and restore the covenant with Jerusalem, despite the fact that there is no mention of remorse on Jerusalem's part, it seems a bit presumptuous on Yhwh's part to assume that Jerusalem would take him back. After all, he has been verbally and physically abusive to her" ("The 'Whore' of Ezekiel 16," 76).

70. See Sheridan, *Language for God in Patristic Tradition*, 42.

71. Similarly, Exum states, "The fact that this is metaphorical violence does not make it less criminal. Indeed, it is extremely injurious: because God is the subject, we—that is, female as well as male readers—are expected to sympathize with the divine perspective against the (personified) woman.... Sexual violence of which God is the perpetrator and the nation personified as a woman is the object, along with its destructive implications for gender relations, is there. It cannot be dismissed by claiming that it is only 'metaphorical', as if metaphor were some kind of container from which meaning can be extracted, or as if gender relations inscribed on a metaphorical level are somehow less problematic than on a literal level" (*Plotted, Shot, and Painted*, 101–2; 119). I see her point, though I do think that the fact that it is metaphorical makes it *less* problematic. She draws attention to such studies as Gordon and Washington, "Rape as a Military Metaphor in the Hebrew Bible"; Galambush, *Jerusalem in the Book of Ezekiel*; and Ellwood, *Batter My Heart*. For metaphor's destructive potential, see also Bal, "Metaphors He Lives By." See also, for Bal's broader project, her *Lethal Love*.

Israel follows, stated in images of sexual violence, but also in metaphors applying to the land and its fertility."[72] Jeremiah 13:22 is likewise impossible for her to accept, given that she thinks that the meaning that readers will receive is "unmistakable," namely that YHWH "acts against Jerusalem in the role of a perpetrator of sexual violence."[73] As Angela Bauer says, "The image of God the rapist haunts theology and biblical interpretation."[74]

Along similarly critical lines, John Barton remarks that "biblical texts do . . . portray God as having a dark side."[75] In his view, the prophetic literature depicts a two-faced God. He warns, "Commentators have always been tempted to fudge the issue of just how unjust the God of the prophets

---

72. Baumann, *Love and Violence*, 223. Alice A. Keefe surveys a number of feminist readings of Hosea, and she criticizes these readings for assuming the correctness of the standard scholarly view that interprets Hosea as attacking the Canaanite fertility religions. Against the standard feminist scholarship on Hosea, she denies that Hosea "is misogynistic literature which assumes and depends upon a view of female sexuality as something intrinsically negative" (Keefe, *Woman's Body*, 154). After all, "the redeemed Israel is still a woman" in Hosea (*Woman's Body*, 154). Indeed, she observes that "in a social context [such as ancient Israel] where the individual is not the primary locus of human meaning and value, body, sex and gender will carry meanings which are quite distinct from our own and the equations most central to feminist analysis will not necessarily hold" (*Woman's Body*, 158). Furthermore, by contrast to modern understanding of sex and sexuality as a private matter, "In a kinship-based society, sexual reproduction, material production and the maintenance of social power constitute intersecting and coordinate dimensions of a unitary sphere of cultural activity. . . . Rather than sex and the society signifying two separate spheres of human activity, in biblical literature, sexual activity carries profoundly social and political meanings" (*Woman's Body*, 159).

73. Baumann, *Love and Violence*, 223. For a less condemnatory perspective, in dialogue with Baumann and others, see Holt, "'The Stain of Your Guilt.'"

74. Bauer, *Gender in the Book of Jeremiah*, 116. Bauer warns that "the pull of a long interpretive tradition that sides with the voice(s) of prophet/YHWH against the people/Israel, that sides in most instances with the male against the female, surrounds emerging [feminist] counter-readings. It continuously threatens their erasure, as textual and intertextual levels diverge. It is contemporary feminist and womanist voices that have been critical of dualistic patterns confining women. Yet not so Jeremiah. Israel of the past is remembered as 'bride' being 'holy' to YHWH (Jer. 2:2–3), or promised to be 'Maiden Israel', dancing in the future (Jer. 31:4). By contrast, the people of the Jeremianic present are accused of acting as a promiscuous woman of uncontrollable sexuality, defiled and defiling (e.g., Jer. 2:20–22, 23–25, 33–34; 3:1, 2–3, 6–10, 19–20), while at the same time rape, a crime of uncontrolled sexual violation, is presented as 'justified' (e.g., 13:20–27). It is contemporary female voices that call for the embracing of ambiguities. Not so Jeremiah. . . . It is contemporary (fe)male voices that search for fluidity of gender, transgression of traditional gender roles, and flexibility of identities, and hear the male prophet speak in a female voice. Not so Jeremiah" (*Gender in the Book of Jeremiah*, 162–63). It seems to me that the main point of Jeremiah about sin and redemption has been lost here.

75. Barton, *Ethics in Ancient Israel*, 262; cf. 265. He directs attention to Wettstein, "God's Struggles."

is when evaluated in human terms—and not simply in our terms . . . but in the moral terms the prophets themselves apply to human conduct. The God of the prophets is often no 'nicer' a character than the God of Joshua and Judges [who commands genocide]."[76] Approvingly drawing upon the work of Andrew Davies, Barton draws attention to the passage from Isaiah 3 that I have quoted above: "Even if we grant that there is something wrong with the women of Isaiah 3:16–4:1, who take such pleasure in their jewelry and cosmetics, it is impossible to find any human moral principle that would justify the cruel and degrading punishment with which the prophet threatens them."[77]

Yet, I think the point of the first chapters of Isaiah is far from unjust: God has abandoned Israel to her enemies, because Israel has become deeply corrupt. As God says in his law case against Israel, "Your princes are rebels and companions of thieves. Every one loves a bribe and runs after gifts. They do not defend the fatherless, and the widow's cause does not come to them" (Isa 1:23). God adds that the "land is filled with idols" (Is 2:8)—as archeological evidence confirms was the case. In sum, I do not agree with Barton insofar as he implies that God's abandonment of Israel—which follows from Israel's abandonment of God—is unjust. The imagery of the smiting of the "daughters of Zion" (Isa 3:15) is paired with similar insistence that the *men* of Israel will be humiliated and punished. As God says through the prophet Isaiah, "The Lord enters into judgment with the elders and princes of his people: 'It is you who have devoured the vineyard, the spoil of the poor is in your houses. What do you mean by crushing my people, by grinding the face of the poor?'" (Isa 3:14–15).

Baumann's concern is a deeper one than Barton's. She wonders how anyone could accept a Scripture as "holy" if it employs images that involve God violating women sexually or images in which God causes women to

---

76. Barton, *Ethics in Ancient Israel*, 251.

77. Barton, *Ethics in Ancient Israel*, 249. See Davies, *Double Standards in Isaiah*, 133. For an opposed viewpoint, discussed appreciatively and at length by Barton, see Lindström, *God and the Origin of Evil*. Barton comments that "[t]here is considerable controversy about the idea of Yahweh as the source of evil. . . . Lindström would say that though Yahweh is presented as the source of punishment and destruction for the wicked (which may include Israel), to call these things 'evil' is to beg the question: precisely because they are sent by a good God they are not seen as evil by the Old Testament writers, but as good" (*Ethics in Ancient Israel*, 257). After pointing out that Lindström's book is weakened by the fact that he only deals with passages where the language of "good" and "evil" occurs, Barton concludes that "I believe Lindström is right to argue that the *general* tenor of the Old Testament is to stress the justice of Yahweh, and to seek to reduce elements of arbitrariness in human experience of the divine. This seems to be the case even in works that evidently arose out of the experience of disaster, such as Lamentations" (*Ethics in Ancient Israel*, 260).

be publicly humiliated in the very ways in which men of the time caused women to be publicly humiliated. The fact that Jerome insists that such metaphors are meant to be interpreted tropologically or as allegories whose meaning is the opposite of what the metaphor implies, may seem only to confirm Baumann's outrage. Baumann notes that from the outset of her research, "the center of my interest in the prophetic imagery of marriage was not YHWH the 'loving husband.'"[78] On the contrary, she always focused on the punitive imagery, which in her view predominates over love in the prophetic literature. She asks, "Is the complex of metaphors of sexual violence really inseparable from the prophetic marriage imagery?"[79]

This question is all the more urgent for her because she finds that in contemporary culture (she lives in Germany), women are subjected to misogyny and violence. In her (mistaken) view, "marriage is the relationship in which it is easiest for violent men to make women their victims."[80] There is also the problem of male fantasies about violence against women, fantasies that are regularly played out in pornography.[81] Her fundamental point is that "[t]he version of God in which 'he' is presented, in connection with the prophetic marriage imagery, as a sexually violent male is just one of the many problematic sides of the biblical God-image."[82] Even if Israel, having abandoned God, deserved its punishment (namely, abandonment by God), how could a good God permit himself to be described in sexually violent and abusive imagery? As Cheryl Exum states, "Claiming that there is a suffering and loving god behind this imagery will not make it go away."[83] Like Baumann, Exum warns against trying to sidestep the problem by "creating a canon within the canon."[84]

By contrast, other biblical scholars have argued that the metaphors must be read as *metaphors* (in light of the actual destruction brought about by invading armies) rather than as descriptions of acceptable behavior. Robert Carroll urges in this regard, "The voice I hear and read in Jeremiah 2–3 (and also in 5.7–8) is a voice expressing strong disapproval of the community or nation's past behaviour as wild, uncontrolled and apostate. . . . The target of the mockery is the male society."[85] For Carroll, it is important to

78. Baumann, *Love and Violence*, ix.
79. Baumann, *Love and Violence*, ix.
80. Baumann, *Love and Violence*, x.
81. See Morrow, "Pornography and Penance," 62–84.
82. Baumann, *Love and Violence*, 2.
83. Exum, *Plotted, Shot, and Painted*, 122.
84. Exum, *Plotted, Shot, and Painted*, 122.
85. Carroll, "Desire Under the Terebinths," 288.

perceive that the metaphorical woman in the prophetic text is not intended to be a real woman, but rather to be a description of the corporate people. He states that "the only women in the chapter [Ezek 23] are metaphors. The narrative is not about women but about cities or communities represented by those cities. . . . [T]he use of metaphors of women for the community, nation, city and land in the prophets may have little to do with the representation of women as such."[86] The metaphors disturb us, but their original readers may not have understood them the way that we do, and, besides, they too would likely have been disturbed. Somewhat similarly, Else Holt thinks it possible to criticize the disturbing metaphors while retaining the overall portrait of God in the book of Jeremiah. She does not think that we have to "distance ourselves from" or repudiate the prophetic books.[87] From the perspective of studies of trauma, Kathleen O'Connor suggests that the disturbing metaphors are understandable given the prophetic task of articulating and giving meaning to the extreme horrors that the people of Jerusalem and Judah experienced during the events that led to the Babylonian exile.[88] This does not mean that today we need to approve the portrait of God as an abusive husband (or of Israel as a nymphomaniac), but we can appreciate some aspects of what the prophet was doing in his own context: dealing with trauma requires naming it boldly rather than repressing it.

All this is a variation of the problem that also faces interpreters of passages such as Joshua 10:40, where Joshua's destruction of "all that breathed" in the cities that he conquered is seen as obedience to God, "as the LORD God of Israel commanded." How could a good God be one who commands Saul to "go and smite Amalek, and utterly destroy all that they have; do not spare them, but kill both man and woman, infant and suckling, ox and sheep, camel and ass" (1 Sam 15:3)? Indebted to Augustine, Thomas Aquinas suggests that actions against non-combatants, which appear to conflict with the Decalogue's commandment against killing the innocent, may justly be undertaken in obedience to divine command, because God "is Lord of life and death: for He it is who inflicts the punishment of death on all men, both godly and ungodly, on account of the sin of our first parent, and if

---

86. Carroll, "Desire Under the Terebinths," 106. For various contemporary approaches to biblical metaphor and to metaphor more broadly, see for example O'Brien, *Challenging Prophetic Metaphor*; Foreman, *Animal Metaphors and the People of Israel*, 4–29; van Dijk-Hemmes, "The Metaphorization of Woman in Prophetic Speech"; Kittay, *Metaphor*; Donoghue, *Metaphor*; and the essays by numerous notable scholars in Sacks, ed., *On Metaphor*.

87. Holt, "'The Stain of Your Guilt,'" 105.

88. See O'Connor, *Jeremiah*; see also O'Connor, *Lamentations and the Tears of the World*.

a man be the executor of that sentence by divine authority, he will be no murderer."[89] I consider this argument to be untenable. Certainly God is the "Lord of life and death," but if he commanded Israelite soldiers to kill pregnant women and babies, God would be culpable for morally warping the soldiers who performed such heinous actions. Unlike the divine retribution caused by disease or natural disaster—in which the agent of the punishment is not a conscious agent—an intrinsically evil action has a distortive impact upon the person who carries it out. Thus, Church Fathers such as Origen were correct to infer that the human author has a purpose in attributing such commands to God (for example, to warn readers against becoming assimilated to the nations and their gods), but that in actual fact that living God revealed in Scripture could not have issued such commands.

With respect to publicly stripping a woman naked, Baumann points out that John Huehnergard's studies of ancient Near Eastern texts indicate that "if a widow remarries she is to be deprived of the property of her first husband and leave his house naked. In Huehnergard's opinion this stripping [an instance of which is found in Hosea 2:3] has a humiliating aspect: its purpose, however, is primarily the protection of the property of the family or clan."[90] Likewise, Thomas Podella has suggested that the lifting of the skirt, such as is found in Nahum 3:5, is connected in the ancient Near East to legal rites surrounding a divorce, so that it is less about humiliation than it is about indicating that a change of status has taken place.[91] Baumann also recognizes that given the ancient Near East's expectations for covenantal treaties, in the prophetic literature "[t]hreats of violence against women are . . . found within the framework of scenarios in which it is prophesied that a vassal, should he prove unfaithful, will be subjected to every kind of fearful punishment imaginable. Rape of women in the ancient Near East is therefore no more to be regarded as part of 'normal' life than are the other curses."[92] She adds that in the context of exile, there are ancient Near Eastern "iconographic witnesses to the fact that deported persons or prisoners in many cases had to strip or be stripped."[93]

Alice Keefe argues that the disturbing imagery arises, in fact, from how profoundly women were valued in biblical Israel. She explains that women had in their power the very survival of the people: "The social character of sex in ancient Israel relates to the pragmatics of survival in a marginal

---

89. Aquinas, *Summa theologiae* I-II, q. 100, a. 8, ad 3.
90. Baumann, *Love and Violence*, 72; see Huehnergard, "Biblical Notes."
91. Baumann, *Love and Violence*, 75; see Podella, *Das Lichtkleid JHWHs*.
92. Baumann, *Love and Violence*, 78.
93. Baumann, *Love and Violence*, 79.

agrarian frontier zone . . . where the survival and strength of the family group depended upon its size. . . . Such a culture would not likely abstract concerns about group strength and survival from its symbolic constructs about woman's body and female sexuality."[94] With regard to the prophets' symbolic references to the female body, Keefe urges that "in Israel the maternal body might also be considered a 'natural place' to display themes relating to fertility, procreation, lineage, kinship and covenant."[95] As she says, it is understandable and, indeed, powerfully resonant that "woman's body" in biblical texts serves "as a sign for the social body," as the prophets and other biblical authors employ "gynomorphic figurations of corporate identity indigenous to [their] world."[96] Keefe reminds us that when we are

94. Keefe, *Woman's Body*, 159. She adds, "Indeed, as Lyn Brechtel argues, in such a group-oriented culture (as opposed to an individual-oriented culture such as the modern West), the very notion of salvation is intimately tied up with the meaning of woman and sex" (*Woman's Body*, 159; referring to Brechtel, "What If Dinah Is Not Raped?"). Keefe concludes, "When feminist (and other) readers look at the inscription of female sexuality in the book of Hosea and see the female body only as an individual body sexually constrained by the powers of patriarchy, they overlook the corporate and corporeal dimensions of human meaning which were constitutive of the fabric of life in ancient Israel and which are at work in Hosea's imagery. This limitation in interpretive vision may be traced to the indebtedness of feminist theory to the world-view of the Enlightenment with its inscription of the body as an object and possession of the autonomous and rational self. For feminist theory, embodiment has to do with individual bodies, and its thinking about the body is primarily concerned with the systems of ideology and power by which these individual bodies are signified and constrained. The female body then means the individual body, which occupies one of two subject positions: either liberated or oppressed (sexually and socially) within the structures of patriarchy. But in Hos. 1-2 one finds an imagination of the female body as a sign for the body social; this symbol needs to be read within the context of a world-view in which corporate rather than individual meanings of the human and human embodiment are primary" (Keefe, *Woman's Body*, 160).

95. Keefe, *Woman's Body*, 178. Keefe here is criticizing the viewpoint of Eilberg-Schwartz, *The Savage in Judaism*. As Keefe says, "The presence of menstrual taboos alone in ancient Israel is not sufficient evidence to warrant the conclusion that this was a misogynistic culture. One could, instead, argue on the basis of abundant textual clues that the primary association of woman's body in ancient Israel was not with pollution or death, but with fertility, lineage continuity and life" (*Woman's Body*, 178-79). Here Keefe is responding to the position of Bal, *Lethal Love*. Keefe finds Bal's position to be overly one-sided. In this regard, Keefe agrees with Biale, *Eros and the Jews*. Keefe is not denying the reality of "patriarchal determinants of biblical texts" (*Woman's Body*, 184).

96. Keefe, *Woman's Body*, 184. Admittedly, says Keefe, "The possibility that woman's body could have a symbolically positive and central location as a sign for the social body in ancient Israel does not easily occur to the modern reader, whose access to the text is filtered through some 2500 years of intensifying misogyny within which woman comes to signify the temptation to sin, the threat of chaos, and all that which is 'other' to the realm of the sacred" (*Woman's Body*, 184). In my view, the connection of woman's body (preeminently Mary) with the social body of the Catholic Church fits

disturbed by the "metaphor of female sexual transgression" as an "image for the negation of Israel's identity," we need to realize that "[t]he adultery metaphor works in this way because it is also a maternal metaphor, and as such, it participates in and effects a reversal of another important dimension of the symbolism that is constitutive of Israelite identity—Israel as generative mother, symbol of the ongoing life of the people."[97] This perspective helps us to appreciate why such metaphorical imagery was employed in the first place, as well as its original positive intent.

This background gives some explanation to the use of such imagery in Scripture, so long as we do not thereby suppose that we are not meant to be disturbed by the imagery. Baumann remains unpersuaded that the imagery can be excused. If God can be said to behave in this way, how can men be told that they cannot behave in this way?[98] This is obviously a problem that applies to genocidal violence as well.

---

with Keefe's analysis of Israel's scriptural texts, and indicates that the past 2,500 years are more complex—though certainly not lacking in misogyny among some misguided Jews and Catholics. Regarding the ancient Near East, Keefe directs attention to Springborg, *Royal Persons*.

97. Keefe, *Woman's Body*, 210. In the book of Hosea, as Keefe observes, "the condition and fate of the nation are figured in graphic images of maternal bereavement, the loss of female fertility, and the death of mothers" (*Woman's Body*, 210). She adds that these "graphic images are certainly rooted in the realities of war which eagerly claims women and children as victims (see also 2 Kgs 8.12; 15.16; Amos 1.13). But more so, as a metonym for the devastation of war, the slaughter of children and mothers and especially, the slitting open of pregnant women, bespeak the more far-reaching corporate consequences of Assyrian invasion: the end of Israel. Mothers with their children figure the nation as a whole, such that their destruction is the nation's. . . . Israel is a woman in Hosea's metaphor not simply because women are wives, whose conjugal obligations to their husbands in patriarchal society are analogous to the demands of a jealous god, but because women are mothers, whose procreativity functions symbolically as a locus of intergenerational continuity, and hence of national identity. . . . The woman of fornications represents at once the wayward people and the land itself, the land then serving as a congruent metaphor of the corporate body. The identity between the woman and the fertile land is suggested again in Hos. 2, when the husband's threat to strip his wife naked fades into images of drought and desolation upon the land" (*Woman's Body*, 211–12, 214; cf. 216–17). Keefe's conclusion is important: "In Hos. 1–2, the female body, the body politic and the fertile land intertwine in a dense symbolic complex that yields no unambiguous correspondences, but which evokes the reality of the contemporary situation as one of betrayal, bloodshed and 'adulterous' political and commercial liaisons. . . . Although the metaphor is predicated upon the legitimacy of patriarchal control of female sexuality, there is a depth dimension in this symbolism of woman that exceeds those determinations" (*Woman's Body*, 217).

98. See Weems, "Gomer," 100; cited in Baumann, *Love and Violence*, 99. See also Weems's *Battered Love*, a book frequently referenced by Baumann. In addition, see Setel, "Prophets and Pornography"; as well as Thistlethwaite, "Every Two Minutes,"; Shields, "Gender and Violence in Ezekiel 23"; Exum, *Plotted, Shot, and Painted*, 109–10.

I agree with Baumann that a God who engages in the ancient Near Eastern practice of physically humiliating and attacking rebellious wives is not an acceptable "God." For scholars such as Exum, this means "doing away with . . . biblical authority" and with the notion that the biblical God is the "'real' god."[99] By contrast, I stand with Jerome and with the other witnesses to the Catholic (and Orthodox) Church's spiritual—allegorical, typological, tropological—reading of parts of the Old Testament's language. A cultural practice of physically abusing wives is being metaphorically attributed by the prophetic authors to God, but this cultural practice is not of God.[100]

This is similar to how many Christians have long interpreted God's biblical commandments regarding the killing of all the persons living in a specific city. It is also similar to how many Christians interpret biblical portraits of God noisily "walking in the garden" or of God inflamed with jealousy and rage, desiring to slaughter his entire people until Moses talks him out of it (Gen 3:8; Deut 32).[101] Such texts are read theologically in light of

---

Exum describes Ezekiel 23 as "the most pornographic example of divine violence," where "the male author seems to take pleasure in picturing the sexual attentions pressed upon them by 'desirable young men' (vv. 12, 23): the handling of their breasts and their defilement by their lovers' lust. He betrays a fascination with sexual prowess and an envy of other (foreign) men's endowment, fantasizing his rivals with penises the size of asses' penises and ejaculations like those of stallions" (*Plotted, Shot, and Painted*, 109; cf. 124–25). See also Brenner, "Pornoprophetics Revisited"; Brenner and van Dijk-Hemmes, *On Gendering Texts*, 167–95; Brenner, "Women's Traditions Problematized."

99. Exum, *Plotted, Shot, and Painted*, 122; cf. 126–27, where she celebrates Jerusalem's insistence upon autonomy vis-à-vis this abusive god. On the positive side, Exum appreciates that male readers (that is, the majority of the intended hearers and readers) would have recognized themselves as "personified Israel" and therefore would have experienced being "placed in the subject position of women and, worse, of harlotrous, defiled, and sexually humiliated women" (*Plotted, Shot, and Painted*, 123). However, the effect is somewhat bleaker when viewed as a whole, as seen in Galambush, *Jerusalem in the Book of Ezekiel*, 161 (quoted by Exum in *Plotted, Shot, and Painted*, 123n62).

100. See also Holt, "'The Stain of Your Guilt,'" 111. Regarding Jeremiah 2–3, she grants the offensiveness of the abusive imagery, but adds that the offensive passages "might even have been meant to be offensive from the beginning. . . . The implied—male—audience is supposed to be offended, emasculated by an imagery that turns them into wayward, nymphomaniacal, unfaithful women. This is how the metaphor is supposed to work by the implied author in a patriarchal society, based on honor and shame. The implied—male—audience is supposed to understand the message that God is still in control, but also that their God is a jealous and violent God. We might not like this picture—but the picture is there on purpose and we need to be able to understand its message" ("'The Stain of Your Guilt,'"112).

101. For the historical development of biblical portraits of God, see Smith, *The Early History of God*; Smith, *The Origins of Biblical Monotheism*. See also his more theological work, *How Human Is God?*, in which he argues that issues such as the divine anger (for example) are caught up in a paradox, rooted in the difficulty of speaking adequately about God and about God's relationship to us in the midst of sin and suffering: "On

the overall biblical witness to the God who makes covenant with Abraham in order to bless Abraham's descendents and ultimately the whole world.

What this kind of exegesis ("allegorical" or "theological") does is allow the abusive metaphorical imagery to be read and understood in its fullest and most proper contexts, while valuing the value of the historical-critical clarifications brought by Keefe and others. Jerome knows that the God who reveals his love in the prophetic books and in Christ Jesus may (and does) justly punish his people—indeed the punishment (exile) is intrinsic to their idolatrous turning away from God—but this God would never abuse a woman, and indeed would never commit any evil action whatsoever. After all, "God is love" (1 John 4:16) and "God cannot be tempted with evil" (Jas 1:13). Quite rightly, Jerome uses his knowledge of the entire Bible to guard against misreadings of the abusive imagery that would turn the just God of mercy and love into the very kind of oppressive and sexually abusive god (prevalent among the nations) that he repeatedly reveals himself not to be.

Recall what happened when the young Augustine, inspired by Cicero's *Hortensius* to seek wisdom about divine realities, applied himself to reading Christian Scripture. For Augustine as a young man, one of the problems with Scripture—especially the Old Testament—was that "[i]t seemed to me unworthy in comparison with the dignity of Cicero."[102] Cicero never thought of God as filled with the passions of jealousy and anger or as plotting actions of violence against women and infants. Later, Bishop Ambrose of Milan advised Augustine to read the Book of Isaiah; but Augustine "did not understand the first passage of the book" and put it down.[103] Augustine's response to the first chapters of Isaiah is easy to sympathize with, given Isaiah's attention to the contemporary politics of his day and the dense culturally embedded style of his writing. But Ambrose's influence won out.

---

the one hand, images of the violent and angry God suffer in *their* limitations as they partake of *our* human language. On the other hand, these images capture helpful dimensions of what the divine is about" (43). In response to David R. Blumenthal's *Facing the Abusing God*, Smith suggests that we proceed by recognizing that what we see in the prophetic texts involves the people's effort to understand their intense sufferings during the conquest in relation to the covenant to which God remains faithful. He states, "Anger and love are strong, powerful emotions that reflect how deeply one feels about another person. In Jeremiah and Ezekiel, this is God and Israel, husband and wife, now suffering from their terrible breakup. Even anger, terrible anger, is part of this tragic love story. Yet even so, this story is never done, because God is never done; God recovers from the wounds inflicted by Israel, and so Israel does as well" (*How Human Is God?*, 52). Attending to the creation passages in the Old Testament, Smith notes that God the Creator is depicted in terms of his power, wisdom, and presence—and this context is the context of the covenant.

102. Augustine, *Confessions*, III.v.9, p. 40.
103. Augustine, *Confessions*, IX.v.13, p. 163.

Augustine reports, "I heard first one, then another, then many difficult passages in the Old Testament scriptures figuratively interpreted, where I, by taking them literally, had found them to kill (2 Cor. 3:6)."[104]

We may also recall Pope Benedict XVI's *Verbum Domini*, where he reflects upon the "'dark' passages" of the Bible, namely "passages in the Bible which, due to the violence and immorality they occasionally contain, prove obscure and difficult."[105] In addressing the problem, Benedict XVI proposes that "it must be remembered first and foremost that *biblical revelation is deeply rooted in history*. God's plan is manifested *progressively* and it is accomplished slowly, *in successive stages*, and despite human resistance."[106] Thus, we should read the prophets' application to God of the metaphor of a husband violently angry with his adulterous wife as the culturally conditioned mode of discourse that it is; it displays an unacceptable view of violence as permissible in such situations. God revealed himself through real human authors writing in particular cultural contexts. But by reading in context (i.e. historical context, the internal context of the prophetic book, and the context of the whole canon and the realities of what God has done in Christ), Christians can perceive that the import of the prophetic texts is not that God is an angry or violent being, but rather that God wishes to be united fully to his unfaithful bride (his people Israel) and that God will not abandon his unfaithful bride whose actions have imperiled the future of the covenant. Instead, with infinite mercy, compassion, and solidarity with sinners, God will ultimately reunite his bride to himself in perfect mutual love.[107]

III. Conclusion

In Christ, a human marriage becomes "a mystical *participation* in the spousal and sacrificial relationship between Christ and the Church," so that we experience more profoundly the reality of the marriage of God and his people.[108] But not all Christian marriages are good ones. Many women, and men too, have experienced physical violence within a bad marriage. In numerous

---

104. Augustine, *Confessions*, V.xiv.24, p. 88.

105. Benedict XVI, *Verbum Domini*, §42, p. 66. See Ramage, *Dark Passages of the Bible*.

106. Benedict XVI, *Verbum Domini*, §42, p. 66.

107. Yvonne Sherwood points out that when Jerome and Augustine turn to the prostitute married by the prophet in the Book of Hosea, both of these Church Fathers insist that the prostitute (Gomer) became completely chaste prior to the marriage. See Sherwood, *The Prostitute and the Prophet*, 51.

108. See Pitre, *Jesus the Bridegroom*, 155.

cultures over the centuries, husbands have been explicitly allowed to abuse their wives physically.

Jerome's approach recognizes the presence in Scripture's plain sense of a wrongheaded depiction of God, since a central point of divine revelation is that God, while just, is not an oppressive and sexually abusive "god" like the ones found in Near-Eastern and Greco-Roman myth. As we saw, Jerome and other Church Fathers make clear that rape and violation are never justifiable and are infinitely far from the holiness of God. Such evil acts or even the threat of such acts may never be literally attributed to God.

Without referring to this patristic approach, Weems in her book *Battered Love* contends that the diversity of biblical portraits of God means that the image of God as husband can be relativized sufficiently to enable readers to perceive the difference between the "marriage metaphor" and the real "object to which it points (God)."[109] Weems is also poignantly cognizant of the truth that, even despite the many hurtful and failed marriages that we see around us, "the marriage metaphor permits us to believe in the most unbelievable of all possible responses to our woundedness, namely, grace. . . . That we risk loving again those who have wounded us, and that others trust us to try again despite the fact that we have broken their hearts—this is grace. It is a breathtaking possibility."[110] The divine grace is rooted in God's undiminished will to marry his fallen but still beloved people.

Given all this, we are free to read the prophetic texts as they were intended. Despite the images of "violence to the woman [Israel]," it is a truly glorious marriage of God and his people that prophetic texts such as Isaiah 54, Hosea 1–3, and Jeremiah 2–3 have at their core.[111] The people of Israel look forward with yearning to the restoration and intimacy with God that will be brought about by this divine-human marriage. As Richtsje Abma states, "The promise that Yhwh will remarry Zion ([Is] 54:5) contributes to the comfort of Zion and is part of the reversal of her fortunes," just as at the conclusion of Hosea 2 we see that "Yhwh is devoted to Israel" and in Jeremiah we find that "Israel is called to a new intimacy with Yhwh and to new conjugal responsiveness, a perspective that is endowed with promises and blessings."[112] Our sins cannot destroy God's plan for the eschatological

---

109. Weems, *Battered Love*, 119.

110. Weems, *Battered Love*, 114–15.

111. Abma, *Bonds of Love*, 29; cf. 257.

112. Abma, *Bonds of Love*, 257. Abma recognizes that in a certain sense this marital imagery is an "anthropomorphism," but it is an anthropomorphism unlike other anthropomorphisms about God in Scripture (such as God having emotions, desiring to do wicked actions, having "a face, mouth, eyes, heart, hands, ears, feet and a voice," and so on [*Bonds of Love*, 258]). The transcendent God can indeed unite a people to himself

marriage of God and his people. Learning how to understand God's scriptural word, we may continue boldly seeking the marital "depths of communion with God for which the human soul yearns" and which the God of Israel offers to us and triumphantly inaugurates in Christ Jesus, in merciful solidarity with sinners but also in his perfect justice.[113]

---

in an intimacy so profound as to be marital. As Abma says, "There is no shade of sexuality or procreation in the relationship with Yhwh ... but there is intimacy between Yhwh and Israel. ... God's love for Israel implies that he takes pleasure in the people and in their being with him (Jer. 2:2). He enjoys Israel as his partner and does not want to lose her (Hos. 2:21–22). There is a sense of joy and delight in God's partnership with Israel (Isa. 62:4). If there has been a temporary estrangement, a new and fresh start is made, indicating that Israel remains the partner after God's heart" (*Bonds of Love*, 259). Israel lives "side by side" with God and enjoys "fellowship" and "companionship" with him (*Bonds of Love*, 259).

113. Ortlund, *God's Unfaithful Wife*, 8.

Chapter 2

Image of God

In the previous chapter, I explored the reality that "Christ has only one immaculate spouse, the church, to whom he is always faithful."[1] Marital intimacy with God is the human vocation. But does this have any impact on what God may intend when, according to Genesis 1:26–27, he proclaims, "Let us make man in our image, after our likeness," which is then glossed by the affirmation that "God created man in his own image, in the image of God he created him; male and female he created them"?

Historical-critically, contemporary biblical scholars find that in its ancient Near-Eastern context, Genesis 1:26–27 taught (as Walter Brueggemann says) that "the image of God reflected in human persons is after the manner of a king who establishes statues of himself to assert his sovereign rule when the king himself cannot be present."[2] On this view, Genesis 1:26–27 reveals that *all* human beings are in the image of God. This royal image of God involves service to each other, not domination by one over all others.

Brueggemann, however, goes further and reasons that "humankind is a community, male and female. And none is the full image of God alone. Only in community of humankind is God reflected. God is . . . not mirrored as an individual but as a community."[3] This latter point suggests that the "image of God" already has something like the Trinity in view, since people

---

1. Kereszty, *The Church of God*, 137. Kereszty notes, "Beginning with Origen, the church-bride is identified with the bride in search of the bridegroom in the Song of Songs" (*The Church of God*, 137). I will return to this connection with the Song of Songs in the conclusion of my book. For Kereszty, the holy bride is preeminently Mary, and with her the blessed souls in heaven.
2. Brueggemann, *Genesis*, 32.
3. Brueggemann, *Genesis*, 34.

can mirror God "as a community" only if God is in some mysterious sense a "community." Moreover, if the community of humankind is preeminently understood as being "male and female" (Gen 1:27)—if the original man and woman (Adam and Eve) are the paradigmatic community—then with Francis Martin we can say that "Adam images God, that is, makes his power and authority present and interacts with God, in the relating of man and woman."[4] If so, then, arguably, the image of God in humankind is found in marriage, which is the intimate "relating of man and woman" that we see already in the original union of Adam and Eve.

In *Engaging the Doctrine of Creation*, I argued that the image of God is found in the rational soul and its powers of knowing and loving (and thus preeminently in Jesus Christ) and also is found in the human body in a participated way, since the human person is a soul-body unity and the human body is made to facilitate and express relational communion.[5] When properly oriented, the powers of knowing and loving direct the human being toward God. Since Christ supremely knows and loves God and supremely embodies love on the Cross, in his humanity Christ is the perfect image of God. I still agree with this position regarding the nature of the image of God. But in the present chapter, I add that a loving and fruitful marriage (a man and a woman, and [potentially at least] a child) *also* exhibits a way in which human beings are made to the image of God. The triune God, in creating humans "in his image" and "male and female" (Gen 1:27), has given us a marital image of himself, in accord with the fact that humans are created for marriage with the Trinity.

---

4. Martin, "Male and Female He Created Them," 259.

5. I treat the image of God in my *Engaging the Doctrine of Creation*, chapter 4. Since I interact with a number of biblical scholars and theologians in that chapter (and also briefly survey the patristic debates about this topic), I can refer readers to that chapter for background to the present chapter. See also my comparative analysis of Thomas Aquinas and David Novak on the image of God in my *Jewish-Christian Dialogue*, chapter 3. For further helpful background, advocating a view of the image of God that accords with the Fathers and Aquinas, see Staniloae, *The Experience of God*, 85–92. Along the lines of the present chapter, Staniloae adds, "The fact that Genesis speaks of the image in connection with the creation of the human person as a couple may have significance for the communitarian character of the image and for its development in common. 'So God created man in his own image, in the image of God He created him; male and female He created them' (Gen 1:27). Moreover, for the connection between the communitarian character of the image and the Holy Trinity, there may also be significance in the fact that immediately before this, Genesis represents God as speaking in the plural when the decision is made to create man in the divine image: 'Then God said, "Let us make man in our image, after our likeness"' (Gen 1:26)" (*The Experience of God*, 100).

In order to make this argument, I will draw especially upon the writings of Hans Urs von Balthasar. My first section explores his understanding of marriage as the best image of the Trinity, in light of his descriptions of the positions advanced by Augustine, Richard of St. Victor, Georg Friedrich Hegel, and Martin Buber. Second, because von Balthasar directs attention to the cognate approach taken by Matthias Joseph Scheeben, I examine Scheeben's proposal. Von Balthasar's position differs from Scheeben's in that von Balthasar is not attempting to show that we can find an image of the Trinitarian processions in (first) Eve's coming forth from Adam and (second) Seth coming forth from Adam and Eve. Instead, von Balthasar argues that a married couple, insofar as the husband and wife act in self-surrendering and fruitful love, image the self-surrendering fruitfulness (difference-in-unity) of the divine Persons. Given von Balthasar's reflection on how the married couple image the selfless and fruitful love of the triune Persons, we will find that the human "image of God" has to do with human self-surrender in spousal love—a spousal love that can equally be enacted by *single* persons, as Christ reveals.

Like von Balthasar, his theological disciple and partner Adrienne von Speyr teaches that the image of God is found in our self-surrendering receptivity and generosity. For von Speyr, as Michele Schumacher says, the image of God is "more 'impressively' apparent in the man-woman relationship."[6] Von Balthasar and von Speyr offer a "united work" or a "common theology," especially with regard to "the overriding mystery of Trinitarian surrender."[7] But in the present chapter, I focus on von Balthasar since it is his writings that I know best. Even so, Schumacher's observation is apropos: "For Adrienne, the entire mystery of the human person might be summarized in terms of loving surrender, because quite simply—as she 'saw' it—this attitude is divine before it is human."[8]

---

6. Schumacher, *A Trinitarian Anthropology*, 268–69.

7. Schumacher, *A Trinitarian Anthropology*, 397.

8. Schumacher, *A Trinitarian Anthropology*, 396–97. Schumacher remarks, "Precisely as the fruit of the marital union and as God's gift to the couple, the child thus points to the fact that more than an extrinsic likeness is implied between the human communion of persons, on the one hand, and the Trinitarian communion of persons, on the other. Creation in the image of God thus means, for Adrienne . . . that the human being is 'complete [*vervollständigt*]' only through the human 'other'—in, that is to say, the communion made possible by the reciprocal surrender of two persons—which in turn is only possible, as we shall see, in each one's opening to God" (*A Trinitarian Anthropology*, 270). Schumacher adds that Adrienne sets forth "characteristically male and female manners of surrender" (*A Trinitarian Anthropology*, 271). In her discussion of Adrienne von Speyr on these themes, Schumacher draws particularly (though not exclusively) upon two works by von Speyr: *Die Schöpfung* and *Theologie der Geschlechter*. Schumacher directs attention to Antoine Birot, whose works relevant to the topic of this

Third, because von Balthasar's position bears some similarity to that of Karl Barth, I will pay some attention to Barth's position as well. Barth highlights the couple's imaging of God's relationality and covenant-partnering. Finally, in a brief fourth section, I engage other recent advocates of marriage as image of the Trinity, including Marc Ouellet, Paul Evdokimov, and Pope John Paul II. Their viewpoint has been well expressed by Timothy Cardinal Dolan: "marriage and the Trinity have *everything* to do with each other."[9]

My conclusion is that although von Balthasar's understanding of marriage as image of the Trinity needs to be complemented and undergirded by the Augustinian-Thomistic understanding of the image of God, von Balthasar's focus on fruitful self-surrendering love is valuable for perceiving how it is that humans are created for marriage with the Trinity. This is the deepest meaning of "the experience of a married couple who goes through life together, ending ultimately in the everlasting embrace of Father, Son, and Spirit."[10]

I. Hans Urs von Balthasar on Marriage and the Trinity

As noted above, Hans Urs von Balthasar considers Christian marriage to be an image of the Trinity. In developing this argument, he begins by observing that because Jesus Christ is the truth—the supreme "image" and "likeness" (Gen 1:26) of the Trinity—this must mean that "the worldly realm must somehow image the trinitarian, and the self-exposing Logos can and must assume the way of this imaging in order to express himself."[11] How does the "worldly realm" image the Trinity? Exploring various possible ways, von Balthasar agrees with Maurice Blondel that the logical distinction between identity and difference requires a third element, namely, the stance from which one identifies difference, or, put another way, the relation between the differing parties. Along similar lines, Paul Claudel holds that each thing exists in relation to a vast set of other things, and, together, this thing and the vast set of other things exist in relation to God. Thus, it is impossible truly to apprehend one thing without apprehending three realities at once. For both Blondel and Claudel, it is impossible to know a thing in its unity

---

chapter include *La dramatique trinitaire de l'amour* and "Le fondement christologique."

9. Dolan, "Why Marriage Matters Most," 70.

10. Dolan, "Why Marriage Matters Most," 70.

11. Von Balthasar, *Truth of God*, 35.

without knowing it triadically; and therefore all worldly things contain a Trinitarian imprint.[12]

Having affirmed the Trinitarian pattern of all things, von Balthasar turns to the two classic analogies for the Trinity—those of Augustine and Richard of St. Victor.[13] He argues that both have value but also weaknesses. With regard to the weaknesses, he states, "The interpersonal model [i.e. Richard's] cannot attain the substantial unity of God, whereas the intrapersonal model [i.e. Augustine's] cannot give an adequate picture of the real and abiding face-to-face encounter of the hypostases."[14] As von Balthasar notes, Augustine holds that the problem with the love shared by two friends is that, although it communicates a triad, it does not communicate absolute unity, and it also does not communicate the unchangeableness of God—since two friends can have a falling out. Desiring to ground the unity of the image at the level of personal consciousness rather than at the level of being, Augustine considers the triad of *mens*, *notitia*, and *amor*; with *notitia* here signifying active "self-knowing."[15] The love that flows from this self-knowing is self-love. This poses a problem, because love of God, not self-love, has to be the highest human imaging of God.

Augustine then speaks of *memoria*, *intellectus*, and *voluntas*. These three are all states or functions of the one soul, but von Balthasar remarks that even Augustine admits that they are not strictly *identical* with the one soul. Drawing upon Book XV of Augustine's *De Trinitate*, von Balthasar argues that in fact what Augustine has given us is "[t]he one 'I' with its three functions."[16] Von Balthasar also contests the connection that Augustine draws between *intellectus* and the Son, on the one hand, and *voluntas* and the Spirit, on the other.[17]

Next, von Balthasar examines Richard of St. Victor's Trinitarian image of two selfless lovers who selflessly love a third person. Appreciatively, he finds that this image expresses "the full selflessness of Christian *caritas*

---

12. For a skillful presentation of this point (without reference to Blondel or Claudel), see Leithart, *Traces of the Trinity*.

13. For discussion see den Bok, *Communicating the Most High*; and Ayres, *Augustine and the Trinity*.

14. Von Balthasar, *Truth of God*, 38.

15. Von Balthasar, *Truth of God*, 38.

16. Von Balthasar, *Truth of God*, 40.

17. Von Balthasar asks, "If each of the Divine Persons possesses the whole Godhead, and if the Godhead itself knows and loves as a 'personality', how can knowledge and love be attributed to the Son and the Spirit except by way of appropriation?" (*Truth of God*, 40). I think that this question can be answered, and in fact is adequately answered by Aquinas. For discussion see Emery, "Essentialism or Personalism?" See also my *Engaging the Doctrine of the Holy Spirit*.

and its perfection in God."[18] In a number of ways, he considers this image to be an advance over Augustine's proposal. He summarizes Richard's position as follows: "For him and his successors, the only relevant principle was the logic of *caritas*, which requires in God the presence of the 'other', that is, the beloved, and of the 'third', the common object of love."[19] But in von Balthasar's view, just as Augustine's image fails to convey adequately the threeness of the divine Persons, Richard's image fails to convey adequately the divine unity. Besides, both images, at their best, offer only "the faintest glimmer of an elucidation of the superabundant triune life that indwells the divine unity."[20] Both images perform a service, but neither can suffice on its own, and even taken together they offer the merest glimmer.

In light of this situation, von Balthasar seeks a new ground for understanding the image of God. A key issue, he contends, is what to think of otherness in God: is it a threat to absolute unity, a "negation of the One or its 'reversal'"?[21] In his view, divine difference (the difference of Persons) grounds human difference, and so difference is positive, not negative; difference in God does not negate the divine unity. Since God is "the God of love,"[22] this requires for von Balthasar (as for Richard and Bonaventure) that there be positive personal difference in God. Positive divine difference, as true intra-Personal divine love, requires that "in God receiving is just as positive as giving."[23] This position grounds his identification of each divine Person with self-surrendering love.

---

18. Von Balthasar, *Truth of God*, 41–42.
19. Von Balthasar, *Truth of God*, 42.
20. Von Balthasar, *Truth of God*, 42.
21. Von Balthasar, *Truth of God*, 43.
22. Von Balthasar, *Truth of God*, 82.

23. Von Balthasar, *Truth of God*, 83. For von Balthasar, the key is "the unconditional self-surrender of each divine hypostasis to the others" so that "none of the hypostases in God overwhelms any of the others with its personal property" (*Truth of God*, 83). I do not think that "unconditional self-surrender" is the best way of describing the relations of the divine Persons. It seems to me more precise to begin with the biblically attested generation of the Word by the Father, and the biblically attested spiration of the Spirit from the Father (and—or through—the Son). The three Persons are not three "selves," nor is "surrender" sufficiently precise to describe the distinctive notional acts to which Scripture attests, without undermining the unity and simplicity of the Trinity. Yet, I appreciate what von Balthasar is getting at. Surely, even if theologians should exercise care in speaking about so great a mystery as that of the Trinity, the Trinity is not less than selfless love. See also the cogent remark of Oakes, "Gathering Many Likenesses," 887fn78: "One of the primary semantic difficulties of this way of speaking is that the Father has no 'self,' either to give or to have or to empty or to surrender, in isolation from the Son and Spirit. However, this semantic difficulty is shared by any account of the divine persons when they are signified by substance or form rather than by relation

Von Balthasar adds that two methods for thinking about the image of the Trinity are possible: "dialectic" and "dialogic." He favors the "dialogic" because it fully allows for the goodness of otherness; humans image God precisely by handing themselves over to the other. To be a creature is to imitate the divine Persons in their self-surrendering love. Beginning with the divine Persons, the "dialogic" approach attempts to show that all creatures image the Trinity by self-surrender of various kinds. As Nicholas Healy puts it, "The Father's eternal generation of the Son, imaged and interpreted by the life and death of Christ, is best understood not by analogy to an immanent act of the mind (Augustine and Aquinas), but in terms of a total-gift-of-self (*Selbsthingabe*) proper to love."[24]

Dialectic proceeds from the opposite direction, and seeks to move from creaturely difference to a Trinitarian difference in God. Here von Balthasar has Hegel in view.[25] Specifically, in *Elements of the Philosophy of Right*, Hegel argues that love's essence consists in realizing that one is only who one is *when one gives oneself entirely to another person*. The person in love discovers the following: "I am not isolated on my own [*für mich*], but gain my self-consciousness only through the renunciation of my independent existence [*meines Fürsichseins*]."[26] In self-surrender, the person finds himself or herself.

Hegel goes on to speak of two "moments" in love. The first moment consists in no longer wishing to be independent, no longer wishing to be for oneself alone. The lover recognizes that such an existence would be "deficient and incomplete."[27] It is through self-surrender that a person attains his or her own unity or complete self-consciousness. The second moment consists in finding oneself in another person and having the other person do the same in oneself. Hegel states: "I gain recognition in this person, who in turn gains recognition in me."[28] Clearly, this is moving close to an image of the Trinity, in which the relations define the Persons without compromising the absolute unity of the Persons.

---

or act, as von Balthasar himself was aware: 'The Father must not be thought to exist 'prior' to this self-surrender (in an Arian sense): he is this movement of self-giving that holds nothing back' (*Theo-Drama* 4:323)."

24. Healy, *The Eschatology of von Balthasar*, 127.

25. See my *Achievement of von Balthasar*, and, much more comprehensively, O'Regan, *The Anatomy of Misremembering*.

26. Hegel, *Elements of the Philosophy of Right*, §158, p. 199.

27. Hegel, *Elements of the Philosophy of Right*, §158, p. 199.

28. Hegel, *Elements of the Philosophy of Right*, §158, p. 199.

Hegel, however, considers the reality of love to be "the most immense contradiction."[29] It strikes him as beyond the realm of understanding, because he cannot see how self-consciousness can be established by surrendering one's own self-consciousness. He cannot see how the realization that one is radically incomplete without the other can be the basis for true completeness in oneself. For Hegel, there is an *opposition* between the negation of self-consciousness (in the lover's self-surrender) and the affirmation of self-consciousness (in the lover's self-surrender). He holds that love resolves this contradiction and establishes an "ethical unity."[30] In the family and the state, one learns that one is fulfilled by being a "member" rather than an independent person who lives for oneself.[31] The dialectical synthesis, then, happens when two persons mutually "consent to *constitute a single person* and to give up their natural and individual personalities within this union," in order to "attain their substantial self-consciousness."[32]

Von Balthasar notes that although Hegel's position here could be developed (as Hegel himself did) in terms of a dialectical logic of "God's attainment of completion through his becoming world and concrete spirit," it could also be developed along the dialogic lines of Franz Rosenzweig, Martin Buber, and Ferdinand Ebner, who identify the "I-Thou relation as the primordial phenomenon," so that the "I" is "something that has always already been addressed by, and addressed, a Thou"—a *"Logos Theou."*[33] Indeed, von Balthasar finds a triad here, since in this line of thought, "the condition of the possibility both of the I and of the Thou is a having been addressed by the very ground of the interpersonal dynamism itself."[34] In Martin Buber, whose work he studied closely,[35] he identifies a full-fledged (though unconscious) image of the Trinity. He explains that for Buber, "spirit reigns between the I and the Thou, who are pure relation to each other, but each one, incommunicable in his core (as the Other), nonetheless (and precisely for this reason) communicates all that he has."[36] The self-communicating "I" and "Thou" share their "spirit" with each other as their mutual bond.

---

29. Hegel, *Elements of the Philosophy of Right*, §158, p. 199.
30. Hegel, *Elements of the Philosophy of Right*, §158, p. 199.
31. Hegel, *Elements of the Philosophy of Right*, §158, p. 199.
32. Hegel, *Elements of the Philosophy of Right*, §162, p. 201.
33. Von Balthasar, *Truth of God*, 45.
34. Von Balthasar, *Truth of God*, 49.
35. See von Balthasar, *Martin Buber and Christianity*; and Sciglitano, *Marcion and Prometheus*.
36. Von Balthasar, *Truth of God*, 55.

Von Balthasar considers this insight into I-Thou-spirit to be valuable but incomplete. In seeking an image that is the most adequate to the mystery of triunity, he suggests that we should proceed farther along the marital lines begun, but not completed, by Hegel. Specifically, he urges that we think in terms of the image of man, woman, and child. Augustine, of course, argued in his *De Trinitate* against the viability of this image. Augustine observes, "I do not find the opinion very convincing which supposes that the trinity of the image of God, as far as human nature is concerned, can be discovered in three persons; that is, that it may be composed of the union of male and female and their offspring."[37] For one thing, by placing the Holy Spirit in the female role, it seems to make the Holy Spirit into a quasi-mother of the Son and a quasi-wife of the Father. This objection can be contested by arguing that we are here speaking of spiritual relations. Augustine grants the validity of this response, and he explains that his own concern lies deeper: if the image of the Trinity is a man, woman, and child, how could each individual human being be in the image of God? It would seem that, individually speaking, a man at best could be the image of the Father, a woman the image of the Spirit, and a child the image of the Son. Besides, even if one insisted that "male and female he created them" (Gen 1:27) means that the image of the Trinity is the man and the woman together, there is here no mention (or existence) of a child. Augustine concludes, "We should not then understand man being made to the image of the supreme trinity, that is, to the image of God, as meaning that this image is to be understood in three human beings."[38]

Like Augustine, Thomas Aquinas calls "absurd" the view that the man, woman, and child collectively comprise the image, on the grounds that the man and woman (even prior to having a child) each fully possess the image of the triune God.[39] Aquinas insists that the image of God is not the product of the conjunction of both sexes, but rather fully "belongs to both sexes, since it is in the mind, wherein there is no sexual differentiation."[40]

In von Balthasar's view, however, it is not necessary to suppose that the image is found in actual childbearing or actual offspring. Rather, he highlights "fecundity" and "fruitfulness," not only bodily, but also spiritual.[41] He sees no need to institute a sharp divide between bodily and spiritual, since in actual marriage we find conjoined "the organic *and* personal fruitfulness

---

37. Augustine, *The Trinity*, XII.2.5, p. 324.
38. Augustine, *The Trinity*, XII.2.9, p. 327.
39. Aquinas, *Summa theologiae* I, q. 93, a. 6, ad 2.
40. Aquinas, *Summa theologiae* I, q. 93, a. 6, ad 2.
41. Von Balthasar, *Truth of God*, 60.

of the two."⁴² In the begetting of a child, God is involved, due to marriage's natural role in the production of God's images. The marital act, which consummates the covenant of marriage, is not bereft of God; on the contrary, at its most fundamental level, it is done in God's name, as an act of self-giving covenantal love. Von Balthasar benefits here from Scheeben's understanding of love as self-giving *ecstasis*: "The lover goes out of himself to the beloved, unites himself to it and gives himself to it in such a way as to rest in it."⁴³ Von Balthasar commends Scheeben's Thomistic approach with respect to this point.⁴⁴

In the fruitful and self-giving love of the spouses, then, von Balthasar discerns the greatest possible creaturely analogue to the self-giving fruitfulness of the divine Persons. Obviously, the divine Persons do not engage in bodily actions, let alone in marriage; but their proper acts are supreme acts of self-giving fruitfulness. Each divine Person is infinite self-giving fruitfulness, and the one Godhead is infinite self-giving fruitfulness in love. Von Balthasar states with regard to marriage, "The relationship described here"—which builds upon the dialogic "I-Thou"—"remains, in spite of all the obvious dissimilarities, the most eloquent *imago Trinitatis* that we find woven into the fabric of the creature."⁴⁵ He argues that the image found in marital fruitfulness "not only transcends Augustine's self-contained I, but also allows the '*condilectus* [co-beloved]' that Richard's model imports from the outside to spring from the intimacy of love itself—precisely as its fruitfulness—while avoiding the dangerous tendency of the dialogicians to allow interpersonal encounter to slide into a mere two-way monologue."⁴⁶ In the fruitfulness modeled by a married couple, von Balthasar finds a very simple "permanent proof of the triadic structure of creaturely logic."⁴⁷

Again, the key here is fecundity, which can be as much spiritual as bodily. According to von Balthasar, "supernatural fruitfulness"—as

42. Von Balthasar, *Truth of God*, 60–61.
43. Waldstein, "Covenant and the Union of Love," 140.
44. See von Balthasar, *Seeing the Form*, 111–12.
45. Von Balthasar, *Truth of God*, 62.
46. Von Balthasar, *Truth of God*, 62.
47. Von Balthasar, *Truth of God*, 62. Von Balthasar cautions, "God's immanencing into the world in Jesus Christ can be neither constructed (Hegel) nor postulated (Baius) starting from the world" (*Truth of God*, 84). This was a mistake that, in von Balthasar's view, the "dialogicians" (Rosenzweig, Buber, Ebner, et al.) tended to make, since for them the I-Thou dimension could not function without "the immanent presence of the divine" (*Truth of God*, 84) Although grace remains sheer grace, however, the fulfillment by self-surrender that belongs to "the ontological language of creatureliness as such"—and that is present already in a high form in natural marriage—is "not foreign to the logic of God" (*Truth of God*, 84).

exemplified in vowed religious and clergy or, in a unique way, in the Blessed Virgin Mary—correlates with "the sacred character of matrimony," and is also foreshadowed by the way in which the I-Thou relationship in spiritual exchange finds fulfillment in "an objective third."[48] Likewise, the virginal Christ is "'image par excellence,'" "the image that God himself finally places before us."[49] Christ is the one who "completes or retrieves the image-character that man has lost and darkened."[50] Von Balthasar supports this point from scriptural texts that present Christ as the true image to which we must be conformed: "we all, with unveiled face, beholding the glory of the Lord, are being changed into his likeness from one degree of glory to another" (2 Cor 3:18); "put on the new man, which is being renewed in knowledge after the image of his creator" (Col 3:10); "Just as we have borne the image of the man of dust, we shall also bear the image of the man of heaven" (1 Cor 15:49).[51] Christ's life was a constant manifestation of "shared existence with one's fellowmen" (or "love of neighbor") and "fruitfulness."[52] By giving positive value to difference and being always "for others," he stands out in his humanity as the supreme image of the self-surrendering Trinity.

Marital friendship and fecundity are not necessary, then, to image the Trinity. Spiritual or virginal friendship and fecundity can accomplish the same thing. But this does not take away the fact that marriage, with its especially intimate and profound friendship between the spouses, embodies a "shared existence with one's fellowmen" and "love of neighbor" that has a unique natural intensity and whose fruitfulness is powerful in the world. In the natural course of human life, the I-Thou bond of marriage, with its self-giving ordering toward fruitfulness, "remains, in spite of all the obvious dissimilarities, the most eloquent *imago Trinitatis* that we find woven into the fabric of the creature."[53]

II. Matthias Joseph Scheeben on Marriage and the Trinity

In describing this "most eloquent *imago Trinitatis*" in *Truth of God*, von Balthasar repeatedly commends the theology of Matthias Joseph Scheeben,

48. Von Balthasar, *Truth of God*, 84.
49. Von Balthasar, *Truth of God*, 72.
50. Von Balthasar, *Truth of God*, 73.
51. See von Balthasar, *Truth of God*, 73.
52. Von Balthasar, *Truth of God*, 85.
53. Von Balthasar, *Truth of God*, 85. For further discussion, see Meuffels, *Einbergung des Menschen*, 441–46.

for whom the marriage of God and humanity is the heart of everything. As von Balthasar observes elsewhere, Scheeben rejoices in "God's central *conubium* with mankind (and, through it, with the whole world) in the Incarnation."[54] Scheeben attends to the physical aspect of marital fruitfulness as much as to the marital friendship in order to underscore that body and soul are united in their imaging of the divine-human marriage that God has accomplished in and through Christ. According to von Balthasar, Scheeben's theology is "one great doctrine of *eros*," rooted in the Trinity as "an interior fruitfulness that pours itself out."[55]

In *The Mysteries of Christianity*, Scheeben places Ephesians 5 at the center of his reflection on the Church: the husband and wife are an image of the self-surrendering, fruitful love of Christ and the Church. The Incarnation itself already is a marriage between God and humanity, but the union envisioned by God comes to full fruition only in the Church. The consummation of the marriage takes place in the Eucharist, which is a perfect communion between the (bridal) baptized and the Lord. Scheeben amplifies the impact of this marital imagery by arguing that fruitful marriage itself is a sign not only of Christ and the Church, but also of the Trinity. Most notably for my purposes, he proposes that the family—man, woman, child—images the unity of the Trinity.[56]

Scheeben tries to demonstrate this by attending at length to the biblical narrative of Adam and Eve in Genesis 2. He states, "In deriving Eve from the side of Adam, God wished to bring about the procession of human nature in the representatives of family unity (father, mother, and child) from one principle, just as the divine nature is transmitted from the Father to the Son, and from the Father and the Son to the Holy Spirit."[57] In the original family, Adam stands in the role of the Father; Eve in the role of the Son (because she comes forth solely from Adam); and their child (still not conceived prior to the fall) in the role of the Holy Spirit, as "the fruit and crown of the union of man and woman."[58] Scheeben thinks that the human family (man, woman, child) images not only the unity but also the Trinity of the divine Persons. In humans, generation must be the work of two persons (male and female), whereas in the infinitely perfect nature that is God, generation is the work of the Father alone.

---

54. Von Balthasar, *Seeing the Form*, 114.

55. Scheeben, *The Mysteries of Christianity*, 109.

56. See also the cognate discussion in Scheeben, *Handbuch der katholischen Dogmatik*, II, 422–23.

57. Scheeben, *The Mysteries of Christianity*, 182.

58. Scheeben, *The Mysteries of Christianity*, 182.

More controversially, Scheeben proposes that the relationship between Father and Son is mediated by the Spirit in a way that is analogous to the way the relationship between a human father and son is mediated by the mother. He states, "As the mother is the bond of love between father and child, so in God the Holy Spirit is the bond of love between the Father and the Son; and as she brings forth the child in unity of nature with the father . . . so the Holy Spirit manifests the unity of nature between the Father and the Son."[59] The Holy Spirit does this as the bond of love between the Father and Son, or, more specifically, as "the fruit" of the "mutual unity and love" of the Father and Son.[60] The generation of Eve here parallels not the generation of the Son (as it did in the derivation of Eve from Adam's side) but rather the spiration of the Spirit. He gives various reasons for this, among them that "as Eve was taken from the side of Adam, from his heart, the seat of love, seeing that the material of her body was taken and given out of love, so we must say of the Holy Spirit that He proceeds not from the bosom, but from the heart of the Father and the Son."[61]

The imaging of the Trinity by the generative love apparent in the original human family—with Adam imaging the Father, the child the Son, and Eve the Spirit—may seem, Scheeben recognizes, to be a *novum* of his fertile imagination. For this reason, he cites various Fathers of the Church with regard to the symbolism of Adam and Eve. He notes that according to St. Methodius, Eve (formed of Adam's rib) symbolizes the Spirit, because the Spirit is the "divine vital principle which constitutes the Church the bride of Christ."[62] When Adam/Christ stands in (death-like) selfless love, from his side comes forth the vital principle that enables his Church to be established. The vital principle is the Holy Spirit, and what comes forth from Adam's side is Eve. But if Adam is here the Father, however, why is it that the new Adam (Christ) is the incarnate Son? Scheeben replies that the generative principle is in fact the Father *and* the Son, God *and* the new Adam. Recall that God draws the vital principle (the rib, or, in the new Adam, the blood) out of Adam's side. Thus, the Spirit comes forth from the union in selfless love of the Father and the Son. In this regard Aidan Nichols comments that "Scheeben's preferred account of the Spirit . . . is an anticipation of Balthasar," since it puts forward (Balthasarian) images of "overflowing fruitfulness."[63]

---

59. Scheeben, *The Mysteries of Christianity*, 183.
60. Scheeben, *The Mysteries of Christianity*, 183.
61. Scheeben, *The Mysteries of Christianity*, 184.
62. Scheeben, *The Mysteries of Christianity*, 184.
63. Nichols, *Romance and System*, 270.

Scheeben also cites Gregory of Nazianzus's Fifth Theological Oration.[64] Gregory links Adam to the Father, Seth to the Son, and Eve to the Holy Spirit. He states, "What was Adam? Something molded by God. What was Eve? A portion of that molded creation. Seth? He was the offspring of the pair."[65] The offspring, the son, was Seth, whereas Eve came directly from Adam without being an offspring. They all share the same nature (Adam's). In this way, Gregory attempts to show that the generation of the Son is not the same as the spiration of the Spirit, even though both derive from the Father. It is not exactly a family image of the Trinity, but it is an argument in which the derivation of Eve helps us to understand the difference between the generation of the Son and the spiration of the Spirit. Richard of St. Victor and Bonaventure provide a similar analogy, though with Eve in the role of the Son and Seth in the role of the Spirit.[66]

Scheeben adds that there is a connection between the Hebrew name "woman" (given to Eve) and the name of the Spirit. He explains that "as the Hebrew word for woman serves to show that the woman ... is joined to him most intimately as a companion and helpmate of like nature, so the name 'Spirit' in the case of the Third Person in God indicates that He proceeds from the other two persons as their most perfect companion," sharing in their nature.[67] He connects this argument to the argument from a perfect family. As in a family the bond between father and son is the mother, who bears the child in her womb and thereby testifies to the fleshly unity between father and son (in a manner that the father cannot do), so also in the Trinity the bond between Father and Son is the Spirit, who "represent[s] the spiritual unity, the unity of spirit, of the spiritual nature between Father and Son; not indeed as its intermediary, but as its flower and culmination."[68] The family image gives the Spirit a place not merely as an intermediary between the Father and Son, but as a fullness of spiritual unity, just as the mother manifests a fullness of fleshly unity between the father and son. With Mary in view, Scheeben adds that "generation in God is virginal; hence the Holy Spirit must be the bond of union between the Father and the Son in virginal fashion."[69]

---

64. See Nichols, *Romance and System*, 270. For a fuller discussion of Scheeben's Trinitarian theology, see Minz, *Pleroma Trinitatis*.

65. Gregory of Nazianzus, "Oration 31: On the Holy Spirit," 124 (§11).

66. For discussion see Ouellet, *Divine Likeness*, 25.

67. Scheeben, *The Mysteries of Christianity*, 186.

68. Scheeben, *The Mysteries of Christianity*, 187.

69. Scheeben, *The Mysteries of Christianity*, 187–88.

For von Balthasar, Scheeben's position that the Holy Spirit is feminine in the Trinity is untenable.[70] But as we have seen, von Balthasar supports Scheeben's emphasis on the family as an image of the Trinity, indeed as the greatest image of the Trinity. The reason consists mainly in the connection between marriage and fruitful self-surrendering love. Spiritual fruitfulness is not impeded when the marriage happens to be childless due to no fault of the couple, even if the fleshly dimension of fruitfulness must not be minimized.[71]

In *The Christian State of Life*, von Balthasar urges that the meaning of Genesis 1:26–28 is that "God's being in the Trinity is an infinite fecundity that reveals itself externally in creation; whatever is made in his image must, of its very nature, have a share in this fecundity."[72] Here, much more than in his trilogy, he also affirms Scheeben's intuition that the origination of Eve from the side of Adam constitutes "a direct physical image of the origin from the Father's substance of the eternal Son who shares his nature."[73] Von Balthasar thinks that the formation of Eve from Adam's side gives the original pair a "spiritual oneness and fecundity" that establishes them from the outset as "the image of the concrete divine oneness of nature and fecundity within the Trinity."[74] Still, the key is not the order of origination so much as it is the imaging of unity and self-surrendering fecundity. Marriage must now obey the self-surrender of the Cross, through "which all desire, insofar as it is disordered and selfish, is vanquished by the selflessness of Christian self-giving."[75]

---

70. Von Balthasar comments with Scheeben's position in view: "because 'generation' is already exclusively reserved as an analogue for the Father-Son relationship, and because the Son, if anyone, would have to represent the feminine element therein, we cannot legitimately argue from the feminine form of the Hebrew words 'spirit' (*ruach*) and 'wisdom' (*kochma*) that the Spirit is the feminine in God" (*Truth of God*, 60; see also 60fn97).

71. See Scheeben, *The Mysteries of Christianity*, 594. Von Balthasar emphasizes that the fruitfulness that pertains to Christian marriage does not require that there be an actual child; it simply requires that the couple be open to God's gift if it comes. See von Balthasar, *The Christian State of Life*, 246.

72. See von Balthasar, *The Christian State of Life*, 226: "God's being in the Trinity is an infinite fecundity that reveals itself externally in creation; whatever is made in his image must, of its very nature, have a share in this fecundity."

73. Von Balthasar, *The Christian State of Life*, 227.

74. Von Balthasar, *The Christian State of Life*, 228.

75. Von Balthasar, *The Christian State of Life*, 248. For von Balthasar, consecrated virgins and married Christian couples can therefore be said to be following the same basic state of life, namely, that of Christ's fecundity in self-surrendering love. Geoffrey W. Bromiley raises an important practical question: "Is it not an illusion to think that the power of sin is broken if, even though we are dead to sin, we have no strength to

III. Karl Barth on Marriage and the Trinity

Although von Balthasar is willing to appeal to the derivation of Eve from Adam in order to ground the unity of the marital image, he focuses his attention upon the fecundity or fruitfulness of self-surrendering love, which in the order of created human nature is best imaged in marriage (and specifically in the sexual intercourse of the married couple). On this view, the acts that most uniquely characterize marriage display a "trinitarian model."[76] Von Balthasar thinks that the concrete difference-in-unity of this marital image and its ability to illuminate Trinitarian self-surrender (by which, in his view, the divine Persons are related to each other) make it more valuable than reflection upon the individual soul's acts (Augustine) or even upon any pair of lovers (Richard).

By following this path, von Balthasar largely turns away from the attention to the derivation of Eve and Seth from Adam that interests some of the Fathers and that also is Scheeben's focus. Instead, acts of fecund self-surrender for the life of another take center stage, thereby ensuring that Christ, without needing to be married in the order of created human nature, can be the perfect image in the order of grace.

This image, focused on acts of self-surrendering love, is concretized by marriage (and in a different way by Christ and by consecrated virgins) along lines that specify the insight of Martin Buber and others that the "I" is "something that has always already been addressed by, and addressed, a Thou"—a "*Logos Theou.*"[77] As noted above, von Balthasar is sympathetic to this I-Thou dialogic image, which he traces ultimately to a modification of Hegelian dialectic. In *The Theology of Karl Barth*, von Balthasar connects this I-Thou image to Barth's approach. As von Balthasar says, Barth identifies "the I-Thou relationship in man" as "an 'analogy' with that between God and man" and which also serves as the basis for Barth's "doctrine of the *imago Dei*."[78]

Whereas von Balthasar focuses upon the (marital) act of fruitful self-surrender in love, Barth (in the second Part of *The Doctrine of Creation*)

---

resist its dying strokes in this interim life but still live as the old sinners we were instead of the new people we now are?" (Bromiley, *God and Marriage*, 51). Bromiley replies against this counsel of despair: "God himself has in fact provided us with the necessary power for mortification and renewal. He has done this through his word and through the faith which it engenders. Indeed, as God the Holy Spirit, he himself is the power" (Bromiley, *God and Marriage*, 51).

76. Von Balthasar, *The Christian State of Life*, 232.
77. Von Balthasar, *Truth of God*, 45.
78. Von Balthasar, *The Theology of Karl Barth*, 89.

emphasizes that for Genesis 1–2, "the account of the creation of man as male and female is the climax of the whole history of creation."[79] Man is always a "partner," never in an isolated condition. The act of encounter is the center of Barth's thought here: "Human being becomes the being in encounter in which alone it can be good."[80] Encounter means being "for" each other; there is no human who is not a *fellow* human, and specifically the male and the female are made for mutual encounter. Barth draws attention to the Song of Songs for understanding man and woman's "being in encounter," rooted in their "distinction and connexion" (difference and unity).[81] The work done in von Balthasar by "self-surrender" is here done by "encounter."

Thus, for Barth the encounter between man and woman, described in Genesis 2 and Song of Songs, symbolizes God's encountering his people. He states that the covenant between God and Israel comes first; the covenant between man and woman is the image of this primordial covenant. The covenant between God and Israel "is the original of which the essence of the human as the being of man and woman can only be the reflection and copy. Man is primarily and properly Yahweh, and woman primarily and properly Israel."[82] In creation, man is already "male and female" and so already has "the basic form of being in the encounter of I and Thou, of humanity as fellow-humanity."[83] The revelation of God's Word, then, shows that "before all time, and in the beginning of time posited by the act of creation, and in the perishing time which stands under the sign of the fall and its penalty, and finally in the new time of freedom which has dawned, the resolve and will of God was and is and will be: 'Christ and the community.'"[84]

How does this relate to the image of God described in Genesis 1:26–27? Essentially, the image consists in our being created as a "reflection" of God's own I-Thou in the Spirit. We are created to be partners, to have fellowship, to encounter a Thou (and a thou). We are created to be "for" the Thou/thou. Barth states, "Man generally, the man with the fellow-man, has indeed a part in the divine likeness of the man Jesus, the man for the fellow-man. . . . God created him in His own image in the fact that He did not create him alone but in this connexion and fellowship."[85] God himself is

---

79. Barth, *Church Dogmatics*, III.2, 291.
80. Barth, *Church Dogmatics*, III.2, 292.
81. Barth, *Church Dogmatics*, III.2, 294, 296.
82. Barth, *Church Dogmatics*, III.2, 297.
83. Barth, *Church Dogmatics*, III.2, 316.
84. Barth, *Church Dogmatics*, III.2, 317.
85. Barth, *Church Dogmatics*, III.2, 323–24.

"I and Thou," Father and Son, united in the Holy Spirit. The Father and the Son "encounter" or "confront" each other while being supremely one in the Spirit. Likewise, "God created man in His own image, in correspondence with His own being and essence,"[86] by creating man male and female so as to be intrinsically ordered to a thou (man to woman, woman to man) and, furthermore, by God's eternal determination, to be ordered as Israel-bride to YHWH-bridegroom. The fullness of the image emerges, therefore, through divine revelation which reveals that from all eternity God wills to unite the Church (which ultimately includes all for whom Christ says "Yes") to himself in Christ. The point is encounter: "God is in relationship, and so too is the man created by Him."[87] At creation, this image is found in man and woman, in their fundamental encounter and being-for each other. Barth sums up, "Because He is not solitary in Himself, and therefore does not will to be so *ad extra*, it is not good for man to be alone, and God created him in His own image, as male and female."[88]

In the first Part of *The Doctrine of Creation*, first published in 1945 (three years before the second Part treated above), Barth says many of the same things but adds a few clarifications that are worth mentioning. He identifies his significant debt to Dietrich Bonhoeffer's 1933 book *Creation and Fall*.[89] For Bonhoeffer, the image of God described in Genesis 1 is found in human freedom, which is a relational freedom, a freedom for worship. This image is not possessed by humans in an autonomous way, but rather is given by God: as Bonhoeffer puts it, "Being free means 'being free for the other,' because the other has bound me to him. Only in relationship to the other am I free."[90] This is shown by the fact that man is created as intrinsically relational, as man and woman; and it is also shown by the relation of human creatures to the Creator.

Bonhoeffer's focus on relational freedom—"bound" to be free—is picked up by Barth in light of Barth's distinctive emphasis on the act of encounter and on being "for" the other. It is this element of Barth that connects with von Balthasar's emphasis on the act of fruitful surrender. Both Barth and von Balthasar ground the image not only in an act, but in an act whose lineaments are best apparent (in the created order) in the marital intimacy and bond of the man and woman. Commenting on Bonhoeffer's view, Barth

---

86. Barth, *Church Dogmatics*, III.2, 324.
87. Barth, *Church Dogmatics*, III.2, 324.
88. Barth, *Church Dogmatics*, III.2, 324.
89. For an English translation of the 1937 edition of *Schöpfung und Fall*, see Bonhoeffer, *Creation and Fall*, trans. John C. Fletcher.
90. Bonhoeffer, *Creation and Fall*, 40.

approves it and adds his own emphasis on encounter or confrontation: created freedom "is expressed in a confrontation, conjunction and inter-relatedness of man as male and female."[91] Like divine freedom, created human freedom is freedom "for": we are to be "for" each other as God is "for" us in Christ. Barth underscores that Genesis 1:27 itself interprets the meaning of the "image of God" precisely by pairing it with "male and female": "in the image of God he created him; male and female he created them" (Gen 1:27). For Barth, therefore, the search for the image of God in the soul (or elsewhere) is absurd; God himself has shown us where to look.

Barth's position, interpreting the image of God as the freedom of the I-thou encounter (especially of man and woman, and therefore especially in marriage), focuses attention on the covenantal encounter, just as von Balthasar focuses attention on self-surrendering fruitfulness. Von Balthasar's position seems to me to offer a deepening of Barth's perspective, insofar as von Balthasar specifies covenantal encounter as fecund self-surrendering love. This accords with the way in which God encounters us in Christ. Again, both von Balthasar and Barth assume the existence of human capacities (the embodied soul's relational powers) and seek to locate the image not in the capacities but in a free act rooted in the "differentiation and relationship between man and woman."[92] The image is the encounter—or the self-surrender—inscribed in marriage. For von Balthasar, the self-surrender of man and woman images the Trinity; for Barth, the encounter of man and woman (in its differentiation and relationship) images the Trinity.

Barth is well aware, of course, that "[t]here can be no question of anything more than an analogy. The differentiation and relationship between the I and the Thou in the divine being . . . are not identical with the differentiation and relationship between male and female."[93] Not surprisingly, he presses this point even further, eager to avoid setting up an "analogy of being" or an image that the creature possesses autonomously. He even maintains that "[m]an is not created to be the image of God but . . . he is created in correspondence with the image of God."[94] He means simply that we are created to copy or imitate the divine copy or image, namely, the Word or Son. Our copying of the Son (who is "Thou" to the Father's "I") is not an autonomous power of our own, but always comes from "the intention and deed" of God, who wills this for man and woman.[95] He explains that "the

---

91. Barth, *Church Dogmatics*, III.1, 195.
92. Barth, *Church Dogmatics*, III.1, 195.
93. Barth, *Church Dogmatics*, III.1, 196.
94. Barth, *Church Dogmatics*, III.1, 197.
95. Barth, *Church Dogmatics*, III.1, 197.

image of God is such that, as the *analogia relationis*, it can never cease to be God's work and gift or become a human possession."[96] The creatureliness of the image requires that the human being, in relation to God, be "absolutely at the disposal" of the Creator rather than ever being "satisfied with itself."[97]

Furthermore, Barth notes that we do not simply pass on the image of God by procreation (by producing copies of ourselves), but rather we pass on the image of God insofar as God himself, in his free mercy, recognizes our children as "Thou." This shows again that the act of encounter always has its foundation in a "direct decision and action on the part of God Himself."[98] Certainly procreation belongs to this process, but God's free covenantal will is the defining reality, not procreation per se. In this regard I find von Balthasar's emphasis on fruitful (marital) self-surrendering more helpful, because it integrates procreation while keeping divine and human action (namely, self-surrender) at the center.

Underlying both self-surrender and encounter, of course, is the relational power of knowing and loving God, which finds its perfect fulfillment in Christ's self-surrender on the cross, where he "fully reveals man to himself and brings to light his most high calling."[99] Whereas Barth insists that "the image of God is exclusively the affair of God Himself in His disposing

---

96. Barth, *Church Dogmatics*, III.1, 201.

97. Barth, *Church Dogmatics*, III.1, 226.

98. Barth, *Church Dogmatics*, III.1, 199. Barth adds, "The Reformation thesis concerning the loss of the *imago Dei* through the fall is understandable and necessary against the background of the Reformation understanding of the *imago* as a *rectitudo animae*, or *status integritatis*, which man had originally possessed but immediately forfeited by reason of his guilt and as its consequence and punishment. But there is no basis for this conception of the *imago* in Gen. 1. The biblical saga knows nothing of an original ideal man either in Gen. 1, Gen. 2 or elsewhere" (Barth, *Church Dogmatics*, III.1, 200). Barth emphasizes that all depends upon God's free will. Nothing that humans do can result in the loss of the image of God, because the image does not belong to humans per se but rather is always at the disposal of God. God's will, furthermore, is free but not arbitrary or erratic: "the divine intention at the creation of man, and the consequent promise and pledge given with it, cannot be lost or subjected to partial or complete destruction. This is proved by the fact that the history of God's fellowship and intercourse with man is not abrogated with the fall as the actualization of man's rejection of this relationship. On the contrary, it really begins with the fall. For although it involves for man a complete reversal of the divine intention and therefore shame and judgment, it is at this point that God acknowledges His intention, addressing man as a Thou and making him responsible as an I, and that men themselves must stand and fall together as I and Thou, as man and woman" (Barth, *Church Dogmatics*, III.1, 200). We can rely upon the fact that "God's free and gracious will" that man and woman image God "is continually fulfilled in man [and woman]," insofar as God continually address man and woman as Thou (Barth, *Church Dogmatics*, III.1, 200).

99. *Gaudium et Spes* §22, 922.

of man in incomprehensible mercy,"[100] von Balthasar's argument that the image of God is found in the man and woman's fruitful self-surrender (as well as in the spiritually fruitful self-surrender of a single person) allows for an image that is truly in the human creature while always being relationally ordered to God. On this view, Christ's fruitful self-surrender in love elevates and perfects our created power of fruitful self-giving by establishing the new creation in the consummated marriage of God and his people.

Barth avers that in Jesus Christ "we have *the* image in face of which the question of the original is finally answered."[101] Indeed, he puts the point even more strongly. Quite simply, we cannot understand Genesis 1:26-27 if we do not read it christologically. The very basis of creation is already God's covenant with the human race, and thus with the whole cosmos, in Christ.[102] In Jesus Christ we discover that God has in fact freely and graciously willed to create *all* humans in God's image, so that the image "passes into man's possession and becomes a human reality."[103] God has made all humans in light of Christ, the new Adam. In making all humans (male and female) "in his own image" (Gen 1:27), God makes all humans in the image of Christ: thus "Jesus Christ is already Adam."[104] Christ, as head of his body, includes his bride the Church, with the result that male and female are from the outset in the image of Christ.[105]

For Barth, the covenant is the primal reality: it is because God makes covenant with the human race in Christ that God creates, and it is because humanity is always to be "God's partner in this covenant" that man has a partner, woman.[106] In this covenant, man freely chooses his partner (as when Adam rejoices when God brings Eve to him), but man thereby also "decides

---

100. Barth, *Church Dogmatics*, III.1, 202.
101. Barth, *Church Dogmatics*, III.1, 202.
102. See Barth, *Church Dogmatics*, III.1, 228-29.
103. Barth, *Church Dogmatics*, III.1, 203.
104. Barth, *Church Dogmatics*, III.1, 203; cf. 219.

105. Commenting on such texts as 1 Corinthians 15:49, 2 Corinthians 3:18, Romans 8:29, and Colossians 3:10 (as well as Colossians 1:15), Barth emphasizes that "the image and the reality are not two different things but the reality is present in the image. The community, Christians, are also present in all that Jesus Christ is, and therefore in the fact that He is the image of God" (Barth, *Church Dogmatics*, III.1, 205). Regarding Paul's theology (with particular attention to 1 Corinthians 11 and Ephesians 3), Barth adds that "all that he had to say about man and woman was seen from this angle, in the light of the relationship between Jesus Christ and His community, and therefore of His divine likeness, and that it is only in this way that it is presented as an 'order of creation.' ... [T]he agreement of Paul's teaching with Gen. 1:26f. must not be underestimated in this respect (where it is often overlooked)" (Barth, *Church Dogmatics*, III.1, 205).

106. Barth, *Church Dogmatics*, III.1, 290.

for the decision that has been made concerning him."[107] God always has decisive priority in the encounter, just as, for von Balthasar, God always has decisive priority in our fruitful self-surrender.[108]

Lastly, the fourth Part of *The Doctrine of Creation* should be mentioned, because Barth treats marriage extensively here. More explicitly than previously, he identifies marriage itself not only as an image of God's interior freedom, but also more precisely as an image of "the twofold freedom of God's Word and Spirit."[109] He also refers to Emil Brunner's view of "the natural trinity of father, mother, and child," which for Brunner serves to make monogamy requisite. In Barth's view an emphasis on this "natural trinity" is in fact "a depreciation of marriage in favour of the family."[110] Thus Barth does not go down the path of Scheeben and others.

---

107. Barth, *Church Dogmatics*, III.1, 293. In his extensive discussion of this decision, Barth emphasizes human freedom in the man-woman encounter—giving a passive relationship to woman, however (in accord with his account of the Church)—by remarking that "man had to complete his own creation according to the will and purpose of God by electing woman and saying Yes to her existence before him, thus also saying Yes to God's whole creation, and finally and supremely to his own humanity. . . . Things have to happen as they do when man and woman love each other and are married; man has to be the one who seeks, desires, sacrifices and is utterly dependent on woman for the fulfilment of his relationship to her, so that to this extent he is the weaker half, because all this is rooted and grounded in the divine creation and therefore in the divine will and purpose. . . . In the manifold meaning of the concept he [man] must really seek and find in her his own glory. And she for her part must desire only to be his glory. The will and purpose of God for both must find realization in this event" (Barth, *Church Dogmatics*, III.1, 305-6). Barth holds that the man is the "weaker partner" (Barth, *Church Dogmatics*, III.1, 306) because the man is in the petitioner's position of seeking the woman.

108. Barth's interpretation of the Song of Songs is also worth noting: "A comparison of Gen. 2 and the Song of Songs does at least reveal that what interested the authors of the creation saga and these love songs was the fact that in the relationship between man and woman—even prior to its character as the basis of the father-mother-child relationship—we have to do primarily with the question of an incomparable covenant, of an irresistibly purposed and effected union. The Song of Songs is one long description of the rapture, the unquenchable yearning and the restless willingness and readiness, with which both partners in this covenant hasten towards an encounter" (Barth, *Church Dogmatics*, III.1, 313).

109. Barth, *Church Dogmatics*, III.4, 216.

110. Barth, *Church Dogmatics*, III.4, 200-1. See Brunner, *Das Gebot und die Ordnungen*, 330.

IV. Other Contemporary Approaches

In his 1994 "Letter to Families," Pope John Paul II broadly shows his agreement with Scheeben's and von Balthasar's proposals—though without naming them personally—by remarking: "The primordial model of the family is to be sought in God himself, in the Trinitarian mystery of his life."[111] Yet, Marc Cardinal Ouellet has complained that "this theme of the family, image of the Trinity, is still far from being unanimously welcomed. It has yet to rally those who follow the long tradition founded upon the authority of Augustine of Hippo and Thomas Aquinas, who preferred the 'psychological' or 'intra-subjective' analogy as an approach to the Trinitarian mystery."[112]

Admittedly, I am unconcerned by this lack of unanimity. According to Ouellet, "the meaning of the relationship between the Trinity and the family depends upon whether or not the man-woman relationship is included within the *imago Dei*. If man—man and woman—is the image of the Trinity, then the communion and participation of the family 'we' in the Trinitarian 'We' goes far deeper."[113] In my view, however, the inclusion of the man-woman relationship within the image is not necessary. Even if the image of God is found in the soul rather than strictly in the man and woman (whether in their fruitful self-surrendering love or their relational and differentiated covenantal encounter), the man-woman relationship can still retain significance. After all, when two images of the Trinity (a man and a woman) are involved in a uniquely intimate relational bond, surely a communion of such persons would also serve to image the Trinity.

---

111. John Paul II, "Letter to Families," §6.

112. Ouellet, *Divine Likeness*, 20. Drawing upon Gendron's *Mystère de la Trinité*, Ouellet notes that in fact the Church's theological tradition has always possessed a family image of the Trinity, although not in a precise or uncontroverted manner. In the West, however, the influence of Augustine brought this image to an end.

113. Ouellet, *Divine Likeness*, 21. Ouellet later points out, "The common fecundity of the divine 'We' and the human 'we' must not be seen exclusively from the angle of fertility. It is not doubt its most creative moment but it also expands to the many relationships of education, sharing, and affection that make up the community life of persons committed one to another and one 'for' another in the family's framework" (*Divine Likeness*, 36). Ouellet is obviously well aware of the two points that von Balthasar singles out, namely self-surrendering love (unity-in-difference, communion) and fruitfulness. Ouellet remarks, "On what precisely does it [the family analogy of the Trinity] hinge? On the correspondence between the persons or the communion of persons? A recurring expression in the writings of John Paul II guides us towards the second hypothesis: the *communio personarum* is the common meeting place of the deeper reality of the family and of the mystery of the Trinity.... This analogy is based fundamentally on the interpersonal love which, by means of gift and reception, engenders persons, maintains them in relation, and allows them to fulfill themselves as persons 'by a sincere gift of self'" (*Divine Likeness*, 34).

Ouellet comments that "Augustine's major objection to this analogy [of the family] is the impossibility of realizing a true unity, that is to say a substantial unity, within a human family; in the three human *hypostases* of man, woman, and child there exists such a disparity that any real unity is inconceivable."[114] Actually, however, the even more pressing problem is that if the best image of the Trinity is found in the married couple and their child, then unmarried individuals are not in the image of God. As we have seen, von Balthasar gets around this problem by simply arguing that marriage exemplifies love of neighbor and fruitfulness but that consecrated virginity does so, too. It follows that even if von Balthasar calls the marital image the "greatest" image of the Trinity, he qualifies this by making clear that individuals who obey God's call to singleness (such as Jesus) also image the Trinity, and indeed do so with supreme perfection insofar as their self-surrendering love and fruitfulness are perfect (as in the case of Jesus).

As Ouellet notes, Augustine recognized that the love of neighbor can produce "a common soul and a common heart among those who love one another," and this unity is a reflection of the unity of the Trinity.[115] This kind of unity-in-difference is what von Balthasar has in view when he highlights self-surrendering love of neighbor and fecundity as the two key elements of the image of the Trinity; and it is also what we found in Barth's model of covenantal encounter, and even in Scheeben's modeling the Trinitarian processions upon the derivation of Eve and Seth from Adam. In a manner that resonates with the insights of both von Balthasar and Barth, Pope John Paul II's "Letter to Families" concludes that "the divine 'We' is the eternal pattern of the human 'we', especially of that 'we' formed by the man and the woman created in the divine image and likeness."[116]

The Orthodox theologian Paul Evdokimov has this same point in view when he states, "'When husband and wife are united in marriage, they are no longer seen as something earthly, but as the image of God Himself.' These words of St John Chrysostom allow us to see in marriage a living icon, a 'theophany.'"[117] Somewhat like Gregory of Nazianzus, Evdokimov emphasizes that just as the divine Persons are of one nature (and are thereby a single subject), so also the married couple, joined by God as the third, make up a single subject. Evdokimov states, "It is therefore nuptial man who is in the image of the triune God, and the dogma of the Trinity is his

---

114. Ouellet, *Divine Likeness*, 22.

115. Ouellet, *Divine Likeness*, 24. Ouellet draws attention here to Augustine's Tractate 39 on the Gospel of John.

116. John Paul II, "Letter to Families," §6.

117. Evdokimov, *The Sacrament of Love*, 118.

divine archetype, the icon of the nuptial community."[118] This is because of the graced bond of love shared by the married couple. Evdokimov remarks, "The human being, as a closed monad, would not be His image."[119] A "closed monad" would, of course, not be a human being, since all humans are intrinsically relational vis-à-vis God and neighbor even if they do not realize this.

The logic that Evdokimov employs justifies the consecrated virgin's being in the image of the Trinity, insofar as the consecrated virgin (preeminently Christ) is filled with self-surrendering love of neighbor and is spiritually fruitful.[120] In *Mulieris Dignitatem*, Pope John Paul II argues along Evdokimov's lines that "man and woman, created as a 'unity of the two' in their common humanity, are called to live in a communion of love and in this way to mirror in the world the communion of love that is in God, through which the three Persons love each other in the intimate mystery of the one divine life."[121] This point is best spelled out by von Balthasar's emphasis on triune self-surrendering love and fruitfulness.

V. Conclusion

Because humans are created to be fulfilled through intimate eschatological marriage with God, Christian marriage is a valuable image of the Trinity. Yet in making this point, we must also affirm, as von Balthasar does, that "the sexual man/woman fruitfulness need be no longer the exclusive model of fruitfulness," since Christ's "suprasexual fruitfulness" brings the Church into being.[122] Von Balthasar appreciates that we can also see this image of the Trinity in the suprasexual fruitfulness of the Virgin Mary. He observes in *New Elucidations* that ultimately "the concept of fruitfulness brings us into a sphere that affects every Christian, without distinction between the married and those who have consecrated their virginity to God."[123]

---

118. Evdokimov, *The Sacrament of Love*, 117.

119. Evdokimov, *The Sacrament of Love*, 115.

120. As Ouellet puts it, Christ is the one who fulfills God's covenant with Israel and who thereby consummates the marriage of God with his people. See Ouellet, *Divine Likeness*, 29.

121. John Paul II, *Mulieris Dignitatem*, §7. For an extended discussion of these matters, see John Paul II, *Man and Woman He Created Them*.

122. Von Balthasar, *Dramatis Personae*, 413.

123. Von Balthasar, *New Elucidations*, 222. In this section of *New Elucidations*, von Balthasar has in view Pope Paul VI's 1968 encyclical *Humanae Vitae*. As von Balthasar says of that encyclical's teaching, in light of scriptural revelation: "For sexuality as Christians understand it—sexuality that takes as its norm the relationship between

Nonetheless, it is specifically Jesus Christ who, through his self-surrender on the Cross as received by Mary at the foot of the Cross (embodying the Marian Church), reveals the full meaning of marriage as an image of the Trinity—and at the same time inaugurates the eschatological marriage of God and his people. In light of this eschatological marriage and especially Ephesians 5, von Balthasar states that "it is from the fruitfulness of Christ and the Church that the model for the married state may be drawn. For the source of this fruitfulness lies in the fact that no limits whatsoever are imposed on self-surrender, either on Christ's part or on that of the Church."[124] Human marriage is a sign of this marriage of Christ and the Church, in which Christ perfectly images the Trinity and enables his followers to do the same and to be eschatologically "married" to the Trinity through the fruitfulness of self-surrender in love. In marriage, the couple's "physical fruitfulness" is conjoined with their "spiritual fruitfulness" or "total surrender to each other."[125] Christian marriage, then, introduces us to "a form of existence in which God's Agape . . . becomes the all-inclusive total meaning of life."[126] Here we find the "form" of the inaugurated marriage of God and his people for which the whole cosmos was created.

The 2009 Pastoral Letter of the United States Conference of Catholic Bishops, *Marriage: Love and Life in the Divine Plan*, remarks about marriage and the Trinity: "As we learn from the mystery of the Trinity, to be in the image and likeness of God is not simply to have intelligence and free will, but also to live in a communion of love. From all eternity the Father begets his Son in the love of the Spirit."[127] Put otherwise, while affirming that the Father's begetting does not depend upon the Spirit (so as not to overthrow the Father's sufficiency as the fount of the Trinity or to undermine the order of origin), we can say that in his eternal act of begetting, "the Father gives himself entirely over to the Son in the love of the Holy Spirit. The Son, having been begotten of the Father, perfectly returns that love by giving himself

---

Christ and his Church—Christ's words hold true: 'Let him grasp it who can.' But Christ is saying something more here than that very few men and women will actually grasp his doctrine. He is issuing us a challenge to serious endeavor, the same challenge, essentially, that rings through the whole of the Gospel: take up your cross every day, sell all you possess, and do not cheat as did Ananias and Sapphira. Why should the sexual area alone offer no challenge to the Christian? Sexuality, even as *eros*, is to be an expression of *agape*, and *agape* always involves an element of renunciation. And only by renunciation can the limits that we set on our own self-surrender be transcended" (*New Elucidations*, 227–28).

124. Von Balthasar, *New Elucidations*, 222.
125. Von Balthasar, *New Elucidations*, 223.
126. Von Balthasar, *Dramatis Personae*, 414.
127. United States Conference of Catholic Bishops, *Marriage*, 35.

entirely over to the Father in the same Spirit of love."[128] On the basis of this Trinitarian theology, the bishops draw the conclusion that to be in the image of God—in the image of the *triune* God—involves being in relational communion. There is no human "image of God" abstracted from the relational call of the God who made us to know and love him by becoming "the Bride, the wife of the Lamb" (Rev 21:9).[129]

---

128. United States Conference of Catholic Bishops, *Marriage*, 35–36. On the importance of the Trinitarian order of origin, see the Introduction to my *Engaging the Doctrine of the Holy Spirit*.

129. The Bishops quote the *Catechism of the Catholic Church*: "the Christian family is a communion of persons, a sign and image of the communion of the Father and the Son in the Holy Spirit" (*Catechism of the Catholic Church*, §2205, cited in USCCB, *Marriage*, 37). On the same page, the Bishops also cite Thomas Aquinas's *Summa theologiae* I, q. 93, a. 3, where Aquinas (in treating the image of God) describes "a certain imitation of God, consisting in the fact that man proceeds from man, as God proceeds from God."

Chapter 3

Original Sin

If the human image of the Trinity is expressed in marital fruitfulness and self-surrender and the human vocation consists ultimately in marriage with God, then it is fitting that original sin was the fall of the first marriage. But when we think of original sin, we generally do not think of the significance of Adam and Eve being a married couple. Why should it matter that the first sin was committed not by one person alone, but by Adam and Eve together? After all, if the first sin was the desire to "be like God, knowing good and evil" without depending upon God (Gen 3:5), then such pride can easily arise in an individual as much as it can in a married couple. Besides, even raising the issue may seem like a stretch. Isn't it already difficult enough to believe that there was an original sin committed by a truly free human being at the dawn of human rationality? Why insist that not solely Eve or solely Adam, but Adam and Eve *as a married couple* were the proud perpetrators of original sin and that this has theological importance?

N. T. Wright comments that after the destruction of the Second Temple by the Romans in 70 AD, Jews such as the authors of 4 Ezra and 2 Baruch came to hold that "the sickness of evil in the world was a deeper disease than anyone had supposed," so deep as to "make subsequent [post-Adamic] sin inevitable, even for Israel."[1] Among Jewish authors *prior* to 70 AD, he

---

1. Wright, *Paul and the Faithfulness of God*, II, 745. Crucially, Wright argues that "*Paul's radical rethinking of creational and covenantal monotheism contained within itself both an intensification of the problem and an equally radical solution.* As the fall of Jerusalem [in 70 AD] sent the apocalyptists back to the scriptures, and ultimately back to Adam, so the events concerning Jesus did the same for Paul" (*Paul and the Faithfulness of God*, II, 747). Put otherwise: "Did Paul come with a 'problem' or 'plight' to which he discovered that Jesus was the 'solution'? Or was part of the shock of the revelation on the road to Damascus the fact that, since Israel's God had apparently provided him

notes, the only one to affirm such a position was Paul. But Paul generally attributes the devastating first sin to Adam alone. Thus, Paul remarks that "as one man's trespass led to condemnation for all men, so one man's act of righteousness leads to acquittal and life for all men. For as by one man's disobedience many were made sinners, so by one man's obedience many will be made righteous" (Rom 5:18–19). Paul makes essentially the same point immediately prior to these verses, when he comments: "If, because of one man's trespass, death reigned through that one man, much more will those who receive the abundance of grace and the free gift of righteousness reign in life through the one man Jesus Christ" (Rom 5:17). This certainly does not sound like someone who considers it important that a married couple committed the first sin.

For Paul, Jesus Christ is the true head of the human race and the source from whom eternal life comes for all humans. This fact leads him to accentuate Adam in parallel with Christ as the new Adam. Christ descends from Adam, but it is Christ who truly stands at the head of the human race. Since the time of Adam, Christ has been awaited by the human race—however unconsciously—as its savior from the terrible condition of corruption and alienation from God and as the one who will lead the human race to its deifying consummation. Paul emphasizes that the ultimate bond of the human race is found not in corporeal descent from Adam but in "the fullness of the blessing of Christ" (Rom 15:29). God calls us to be "one body in Christ, and individually members one of another" (Rom 12:5). In Christ, all who have since Adam's fall been "under the power of sin" (Rom 3:9) "have now received our reconciliation" (Rom 5:11).

Paul proceeds along the same lines in 1 Corinthians 15, again focusing solely on Adam rather than on both Adam and Eve. He begins by recounting the fact that Christ, after dying "for our sins in accordance with the scriptures," rose from the dead (1 Cor 15:3). He then chastises some of the Corinthians for accepting that Christ rose from the dead but denying that other humans will rise from the dead. He explains that "as in Adam all die, so also in Christ shall all be made alive" (1 Cor 15:22). Adam stands at the root of the human race in terms of fallen life (which leads to death); while Christ stands at the root of the human race in terms of risen life (which leads to

---

with a 'solution', there must have been some kind of hitherto unsuspected 'plight'?" (*Paul and the Faithfulness of God*, II, 747). Wright argues that neither approach is correct; instead, Paul began with "the problem generated by creational and covenantal monotheism: why is the world in such a mess, and why is Israel still unredeemed? The revelation of Jesus as the crucified and risen Messiah meant, for Paul, that the covenant God had offered the solution to these problems—but, in offering the solution, Israel's God had redefined the problems, had revealed that they had all along been far worse than anyone had imagined" (*Paul and the Faithfulness of God*, II, 749).

resurrection). Citing Genesis 2:7 regarding the creation of Adam, he states that the difference consists in the kinds of bodies that pertain to earthly life and risen life: the latter kind characterizes Christ's glorified flesh. In this respect, he contrasts "[t]he first man Adam" with "the last Adam" (1 Cor 15:45). Adam is the "first man," who is ultimately "the man of dust"; Christ, the Son of the Father, is "the second man," who is "the man of heaven" (1 Cor 15:47–48). The second Adam is far more powerful and determinative than the first Adam. The first Adam was always, in God's providence, "a type of the one who was to come" (Rom 5:14).

Does Paul, then, know only "the transgression of Adam" (Rom 5:14)? In fact, Paul knows well the Genesis story in which Eve, knowing God's command that "of the tree of the knowledge of good and evil you shall not eat" (Gen 2:16), freely takes the fruit of that very tree, eats of it, and gives it to Adam to eat. In 2 Corinthians 11, Paul shows his awareness that the first sin was not only Adam's but also Eve's. Attempting to guide his recalcitrant flock at Corinth, Paul states that "I am afraid that as the serpent deceived Eve by his cunning, your thoughts will be led astray from a sincere and pure devotion to Christ" (2 Cor 11:3). His point is that the cunning of a false preacher (parallel to the serpent's cunning) would not absolve the Corinthians of their guilt in turning away from what Paul has taught them about "a sincere and pure devotion to Christ." Just as any Corinthians who followed the false preacher would thereby separate themselves from Christ, so also Eve committed a sin whose guilt, despite her efforts, cannot be pinned on the serpent.

Similarly, in 1 Timothy 2:13–14, we find another passage that recognizes Eve's sin, whether or not the author is Paul. Indeed, in this passage it might seem that the sin and guilt belong entirely to Eve, which would be the opposite of the impression given by Romans 5. The passage states, "For Adam was formed first, then Eve; and Adam was not deceived, but the woman was deceived and became a transgressor."[2]

---

2. John J. Collins remarks, "In Genesis, Adam and Eve are both responsible for the act of disobedience. If either bears greater responsibility, it is Adam, insofar as he seems to hold primacy, and in fact the act became known traditionally as the 'sin of Adam.' Nonetheless, we read in the Book of Ben Sira (early second century BCE): 'From a woman sin had its beginning and because of her we all die.' Even more egregiously, 1 Timothy 2:14 says: 'Adam was not deceived, but the woman was deceived and became a transgressor.' Such claims cannot be justified by exegesis of Genesis. Adam may not have been deceived by the snake, but he was deceived by Eve, and he was just as much a transgressor as she was. At this point, the text seems to be subordinated to the cultural prejudices of a later era" (*What Are Biblical Values?*, 88). For discussion of the authorship of 1 and 2 Timothy, tentatively favoring Pauline authorship against the majority of scholars, see Johnson, *The Writings of the New Testament*, 255–57, 381–89.

It is clear that Paul recognizes that Adam and Eve committed the first sin, even if they played different roles in it and even if Paul highlights Adam in order to accentuate Christ. David Cloutier puts the matter with eloquent understatement: "[B]y giving us the naked man and woman, the story hints that things now are not like they were then."[3] The relationship between man and woman in marriage is not now like it was prior to sin. It is clear that the fall has done something to marriage (see Gen 3:16), even if it is not clear that Adam and Eve's status as a married couple has any theological significance with regard to the first sin.

Cloutier does not ask whether it matters that Adam and Eve (husband and wife) together committed the first sin. Can any insight be gleaned from Genesis 1–3 in this regard? Certainly original sin is the fall of the "image of God," and the image of God is "male and female" (Gen 1:27). When God fashioned Eve for Adam, he greeted her joyfully as "bone of my bones and flesh of my flesh" (Gen 2:23) and they enjoy a relationship so intimate as to be "one flesh" (Gen 2:24). When Eve eats from the forbidden tree, the next thing we read is that "she also gave some to her husband, and he ate" (Gen 3:6). The description "her husband" seems significant, as does the fact that it is only after *both* Adam and Eve have eaten that "the eyes of both were opened, and they knew that they were naked" (Gen 3:7). Looking back from the vantage point of Ephesians 5 and Revelation 21, it is clear that the vocation of the first married couple was to serve as a sign of the eschatological marriage of God and his people. They failed in this vocation, and thus also failed to image God as they were called to do. But can we say that the dimension of marriage informs the theological significance of the fall according to Genesis itself?

In order to investigate this question, I will first examine three recent Christian commentaries on Genesis, all of which are insightful regarding human yearning for communion with God and regarding the broken relationship of Adam and Eve. These contemporary commentators, however, do not focus on original sin as the sin of a marriage, although R. R. Reno's commentary does perceive the crucial link between a harmonious marriage and its ordering toward the eschatological marriage of God and creation. Turning from these contemporary commentaries to earlier ones, I explore the discussions of Genesis 2–3 offered by Ephrem the Syrian, John Chrysostom, and Augustine. The marriage of Adam and Eve prior to and during the first sin is at the forefront of these Church Fathers' minds when they interpret the fall. In light of the existential insights of the modern commentaries, the patristic commentaries on Genesis 2–3 encourage deeper reflection upon

---

3. Cloutier, *Love, Reason, and God's Story*, 65.

why it matters that the first sin was committed not by two individuals, but by a married couple.

Gordon Wenham remarks about Genesis 2:21–25: "Here the ideal of marriage as it was understood in ancient Israel is being portrayed, a relationship characterized by harmony and intimacy between the partners. . . . [T]he first days of the first marriage remain a goal to which Israel hoped to return when the promises to Abraham were fulfilled."[4] Fully to appreciate this eschatological goal requires appreciating that Adam and Eve's sin is an act of a married couple that distorts the idyllic marriage. Commenting upon Augustine's *City of God*, John Cavadini identifies what is really at stake: "Original sin is the sin of Adam . . . , namely, the *willing of and the creation of a fallen solidarity*."[5] Having been made for selfless solidarity—ultimately for eschatological marriage with God—Adam and Eve freely choose instead to engender a fallen solidarity rooted in self-centered pride. It is this fallen marital communion that the divine Bridegroom renews and elevates, as Cavadini says, "by the re-forming power of Christ's love."[6]

I. Contemporary Biblical Scholarship: Arnold, Reno, Cotter

Do contemporary biblical scholars give much attention to Adam and Eve as a married couple? Specifically when it comes to thinking about the first sin, how do scholars today account for the role of Adam and Eve's relationship?

Bill T. Arnold

Commenting on Genesis 2:21–23, in which God creates the woman, Bill T. Arnold devotes significant space to arguing that an egalitarian understanding of men and women is in view here. He suggests that this fits the situation

---

4. Wenham, *Genesis 1–15*, 69. Wenham notes that the one-flesh union described in Genesis 2:24 has to do not simply with sexual union or children or spiritual communion (important though these are), but with a new and enduring "kinship relation" between the man and the woman (*Genesis 1–15*, 71). For analysis of the way in which the theme of kinship unfolds biblically, see Hahn, *Kinship by Covenant*. I add that other than speaking of the "primeval act of disobedience of the first human couple" (Wenham, *Genesis 1–15*, 55), Wenham does not devote attention to the significance of the fact that the first sin was committed by a married couple.

5. Cavadini, "Spousal Vision," 219.

6. Cavadini, "Ideology and Solidarity," 101.

of "the highland villages of early Israel," before the rise of the monarchy.[7] He notes that the man's response to the creation of the woman shows that "[t]he man and the woman are uniquely each other's in a way that defines what it means to be human, which also distinguishes them from the animals."[8] When the narrator announces, "Therefore a man leaves his father and his mother and cleaves to his wife, and they become one flesh" (Gen 2:24), Arnold interprets this as the institution of marriage, which he suggests arises (in the narrative) from the need to reunite "two parts of a sexual whole" in a "one flesh" union—since Eve was originally taken out of Adam.[9] Here marriage is seen as a reuniting, rather than simply as two individuals getting together. Arnold speaks of "the primordial communal unity of the first two humans, which becomes the paradigm for all marriages."[10]

Arnold devotes some space to arguing that we need to recognize that Genesis 3:1–7 does not use the word *fall* or speak about the infecting of all later humans with a fallen condition due to the loss of grace. He attributes such concepts to Second Temple Judaism and to Paul, as well as to the thought of Augustine. In my view, he pushes too quickly past the reasons—grounded in Genesis 3:1–7 itself—for why Second Temple Judaism developed the conceptual language of the "fall." Be that as it may, he similarly notes that the association of the "serpent" with "Satan" is the product of Second Temple Judaism. He argues that in Genesis 3 the serpent is likely the Canaanite god Baal, presented here in a symbolic form.

When Arnold turns to the sin itself, he summarizes it quickly. He states simply, "The misdeed was infectious and communal: 'and she also gave . . . and he ate' (3:6)."[11] Other than mentioning that the sin was "communal," he does not refer to the fact that the sin occurs from within what he earlier called "the primordial communal unity" of the marriage of Adam and Eve. He moves directly to the results of the sin, which include Adam and Eve's acquiring "the serpent's shrewdness," losing their innocence, and trading obedience to and "right relationship with" God for a bodily pleasure.[12]

Thus, Arnold does not explicitly contemplate the possibility that the fact that the sin was committed by the first married couple, within the first marriage, has significance for the meaning of the sin. He recognizes that the

---

7. Arnold, *Genesis*, 60. He is drawing here upon the research of Carol L. Meyers, especially *Discovering Eve*.

8. Arnold, *Genesis*, 61.

9. Arnold, *Genesis*, 61.

10. Arnold, *Genesis*, 61.

11. Arnold, *Genesis*, 66.

12. Arnold, *Genesis*, 66.

sin is "communal," but this is as far as he goes in the direction of seeing any significance to the fact that the first sin was not committed by one person alone. Arnold concludes that Genesis 3 "is primarily interested in why the individual human, *by nature of his or her humanity*, is forever afflicted by alienation, guilt, and the inevitability of death, and yet why humans still have this potential for life with God."[13]

R. R. Reno

In his expressly theological commentary on Genesis, R. R. Reno makes a crucial point with regard to Genesis 2:18–20: "The primal loneliness of the first man and his desire for a fuller fellowship foreshadow the great biblical theme of consummation."[14] In Genesis 2, this "primal loneliness" is highlighted when, after the man names all the animals, we find that "for the man there was not found a helper fit for him" (Gen 2:20). Reno underscores that the consummation of this "desire for a fuller fellowship" must be bodily rather than a flight from the body. In fact, the consummation will involve an embodied covenantal history, the incarnation of the Son, and the sacraments of the Church.

When Eve is created from Adam's rib (Genesis 2:21–23), Reno notes that Adam has at last "found the one whom he has desired."[15] He remarks that Adam and Eve, however, do not consummate their (physical) desire, or at least the narrative does not describe such a consummation, although it does speak more broadly about a married couple becoming "one flesh" (Gen 2:24). Reno argues that the lack of a concretely described sexual consummation signals something important: *eros*, human desire, aims not only at sexual intercourse but at companionship, and ultimately at companionship with God. Reno holds that "we cannot treat marriage and sexual desire as simply natural aspects of life, any more than we can treat acts of the will or efforts of the intellect as merely biological."[16] Instead, "marriage and sexual desire" are ordered to "our supernatural vocation, which is our entrance into the seventh day, the future of living in fellowship with God."[17] *Eros* points us toward this divine fellowship; we are not going to be satisfied with less. As Reno puts it, "Love presses toward the infinite."[18] In the love of a man and

13. Arnold, *Genesis*, 73.
14. Reno, *Genesis*, 74.
15. Reno, *Genesis*, 75.
16. Reno, *Genesis*, 75.
17. Reno, *Genesis*, 75.
18. Reno, *Genesis*, 76.

a woman, we often find the desire for and profession of everlasting love, a desire that goes well beyond what earthly life can offer. Marital love expresses our sense that we are made for an everlasting love, for a "transcendent purpose," one that is radically "open-ended" and therefore possible only in God.[19] The love between a man and a woman leaves behind the strictly "natural" realm and conveys our "human dynamism toward fellowship with God," who is the "beloved" in whose arms we ultimately desire to rest.[20]

Reno has here identified what I consider to be the key point. At the same time, of course, the love between a man and a woman in marriage is not simply a stand-in for spiritual desire for God. Reno notes that for Genesis 2, "The emotional and physical bond between male and female reaches toward new life in children."[21] The creative dynamism of God in Genesis 1–2 is reflected by the creative dynamism found in the love of a man and a woman. Again, each of us strives toward "something more, something fuller, something that evokes the 'at last' of our spiritual desire."[22] Marriage, with its male-female *eros* and with its ordering toward the next generation, is filled with the "forward push of desire, the restlessness of human loneliness, the future-oriented reality of procreation."[23] These bodily and spiritual dynamisms are integrally related, and all of them flourish only when we are in fellowship with God, who alone can sate our forward-looking thirst for eternal communion. When we exercise our desire outside of fellowship with God, it becomes a destructive force, tearing down communion rather than building it up. A constant theme of Reno's commentary is that the good ordering of human love in marriage and in relationship with God that we find in Genesis 2 is deeply fragile in the fallen world, where real communion (of any kind) often seems so difficult to obtain or sustain. He states, "The restless heart and its desire for fulfillment can rage against the limitations of the present, and driven by a longing for something more, we can seek perverted, false forms of rest, clinging to false loves."[24]

When he comes to the sin of Adam and Eve, he attends to the fact that Eve talks too much with the serpent. Eve also adds to God's commandment an element that God did not command, namely, that they could not even *touch* the fruit of the tree. Reno reflects here on the character of sin, which is a "perverted love of a finite good, and therefore has no stable, fundamental

19. Reno, *Genesis*, 75.
20. Reno, *Genesis*, 76.
21. Reno, *Genesis*, 76.
22. Reno, *Genesis*, 76.
23. Reno, *Genesis*, 76.
24. Reno, *Genesis*, 76.

form."[25] In his view, the sin of Adam and Eve cannot be set down to one and only one root, such as pride. But the sin of Adam and Eve does express, he says, our tendency to desire a this-worldly good over the good of relationship with God. Reno observes that "we are tempted to rest in countless finite goods, and the temptation is strong."[26] Adam and Eve give in to this temptation.

Although Reno does not discuss the marital context of the first sin, he does ask the question of who is to blame. Romans 5 suggests that the sin is Adam's, whereas 1 Timothy 2 suggests that the sin is Eve's. Reno argues that, in fact, the key point is that neither Eve nor Adam originates wickedness in the world. Both act in a world where disobedience is already present. Only the serpent, Satan (whom Reno understands to be a fallen angel), originates evil. Yet by freely choosing to repeat this evil, to disobey God, both Adam and Eve sin against God and are fully culpable for their sin.

Interpreting Genesis 3:7, "the eyes of both were opened, and they knew that they were naked," Reno does not mention marriage or its symbolism. However, he does argue that fallen Adam and Eve's spiritual vision is obscured by carnal vision. He states, "Everything is now seen in terms of the project of bodily existence, one that involves satisfying transient desires and ensuring survival."[27] This suggests (although Reno does not make it explicit) that Adam and Eve's marital life now becomes sadly constricted, turned away from God and from ultimate goods of love. Love, which seeks everlasting communion, has been traded for lust. Reno observes that the shame that Adam and Eve feel indicates that they "are living carnally, living as if the material world was the final truth that constrains and governs human life."[28]

Reno concludes that "Adam and Eve choose loyalty to the lie—life according to its physical reality—and this sends them marching away from the Sabbath fulfillment for which they were created."[29] This is an excellent way to put it. The ultimate "Sabbath fulfillment," as Reno knows (though without stating it here), is the marriage of God and humanity that is accomplished in Christ and that will be brought to perfect fulfillment at the end of time. In sinning, the first married couple distorts the love that properly orients marriage to the Sabbath consummation, and that enables marriage to be fully itself.

25. Reno, *Genesis*, 88.
26. Reno, *Genesis*, 89.
27. Reno, *Genesis*, 92.
28. Reno, *Genesis*, 92.
29. Reno, *Genesis*, 97.

David W. Cotter, O.S.B.

Treating Genesis 2:18, "It is not good that the man should be alone; I will make him a helper fit for him," David Cotter proposes that the original "man" (or human) is suffering from a serious threat: "solitude," loneliness.[30] Creation in Genesis 1 is declared to be "very good" (Gen 1:31), but loneliness is "not good." Indeed, Cotter considers that loneliness, if allowed to fester, "will cause the human to die."[31] The human requires a helper or partner. The result is human maleness and femaleness, so that the human has what it takes to sustain life rather than to die in sterility. Cotter states that the man's glowing words upon seeing the woman express the "nearly universal" human experience of "finding another person with whom one shares such an intense kinship and intimacy that, in meeting the other, one feels as though a hitherto lost and unknown part of oneself is being discovered, that two people seem to share, in some mysterious fashion, a single personhood."[32] Such a friendship, in the way that Cotter describes it, need not be between a man and a woman. Yet, Cotter has noted the way in which the creation of the woman overcomes the sterility that would otherwise doom the human race, and so his description of the "nearly universal" experience of finding a friend is in accord with the male-female aspect of the narrative.

Cotter then describes the friendship of Adam and Eve. On the basis of their nakedness and absence of shame, he comments that "[t]heir communion is total and their intimacy unbarred."[33] Cotter does not specify what precisely he thinks is entailed by Genesis 2:24's reference to the man and the woman becoming "one flesh," nor does he say anything further about marriage itself. Regarding Genesis 2:24, he says simply that "[o]ne might well read what follows just as an etiology for marriage, but it is not merely that."[34] Unlike Arnold and Reno, however, Cotter's discussion of the *sin* of Adam and Eve mentions their marital relationship, even if quite obliquely. In his very brief commentary on Genesis 3:1–5, Cotter refers to both Adam and Eve even though the serpent here is talking only with Eve. Cotter states, "Desirous of real wisdom, the couple mistakenly thinks that the snake's slyness is what they seek."[35]

---

30. Cotter, *Genesis*, 31.
31. Cotter, *Genesis*, 31.
32. Cotter, *Genesis*, 33.
33. Cotter, *Genesis*, 33.
34. Cotter, *Genesis*, 32–33.
35. Cotter, *Genesis*, 34.

Commenting on Genesis 3:7, where Adam and Eve's eyes are opened and they discover their (shameful) nakedness, Cotter states that Adam and Eve "have learned . . . that they are not to be trusted, if not with God's gifts, then certainly not with each other."[36] Their mutual disobedience turns their lives upside down. Cotter does not probe further into the significance of the marital context of the sin.

II. Fourth- and Fifth-Century Fathers of the Church on Genesis 2–3

Ephrem the Syrian (d. 373)

Thus far, we have seen significant appreciation for the communion of Adam and Eve and for the way in which their desire for a partner (and friendship) bears upon their desire for intimate and indeed everlasting communion with God, but not much attention to the direct import of the marital context of the first sin—although Reno recognizes that whenever a couple stops pursuing communion with God, the couple's own relationship (which then becomes the ultimate good) will suffer. What do patristic commentators add to our understanding of marriage and original sin?

Let me begin with Ephrem the Syrian. Describing the garden of Eden as "the land of Paradise,"[37] Ephrem supposes that this Paradise is a mountain somewhere in the middle of the ocean. Ephrem is not averse to using his imagination to fill in details. Nor is he averse to asking difficult questions, such as how, when God placed Adam in the garden of Eden, Adam could "till it and keep it" (Gen 2:15), since after all Adam had no "agricultural implements" and no robbers needed to be kept at bay.[38] He describes Adam functioning as "a loving shepherd" by naming all the animals, who in Ephrem's view did not at this juncture prey upon each other.[39] Ephrem emphasizes that Adam ruled wisely and peacefully in Eden, in accord with Adam's God-given authority. For Ephrem, the crucial thing is to perceive the wonderful gifts that God gave to Adam. He states that "God gave Adam authority, made him share in the act of creation, wrapped him in glory, and gave him the Garden."[40] God did all this even before giving Adam the greatest gift of all, Eve.

---

36. Cotter, *Genesis*, 35.
37. Ephrem the Syrian, *The Commentary on Genesis*, 200.
38. Ephrem the Syrian, *The Commentary on Genesis*, 202.
39. Ephrem the Syrian, *The Commentary on Genesis*, 203.
40. Ephrem the Syrian, *The Commentary on Genesis*, 204.

Ephrem considers that Adam needed a "helper" (Gen 2:20) and that Eve amply fulfilled this role. What Ephrem has in view are the tasks that a wife on a flourishing ranch would possess. He comments that "Eve looked after things inside, caring for the sheep, oxen, herds, and flocks in the field"; and in addition to this, Eve helped Adam "with the buildings and the sheepfolds, and with the crafts that he invented."[41] Ephrem is obviously filling in some details here, but he certainly does not present Eve as a mere hanger-on or ornament. He assures us that Eve assisted Adam "in all sorts of ways."[42] Essentially, they co-worked the ranch.

With respect to God's creation of Eve out of Adam's rib, Ephrem observes that, having made Eve to be beautiful, "God then took her and brought her to Adam who was both one and two: he was one because he was Adam, he was two because he was created male and female."[43] Adam can be said to be "created male and female" because, in himself, he had the potency for Eve; or at least he had this when God miraculously made Eve from his rib. Ephrem's main point here is that the human being involves unity and distinction: humans are one in that we are human, but humans are divided into male and female. Ephrem therefore sees the one-flesh marital union as indicating a return to primal unity. Commenting on Genesis 2:24, "Therefore a man leaves his father and his mother and cleaves to his wife, and they become one flesh," Ephrem states that when this occurs, "the two of them become one, without division, as they were originally."[44] He adds that Adam and Eve were certainly not children, but adults fully endowed with wisdom and strength.

For Ephrem, the temptation came from the beauty of the Tree, which prompted Adam and Eve's greed. By comparison, the serpent's effect was negligible, though Adam and Eve sought to blame the serpent. Prior to the arrival of the serpent, however, Eve had not yet experienced any trouble. She had not yet "been tormented by any struggle over the Tree's beauty."[45] In Ephrem's view, a key step taken by the serpent was to lure Eve to look directly at the Tree and thereby become entranced by its beauty. But more important for my purposes are the connections that Ephrem draws between her sin and her marriage.

---

41. Ephrem the Syrian, *The Commentary on Genesis*, 204–5.
42. Ephrem the Syrian, *The Commentary on Genesis*, 205.
43. Ephrem the Syrian, *The Commentary on Genesis*, 205.
44. Ephrem the Syrian, *The Commentary on Genesis*, 206.
45. Ephrem the Syrian, *The Commentary on Genesis*, 210.

Commenting on Genesis 3:6, "she took of its fruit and ate," Ephrem suggests that "she ate furtively, away from her husband."[46] What did she have to gain from doing this? In light of the serpent's promise that eating from the "tree of the knowledge of good and evil" (Gen 2:17) would make her "like God, knowing good and evil" (Gen 3:5), Ephrem proposes that she imagined that "she would return clothed in divinity to her husband whom she had left as a woman."[47] Ephrem's idea is that Eve decided to reverse the order of marital headship, "so that she might become head over her head, and that she might be giving orders to him from whom she received orders."[48] She sought to be "like God" (Gen 3:5) by contrast to Adam. She would "become senior in divinity to Adam to whom she was junior in humanity."[49]

In my view, by supposing that Adam naturally should "give orders" as Eve's "head," Ephrem has imported the later punishment for sin into the state of innocence. Nonetheless, Ephrem is correct to perceive the sin in the context of marriage. In marriage, as in any society of persons, the struggle for power can become acute. Instead of self-giving lovers, married persons can become manipulators. The desire to gain power over another person, as distinct from the desire to serve another person, devastates a marriage. It turns what should be a self-surrendering communion of "one flesh" (Gen 2:24) into a self-serving power-grab.

Ephrem's suggestion that the first sin, committed from within a marriage, turned marriage into its opposite—into a power struggle—is therefore a profound insight. Indeed, Ephrem's insight also shows what sin does to our relationship with God. Instead of being the one who wondrously calls human beings to a marriage with himself, God becomes someone with whom we now think we are locked in a power struggle.

Ephrem remarks that having eaten the forbidden fruit, Eve discovered that she did not in fact become "like God." Why then did she give the fruit to Adam to eat? For Ephrem, she played the role in relation to Adam that the serpent had played in relation to her. Nonetheless, she is not to blame for Adam's sin, since Adam knew that God had commanded that this fruit not be eaten. Adam did not have to take orders from Eve; he could have said no. Thus, Adam showed his own culpable lack of "love for, or fear of, Him who gave the commandment."[50]

---

46. Ephrem the Syrian, *The Commentary on Genesis*, 212.
47. Ephrem the Syrian, *The Commentary on Genesis*, 212.
48. Ephrem the Syrian, *The Commentary on Genesis*, 212–13.
49. Ephrem the Syrian, *The Commentary on Genesis*, 213.
50. Ephrem the Syrian, *The Commentary on Genesis*, 213.

The tragic irony was that God had wished to give Adam and Eve all that they lost by trying to seize it. Ephrem argues that the presence of the two Trees indicates God's will for humans, a will that was later fully revealed in Jesus Christ. Ephrem states, "For had the serpent been rejected, along with the sin, they would have eaten of the Tree of Life, and the Tree of Knowledge would not have been withheld from them any longer; from the one they would have received infallible knowledge, and from the other they would have received immortal life. They would have acquired divinity in humanity."[51]

Ephrem interprets God's punishment of Eve in Genesis 3:16 as follows: "'And you shall turn to your husband'—to be counseled, and not to counsel—'and he shall have authority over you'—since you imagined that by eating the fruit you would from then onward have authority over him."[52] The suggestion here is that the sinless marriage of Adam and Eve would have been lived in a mutual self-giving way, rather than being experienced as a power struggle. The problem with the human race, at its root, is a failure in marriage that impedes the first humans from attaining the eschatological marriage.

John Chrysostom (d. 407)

I begin with Chrysostom's commentary on Genesis 2:16, "And the LORD God commanded the man, saying, 'You may freely eat of every tree of the garden, but of the tree of the knowledge of good and evil you shall not eat, for in the day that you eat of it you shall die.'" Chrysostom emphasizes first not the negative commandment, but the "generosity" and "great kindness" of God.[53] God gives the whole garden for the man to enjoy, with the exception of only one tree. God holds back the one tree not out of stinginess but simply to give the man the opportunity to acknowledge God as the giver of gifts. Chrysostom urges, "Notice in this case as well as others God's goodness."[54] He adds that God emphasizes "right from the outset that man and woman are one," in a hierarchical unity of mutual love.[55]

By determining to create the woman to be Adam's companion, says Chrysostom, "the good God does not stop short, but adds kindness to kindness, and, in an abundance of riches, wants to clothe this rational being

---

51. Ephrem the Syrian, *The Commentary on Genesis*, 214.
52. Ephrem the Syrian, *The Commentary on Genesis*, 220.
53. Chrysostom, *Homilies on Genesis*, 188.
54. Chrysostom, *Homilies on Genesis*, 188.
55. Chrysostom, *Homilies on Genesis*, 188.

[Adam] in every degree of esteem, and along with this esteem to regale him with a life of ease."[56] The description of Eve as "a helper fit for him [Adam]" (Gen 2:18) shows Chrysostom that the woman is on par with Adam: she too is "possessed . . . of reason."[57] Adam and Eve did not sin because of immaturity or because God refused to grant them the necessary wisdom.

Reflecting further upon the creation of the woman as a "helper" (Gen 2:18), Chrysostom notes that many animals help humans in manifold and irreplaceable ways, by pulling loads, producing milk, giving wool for clothes, and so forth. If all that the woman did was to do such menial tasks for the man, then the man would have already found his "helper." The point is that to consider the woman's contribution along menial lines would be absurd. Chrysostom states that "the help provided for Adam by woman is different and immeasurably superior."[58] Chrysostom defines Eve as "like man in every detail—rational, capable of rendering him what would be of assistance in times of need and the pressing necessities of life."[59]

In Chrysostom's view, Adam and Eve did not have sexual intercourse until after the fall, nor would they have wanted to do so, since "they were living like angels in paradise and so they were not burning with desire."[60] As evidence, he notes that they were not wearing clothes and were without shame (Gen 2:25). He sees this "angelic way of life" as further indication of God's enormous generosity toward the first humans. They were not pressed by a need for food or shelter, by the impulses of sexual desire, or by any fear whatsoever.

Yet, Adam was Eve's true "husband," even though the marriage was unconsummated.[61] The arrival of the serpent (the devil), however, threw things out of kilter. Chrysostom is surprised that Eve wished to talk with the serpent rather than with Adam. After all, Adam was "the person for whose sake she came into being, with whom she shared everything on equal terms, and whose helpmate she had been made."[62] Something is awry if she chooses to talk at length to the serpent. Moreover, Eve does not perceive the way in which the serpent twists God's words, and Eve also reveals God's commandment to one who cares nothing for God. The serpent even

---

56. Chrysostom, *Homilies on Genesis*, 189.
57. Chrysostom, *Homilies on Genesis*, 190.
58. Chrysostom, *Homilies on Genesis*, 197.
59. Chrysostom, *Homilies on Genesis*, 200.
60. Chrysostom, *Homilies on Genesis*, 202.
61. Chrysostom, *Homilies on Genesis*, 215. In his *On Virginity*, Chrysostom indicates that the marriage of Adam and Eve—insofar as it was sexually consummated—was a concession given due to the fall: see Chrysostom, *On Virginity*.
62. Chrysostom, *Homilies on Genesis*, 210.

contradicts God flatly, implying that God is a liar, and still Eve does not turn away.

Chrysostom emphasizes that Eve's problem was not lack of rational power. Eve could easily have known that the serpent's words were false, but she chose to listen to him, "puffed up as she was with the hope of being equal to God and evidently dreaming of greatness."[63] Her motive was to move beyond mere human rationality and to attain divinity. She wanted "honor equal to the Creator" and attainment of "the very pinnacle of power."[64] In considering such a thing possible, she was being irrational, but it was an irrationality rooted in the greatness of the gifts that God had already bestowed.

Chrysostom underscores Eve's equality with Adam, "in whose dignity" Eve "had equal share," and with whom Eve was one "in being and one in language."[65] For his part, Adam ate the forbidden fruit at Eve's request. But Chrysostom does not blame Eve for Adam's action. On the contrary, he thinks that Adam, too, supposed that by eating the forbidden fruit he could become "like God" (Gen 3:5). The result was that Adam "readily shared in the food," notwithstanding God's commandment.[66] Thus, the actual eating of the forbidden fruit was merely the outward symbol of an inward rebellion against God. Chrysostom denies that Adam and Eve, prior to eating the forbidden fruit, lacked the "knowledge to discriminate between good and evil."[67] They were deeply knowledgeable; had they not been, Adam could not have named the animals. They knew it was evil to disobey God's commandment but freely did it anyway.

God included the tree in the garden in order to show Adam and Eve, by giving them a "slight command," that God was indeed in charge of the garden.[68] Had God not included a forbidden tree in the garden, Adam and Eve might have imagined that "visible things" are "self-sufficient."[69] The tree served as a reminder that neither the garden nor Adam and Eve themselves could exist autonomously from the Creator God. As Chrysostom observes, therefore, "it was not the tree that caused the harm, but slothful will and contempt displayed for God's command."[70] Nor does God punish Adam

---

63. Chrysostom, *Homilies on Genesis*, 213.
64. Chrysostom, *Homilies on Genesis*, 214–15.
65. Chrysostom, *Homilies on Genesis*, 214.
66. Chrysostom, *Homilies on Genesis*, 216.
67. Chrysostom, *Homilies on Genesis*, 218.
68. Chrysostom, *Homilies on Genesis*, 219.
69. Chrysostom, *Homilies on Genesis*, 219.
70. Chrysostom, *Homilies on Genesis*, 220–21.

and Eve mercilessly. After Adam and Eve cause their own loss of dignity by their rebellion, and God, as a "loving father," has "pity" on them and comes to their side like a physician.[71]

In sum, for Chrysostom, the context of marriage (albeit unconsummated marriage) matters for original sin primarily because God's greatest gift to Adam is Eve, whom God lovingly fashions with all perfections. In desiring to be equal with God, however, Adam and Eve distort their union. The result is that Adam and Eve, "who previously passed their life like angels on earth," are reduced to stitching together "fig leaves" to cover their private parts, because they are ashamed of their lust.[72] Having sought to divinize themselves, they find themselves cut off from the very consummation toward which they were supposed to help each other.

Augustine (d. 430)

Augustine examines our topic in *City of God*. Before their rebellion, says Augustine, Adam and Eve "lived in a partnership of unalloyed felicity; their love for God and for each other was undisturbed."[73] This is a portrait of a perfect marriage. Augustine explains that Adam and Eve, as a married couple, experienced their love as "the source of immense gladness, since the beloved object was always at hand for their enjoyment."[74] In their marriage, no prospect of or interior inclination to sin was present, nor was there a prospect of death. Instead they enjoyed together "a serene avoidance of sin; and as long as this continued, there was no encroachment of any kind of evil, from any quarter, to bring them sadness."[75] In Augustine's view, we can

---

71. See Chrysostom, *Homilies on Genesis*, 222–23.

72. Chrysostom, *Homilies on Genesis*, 220.

73. Augustine, *City of God*, XIV.10, 567. On a number of the issues discussed in this section, see Cavadini, "Feeling Right,"; Cavadini, "Reconsidering Augustine on Marriage and Concupiscence." In his "The Sacramentality of Marriage," Cavadini remarks, "To Augustine's mind, there is something naive about a view of marriage that treats sexual desire as a relatively uncomplicated *eros* that education and ascetic living can easily channel into the pleasures of home and family. For Augustine, sexual desire as we know it is anything but uncomplicated. To people accustomed to thinking that sexual desire and the pleasure it seeks are obvious and uncomplicated goods that contribute, in a straightforwardly positive way, to the bonding and happiness of a married couple, Augustine's views will look pessimistic. Yet, Augustine would probably insist that it is simply realistic. Sexual pleasure is not a fixed quantity, unambiguously and obviously good as we experience it in a fallen world" (161).

74. Augustine, *City of God*, XIV.10, 567.

75. Augustine, *City of God*, XIV.10, 567.

today hardly imagine the contentment of Adam and Eve prior to their sin, and this contentment was entirely the gift of the Creator God.

Adam and Eve therefore had "true freedom," which is only possible when the will is "not subservient to faults or sins."[76] It might seem that if Adam and Eve had to obey God's will in the case of the forbidden tree, then they were not truly free: they were under compulsion and their will's freedom was hampered by a threat. But Augustine argues the opposite. Freedom is linked with doing the good, with doing what *fulfills* the human will and what leads to the flourishing of the human person. God's will, which is always good, always conforms with what the rational human person would want for his or her own flourishing, assuming that the person's will is good. The perfect goodness of God's will does not compete with or hamper the exercise of the human will. On the contrary, as Augustine says, "the rational creation has been so made that it is to man's advantage to be in subjection to God, and it is calamitous for him to act according to his own will, and not to obey the will of his Creator."[77] In the original state, humans would have considered it crazy to rebel against the good will of the Creator, because their own desire would have accorded fully with God's good desire for their flourishing.

Augustine teaches that "God instituted marriage from the beginning, before man's Fall, in creating male and female."[78] He observes that after creating human beings "male and female," "God blessed them, and God said to them, 'Be fruitful and multiply'" (Gen 1:28). The point is that human sexual intercourse is willed by God, and not simply (as Chrysostom thought) as a concession after the fall. Augustine argues that "it would be a manifest absurdity to deny the fact that male and female were created for the purpose of begetting children, so as to increase and multiply and fill the earth."[79] Recall that Chrysostom held that prior to the fall humans would not have desired to have sex. Augustine affirms the opposite. He points out, "If anyone says that there would have been no intercourse or procreation if the first human beings had not sinned, he is asserting, in effect, that man's sin was necessary to complete the number of the elect."[80] He argues, however, that marital intercourse prior to sin would have been free of the element of lust.[81]

76. Augustine, *City of God*, XIV.11, 569.
77. Augustine, *City of God*, XIV.13, 571.
78. Augustine, *City of God*, XIV.22, 584.
79. Augustine, *City of God*, XIV.22, 584.
80. Augustine, *City of God*, XIV.23, 585. Note that earlier in his career, Augustine himself had supposed that sexual intercourse (assuming Adam and Eve had not fallen) would not have existed in Eden.
81. Augustine, *City of God*, XIV.23, 586. Lust differs, of course, from rightly ordered

Having himself experienced the chains of lust, Augustine knows that it does not conduce to self-giving love and communion but rather conduces to the using of one's partner and to looking at other persons with lust. Augustine refers in this regard to Jesus' warning, "I say to you that every one who looks at a woman lustfully has already committed adultery with her in his heart" (Matt 5:28).

Confronted with the question of why the first humans sinned, Augustine argues that the answer is pride, which is the "longing for a perverse kind of exaltation."[82] The first humans must have become "self-complacent," choosing themselves over the divine good.[83] In his view, the actual eating of the forbidden fruit was the manifestation of an already existing pride. Likewise, Eve's willingness to believe the serpent was a manifestation of interior fallenness. Augustine considers that "if the will had remained unshaken in its love of the higher changeless Good, which shed on it light to see and kindled in it fire to love," then "the will would not have been so darkened and chilled in consequence as to let the woman believe that the serpent had spoken the truth."[84]

Augustine explicitly reflects upon the fact that the first sin took place in a marital context. The devil, in the form of the serpent, chose first to speak to Eve, on the grounds that Eve, in the devil's view, was "the inferior of the human pair."[85] Although he holds that Eve would never have been willing to believe the serpent's words had not she been disarmed interiorly by pride, Augustine does place her in the position of inferiority. He suggests that Adam, due to pride, chose his marriage over God, thereby corrupting the first human communion. As Augustine puts it, Adam "fell in with her [Eve's] suggestions because they were so closely bound in partnership."[86] Along lines reminiscent of what Augustine might once have been tempted to do with regard to his long-time mistress, "Adam refused to be separated from his only companion, even if it involved sharing in her sin."[87] Adam freely chose, with equal pride and equal culpability as that of Eve, "to put

---

sexual desire, although Augustine thinks that in our fallen state we cannot keep our sexual desire entirely free of lust.

82. Augustine, *City of God*, XIV.13, 571.
83. Augustine, *City of God*, XIV.13, 571.
84. Augustine, *City of God*, XIV.13, 572.
85. Augustine, *City of God*, XIV.11, 570.
86. Augustine, *City of God*, XIV.11, 570.
87. Augustine, *City of God*, XIV.11, 570.

his wife's will above God's commandment" and to refuse "to desert his life's companion even though the refusal entailed companionship in sin."[88]

For Adam in his pride, his marriage with Eve mattered more than obedience to God's commandment—and this caused damage to marriage itself, by turning what should have been a sign of the eschatological union of God and humankind into a sign of our inability properly to give ourselves in love, a sign of our tendency to use and abuse even our spouse. Augustine pins the blame not on marriage, of course, but on the fact that Adam and Eve had become focused on themselves, on their "own light" rather than God's light.[89] Cavadini points out, "That Adam had some alternative is clear from the contrasting story of the second Adam."[90] When Adam joined Eve in acting as he did, he did not save his marriage. On the contrary, he deeply wounded it (see Gen 3:16). Yet, in the fall of human marriage, we also see the seeds of the self-sacrificial divine love that restores and renews marriage, establishing "the Bride, the wife of the Lamb" (Rev 21:9; cf. Gen 3:15 and Rev 12:1–6).

III. Conclusion

Let me take stock of the contributions of the modern and patristic interpreters to the question of whether it matters that the first sin was committed by a *married* couple. Arnold describes the first man and woman as equals who represent the primordial unity of human beings. He also describes the first sin as a "communal" sin. This, as we have seen, is an extremely important insight. Reno, too, emphasizes the "primal loneliness" and desire for fellowship that characterize humans as creatures made for communion in love. Reno shows how *eros* gives us a drive not solely toward human marriage but toward supernatural communion with God. He points out that the difference between love and lust is that love seeks for everlasting communion and lust for mere transient ends. Cotter remarks upon God's description of our solitude as "not good," and he depicts the feeling that we have when we find a true friend. Cotter portrays Adam and Eve's marriage, prior to sin,

---

88. Augustine, *City of God*, XIV.13, 572. For discussion of how Augustine here attempts to integrate Romans 5:12–21 and 1 Timothy 2:14, see Anderson, *The Genesis of Perfection*, 105–7.

89. Augustine, *City of God*, XIV.13, 573.

90. Cavadini, "Spousal Vision," 218. As Cavadini observes, "Commentators have generally been harsh on Augustine for seeming to imply that Adam should have abandoned Eve rather than enter into a *societas* characterized by sin. . . . It is true that Adam preferred to enter a fellowship of sin rather than to abandon Eve, but, in fact, these were not the only alternatives available to him" ("Spousal Vision," 218).

as marked by perfect intimacy and communion. When he turns to what motivated the first sin, he suggests that the couple sought to obtain God's wisdom for themselves, so that their communion would be self-sufficient rather than oriented toward God.

To these valuable insights from the modern commentators, the specifically marital dimension of original sin is added more explicitly by the Church Fathers. Ephrem depicts Eve as Adam's co-worker, and he describes the one-flesh unity of marriage as a return to the primal unity of humanity. He supposes that Eve decided to eat the forbidden fruit precisely in order to upend the marital hierarchy: she wanted to be deified in order to be able to lord it over Adam! In other words, the first sin flows from the choice to view marriage in terms of self-serving power rather than self-surrendering love.

Chrysostom emphasizes the extraordinary generosity and goodness of God, and he highlights the fact that Eve possesses wisdom and that she helps Adam in the ways that only another rational human could. After describing the (sexually unconsummated) marital friendship of Adam and Eve, he shows that original sin distorts this friendship by coloring it with lust. For Chrysostom, marriage provides an important context for the first sin because it exhibits the greatness of God's gift to Adam (namely, Eve) and it exhibits the primordial distortion of friendship.

Augustine argues that Adam chose to eat the fruit because he did not want to be separated from his companion Eve. In so doing, he brought about the fall not merely of individuals but of human marriage itself, which henceforth is marked by power struggles, lust, and so on. Since the fall was the fall of the primordial marriage, it makes sense that the restoration of all things will come from the divine Bridegroom renewing his Bride, in the perfect *societas*.

In Christ, God calls husband and wife to learn self-surrendering love within the communion of marriage and, through this graced love, to be united not merely to the human spouse but to God himself in the supernatural marriage of Christ and his Church. Ultimately, the first married couple's sin shows what happens when an interpersonal relationship closes in upon itself in pride and power-seeking. As Genesis 2–3 shows, marriage is the greatest creaturely gift that God gives. The gift of the woman goes infinitely beyond any other gift that God gives to Adam, besides God's own self. Both the patristic and the modern commentators recognize that the marital friendship with one's spouse and friendship with God are profoundly connected: marriage should point us outward toward communion with God (ultimately the marriage of God and his people), rather than turning us inward. Original sin is *the sin of a married couple* because original sin destroys the communion for which we are made; and we are made for marriage with

God. The distortion of the vocation of human marriage is a distortion of the everlasting vocation: the marriage of God and creation.

In proclaiming the beauty of the first marriage and the tragedy of the married couple's sin, Genesis 2–3 offers the bad news that we have traded self-surrendering love for a simulacrum of power, and fruitful wisdom for sterile pride. We have failed to image God as we should, because we have imagined him to be power-hungry rather than self-surrendering. But Genesis 2–3 also offers the good news that, in our shame, we can discover the greatness of God's mercy and love. Far from giving up on marriage, God proceeds even more boldly with the constitution of his eschatological Bride.

Chapter 4

Cross

If the first sin was committed by a married couple who distorted their vocation of eschatological marriage with God, then the means by which humanity overcomes this sin—namely the redemptive action of Jesus Christ on the Cross—should profoundly inform marriage. The Second Vatican Council's Pastoral Constitution on the Church in the Modern World, *Gaudium et Spes*, devotes significant attention to the presence of Christ in marriage. It begins by stating, "Just as of old God encountered his people with a covenant of love and fidelity, so our Saviour, the spouse of the Church, now encounters Christian spouses through the sacrament of marriage."[1] Does this encounter, however, have anything to do with Christ's Cross?

Gaudium et Spes first emphasizes the risen and ascended Christ's presence, his abiding with the married couple and directing them toward the eschatological consummation of the union of Christ and the Church. Christ "abides with them in order that by their mutual self-giving spouses will love each other with enduring fidelity, as he loved the Church and delivered himself for it."[2] This presence befits the self-giving love and fidelity that Christ displayed preeminently in his Cross. *Gaudium et Spes* makes clear, therefore, that the married couple is "directed and enriched by the redemptive power of Christ."[3] The married couple will "practice a love that is firm, generous, and prompt to sacrifice" and this love will involve "a free and mutual giving

---

1. *Gaudium et Spes*, §48, 950.
2. *Gaudium et Spes*, §48, 950–51.
3. *Gaudium et Spes*, §48, 951.

of self."[4] These statements reflect the depth and selflessness of Christ's love for us on the Cross.

Gaudium et Spes concludes its section on marriage by observing of the Christian married couple that "in the footsteps of Christ, the principle of life, they will bear witness by their faithful love in the joys and sacrifices of their calling, to that mystery of love which the Lord revealed to the world by his death and resurrection."[5] This concluding statement explicitly refers to Christ's Cross, to which the spouses bear witness by their mutually self-surrendering love, and it also reveals the consummation of divine love that is begun by Christ's Resurrection.

Yet, it would be a stretch to argue that *Gaudium et Spes* places Christ's Cross at the very center of its account of marriage. The Council Fathers may have feared making marriage itself, whose great dignity they wished to promote, sound like a crucifixion![6] Such a negative view of marriage would be a profound distortion of what Christian marriage is.

---

4. *Gaudium et Spes*, §49, 952–53.

5. *Gaudium et Spes*, §52, 957.

6. See Browning, *Marriage and Modernization*, 44–49, 97–98. Browning compares Luther and Aquinas on this point, noting that Luther's reading of Ephesians 5 emphasizes marital self-sacrifice, whereas Aquinas's reading of Ephesians 5 emphasizes marital mutual love or friendship. Browning favors Aquinas, insofar as he understands him: "I agree with both Luther and Aquinas. Overcoming the male and female problematics [namely, the tendency of men to separate from the mother and child, and the tendency of women willingly to raise children without male help] requires love as sacrificial love. But I cast my lot more with Aquinas than Luther. The love that truly enriches the marital relation is not one that makes sacrificial love an end in itself. It is a love that celebrates the mutuality of love as equal regard and employs the sacrificial moment as the extra effort, done with the grace and help of God, that is required to restore strained relations to mutuality once again. Christ gives up his life not as an end in itself but as a step toward fellowship with the church. Husbands and wives do not sacrifice for one another as an end in itself but as a step toward restoring love as mutuality" (*Marriage and Modernization*, 98). See also his claim elsewhere that "[t]he sacrificial or self-giving love of the cross functions for us to revitalize and restore love as equal regard and mutuality," so that "sacrificial love (the meaning of the cross)" is "not an end in itself but . . . the second mile of enduring love sometimes needed to restore the core of love, that is, love as equal regard and mutuality" (Browning, "The Relation of Practical Theology to Theological Ethics," 404). I think that in the fallen world, however, love as mutuality will be self-sacrificial love. Aquinas recognizes this giving of oneself when in the *Summa theologiae* he describes the selflessness of charity: "we love God, not for anything else, but for Himself" (II-II, q. 27, a. 3). But of course, as Browning points out, selfless love finds its consummation in friendship, properly understood: "friendship consists in loving rather than in being loved. Now charity is a kind of friendship. Therefore it consists in loving rather than in being loved" (II-II, q. 27, a. 1, *sed contra*). For discussion of Aquinas's theology of charity, see Mansini, "Aristotle and Aquinas's Theology of Charity."

For its part, the 1997 *Catechism of the Catholic Church* explains that "[i]t is by following Christ, renouncing themselves, and taking up their crosses that spouses will be able to 'receive' the original meaning of marriage and live it with the help of Christ."[7] In this sentence, the *Catechism* affirms the centrality of Christ's Cross in Christian marriage, since by his Cross Christ gives us the grace to imitate his self-surrendering love. But the *Catechism* does not expand upon this point.

The United States Catholic Conference of Bishops' 2009 Pastoral Letter, *Marriage: Love and Life in the Divine Plan*, similarly addresses the Cross of Christ, though only briefly. First, citing the *Catechism*, the bishops explain that marriage was distorted by original sin; then the bishops note that in Christ "the Holy Spirit heals men and women from sin and elevates them to share in God's very own divine life."[8] The inauguration of the kingdom has consequences for marriage. Namely, Christ "heals marriage and restores it to its original purity of permanent self-giving in one flesh (see Mt 19:6)," and Christ makes marriage into a sacramental image of (and graced participation in) the eschatological union of Christ and his Church, exhibiting "self-giving love modeled on God's inner life."[9] In describing the supreme self-giving love that Christ showed for the Church—and by which Christ redeemed his people—the Pastoral Letter remarks with reference to Ephesians 5:25–27 that this love was "most completely expressed by his death on the Cross."[10] Rather than further describing marriage in relation to the Cross, however, the Pastoral Letter turns instead to the way in which the marital love of Christians is an image of the Trinity's communion of fruitful love—although toward the end of their Pastoral Letter, the bishops specify this participation in the Trinitarian communion in terms of participation in the love of Christ on the Cross.[11]

The themes touched upon by *Gaudium et Spes*, the *Catechism*, and the Bishops' Pastoral Letter are at the center of the Reformed pastor Timothy Keller's *The Meaning of Marriage*. Like the *Catechism* and the Pastoral Letter, Keller is aware that in contemporary culture the Cross no longer seems relevant to marriage in the minds of many ordinary believers. This is at least partly because in the period between 1960 and 1990, there was (in the

---

7. *Catechism of the Catholic Church*, §1615.

8. United States Conference of Catholic Bishops, *Marriage*, 30.

9. United States Conference of Catholic Bishops, *Marriage*, 30. The bishops add, "Marriage is a call to give oneself to one's spouse as fully as Christ gave himself to the Church. The natural meaning of marriage as an exchange of self-giving is not replaced, but fulfilled and raised to a higher level" (*Marriage*, 32).

10. United States Conference of Catholic Bishops, *Marriage*, 32.

11. United States Conference of Catholic Bishops, *Marriage*, 46.

words of Don Browning) "a colossal cultural shift within a single generation from valuing an ethic of self-sacrifice in marriage and families to an ethic that values mutuality."[12] Of course self-sacrificial love and mutual love are not in competition, since in fact in this life they are two sides of the same coin. But given the necessity in marriage that both the man and the woman sacrifice for the other person and for the family, stable marriage—marriage that bears witness to the union of Christ and the Church—will be in trouble without appreciation for the self-sacrificial dimension.[13]

Keller argues that "the main enemy of marriage" is "sinful self-centeredness," and his first chapter begins with the sentence, "I'm tired of listening to sentimental talks on marriage."[14] He points to some statistics that show the difficulty of marriage in modern America: for example, in the past sixty years the percentage of married adults has decreased by almost a quarter; the divorce rate has doubled; and around 60 percent of people live with a partner before getting married—even though Keller also notes (quite tellingly, in terms of modern American class divisions) that "by far the greatest percentage of divorces happen to those who marry before the

---

12. Browning, *Marriage and Modernization*, 46; citing polling research completed in 1996 in preparation for Browning et al., *From Culture Wars to Common Ground*. Browning comments: "Fifty-five percent of Americans today believe that a successful marriage correlates with mutuality. Only 38 percent believe it correlates with love as self-sacrifice and 5 percent believe a good marriage correlates with an individualistic love ethic emphasizing self-fulfillment. . . . But our respondents believed that their fathers and mothers saw love and family life very differently. Only 29 percent thought their mothers would have correlated a good marriage with mutuality. Fifty-six percent thought that their mothers and 40 percent thought that their fathers would have valued love as self-sacrifice" (*Marriage and Modernization*, 46–47). See also Browning and Rodriguez, *Reweaving the Social Tapestry*.

13. Later in *Marriage and Modernization*, Browning mentions marriage-promotion books and programs that ground themselves in the economic and personal-happiness benefits of marriage, including Hendrix, *Getting the Love You Want* and Waite and Gallagher, *The Case for Marriage*. For criticism of Browning's project in *From Culture Wars to Common Ground*, see Waters, *The Family*, 241–44. Waters contends that the "critical familism" of Browning and his co-authors fails because it is theologically thin and thereby incapable of accounting for self-sacrificial love as anything more than a temporary restorative measure in a marriage. In *Marriage and Modernization*, Browning is aware of the central importance of self-sacrificial love, even if, by comparison with Waters, Browning is much more sociological and not theologically careful. For criticisms of Browning—and also of the notion of the family as "domestic church"— similar to those offered by Waters, see Bennett, *Water Is Thicker Than Blood*, chapter 1. Bennett warns that through his social-justice enthusiasm for marriage, Browning (and others involved in his project) risk making a "good marriage . . . *necessary* for modern Christians," rather than viewing marriage first in relation to Christ and understanding it as a subordinate and impermanent good (*Water Is Thicker Than Blood*, 9).

14. T. Keller and K. Keller, *The Meaning of Marriage*, 5, 9, 13.

age of eighteen, who have dropped out of high school, and who have had a baby together before marrying."[15] Drawing upon Stanley Hauerwas's work, Keller goes on to critique the contemporary emphasis on "marriage-as-self-realization" with one's "soul mate," which neglects the truth that marriage is an institution in which the man and woman unite for a shared purpose, ultimately a transcendent one.[16]

When Keller turns to identifying what he calls the biblical "secret" of marriage, it comes from Ephesians 5: husbands should love their wives as Christ on the Cross loved the Church. He explains that "Jesus's sacrificial service to us has brought us into a deep union with him and he with us," and so the key to a good marriage is for both spouses to imitate Jesus' self-sacrificial love.[17] Indeed, this is the key to a good life as well: in faith and charity, we must be configured to Christ's Cross, dying to ourselves and submitting to the loving will of God. Put simply, the gospel of Christ provides "both the power and the pattern" for a good marriage.[18] As Keller explains, "God's saving love in Christ . . . is marked by both radical truthfulness about who we are"—namely, sinners—"and yet also radical, unconditional commitment to us."[19] When we recognize *ourselves* as sinners who are loved by Christ, we are freed to recognize and accept our spouse's sinful weakness in "Spirit-generated selflessness," without thereby ceasing to love our spouse.[20] Receiving such love from us in Christ, our spouse too will be freed (in Christ) to love.[21]

---

15. T. Keller and K. Keller, *The Meaning of Marriage*, 16.

16. T. Keller and K. Keller, *The Meaning of Marriage*, 28, 32–33. See Hauerwas, "Sex and Politics." Among the many exponents of "marriage-as-self-realization" (and therefore persons who are deeply disappointed with "marriage"), Keller names Laura Kipnis, *Against Love*; and Pamela Haag, *Marriage Confidential*. See also Russell, *Marriage and Morals*.

17. T. Keller and K. Keller, *The Meaning of Marriage*, 42. Love "is sacrificial commitment to the good of the other. If we think of love primarily as emotional desire and not as active, committed service, we end up pitting duty and desire against each other in a way that is unrealistic and destructive" (*The Meaning of Marriage*, 81).

18. T. Keller and K. Keller, *The Meaning of Marriage*, 44.

19. T. Keller and K. Keller, *The Meaning of Marriage*, 44.

20. T. Keller and K. Keller, *The Meaning of Marriage*, 66.

21. The opposite counsel, Keller points out, is to focus on self-realization (rather than uniting oneself as a sinner to the power of Christ's Cross). He explains, "There is a more secular approach to marriage that says that the real problem in marriage is that you have to get your spouse to recognize your potential and help you to develop it. You must not let your spouse trample all over you. Self-realization is the goal. You've got to develop yourself in your marriage, and if your spouse won't help you do it, you've got to negotiate. And if your spouse won't negotiate, you've got to get out to save yourself" (*The Meaning of Marriage*, 66). Keller adds a crucial point with respect to the impact

The contemporary Catholic theologian Alexandra Diriart has also addressed the relationship of marriage and the Cross, in her essay "Un amour sauvé: la forme pascale de la vie conjugale" ("A redeemed love: the paschal form of the married life").[22] She draws inspiration from the Gospels, where coming to know Christ often requires overcoming an interior impediment. She also benefits from Pope Benedict XVI's encyclical *Deus Caritas Est*, which speaks of the progression from an *eros* rooted in this world to an *eros* that finds what it desires in God, through a "path of ascent and purification" that enables love to "fully realize its human and divine promise."[23] Much like Keller, but appealing to the powerful biblical reality of the new exodus, Benedict XVI describes growth in love as "an ongoing exodus out of the closed inward-looking self toward its liberation through self-giving, and thus toward authentic self-discovery and indeed the discovery of God."[24]

Along these lines, then, Diriart notes that in marriage there is often an element of self-seeking, of desire to be loved and to possess the other person. The married couple must therefore move through self-seeking love to attain self-giving love, the perfection of the image of God. Arguing that "*[t]he logic of true love . . . is that of the paschal mystery,*" Diriart applies this point to marriage, in which each spouse will find that "[t]he experience of the other in his defection, in his vulnerability, in his limitation but also in the unknowable excess of his otherness, equally reflects, as in a mirror, one's own inadequacy, one's own defection, one's own narcissism, and one's own incapacity to love the other as other."[25] This experience, Diriart proposes, awakens one to one's own need for the healing power of Christ's Cross. It initiates a path by which one's love for the other truly becomes self-giving (other-oriented) love rather than selfish self-love.

Diriart next draws upon the theologies of marriage of Thomas Aquinas and Pope John Paul II. In his treatment of marriage in the *Summa*

---

of sin: "each of us comes to marriage with a disordered inner being. Many of us have sought to overcome self-doubts by giving ourselves to our careers. That will mean we will choose our work over our spouse and family to the detriment of our marriage. Others of us hope that unending affection and affirmation from a beautiful, brilliant romantic partner will finally make us feel good about ourselves. That turns the relationship into a form of salvation, and no relationship can live up to that" (*The Meaning of Marriage*, 73).

22. Diriart, "Un amour sauvé"; all translations from this text are my own. See also Kasper, *Theology of Christian Marriage*, 35–36.

23. Benedict XVI, *Deus Caritas Est*, §6, cited in Diriart, "Un amour sauvé," 278. See also Cloutier, "Marriage and Sexuality," 324.

24. Benedict XVI, *Deus Caritas Est*, §6, cited in Diriart, "Un amour sauvé," 278. See also Noriega, *Eros e Agape*.

25. Diriart, "Un amour sauvé," 282. See also Zolli, *Prima dell' alba*.

contra gentiles, Aquinas teaches that "in this sacrament a grace is conferred on those marrying, and . . . by this grace they are included in the union of Christ and the Church."[26] Likewise, in paragraph thirteen of *Familiaris Consortio*, John Paul II emphasizes that Jesus, by liberating humans from sin through his sacrificial love on the Cross, frees us to live the truth of marriage. In Christ, says John Paul II, the "marriage of baptized persons" becomes a "real symbol of that new and eternal covenant sanctioned in the blood of Christ," and Christ's Spirit enables the married couple to love "one another as Christ has loved us."[27] Most important for Diriart is John Paul II's

26. Aquinas, *Summa contra gentiles*, Book IV, ch. 78, 296. As Diriart says, "It did not suffice [for Aquinas], therefore, to say in the *Commentary on the Sentences* that the *res contenta* (the grace contained) consisted in a help for facilitating the accomplishment of the purposes of marriage. It was necessary to go a step further by saying that this grace makes possible the accomplishment of the purposes of marriage *because* this grace is the gift of the very measure of the love of Christ for his Church. Even if Thomas does not explicitly have recourse to the term '*res contenta*,' this is indeed what he has in view: not that the sacrament of marriage contains the union of Christ and the Church *substantialiter*, but rather by way of *participation*" (Diriart, "Un amour sauvé," 290). In the same context, Diriart points to *Summa theologiae* III, q. 65, a. 3, where Aquinas describes the sacraments (other than the Eucharist) as containing an instrumental power that participates in Christ.

27. John Paul II, *Familiaris Consortio*, §13 (www.vatican.va). From a Protestant perspective, Brent Waters praises the main lines of *Familiaris Consortio*, noting that "this apostolic exhortation may be characterized as an attempt to ground a theological account of the family in a dynamic relationship between providence and eschatology. Christ's new creation entails a transformation of the old instead of its negation; the new is born out of the old, preserving a degree of continuity" (Waters, *The Family*, 245). But for Waters, *Familiaris Consortio* is marred "by its portrayal of the family as a *domestic church*" (*The Family*, 245). He notes that one problem is that "since both the family and the church share a common eschatological witness, singleness is reduced to a prerequisite lifestyle that enables a person to devote more time to the larger church. Consequently, singleness cannot, by way of contrast, both affirm *and* temper the providential witness of the family" (*The Family*, 246). Unlike Waters, I see no fundamental problem with calling the Church the adoptive "family" of God, since believers are "sons of God" and "children of God" in Christ (Rom 8:14, 16). But the analogy can be abused, and I agree with Waters's emphasis that we must take care not to "ease the tension between family and church" (*The Family*, 247) by mixing up the specific tasks of the family with those of the Church (or with those of consecrated single people). In his *Vocation to Virtue*, 147–53, Kent Lasnoski identifies some recent abuses of the term "family" (extending it too univocally to religious orders), and he draws upon salutary concerns raised by Schneiders, *Selling All*, and by McAllister, *Living the Vows*. Yet Lasnoski falls into the problem identified by Waters when he (Lasnoski) proposes, "Integrating single celibates with married Christians in one living situation might allow for a fuller sharing of prayer and apostolate and a more direct witness and accountability between the two" (*Vocation to Virtue*, 154). Similarly, Jana Bennett, in a generally quite helpful book, argues that it is best to think theologically about families not primarily in terms of a sacramentally married man and woman with children, but primarily in terms of "Christian households," which includes monasteries, intentional communities, and

conclusion: "Conjugal love reaches that fullness to which it is interiorly ordained, conjugal charity, which is the proper and specific way in which the spouses participate in and are called to live the very charity of Christ who gave Himself on the Cross."[28] Here John Paul II restates paragraph eleven of *Lumen Gentium*, which teaches that the sacrament of marriage enables the married couple to "signify and share" (or participate in) the wondrous reality of "the unity and faithful love between Christ and the Church."[29]

Thus, Diriart shows that the key to living out the gift of the sacrament—to allowing the sacrament to bear its full fruit—is to discover in it the "paschal form of love."[30] If the couple is unaware that, in marriage, love must mature by following the path of the Cross and moving from self-seeking love to self-surrendering love whose ultimate goal is eschatological, the couple will be unable to find the fruitfulness of Christian marriage. A marriage serves its true purpose, and expresses its sacramental power, only when, as the Baptist theologian Gary Thomas says, we "grow in our service, obedience, character, pursuit, and love of God"—and this comes by and through the Cross of Christ, which transforms our "self-centered view" of ourselves and our marriage into a "God-centered view."[31]

"parents and children in all the variety of what that means in contemporary society" (Bennett, *Water Is Thicker Than Blood*, 30). This seems a mistake, for the reasons that Waters indicates.

28. John Paul II, *Familiaris Consortio*, §13, cited in Diriart, "Un amour sauvé," 290.

29. *Lumen Gentium* §11, 362, cited in Diriart, "Un amour sauvé," 291–92.

30. Diriart, "Un amour sauvé," 292. In a nutshell, she emphasizes the "*real participation*" in the indissoluble union of Christ and the Church that is bestowed by the sacrament of marriage.

31. Thomas, *Sacred Marriage*, 12, 33. See also the observation of Richard R. Gaillardetz: "faithful Christian marriage has an undeniably ascetical dimension. Those who choose to marry also embrace a vowed life. Marriage draws them as well into a public commitment to enter into the paschal mystery through a real renunciation of goods" (Gaillardetz, *A Daring Promise*, 55). I agree with Gaillardetz that in general, "not enough is said about the ascetical character of marriage," namely the way in which marriage embodies "a free embrace of the dying and rising of Christ" (*A Daring Promise*, 54–55). David S. Crawford argues that marriage, like consecrated virginity, is a form of the "*sequela Christi*" and thus a "state of perfection," since marriage too is "a giving away of everything that one has and is to belong 'wholly to the Lord,' although analogously, through the sacramental mediation of the other" (Crawford, *Marriage and the* Sequela Christi, 26; cf. Crawford, "Christian Community"). I do not think that marriage is a "state of perfection" in the sense of consecrated virginity (with its poverty, chastity, and obedience). For helpful discussion of this point, see Farley, "Celibacy under the Sign of the Cross," 140–43. Even so, I can agree with what Crawford is getting at when he says that "just as virginity reveals the depth and interior meaning of marriage and nuptial desire as ('paradoxically') fulfilled only in self-emptying (i.e., as possessing the interior form of the counsels), so too marriage discloses the interior meaning of virginity's self-emptying as (again, 'paradoxically') a radical fulfillment of nuptial desire (and therefore

Let me be clear about the meaning of the Cross of Christ. Garry Wills has voiced a common concern when he argues that Anselm's theology of the Cross inevitably entails that God (the Father) killed or murdered God (the incarnate Son) in order to save humankind.[32] Wills sums up his understanding of Anselm's position: sinful humankind deserved the penalty of death and damnation; God could spare all humankind this penalty only if his innocent Son took flesh and bore the punishment for all of us; God the Father therefore inflicted the punishment of death upon his willing Son, Jesus Christ.

In fact, Wills has gotten things backward. The Cross, as an event willed by God, is Jesus' free act of supreme love in solidarity with the fallen human race, who heals us by entering into our alienated condition and reversing our selfish self-love by his supreme self-surrendering love.[33] What God wills is love (the perfection and true flourishing of the human image of God), not death per se. Perry Cahall comments that "Christ's sacrifice out of love for his bride . . . is not a sacrifice of desolation, but a sacrifice of oblation, pouring himself out in love."[34] To associate marriage with the Cross in no way means that a Christian spouse should willingly be abused by his or her spouse, since this would merely be to encourage sin (to the *detriment* of one's abusive spouse). Instead, spouses must follow the path of the Cross in the sense of being "willing to sacrifice [their] own wants and sometimes even needs for the sake of the beloved," in imitation of Jesus' love and mercy.[35] Spouses have to learn the value of suffering out of love—both in selflessly caring for one's beloved, and in emerging from one's own self-centeredness. As St. Paul says of Christians, we are "fellow heirs with Christ, provided we suffer with him in order that we may also be glorified with him" (Rom 8:17).

In order to contribute to retrieving the centrality of Christ's Cross for Christian marriage (understood in relation to the eschatological marriage),

---

as possessing the interior form of spousal love)" (*Marriage and the Sequela Christi*, 27). Here a remark of Hans Urs von Balthasar, whose work informs Crawford's, is apropos: "the lay person . . . must translate *the example and ways of the state of the counsels into his own life*" (von Balthasar, *Christian State of Life*, 341). See also Roberts, "Christian Marriage," 103–6.

32. See Wills, *Why Priests*, chapter 14: "Who Killed Jesus?" For a scholarly statement of these concerns about Anselm's approach (and later approaches such as Thomas Aquinas's), see Lombardo, *The Father's Will*.

33. For different but still largely complementary approaches to the mystery of the Cross, see Fleming Rutledge, *The Crucifixion*, especially 530–33; White, *The Incarnate Lord*, 308–39.

34. Cahall, *The Mystery of Marriage*, 348.

35. Cahall, *The Mystery of Marriage*, 349.

the remainder of this chapter will proceed in three steps. First, I attend to Catherine of Siena's insistence upon Christ's Cross—his self-sacrificial love—as the heart of Christian marriage. Catherine's imagery in her letters to a married couple challenges the couple to embrace the Cross and (in Cahall's words) "to enter into Christ's Paschal act of self-donation and become a living sign of his sacrificial giving of himself to his Church."[36] With Catherine's words in view, the second section of this chapter briefly examines some Pauline testimony to living in accord with the Cross in married life. Third and finally, I explore insights offered by Karol Wojtyła (the future John Paul II) in two of his pre-papal writings about marriage: *Love and Responsibility* and *The Jeweler's Shop*. Throughout the chapter, I ask whether it is actually true that marriage is renewed by Christ's Cross, given that the Cross, while a sign of God's eschatological love for his bride, is also a sign of great suffering in this fallen world.

I. Catherine of Siena: Letters to Agnesa and Francesco di Pipino

Catherine of Siena's letters to her married friends Agnesa and Francesco di Pipino can be rather bracing. Agnesa and Francesco became Catherine's friends and disciples in 1376, and they hosted Catherine in their home for some weeks during her 1378 visit to Florence. Her letters to Agnesa and Francesco, written in 1378 toward the end of her short life, provide a window into her understanding of the Christian vocation of marriage.

The first letter that we possess is from Catherine to Agnesa. Catherine greets Agnesa by urging her to be "persevering in virtue" and "bound in the gentle bond of charity."[37] This sounds bland enough, but Catherine makes it more specific in a startlingly challenging fashion. She adds, "But so you may better grow and preserve yourself in love for virtue, I want you and

---

36. Cahall, *The Mystery of Marriage*, 352. Much like Diriart, Cahall adds that "one's spouse is rarely the main cause of suffering in marriage. Instead, the main suffering of marriage is suffering the process of conversion that the Holy Spirit wants to work in oneself. In his plan, God intends marriage, and especially sacramental marriage, to foster the spouses' growth in virtue and their ability to be self-gift through self-denial, by calling them to focus on serving the good of each other and their family. This means that the real laying down of one's life in marriage is in the moral and spiritual life, and the real suffering of marriage is suffering a death to self for the sake of one's beloved. Selfishness in all of its forms is the enemy of love.... Spouses must struggle against this selfishness to win a victory over self for the sake of the beloved.... However, we need to realize that dying to self is not a work of senseless suffering and desolation, but a work of life, beauty, and joy" (*The Mystery of Marriage*, 355–56).

37. Catherine of Siena, *The Letters* III, 145.

Francesco to hide yourselves in the open side of Christ crucified in holy desire."[38] According to Catherine, the place to live out the married vocation is found "in the open side of Christ crucified" and in desiring union with him. From Christ's open side come the sacraments of baptism and the Eucharist, and Christ's open side represents his salvific act of love for our salvation.

The next letter is from Catherine to Francesco and Agnesa, and it begins with a salutation that is standard for her. She writes, "I Caterina, servant and slave of the servants of Jesus Christ, am writing to you in his precious blood. I long to see you lovers of virtue, for there is no other way you can have the life of grace or share in the blood of God's Son."[39] Like Paul in Romans 3:25 and elsewhere, she summarizes Christ's saving work by reference to Christ's "blood." Believers must be configured to Christ's Passion in order to be able to obey Christ's commandment of love. Catherine urges Francesco and Agnesa: "Be mirrors of virtue for me. Tread the world and all its pleasures underfoot and follow Christ crucified."[40] This seems like difficult advice; what would it mean for a married couple, living in the world, to tread underfoot the world and its pleasures? Our (marital) union with Christ must begin even now, by sharing in his suffering so as to share in the glory of his love.

The next letter—directed to Agnesa—was written later in the same month (August 1378), and shows that treading the world's pleasures underfoot does not mean giving up food and wine. This time, Catherine's salutation praises perfect humility, and urges Agnesa to "embrace this glorious virtue" through the power of the humble Christ's Cross.[41] The goal of humility is not to make Agnesa docile to people who have power over her. Rather, the goal is to enable Agnesa to "[l]ove everyone in charity."[42] Here Catherine warns Agnesa against excessive fasting. Aware of the permanent physical damage caused by her own period of inordinate fasting, Catherine states, "I ask and order you not to fast—except, when you are able, on the days prescribed by holy Church."[43] Catherine urges Agnesa to drink wine at least once a day. Since everlasting charity is the only true goal, fasting and other evidences of treading the world and its pleasures underfoot must never be mistaken as the goal.

38. Catherine of Siena, *The Letters* III, 146.
39. Catherine of Siena, *The Letters* III, 175.
40. Catherine of Siena, *The Letters* III, 176.
41. Catherine of Siena, *The Letters* III, 181.
42. Catherine of Siena, *The Letters* III, 181.
43. Catherine of Siena, *The Letters* III, 181.

In September 1378, Catherine wrote another letter solely to Agnesa. Her salutation conveys, in her usual style, her longing to see the recipient of the letter "clothed in true solid virtues," and she urges that such virtues can only be possessed by one who possesses charity.[44] Charity, she notes, requires looking to "the gentle loving Word," and this in turn means sharing in "the tree of the most holy cross."[45] She sees no need to develop a sharply different spirituality for married persons: married persons, like single persons and consecrated religious, have a vocation that is nourished by Christ's Cross. Catherine turns again to the image of hiding oneself in Christ's open side, and she explains more fully what she means by it. It means dwelling in Christ and being washed by Christ's salvific blood. It also means acquiring self-knowledge and knowledge of Christ's love. She urges Agnesa to "make it [Christ's open side] your lovely dwelling place in holy knowledge of yourself and true knowledge of the generosity of his goodness."[46] Through the knowledge gained by dwelling in the crucified Christ, Agnesa will understand how much Christ loves sinners, and, as a way of honoring Christ, Agnesa will pray for the salvation of souls in Christ's bride the Church. The salvation of our neighbors becomes the focus of those who dwell in Christ. Proclaiming "Gentle Jesus! Jesus love!," Catherine urges Agnesa to show this love to others, not least by "offering sweet loving desires for them in God's presence."[47]

In October 1378, Catherine wrote another letter to Agnesa. Many of the same themes appear: bathing in the blood of Christ in order to give one's own blood and life for the sake of others, offering prayers for the needs of the world, hiding in the open side of the crucified Christ in order to be able to lead a self-sacrificial life of love. We again find clear commands not to equate cleaving to the Cross with ever stricter physical penance.

A few days later, Catherine addressed a letter to Francesco. His problem appears to be the opposite from that of his wife Agnesa. Although he had spiritual fervor, it is dimming—perhaps due to Agnesa's severe overexertions! In her letter, Catherine suggests that he may be suffering from apathy, from a lack of desire to grow spiritually. She makes clear to him that the goal is simply that he love God and neighbor. This is what the Christian life is about. She urges him, "Let me see you growing in hunger for God's honor and the salvation of souls."[48] She asks him especially to pray humbly

---

44. Catherine of Siena, *The Letters* III, 207.
45. Catherine of Siena, *The Letters* III, 207.
46. Catherine of Siena, *The Letters* III, 207–8.
47. Catherine of Siena, *The Letters* III, 208.
48. Catherine of Siena, *The Letters* III, 293.

for "the salvation of the whole world, and in particular for the reform of Christ's dear bride [the Church], whom we see coming into such darkness and disaster."[49]

A further letter in October 1378 is addressed not only to Francesco and Agnesa, but also to their close friends Bartalo and Orsa Usimbardi. In this letter to the two married couples, Catherine's salutation urges the acquisition of "the fire that in burning does not consume us but makes our soul fat, and unites us with and transforms us into itself, a fire of divine love."[50] As her strategy for growing in charity, Catherine suggests that the married couples should first recognize God to be the giver of our being and the giver of all other gifts that we possess, including the gift of his own Son who rescues us from slavery to Satan. She encourages them to meditate upon Christ's victory over the power of the devil through the power of love. She invites them to rejoice in the love of God: "Oh boundless love! Oh immense charity! Oh fire of divine charity!"[51] Notably, having in a previous letter cautioned Francesco about apathy, she now warns not only Francesco, but also Agnesa (and Orsa), to awaken "from the sleep of apathy."[52] She urges them all to look at Christ's fiery love, since if they have truly seen it, they will love God in return. When they are filled with charity due to the love that shines forth from Christ's Cross, they will be willing "to carry any heavy load for God" and they will reach out to their "neighbors—who are what God loves most."[53] Their marriages will be filled with the love of Christ, and their love for Christ will expand to a marvelous love of each other and of their neighbors. Looking at Christ crucified ensures that a couple's married love does not turn inward or dissolve in apathy, but turns outward toward the loving service of God and neighbor. Catherine closes the letter by asking Orsa to "[b]less your children and encourage Bartalo" and by asking Francesco and Agnesa to "bless Bastiano," their son.[54]

In late October 1378, Catherine wrote another letter to Francesco and Agnesa. In part, her letter is a response to letters that she has received from them. She is also asking a favor of Francesco, namely, to deliver six letters by hand to other people with whom Catherine is corresponding. Her salutation calls them to be united to "Christ crucified" by "persevering even to the

---

49. Catherine of Siena, *The Letters* III, 293.
50. Catherine of Siena, *The Letters* III, 311.
51. Catherine of Siena, *The Letters* III, 312.
52. Catherine of Siena, *The Letters* III, 312.
53. Catherine of Siena, *The Letters* III, 312.
54. Catherine of Siena, *The Letters* III, 313.

point of death" and following "the way of truth."[55] She observes that they can grow in "holy desire" for God by recalling all the blessings that they have received from God, preeminently "the gift of the blood of the Word ... which reveals to us God's indescribable love for us."[56] When we meditate upon God's mercy and love, we will want to emulate God in his selfless love for sinners, and we will turn against "our selfish sensuality which is the cause of our sins."[57] Rejecting "selfish sensuality" and becoming "true servants of Christ crucified" is not only for vowed religious or celibates, but also for married people.[58]

Around the same time, Catherine sent a letter to Francesco and Agnesa whose tone is darker. In Catherine's view, the married couple's behavior has now been influenced for the worse by worldly friends. She warns them against associating "with those who live without fear of God," on the grounds that such friendships will dull our conscience and cause us to be more focused "on the empty pleasures of the world."[59] For Catherine, living in accord with Christ's Cross means devoting time to prayer and showing "familial charity ... for everyone."[60] Although Catherine does not command sexual abstinence to Francesco and Agnesa,[61] she does urge Francesco and Agnesa to cherish their "purity" and "holy modesty" with respect to their "physical feelings."[62] But her main point in this letter is that they should be careful about their friendships. It stands to reason that the behavior of a married couple depends to a certain degree upon whether their friends are devoted to the service of Christ and Christ's poor. She concludes with an exhortation: "Keep living in God's holy and tender love."[63]

I note that Catherine requires of consecrated religious the same Christ-like selflessness that she asks of married couples, although she understands that the married state involves different responsibilities, such as raising a family. Writing in November 1378 to Niccolò di Romagna, a hermit in Florence, she tells him in her salutation: "I long to see you completely surrendered to divine providence and stripped of every earthly attachment

---

55. Catherine of Siena, *The Letters* III, 314.
56. Catherine of Siena, *The Letters* III, 314.
57. Catherine of Siena, *The Letters* III, 315.
58. Catherine of Siena, *The Letters* III, 315.
59. Catherine of Siena, *The Letters* III, 316.
60. Catherine of Siena, *The Letters* III, 317.
61. In this regard see for example her two letters to Ristoro Canigiani (who was married to Alessandra Quaratesi): Catherine of Siena, *The Letters* III, 209–12, 332–37.
62. Catherine of Siena, *The Letters* III, 317.
63. Catherine of Siena, *The Letters* III, 318.

(even to your very self) so that you may be clothed in Christ crucified."[64] This is the very thing that, in her view, makes for a good marriage as well: our attachment must be Christ, to whose reign we must be "completely surrendered."

Lastly, in a letter of late November 378 to Agnesa (jointly with Orsa, wife of Bartalo Usimbardi), Catherine explains that "[w]e have to turn our energies constantly toward God, scorning the world with all its pleasures, loving virtue, and accepting with true patience whatever divine Goodness sends us, understanding that what God gives he gives for our good, so that we may be made holy in him."[65] This "true patience" does not mean passivity, though it does mean discernment. In the face of threats and calamities, Catherine often acts strongly and decisively. Yet, she exercises patience insofar as she does not allow her spiritual serenity to rest upon particular outcomes.

Likewise, her advice to scorn "the world with all its pleasures" does not mean living in a super-ascetic fashion. She recommends drinking wine and partaking in other pleasurable things. She is well aware, however, that we are tempted to live solely for worldly pleasures and that we become impatient if we are threatened by deprivation of such pleasures. Furthermore, when we see the Church in crisis, we too easily excuse our own apathy and lack of faith. We can turn inward rather than surrendering ourselves in love to God. But a good spouse cannot be self-centered. Catherine tells Agnesa and Orsa that they must be free interiorly to surrender everything, even all the way "to the point of death," out of love for God and neighbor.[66] Their marriage must serve them in their eschatological destiny of marital union with the God who on the Cross loved us to the end.

Catherine's exhortations for her married friends are rooted not only in earlier Christian authors and her own mystical experience, but also and above all in the New Testament. Let me now turn to explore briefly the testimony of Paul to the way of the Cross as the path of a flourishing Christian marriage.

II. Pauline Testimony to the Cross and Marriage

Let me begin with Ephesians 5, a central text for understanding the distinctiveness of Christian marriage. Paul urges us to "be imitators of God" (Eph

---

64. Catherine of Siena, *The Letters* III, 343.
65. Catherine of Siena, *The Letters* III, 347.
66. Catherine of Siena, *The Letters* III, 348.

5:1).[67] Immediately, he specifies this imitation in terms of Christ's Cross. We are called to "walk in love, as Christ loved us and gave himself up for us" (Eph 5:2). To "walk in love" is to be willing to give our own selves for the sake of the good of those whom we love. Paul warns that what is at stake is nothing less than our membership in Christ's kingdom. He states, "Be sure of this, that no immoral or impure man, or one who is covetous (that is, an idolater), has any inheritance in the kingdom of Christ and of God" (Eph 5:5). The reason for this exclusion is not an extrinsic one; it is not as though Christ were standing at the gates of his kingdom in order to keep out immoral people. On the contrary, the problem with immorality is that it turns our love inward upon ourselves and thereby cuts us off from union with the self-surrendering love that is God.

In order to "walk in love," a married couple must imitate what Christ has done for us on the Cross. Paul applies this point most explicitly to husbands. He calls upon husbands to "love your wives" precisely "as Christ loved the church and gave himself up for her" (Eph 5:25). By acting with self-sacrificial love toward the Church, Christ enabled the Church to act in the same way toward himself. The one-flesh unity between husband and wife means that if a husband does not selflessly love his wife, he is hurting not only his wife but his own self.

Paul compares the one-flesh union of husband and wife, at whose fruitful center must be selfless love, with the one-flesh union of Christ and his "body" the Church. He states, "For no man ever hates his own flesh, but nourishes and cherishes it, as Christ does the church, because we are members of his body" (Eph 5:29–30). He adds that Genesis 2:24 teaches that "a man shall leave his father and mother and be joined to his wife and the two shall become one flesh" (see Eph 5:31). The one-flesh union of husband and wife, says Paul, symbolizes a "great mystery" or "great sacrament," which Paul specifies as the union of "Christ and the church" (Eph 5:32). In this union, the Cross is not peripheral but rather is central, because Christ unites the Church to himself everlastingly through his selfless love on the Cross.

Paul commands husbands to show this selfless love in marriage: "let each one of you love his wife as himself" (Eph 5:33). Does Paul also urge that wives show selfless love toward their husbands? He does so, although in terms that are more controversial today. After teaching both husbands and wives to "[b]e subject to one another out of reverence for Christ," he exhorts: "Wives, be subject to your husbands, as to the Lord. For the husband is the

---

67. For the (majority) position that Ephesians was not written by Paul, see Schnackenburg, *The Epistle to the Ephesians*, 24–28. I see no theological reason to take a stand on this matter: the truth and authority of the letter to the Ephesians do not rest upon authorship (though I am not persuaded by those who deny Pauline authorship).

head of the wife as Christ is the head of the church, his body, and is himself its Savior. As the church is subject to Christ, so let wives also be subject in everything to their husbands" (Eph 5:21–24).

If the Church is subject to Christ, is Christ also subject to the Church? In a certain sense the answer is yes, because Christ "nourishes and cherishes" the Church and, on the Cross, "gave himself up for her" (Eph 5:25, 29). Thus, in Paul's analogy, the wife is subject to the husband and the husband is also subject to the wife. Furthermore, the measure of what subjection means is the Cross: not a merely passive or senseless act of endurance, but a self-giving act of love for the true good of his beloved.

Paul holds that sufferings serve his configuration to Christ. He even states that "we rejoice in our sufferings, knowing that suffering produces endurance, and endurance produces character, and character produces hope, and hope does not disappoint us, because God's love has been poured into our hearts through the Holy Spirit who has been given to us" (Rom 5:3–5). This is a description of the spiritual growth of a charitable person. The gift of the Holy Spirit and the infusion of love come first. When a person is united to Christ by his Spirit and filled with love, then sufferings can be occasion of spiritual development. The selfless love that Christ reveals on the Cross, in the midst of his own suffering, is the love to which we must be configured.[68]

The married couple, then, must live by the self-sacrificial love of Christ on the Cross. Both husband and wife must refuse to "be overcome by evil" and must instead strive to "overcome evil with good" (Rom 12:21). This is an active task. At no time may the Christian husband or wife do what contradicts true love. Rather than violate the love of Christ, we must bear the "cross" of the suffering that comes from following Christ's radical path.

At weddings, Paul's hymn to love in 1 Corinthians 13 is often read. In the earlier chapters of 1 Corinthians, however, Paul focuses first on the crucified Christ. He states, "When I came to you, brethren, I did not come proclaiming to you the testimony of God in lofty words or wisdom. For I decided to know nothing among you except Jesus Christ and him crucified" (1 Cor 2:1–2). Among his fellow Christians, Paul seeks to point to Christ's Cross. It may seem that those who are configured to Christ's Cross are merely configured to weakness, so that they will be destroyed by those who are powerful. Paul knows that the gospel of "Christ crucified" will be "folly to Gentiles" (1 Cor 1:23), because it appears to be sheer weakness. But in fact, as Paul teaches, Christ crucified is none other than "the power of God and

---

68. The scholarship on Pauline theology is vast. On Paul's theology of suffering, see the discussion (and the numerous works cited) in my endnotes on pages 246–50 of *Dying and the Virtues*. See also the important book that has since appeared: Pitre, Barber, and Kincaid, *Paul, A New Covenant Jew*, especially chapters 4 and 5.

the wisdom of God" (1 Cor 1:24). In Christ, we discover that self-giving love is the only true power, so that "the foolishness of God is wiser than men, and the weakness of God is stronger than men" (1 Cor 1:25).

The married couple that has the Cross at the center of their marriage, therefore, has the most powerful bond of unity and the most fruitful bond of love. Building upon his faith in Christ's Cross, Paul in 1 Corinthians 13 describes the attributes of love. He emphasizes that Christ-like love, whether exercised by a man or by a woman, is neither domineering nor passively weak. Love has the strength to endure. Paul comments, "Love is patient and kind; love is not jealous or boastful; it is not arrogant or rude. Love does not insist on its own way; it is not irritable or resentful; it does not rejoice at wrong, but rejoices in the right. Love bears all things, believes all things, hopes all things, endures all things" (1 Cor 13:4–7). Paul makes clear that Christ-like love is the greatest action anyone can accomplish.[69] More important than having at one's command all "the tongues of men and of angels" or than having "prophetic powers" of understanding or than having the willingness to give away all one's possessions (1 Cor 13:1–3) is the simple act of real love. As Paul puts it, "if I have all faith, so as to remove mountains, but have not love, I am nothing. If I give away all I have, and if I deliver my body to be burned, but have not love, I gain nothing" (1 Cor 13:2–3). In acts of sincere Christ-like love, the Christian married couple performs the greatest possible actions.

In 1 Corinthians 7, Paul adds another element with regard to Christ's Cross in Christian marriage. Namely, Paul thinks that since Christ has undergone the tribulation on behalf of the people (and has been raised as the first fruits of the general resurrection), his followers are now sharing in the eschatological tribulation. In this tribulation or period of suffering prior to the consummation of all things, the primary thing will be to cling to Christ, to endure with faith and charity. Thus Paul argues that "from now on, let those who have wives live as though they had none, and those who mourn as though they were not mourning, and those who rejoice as though they were not rejoicing, and those who buy as though they had no goods, and those who deal with the world as though they had no dealings with it" (1 Cor 7:29–31).

Is Paul thereby contradicting his earlier counsel in 1 Corinthians 7 that "[t]he husband should give to his wife her conjugal rights, and likewise the wife to her husband" (1 Cor 7:3; cf. 1 Cor 7:5–6)? I think not. Certainly, Paul advocates detachment from the things of this world, given that "the form of this world is passing away" (1 Cor 7:31). But Paul affirms not only

---

69. This is also the point of Thérèse of Lisieux, *Story of a Soul*.

sexual intercourse within marriage but also the fact that Christians continue to marry. His point is simply that married couples must not relax into daily routines and imagine our daily work and activities, rather than eschatological union with Christ as his bridal Church, to be the central purpose of life.

In this brief section, I have identified Pauline grounding to Catherine of Siena's insistence that Christ's Cross must stand at the heart of Christian marriage. The next section undertakes a similar task, but now with respect to philosophical reflection. I draw Karol Wojtyła into the discussion, since his philosophical analysis of marital love makes an important contribution.

III. Karol Wojtyła: Philosophical and Dramatic Reflections on Marital Love

Love and Responsibility

Love and Responsibility's focus is on love between a man and a woman. Wojtyła seeks to analyze what such intimate love must involve. He first explores attraction, in which one person sees another person as good. Attraction manifests itself in "emotional-affective reactions," and attraction is not simply to the other person's body but to the other person as "at once a corporeal and spiritual good."[70] Turning to desire, he appropriates Immanuel Kant's dictum that persons can never rightly be used as means to an end; persons are always an end in themselves. Proper desire, then, is a desire for someone as good for us, but not in a utilitarian or self-centered way. Just as we can desire God as a good for us without making God into a mere means, so also we can desire another person as a good for us without making the other person into a mere means. In the love of a man and a woman, there must be a longing not only for one's own good but also for the other person's good. Love that "depends merely on pleasure or self interest" will fall apart as soon as the pleasure or calculated self-interest dissipates.[71]

For real love to exist between a man and a woman, there must also be friendship, which is deeper than sympathy because it involves not feelings but the will. Wojtyła also addresses what he calls "comradeship," in which a couple is bonded by shared work or shared goals. The value of comradeship

---

70. Wojtyła, *Love and Responsibility*, 76. For a helpful popular presentation and application of this text in today's American culture, see Sri, *Men, Women, and the Mystery of Love*. For scholarly engagement and background, see Schmitz, *Center of the Human Drama*; Reimers, *An Analysis of the Concepts of Self-Fulfillment and Self-Realization*; Kupczak, *Gift and Communion*; Kupczak, *Destined for Liberty*; Zimmermann, *Facing the Other*.

71. Wojtyła, *Love and Responsibility*, 87.

consists in its contribution to grounding a friendship, but comradeship alone lacks the depth to be the basis of enduring shared love between a man and a woman.

These elements prepare Wojtyła to discuss what he terms "betrothed love." He argues, "Its decisive character is the giving of one's own person (to another). The essence of betrothed love is self-giving, the surrender of one's 'I.'"[72] Wojtyła differentiates this self-surrender from that characteristic of friendship. In friendship, we desire what is good for our friend. In "betrothed love," we give our self to our friend and this self-gift is reciprocated.

What is meant by the gift of self? After all, no person can give himself or herself away so as no longer to be a person. Nor can one self really enter into the depths of another self, since our innermost depths cannot be plumbed by another human person. Even so, in the order of love self-gift to another person and to God is indeed possible. In fact, the true realization of the self comes about through the gift of self in love.

Wojtyła explains that in giving ourselves, we become what we are meant to be. He points out that something of this can be seen in the care of a doctor for his or her patient, or of a teacher for his or her student. In such instances, of course, it may be simply a case of doing one's duty. "Betrothed love" goes much further than such instances, since in marriage a man and a woman give themselves in a profound way to each other, thereby establishing a unity constituted by "reciprocal self-giving" or "mutual self-surrender."[73] The intimacy, intensity, and exclusivity of this mutual self-giving find expression in sexual intercourse, but involve the whole person.

Having reached this stage, Wojtyła begins anew from a different angle, approaching the love of a man and a woman from the standpoint of human subjectivity. Without freedom, he observes, there can be no real love. This means that love must be analyzed not only psychologically, but also ethically. Rejecting "situation ethics," which fails to appreciate the objective structure of love, he reiterates that the key point is that a person, unlike a thing, cannot be treated as a means to an end. The freedom of each person cannot rightly be compelled. In love, the person freely gives away his or her own will, in the sense that "[t]he person no longer wishes to be its own exclusive property, but instead to become the property of that other."[74] In loving another person, a person freely chooses "the renunciation of its autonomy and its inalienability."[75] This is what it means to give oneself or to

---

72. Wojtyła, *Love and Responsibility*, 96.
73. Wojtyła, *Love and Responsibility*, 99.
74. Wojtyła, *Love and Responsibility*, 125.
75. Wojtyła, *Love and Responsibility*, 125.

surrender oneself to another person, with whom one forms a unity in love. It means that rather than having one's own will, one desires the good of the other with such intensity that one is willing to renounce one's own good if necessary to serve the true good of the beloved. One is no longer governed by what is good for me (egoism), but now by what is good for the beloved (self-surrendering love). Wojtyła states, "Love proceeds by way of this renunciation, guided by the profound conviction that it does not diminish and impoverish, but quite the contrary, enlarges and enriches the existence of the person."[76]

If one renounces one's own autonomous free will in order to serve the good of the beloved, how is it that this action does not impoverish oneself? In a relationship of mutual love, both parties act in this way; it is not a subordination of one's personality to a tyrant. In mutual love, an interpersonal communion is formed that takes the man and woman out of their egoism. It turns out that because humans are made for interpersonal communion, we are most fully ourselves when we are for others in love, rather than being stuck egoistically within ourselves. Wojtyła comments, "What might be called the law of *ekstasis* seems to operate here: the lover 'goes outside' the self to find a fuller existence in another."[77]

This "law of *ekstasis*" characterizes the love between a man and a woman in "betrothed love" and in a well-ordered marriage. The man and the woman must commit their whole selves to each other, in order to form a true unity of persons. Wojtyła notes that "we should rightly speak of the mutual surrender of both persons, of their belonging equally to each other."[78] Only this mutual surrender ensures that their relationship is not based on self-interest, on the use of the other person.

It seems to me, however, that one must ask whether such a union of persons is possible. Put simply, in a fallen world, who would trust another person to surrender himself or herself in a permanent commitment of love? If the other person does not give himself or herself, then the person who does so is played for a fool. The self-surrendering person gets used, rather than loved. Even if the two persons truly give themselves mutually to each other, it is not uncommon that one of these persons will later turn away from this original decision and abandon his or her (former) beloved.

As noted above, Wojtyła holds that the free, "reciprocal gift of self" constitutes a binding "unification" of the persons in which the man and the woman are fulfilled in their deepest core, as creatures made for interpersonal

---

76. Wojtyła, *Love and Responsibility*, 125–26.
77. Wojtyła, *Love and Responsibility*, 126.
78. Wojtyła, *Love and Responsibility*, 126.

communion and self-giving love.[79] But do we not see plentiful evidence in the real world that a person's free will, having surrendered itself to a beloved, often later changes its decision and rescinds that surrender?

Wojtyła recognizes that a hidden egoism can be present in an ostensibly self-surrendering lover. If present, this egoism will eventually manifest itself, and "[i]t is one of the greatest of sorrows when love proves to be not what it was thought to be, but its diagonal opposite."[80] But he points out that if we try to protect ourselves by refusing to be vulnerable, then we rule out for ourselves the true fulfillment that is love. As he observes, "Take away from love the fullness of self surrender, the completeness of personal commitment, and what remains will be a total denial and negation of it"—all that will remain is the use of another person.[81] What we must look for is whether the other person recognizes our value as a person, and we must be sure that we, too, recognize our value as a person. Wojtyła adds that each lover bears a profound responsibility for the other person's good. Here the test often boils down to whether one sees in the other person simply a partner for pleasure, whether sexual or otherwise.

At stake, as Wojtyła recognizes, is personal self-realization, which can only occur through self-gift, since we are created to love. He emphasizes that love's radical responsibility for another person does not crimp the lover or limit the lover's self-actualization. On the contrary, it is a necessary escape from the chains of egoism. This point does not mean that giving ourselves to another person is always a good idea. On the contrary, he reiterates that we have a responsibility in our choosing. We need to have a deep interior connection with that person.

Wojtyła acknowledges that a couple's love will be "put to the test most severely when the sensual and emotional reactions . . . grow weaker."[82] When this happens, a relationship based in egoism will fail, but a relationship based in love for the whole person will "grow stronger, and sink deeper roots."[83] Wojtyła speaks of a love based on mutual love for the whole person as being "serene and confident," freed from the anxiety that plagues love based on idealized sentiment or sensuality.[84] The serenity flows from an objective knowledge of the truth of the person whom one has chosen: one

---

79. Wojtyła, *Love and Responsibility*, 127.
80. Wojtyła, *Love and Responsibility*, 128.
81. Wojtyła, *Love and Responsibility*, 128–29.
82. Wojtyła, *Love and Responsibility*, 134.
83. Wojtyła, *Love and Responsibility*, 134.
84. Wojtyła, *Love and Responsibility*, 134.

knows the person's value "as he or she really is."[85] When love is grounded in this deep fashion, Wojtyła argues, it is even true to say that "[t]he strength of such a love emerges most clearly when the beloved person stumbles, when his or her weaknesses or sins come into the open."[86] It might seem that this would be the time when one spouse would have to rid himself or herself of the offending spouse. But Wojtyła observes that "[o]ne who truly loves does not then withdraw his love, but loves all the more, loves in full consciousness of the other's shortcomings and faults, and without in the least approving of them. For the person as such never loses its essential value."[87] Having chosen a person in love, one does not throw away that person.

Although love makes true self-actualization possible, it also involves limitation: "it is a giving of the self, and to give oneself means just that: to limit one's freedom on behalf of another."[88] Such limitation is in love not felt as restrictive, but rather is felt as "a positive, joyful and creative thing."[89] This is because the human free will was made for precisely such love, for precisely such giving oneself away to serve and rejoice in the good of another. Although love typically begins with sensuality and sentiment, love comes to be when "the will, with its natural aspiration to the infinite good which is happiness," starts "wanting this good for another person too."[90]

Wojtyła adds that this "infinite good" or "happiness" is in fact God, who alone can truly fulfill us. Implicitly at least, marriage is therefore ordered from the outset to God. Moreover, it is when we realize that we truly desire the good of happiness for another person that we realize how expansive our volitional power is; we move from being locked in our ego to realizing that we can go out of ourselves and truly love another person—and

---

85. Wojtyła, *Love and Responsibility*, 135.

86. Wojtyła, *Love and Responsibility*, 135.

87. Wojtyła, *Love and Responsibility*, 135. Cahall remarks along similar lines, "Throughout married life, as Christ seeks to make them fit for eternity with him, spouses will experience suffering at each other's hands as each of them struggles to overcome selfishness in its many forms. . . . Sadly, in this life, it is true that we will hurt those whom we love the most. This is because our callous words and hurtful actions sting harder those who are closest to us. It is important for couples to know that because they are both sinners living in a fallen world, it is inevitable that they will cause suffering to each other. However, the real question is what couples do after they have hurt each other. Will they bear this suffering in tenderness or will they retreat from their relationship? In the Sacrament of Marriage, Jesus offers couples the grace to bear this suffering so that they may overcome sin through each other" (Cahall, *The Mystery of Marriage*, 357).

88. Wojtyła, *Love and Responsibility*, 135.

89. Wojtyła, *Love and Responsibility*, 135.

90. Wojtyła, *Love and Responsibility*, 137.

thus that we can truly love God. We come to see not only the real value of the other person but also the real value of ourselves. Wojtyła emphasizes that this often happens not all at once, but gradually, as we are educated in love over time and come to understand the task of committed self-giving love. This education in love, in order to form a "great love," will also be the work of divine grace, with which the married couple cooperates.[91]

In light of the "insidious possibility of disintegration in relationships between men and women," Wojtyła explores chastity as the fundamental path by which "the love of man and woman can guard against disintegration."[92] Given the constant threat of unchastity—consider the number of marriages destroyed or deeply damaged by pornography use or by adultery—is the risk of self-gift truly a risk that a person today can prudently take? In Christian marriage, a couple is called to give themselves entirely to each other, being "subject to one another out of reference for Christ" (Eph 5:21). But this means giving oneself entirely to a fellow sinner. How can we entrust ourselves to a sinner who is liable to sin against us and deeply wound us? As sinners, moreover, how can we trust ourselves not to sin against and wound our spouse? Wojtyła poses the fundamental problem for sinners: "*Genuine reciprocity cannot arise from two egoisms.*"[93] We must give ourselves in order to attain human fulfillment, and yet our problem is that as sinners we tend to be egocentric, untrustworthy in relation to others. As Wojtyła says, "Love between man and woman cannot be built without sacrifices and self-denial."[94] But do we not often see marriages where one spouse does all the sacrifice and is essentially used by the other spouse?

The Jeweler's Shop

Here, Wojtyła knows that his philosophical arguments have reached their limit. At a certain point, he suggests, one has to make a decision for or against Christ's Cross. Either Christ's humbling of "himself . . . unto death, even death on a cross" (Phil 2:8) is a transformative path worthy of our participation, or it is not. Christians believe that the power of Christ's Cross *heals* sinners. United by faith to his Cross, we are filled by the Holy Spirit with his charity. The presence of the Cross at the heart of a marriage, even if at first manifested only in one spouse, has transformative power.

---

91. Wojtyła, *Love and Responsibility*, 140.
92. Wojtyła, *Love and Responsibility*, 140.
93. Wojtyła, *Love and Responsibility*, 88.
94. Wojtyła, *Love and Responsibility*, 208.

When Wojtyła wants to make this insight clear, he does so in literary form in his play *The Jeweler's Shop*. Anna is the aggrieved party: having been deeply wounded by her husband Stefan, she wants to be rid of her wedding ring. In the play, Anna meets Adam in the street; he tells her that "soon the Bridegroom will pass by."[95] Adam urges her to hear Christ's words of personal love for her: "beloved, you do not know how deeply you are mine, how much you belong to my love and my suffering—because to love means to give life through death; to love means to let gush a spring of the water of life into the depths of the soul, which burns or smolders, and cannot burn out."[96]

When she actually sees the Bridegroom Christ's face, to her great dismay it is Stefan's face. In the sinner whom we are to love, we see Christ. The experience changes Anna, though she remains wounded. She discovers the source of forgiveness. She tells Adam at the end of the play, "I ceased to despise him [i.e. Stefan], ceased to bear a grudge, that terrible grudge at my life which he had wasted. I began to look for guilt in myself as well. It was there."[97] Adam sums up what has occurred in Anna's heart: "A new love could begin only through a meeting with the Bridegroom. What Anna felt of it at first was only the suffering. In the course of time a gradual calm came. And something new that was growing, was still intangible, and, above all, did not 'taste' of love."[98] What the new love sparks, however, is a deepened humility and a growing merciful reconciliation through which, in the end, both Anna and Stefan are able to recognize themselves as loved unconditionally and freely in Christ. This is the power of Christ's Cross at the center of marriage, leading onward to eschatological union with Trinitarian love.

IV. Conclusion

How many marriage-preparation sessions ask the couple if they are prepared to follow the way of Christ's Cross and to place the Cross at the center of their marriage? A man and woman preparing to be married are not likely to think of their coming marriage as a mutual crucifixion. Nor should they. Yet, if married persons are to move beyond egoistic use of each other, they

95. Wojtyła, *The Jeweler's Shop*, 55.

96. Wojtyła, *The Jeweler's Shop*, 64.

97. Wojtyła, *The Jeweler's Shop*, 86. Cahall states, "The more spouses are able to approach the Sacrament of Penance to receive forgiveness from the Bridegroom, the easier they will find it to ask for and offer forgiveness to each other. . . . There is no greater way for a married couple to be tender with each other than to offer forgiveness and mercy to each other" (*The Mystery of Marriage*, 362–63).

98. Wojtyła, *The Jeweler's Shop*, 87.

must commit to self-surrendering love that puts the other ahead of the self. For this, people need the healing and transformation brought by Christ's Cross. Both partners in a marriage are sinners, and so forgiveness and healing are going to be necessary, especially when a (temporary or permanent) separation becomes necessary. Such forgiveness and healing, as well as real hope for transformation, have enduring and efficacious roots in the Cross of Christ.

As we have seen, these points have not been overlooked in the Christian tradition. Recall the insistence of John Paul II's *Familiaris Consortio* that "[c]onjugal love reaches that fullness to which it is interiorly ordained, conjugal charity, which is the proper and specific way in which the spouses participate in and are called to live the very charity of Christ who gave Himself on the Cross."[99] To love each other as they should, the married couple must love with the love of Christ. This is what Catherine of Siena means when she tells her married friend Agnesa that "I want you and Francesco to hide yourselves in the open side of Christ crucified in holy desire."[100]

Her words sound almost too stern for marriage; we might be tempted to think that consecrated religious can make this kind of sacrifice, but not a married couple. But in fact the merciful and transformative Cross of Christ is exactly what modern married couples need. With his Cross in view, Jesus commands his disciples to "love one another as I have loved you" (John 15:12). This is the path of the couple whose marriage embodies self-surrendering love.

Analyzing "betrothed love" from various angles, Wojtyła concludes that its core "is self-giving, the surrender of one's 'I'."[101] As noted above, he is well aware that this is a risk that many people today fear to take, because it can result in deep emotional hurt. But Wojtyła insists, "Love proceeds by way of this renunciation."[102] We become truly free only when we love the other person for the other person's sake. To love in this way, we must surrender ourselves. To undertake such self-surrender, however, requires more strength than we have, given our egoism and weakness. It becomes possible when we draw our strength from the transformative and life-giving Cross of Christ. When we open ourselves to the love of the crucified Christ, we find the freedom to take the risk of love.[103]

---

99. John Paul II, *Familiaris Consortio*, §13, cited in Diriart, "Un amour sauvé," 290. See also Hogan and LeVoir, *Covenant of Love*.

100. Catherine of Siena, *The Letters* III, 146.

101. Wojtyła, *Love and Responsibility*, 96.

102. Wojtyła, *Love and Responsibility*, 125.

103. As Brent Waters says, "The family is not so much a place for applying negotiating skills as practising the sacrificial virtues that give love its greatest breadth and depth"

Such risky love is a portal not only to human married love but also to the recognition that God, in Christ, loves us as his Bride. Indeed, by God's grace, our self-surrendering love has an inbuilt reward: imaging and sharing in the communion of God's triune love. In love, we perceive that Christ's Cross, at the heart of marriage, is not the endpoint: it leads to resurrection and eternal life, in the everlasting marriage of God and his people.[104]

(Waters, *The Family*, 242). Waters directs attention in this regard to Lasch, *Haven in a Heartless World*, whose main points Waters summarizes in *The Family*, 90–95. Where Lasch is at his strongest is when he talks about the role of experts and therapeutic governance in contemporary marriage and family.

104. See also Cavadini, "The Sacramentality of Marriage." As Cavadini observes, by contrast to some popularizers of Pope John Paul II's theology of the body, "Augustine finds a way to make the 'self-donation' of the spouses a function not primarily of natural inclination, but of the long, hard, purifying pedagogy in the loving humility of Christ, which begets the only true joys" ("The Sacramentality of Marriage," 175).

Chapter 5

Procreation and Mutual Love

All this may be well and good: God calls us to an eschatological intimacy with him so profound as to be a "marriage"; we enter into this intimacy through union with Christ's self-surrendering love in graced imaging of God; the fall distorted the primordial human marriage as it turned inward rather than reaching outward to God; and the Cross heals and elevates human marriage and orders the spouses to the eschatological marriage of God and creation. But it may still be asked: why must "marriage" be separated sharply from other forms of human friendship? After all, Jesus was single and had close friendships with men and women. Why focus on marriage when Jesus shows the importance, for the eschatological kingdom, of all sorts of friendships, especially given that Jesus declares that human marriage will not exist in the consummated kingdom?

The Catholic moral theologian Julie Hanlon Rubio suggests that "[c]hildren are not the reason . . . Christians get married. They marry, if at all, to work together in service of the kingdom of God."[1] But there are other ways of working together "in service of the kingdom of God," so this cannot be all that defines marriage. What is unique about human "marriage" and why is human marriage so distinctive as to be analogically employed to describe God's very purpose in creation and redemption?

Brent Waters points out that in what he calls contemporary "late liberal social and political thought," it is assumed that gender roles are social constructs that threaten individual self-fulfillment, and also that human

---

1. Rubio, *A Christian Theology of Marriage*, 57. I note that Rubio certainly gives a significant place to children as well, in her portrait of married couples' "dual vocation" to family and society. See also her "Living the Dual Vocation."

sexuality, as a bodily reality, has no intrinsic meaning.[2] From this perspective, it becomes even more difficult to figure out what differentiates marriage from other friendships and lifestyles. Scott Hahn makes the further point that "we've been trained to think of procreation as a kind of bonus we can *choose* to add on to sex—like upgrading to first class—rather than being inherently part of human sexuality. The modern view is that sex is inherently sterile and only becomes procreative by accident or by the choice of the participants."[3] If so, then the bodily ordering of man and woman toward the conception of a child does not appear to mean anything for determining the nature of marriage.

Defining what marriage entails, Anthony Esolen has argued that a marriage can only occur when "a man and a woman give themselves, *as man and woman*, to one another without reserve and forever."[4] Yet, it is incontestable that in human history and today, "marriage" has taken different forms. The most evident example is polygamy, where a man contracts marriage with a woman while also being married to one or more other

---

2. Waters, *The Family*, 99. Waters describes the arguments of Nelson, *Embodiment*, and Thatcher, *Marriage after Modernity*. See also Catholic Theological Society of America, *Human Sexuality*. Note that, as Waters says, Thatcher (unlike Nelson) "insists that marriage is oriented towards procreation and childrearing" and "contends that Christian discourse on marriage should begin with children" (*The Family*, 104). For Thatcher, however, "the marital covenant should be extended to same-sex couples" and there should also be a Church-approved "betrothal" period in which the couple can licitly live together and have sexual intercourse without yet having made up their minds about whether to proceed to marriage (*The Family*, 104–5). Central to this perspective is the view that it is morally acceptable for children to be deprived at the outset of a father or mother, because for same-sex relationships to be ordered toward children (as Thatcher thinks they must) in-vitro and surrogacy methods will be needed in the background, along with adoption policies that provide for two "mothers" or two "fathers." For a position similar to Thatcher's, see Cahill, "Same-Sex Marriage and Catholicism." For a response to Nelson's Christian promotion of non-marital and extra-marital sexual acts as well as to Nelson's sharp distinction between personhood and bodiliness, see Turner, *Sex, Money and Power*, 38–44.

3. Hahn, *The First Society*, 89. Given that sex's primary end is procreation, Hahn perceives that this means that marriage is intimately tied to the common good (social justice).

4. Esolen, *Defending Marriage*, ix. Adrian J. Walker and Rachel M. Coleman argue that modernity, despite its emphasis on diversity, seeks to stamp out real diversity—that is, diversity grounded in something other than free choice. In their view, with which I agree, "by attempting to write the sexual difference out of the essential constitution of marital society, so-called 'same-sex marriage' strikes at the natural root from which all other inter-human differences derive and in which they find a horizon and measure. In this sense, the ideal of 'diversity' represents . . . a certain radicalization of the logic of liberalism, which locates man's dignity chiefly in the pure formality of his potential for choice, detached from, and opposed to, what man actually is by nature," namely, male and female (Walker and Coleman, "The Saving Difference," 185).

women. In almost all cultures, too, divorce has always been a possibility and so marriage is not considered to be "without reserve and forever." Additionally, some people marry each other for the purpose of having children together, whereas other people marry each other when they are quite old, well past child-bearing years and without any real intention of having children together. Florence Caffrey Bourg contends that Catholicism has only recently appreciated "the unitive purpose of marital sexuality" and thus has only recently granted the moral validity of marital "sex without intending to procreate."[5] Although I think this claim is mistaken, it raises the question of whether the Catholic Church has properly understood the sacrament of marriage and thus whether the Church knows what distinctively constitutes a marriage.

Does God, in Scripture, give us any insight into the purpose or purposes that distinguish marriage from other human friendships? Answering in the affirmative, David Cloutier observes that in Genesis 1 "humans are created male and female specifically so that they can 'be fruitful and multiply' [Gen 1:28]," and, furthermore, "as the story of Israel unfolds in the Old Testament, this procreative purpose stands at the center of the story."[6] Although sin wounds marriage, marriage remains the main context for the

---

5. Bourg, "Multi-Dimensional Marriage," 167. Bourg's essay insists on the goodness of marital sex in which the procreative end is deliberately suppressed. I understand her sense of relief about not having to fear conceiving a child at an unwelcome time, but I think that she underestimates the spiritual and relational importance of ensuring that sexual intercourse expresses, as a soul-body act, both ends of marriage (not necessarily by conceiving a child, but by being open, consciously or unconsciously, to the possibility of conceiving a child). See also, in the same volume, Therrien's helpful "The Practice of Responsible Parenthood," 173–205.

6. Cloutier, *Love, Reason, and God's Story*, 164. Cloutier goes on to nuance his position and to criticize the traditional position somewhat. In his "Jewish Marriage," David Novak affirms that Genesis 1:28 shows that the orientation to the begetting and raising of children distinguishes the kind of relationship that marriage is. He makes clear also that a man and a woman who are unable to beget children (due to age or to other physical defects) can get married, so long as they are open to children if miraculously they come. Of course, entering into the state of marriage, and thus the childbearing that typically comes with marriage, is not a *necessity* for Christians, although in choosing to get married (rather than to live a celibate life) the man and woman express their openness to having children. Philip Reynolds points out that for Augustine, "The obligation to increase and multiply (Gen 1:28), which was urgent throughout the period of the Old Covenant, passed into abeyance with the advent of Jesus Christ" (Reynolds, *How Marriage Became One of the Sacraments*, 102). By contrast, Novak points out that "in Judaism, marriage itself is a duty owed the community by those able to reproduce its members" (Novak, "Jewish Marriage," 103). Not surprisingly, Rabbinic Jewish understanding of marriage—according to Novak—reflects "the covenantal marriage initiated at Sinai between God and the people Israel," whose eschatological end is the fullness of the world-to-come ("Jewish Marriage," 123).

raising of children, and from ancient times to today it has been shaped by "real affection between husband and wife."[7]

The association of marriage with the procreation and raising of children is treated by the Bible as a self-evident element of human life. When a married couple cannot conceive a child, this leads to sadness. In numerous biblical instances, God brings about the miraculous conception of a child. This is part of the stories of Abraham and Sarah, Jacob and Rachel, and other significant biblical couples. In a poignant moment, the hapless husband Elkanah tells his childless wife, "Hannah, why do you weep? And why do you not eat? And why is your heart sad? Am I not more to you than ten sons?" (1 Sam 1:8). Of course he is not!

Can biblical threads such as these help us with regard to understanding the nature of marriage? I think so. Notably, they have done so within the Catholic tradition of reflection upon marriage, illuminated by philosophical reasoning that begins with the facts on the ground: across cultures, marriage has long been identifiable, in Robert Jenson's words, as "the coincidence of the most complete possible bodily union between existing human persons, with equally bodily unity between old and new human persons."[8] The connection of these two unities has not been a mere happenstance. Arguably, the connection arises from what constitutes human flourishing, both as individual human beings and families and as the human race as a whole in its life together. The two unities—between the man and the woman, on the one hand, and the father, mother, and child on the other—go together.

From a Thomistic perspective, Nicanor Austriaco notes that humans possess, whether consciously or not, certain ends or goals that perfect human nature. These ends include life, procreation, community, and knowing truth. Whether or not particular individuals seek these ends in every instance, they nonetheless are "ordered" toward them due to their constitution as human beings, because of what it means for the human race and its members to flourish. Without life, there could be no humanity; without

---

7. Cloutier, *Love, Reason, and God's Story*, 165. He points out, "Some have suggested this means that ancient marriages were loveless, but the evidence quite clearly points in a different direction" (*Love, Reason, and God's Story*, 165). Yet, as he says, in ancient Greece and Rome (and in many earlier and later societies as well) "affection was neither the foundation nor the purpose of the relationship, but a natural consequence as husband and wife ran a household and raised children together" (*Love, Reason, and God's Story*, 165).

8. Jenson, *The Triune Story*, 330. Jenson goes on to describe the same phenomenon as "the union of humanity's synchronic unity with its diachronic unity, of the bodily unity of two existing persons with the bodily unity of successive human persons" (*The Triune Story*, 331). He affirms that marriage "is the place where the two societally constituting modes of social unity coincide, and do so in the flesh" (*The Triune Story*, 332).

procreation, the human race would cease to exist. Without community and truth, the social and rational aspects of human flourishing would be left unfulfilled, stunted by loneliness and ignorance. Since human procreation takes place through the uniting of sperm and egg, and since child-raising is a long-term project on the part of the mother and the father, the communal dimension and the procreative dimension of human flourishing are not separable. Austriaco therefore argues that "a reasoned reflection upon the personal and biological meaning of human sexuality reveals that conjugal love is ordered towards two complementary ends, the procreation of children and the union of the spouses."[9]

In addition to these two *ends*, the Catholic tradition has also generally noted three *goods* of marriage. Perry Cahall explains that "the three aspirations of conjugal love—fidelity, indissolubility, and fruitfulness—are the goods (*bona*) that marriage allows the spouse to realize in their relationship."[10] The "goods" of marriage pertain to what the man and woman, in marrying, promise to give each other. In the Catholic rite of marriage, the man and woman promise that their marital communion will involve fidelity, indissolubility, and openness to children. By contrast, the "ends" of marriage describe the purposes of marriage as a human institution, that is to say, what marriage is for and what makes it distinctive among other kinds of human friendships.

Most people marry with the implicit or explicit expectation of bearing and raising children within a stable and loving union, and this expectation regularly (though certainly not always) comes to pass. Yet, this does

---

9. Austriaco, "Understanding Sexual Orientation as a *Habitus*," 105. Austriaco directs attention here to the teaching of the Second Vatican Council's Pastoral Constitution on the Church in the Modern World, *Gaudium et Spes*. He also makes the point, with regard to homosexual acts, that studies conducted in the United States, the Netherlands, and New Zealand, respectively, have shown a vastly higher rate of mental distress and self-destructive behavior among homosexuals than among heterosexuals, which cannot be correlated with societal oppression since societies with different levels of toleration of homosexual acts do not evince different mental health results. He observes that, according to a study done in the Netherlands, male homosexuals with steady partners average eight casual sexual partners per year and male homosexuals without steady partners average twenty-two casual partners per year. Lesbians show a significantly higher rate of alcohol abuse and other problems. Austriaco is responding to Johnson, "Scripture and Experience." See also Browning, "Can Marriage Be Defined?," Gallagher, "The Case Against Same-Sex Marriage," especially 96, 161, 169–70.

10. Cahall, *The Mystery of Marriage*, 82. Cahall differentiates these three goods from the "ends" of marriage by recourse to the *Catechism of the Catholic Church*, which defines marriage as "by its nature ordered toward the good of the spouses and the procreation and education of offspring." See *Catechism of the Catholic Church*, §1601, cited in Cahall, *The Mystery of Marriage*, 83. The *Catechism of the Catholic Church* here draws upon the *Code of Canon Law*, 1055.

not mean that a loveless marriage, or a marriage that is unable to produce children, is not a marriage. Cahall aptly points out in this regard that "the ends of a thing may not be able to be realized by the agent," without the end thereby ceasing to be present.[11] Admittedly, as Kent Lasnoski has commented, it is often the case today that "marriage is seen as a relationship of a particular kind rather than primarily an institution defined by an essential end."[12] In my view, this is a mistake, largely rooted in imagining the procreative end to be solely "biological" rather than personal.[13] As *Gaudium et Spes* remarks, not only are "[m]arriage and married love . . . by their nature ordered to the procreation and education of children," but also "children

---

11. Cahall, *The Mystery of Marriage*, 88. Cormac Burke recalls that for centuries, the Church and its theologians "presented the ends of matrimony in a clear hierarchical manner: a 'primary' end (procreation) and two 'secondary' ends (mutual help and the remedy for concupiscence)" (Burke, *The Theology of Marriage*, 50–51). These "secondary" ends were insufficiently personal, in Burke's view, due in part to the fact that the inquiry of moral theology into marriage "principally centered on the ethical aspects of physical sexuality," while the canonists focused on issues regarding "the validity of matrimonial consent" (*The Theology of Marriage*, 51). By contrast, building upon the emphasis on mutual love found in *Gaudium et Spes*'s treatment of marriage, the new *Code of Canon Law* takes a new approach by defining the "second" end as "the good of the spouses [*bonum coniugum*]," thereby ensuring that mutual love receives an appropriate place. Burke defines the *bonum coniugum* as "the good of learning to love, of preparing for heaven, of seeking holiness," and he remarks (indebted to *Lumen Gentium* §11) that the *bonum coniugum* cannot be separated from openness to children or from indissolubility (*The Theology of Marriage*, 96). He also bemoans the fact that the "*bonum coniugum*" is often defined without any reference whatsoever to the procreative end, as in Wrenn, "Refining the Essence of Marriage" and Pfnausch, "The Good of the Spouses." See Burke, *The Theology of Marriage*, 98. In my view, "mutual help" and the "remedy of concupiscence," which are the two traditional secondary ends, are implied by "the good of the spouses" or "mutual love."

12. Lasnoski, *Vocation to Virtue*, 9. As an example, he cites Hogan, *Marriage as a Relationship*. Lasnoski's goal is "to understand marriage as a consecrated way of holiness in the Church, a way that participates in the same principles of Christian householding as consecrated religious life and requires the same evangelical virtues as consecrated religious life" (*Marriage as a Relationship*, 5). See also Hadjadj, *Qu'est-ce qu'une famille?* and Berry, "Sex, Economy, Freedom, and Community."

13. Burke is right that "to maintain that a procreative understanding of marriage is not personalist reveals a major defect in anthropological thinking. The contemporary loss of the sense of the goodness of human procreativity, of the uniqueness of the conception of each child, or of a spouse becoming a parent, suggests a devalued conception of life itself" (Burke, *The Theology of Marriage*, 135). For an effort to reconsider the "goods" and "ends"—a reconsideration that in my view is not particularly necessary, in part because the distinction between them does not rule out by any means their intimate relation—see Lowery, "The Nature and Ends of Marriage."

are the supreme gift of marriage and greatly contribute to the good of the parents themselves."[14]

My argument in this chapter on human marriage proceeds in three steps. First, I inquire into marriage's goods and ends with the help of the contrasting perspectives of Plato and his student Aristotle. These two thinkers, the former by marginalizing marriage and the latter by valuing marriage, shed light on what is at stake in discussions of marriage and procreation. Second, I set forth the basic elements of the Christian tradition on marriage's goods and ends. Here I begin by treating Peter Lombard, who was influential at the time in which marriage's sacramental nature was being codified by the Church. The bulk of the section is devoted to two Fathers of the Church, Augustine and John Chrysostom. I read Chrysostom's reflections on marriage in light of Augustine's three goods of marriage.

Third, I examine the beginnings of "personalism" in Catholic theology of marriage as found in Pope Pius XI's encyclical *Casti Connubii*. I then critically engage the approaches to marriage set forth by the Catholic scholars Dietrich von Hildebrand and Cormac Burke, respectively. Here my focus turns explicitly to the ends of marriage and to procreation's status therein.[15] While the chapter only occasionally addresses the eschatological

---

14. *Gaudium et Spes*, §50, 953. For discussion see Kaczor, "Being in Love." *Gaudium et Spes* adds the clarification that, of course, "marriage is not merely for the procreation of children: its nature as an indissoluble compact between two people and the good of the children demand that the mutual love of the partners be properly shown, that it should grow and mature. Even in cases where despite the intense desire of the spouses there are no children, marriage still retains its character of being a whole manner and communion of life and preserves its value and indissolubility" (§50, p. 954).

15. James V. Brownson says, "Scripture regularly speaks of a good marriage as one that has children, but marriage does not cease to exist in the absence of procreation, nor is a marriage without children always portrayed in a negative light" (Brownson, *Bible, Gender, Sexuality*, 115-16). Brownson contends that "the most extended meditation on sexual love in the entire Old Testament, the Song of Songs, makes no mention of issues related to procreation at all, focusing entirely on the delights of physical love. If procreation is the essential purpose of sex and marriage, one is hard-pressed to explain its absence from this entire book of the Bible that is devoted to sex and marriage" (*Bible, Gender, Sexuality*, 116). Yet the procreative end is on full display in the Song of Songs: the sexual imagery clearly indicates the union of male and female sexual organs whose "end" (even in men and women who cannot conceive a child) is procreative (see for example Song 5:4-5). Discussing marriage in the New Testament, Brownson emphasizes, "In this 'interim' period, marriage continued to be valid, but procreation moved to the periphery of the meaning of life in general—and thus of marriage in particular" (*Bible, Gender, Sexuality*, 117). But neither Jesus nor Paul give marriage a new "end" that replaces the procreative end; the ultimate end of God's kingdom does not mean that human marriage no longer has a natural order to the procreative end. In his defense of extending Christian marriage to same-sex couples, Brownson concludes, "Roman Catholic social teaching assumes that the central and essential purpose

marriage of Bridegroom and Bride, it will be clear that part of what is at stake is the "great mystery" of Christ and the Church as signified by the man and woman in marriage.

I. Plato and Aristotle: Is Marriage Needed at All?

Plato

In Plato's *Republic*, Socrates proposes to eliminate marriage entirely among the city's elite governing class, and to reduce marriage to a scheme for controlling breeding among the city's citizens.[16] In Book V of the *Republic*, Socrates argues that sex or gender is not determinative of the qualities and abilities that a man or a woman will possess. Building upon this point, he proposes a gender-neutral ruling class of the city. Athletic and warlike women should be "selected to cohabit with men of this kind and to serve with them as guardians since they are capable of it and akin by nature."[17] The

---

of marriage is procreation, a conclusion that the biblical texts simply do not confirm. Instead, the study of text . . . leads to the conclusion that the unitive purpose of marriage (i.e., conjugal love and faithfulness) is essential, and the procreative purpose of marriage, while important, is not essential in the same way to marriage itself" (*Bible, Gender, Sexuality*, 121). This conclusion is rooted both in misunderstanding the nature of an "end" of marriage and in misreading the biblical texts. He argues that "the one-flesh union spoken of in Genesis 2:24 connotes not physical complementarity but a kinship bond" (*Bible, Gender, Sexuality*, 38), when in fact it connotes both. See Hill's "Gunning for Complementarity," a review of Brownson's book; as well as Gathercole's "Sin in God's Economy," 163–64 (cited by Hill).

16. For a succinct discussion of Plato and Aristotle on marriage—favoring Aristotle's position though attuned to its serious inadequacies (above all, Aristotle's view of women as lesser than men)—see Browning, *Marriage and Modernization*, 102–3. For a matter-of-fact synopsis of Plato's position, see Bobonich, "Plato's Politics," 323. It is helpful also to keep in mind Plato's overall purpose in the *Republic*: "Like the *Symposium*, the *Republic* forms a hierarchy out of the lower physical loves (e.g., for bodies and wine), the middle-level love of honor (*philotimia*), and the highest or culminating level: *philosophia* (Rep. 475a-b; cf. 581a-c)" (Ludwig, "Eros in the *Republic*, 220). For the path by which Socrates persuades his shocked audience with respect to the feasibility (however remote) of his plan, see Yunis, "The Protreptic Rhetoric of the *Republic*," 20–24. By contrast, for an insistence upon the impossibility of what Socrates describes, see Benardete's *Socrates' Second Sailing*. Inspired in part by Leo Strauss's engagement with Plato's *Republic*, Benardete argues that "[t]he communism of women, in which not all women belong to every man but no woman belongs to any man, prepares the way for love in the abstract" (*Socrates' Second Sailing*, 110). In Benardete's view, the *Republic* in this section ruthlessly suppresses the knowledge of teleological natures. The goal is to construct a society in which "*erōs* is never particular; it has the same characteristics as mind" (*Socrates' Second Sailing*, 112).

17. Plato, *Republic*, 456b, p. 695. In her *Women and the Ideal Society*, Natalie Harris

guardians, each of whom must be athletic and warlike, will all be educated together. The women will participate in the naked athletic training alongside the men, and the women will "take their part with the men in war and the other duties of civic guardianship and have no other occupation."[18] Given that the men will be physically somewhat stronger, male and female guardians may do some different tasks, but insofar as possible their tasks should be the same.

Regarding marriage and procreation, Socrates says of the guardians "that these women shall all be common to all these men, and that none shall cohabit with any privately, and that the children shall be common, and that no parent shall know its own offspring nor any child its parent."[19] How can this be possible in practice? Socrates recognizes that the male and female guardians, doing everything together, will also wish to have sexual intercourse with each other. The guardians will have sexual intercourse with different partners and will form no permanent or exclusive relationship.[20]

Since random coupling would in general be disorderly, the city otherwise should arrange that men and women are married off to each other at the best times of life and in a manner that ensures that the next generation will be strong and intelligent. Just as horses or dogs are bred, so should humans be bred. Socrates states that "the best men must cohabit with the best women in as many cases as possible and the worst with the worst in the fewest."[21] With regard to the warrior class, the city should ensure that "the young men . . . who excel in war and other pursuits" should be more frequently in the company of the women, in order that they might "beget as many of the children as possible."[22]

Bluestone summarizes the general history of the reception of Plato's idea.

18. Plato, *Republic*, 457a, p. 696. Regarding the philosophical reception of this idea, Dominic J. O'Meara comments, "To the ordinary male reader of the *Republic* in Antiquity, it must have seemed that one of the most outlandish of Plato's revolutionary ideas was that of including women among the rulers of an ideal state. It should not surprise us, however, that Neoplatonists took notice of and defended this idea" (O'Meara, *Platonopolis*, 83). O'Meara discusses the views of Proclus and Theodore of Asine, the latter of whom is more in line with the viewpoint presented in the *Republic*.

19. Plato, *Republic*, 457c–d, p. 696.

20. Against the view that this is impossible or unworkable in practice, Bluestone suggests that its possibility and workability is confirmed by "the current divorce rate and the statistics on multiple partners for both sexes in today's America" (Bluestone, *Women and the Ideal Society*, 27). She contests A. E. Taylor's argument that "the impulses of sex and family affections are for humans intrinsically, that is, naturally, connected" (*Women and the Ideal Society*, 31). For fourth-century BC Greek understanding of sexual desire, see Calame, *The Poetics of Eros*.

21. Plato, *Republic*, 459d, p. 699.

22. Plato, *Republic*, 460b, p. 699. David Ross comments that for Plato, "the

An important element of Socrates's plan is that among the guardians at least, the father and mother should not be allowed to raise their own children.[23] Instead, the infants will be taken "to certain nurses who live apart in a quarter of the city" and will be raised by the nurses.[24] Infants born with a birth defect will be secretly left to die. A crucial aspect of the plan is that a mother should not be allowed to recognize her child. If the father and mother raised their own children, this would focus their love and interest on a few specific children, rather than strengthening the city by ensuring that "all the citizens rejoice and grieve alike at the same births and deaths."[25] Socrates reasons, "That city . . . is best ordered in which the greatest number use the expression 'mine' and 'not mine' of the same things in the same way."[26]

But if parents do not know who their children are, what about the inevitable problem of incest? Socrates partially solves this problem by proposing that *all* children born within seven to ten months after a man and woman's marriage will be known as their "sons" and "daughters," and furthermore that "all children born in the period in which their fathers and mothers were procreating will regard one another as brothers and sisters."[27] Of course, this means that the guardians will have to resign themselves to allowing brothers and sisters (in this broad sense, and even perhaps in the stricter sense) to marry each other, but Socrates deems this to be acceptable

---

community of wives and children" only holds for "the ruling and warrior classes" (Ross, *Aristotle*, 253). In my view, Plato seems to imply that the warrior class will marry, but my argument does not hinge upon this point; I recognize that Ross is likely to be correct.

23. For a critique of Plato's dismissal of the value of the labor that goes into a thriving family life (as well as other aspects of Plato's thought), see Elshtain, *Public Man, Private Woman*, 20–41. Bluestone offers a scathing response to Elshtain in *Women and the Ideal Society*, 126–54 (she also critiques other thinkers in these pages, among them Carol Gilligan and Mary Midgley). Bluestone especially highlights the fact that, despite Elshtain's insistence upon the universal status and value of the nuclear family, "a large number of Americans . . . no longer live in a nuclear family" (*Women and the Ideal Society*, 132) and most women, during their lifespan of seventy-plus years, spend relatively few of these years with young children as dependents. Bluestone states with regard to Midgley: "Midgley, like so many commentators before her, finds the family arrangements proposed for the guardians hopelessly unnatural" (*Women and the Ideal Society*, 148). This shows Midgley's good sense, in my view. For a defense of the nuclear family as not a "modern" invention and as important for the moral formation of children, see Berger and Berger, *The War over the Family*, although the Bergers stretch a point by arguing that the nuclear family serves liberal democratic values.

24. Plato, *Republic*, 460c, p. 699.
25. Plato, *Republic*, 462b, p. 701.
26. Plato, *Republic*, 462c, p. 701.
27. Plato, *Republic*, 461d, p. 700.

so long as the strongest and most capable men are still marrying the strongest and most capable women.

Socrates adds that the guardians will live together in common homes; they will "not possess houses of their own or land or any other property."[28] Were it otherwise, then among the city's guardians there would form strong and wealthy families, threatening the city's unity. Since the guardian class will share each other sexually without establishing exclusive relationships, Socrates extols "the community of wives and children among the guardians" as key to their having "one and the same thing in common which they will name *mine*," rather than being divided by the interests of a specific marriage and family.[29] If the guardians each had their own spouse and their own identifiable children, then they would focus not on the state and its unity, but on the divisive "pleasures and pains" of their individual families.[30]

In sum, Socrates does not think that marriage is necessary for the proper raising of children. In his proposed ideal city, therefore, marriage is utterly transformed. The only reason he retains marriage for the citizens is so that disorder does not reign and so that the guardians can eugenically control the breeding of the citizens.[31]

28. Plato, *Republic*, 464b–c, p. 703.
29. Plato, *Republic*, 464a, p. 703.
30. Plato, *Republic*, 464d, p. 703.

31. Note that Leo Strauss influentially (in some circles) argues that Plato's proposal regarding the lives of male and female guardians was not meant as a serious proposal, but rather was (as Bluestone summarizes Strauss's view) merely "Plato's way of showing us that the just city could never come into being. Regardless of what Socrates actually says, Plato's real intention was for us to recognize that his utopia was ultimately unrealizable" (Bluestone, *Women and the Ideal Society*, 35). See Strauss, *The City and the Man*, 127. For the view that Plato did not intend his proposal to be taken seriously, see also Crombie, *An Examination of Plato's Doctrine*, vol. 1. For a critique of Plato's proposal and a defense of marriage and family life, along lines broadly influenced by Strauss (inclusive of Strauss's view that Plato's proposal was not meant to be taken literally), see Allan Bloom's "Interpretive Essay" in his translation of Plato's *Republic*. Bluestone criticizes Bloom, remarking that "[t]he strength of what Anna Freud has called 'psychological parenting,' so that in her view the parent is not necessarily the one who contributes the sperm but the one who nurtures the child emotionally, is not even considered [by Bloom]. Nor does he consider animal evidence. We know that there are biological species where there is no parental investment in the offspring, as well as animals where the young are cared for by what we would call foster parents. I am not suggesting that animal data is ultimately decisive. However, any commentator in the 1960s who wishes to pronounce on the naturalness of parental feeling, and therefore on the impossibility of communal rearing for males at least—he mentions only fathers—might be expected to adduce anthropological or biological information to support his view. Instead, his assumptions are baldly stated; he appeals evidently to 'common sense'" (Bluestone, *Women and the Ideal Society*, 35–36). We now have plentiful scientific and sociological evidence to support Bloom's basic line of critique. See for example Raeburn, *Do Fathers*

PROCREATION AND MUTUAL LOVE

Aristotle

In Aristotle's *Politics*, he replies to Plato's *Republic* on the topic of marriage. He extends Plato's thought experiment by inquiring into the question of whether not only the guardians, but indeed "the citizens might conceivably have wives and children and property in common."[32] Aristotle reasons that the city would thereby become a big family, even a quasi-individual. In Aristotle's opinion, however, the purpose of a city does not consist in striving for this kind of unity. A city should rather include a diversity of people. Its self-sufficiency derives not from its unity, but from its diversity. When sexual partners and children are shared, the result is to impede this diversity.

Furthermore, while a person in such a city could indeed say that the women (or the men) are possessed sexually by all, what could not be said is that each individual person possesses all the women (or all the men). In fact, the result would be that no individual person actually possesses anything. None of the women would be a man's wife, and a man would be the husband of no woman. The same would hold for the possession of children.

Grave problems will arise from this situation, according to Aristotle. As he points out, each person inevitably thinks primarily of his or her own self, his or her own interests. If the children are the responsibility of all, then no one will end up taking much of an interest in the children, because no man or woman will be united to any particular children. It is when one can say that children are one's own that one takes a strong interest in them. Other people's children generally are not of urgent interest to individual men and women. Aristotle observes that "anybody will be equally the son of anybody, and will therefore be neglected by all alike."[33]

The first purpose for which Aristotle values marriage, therefore, is for the care of children.[34] When a man and a woman become father and

---

Matter?; Pruett, *Fatherneed*. See also Hines, *Brain Gender*. For an attempt to counter the evidence, see Fine, *Delusions of Gender*.

32. Aristotle, *Politics*, 1261a, p. 80. Ross notes, "Here Aristotle seems to forget Plato's actual arrangements," since Plato does not conceive of *all* the citizens sharing wives, children, and property in common (Ross, *Aristotle*, 253). Seth Benardete comments, "Aristotle's objections to the communism of women and children are so obvious that it is hardly necessary to prove that Socrates was as aware of them" (Benardete, *Socrates' Second Sailing*, 117).

33. Aristotle, *Politics*, 1262a, p. 84. See Ross, *Aristotle*, 253.

34. In *Love and Friendship in Plato and Aristotle*, A. W. Price criticizes Aristotle's understanding of women (for example, Aristotle holds, quite unfortunately, that the most significant female virtue is silence, and Aristotle insists upon women's subordination to men and women's relegation to the home), but also remarks that "Aristotle's depiction of the marital relation is redeemed, to an extent, by his enthusiasm for it. . . . Aristotle, quite sensibly, associates a steady sexual drive with connubiality, not

mother, they will care for their children if they can identify them and if the children belong to their family. Otherwise, the mother and father will neglect them, not being able to identify and raise them as theirs. Besides, how much better it is for a child to be able to know his or her father and mother! Aristotle notes that no one would want to be a "son" of a citizen if that citizen had a thousand other sons and if one was also a "son" of a thousand other citizens. In such a case, being a "son" would be a near-meaningless designation. A child needs the benefit of belonging to a specific family, and having a relationship with his or her actual father, mother, siblings, uncles and aunts, cousins, grandparents and, so on.[35]

Aristotle points out, furthermore, that even if Plato (or Socrates) thinks he can sever the tie between a father and mother and their actual children—by having the children raised anonymously and communally—the fact is that in many cases the parents will bear a physical resemblance to the children. In such cases, the parents will likely recognize their own children and seek to give them special care. Aristotle claims to know of a place in North Africa where men share women in common. Even there, he says, "the children who are born are assigned to their respective fathers on the ground of their likeness."[36] The implication again is that otherwise the men would not care for the children, or at least would not care as much about them.

Another reason that Aristotle gives for valuing marriage consists in the fact that when we know to whom we are related, we can more easily avoid physical fights or lovemaking with our biological parent or sibling or near relation. Aristotle considers it to be deeply unfitting for near-relatives to engage in sexual relationships, or for a son to fight his father.[37]

Aristotle also affirms that marriage serves the good of friendship. In Aristotle's view, friendship is a good for the whole city. A good city fosters friendships, and such friendships strengthen the city against revolution. For friendship to be possible, real distinction is needed. If everyone is my friend,

---

promiscuity (whose source is rather boredom).... Morally, Aristotle places the relation of man and wife, if they are good, within the friendship of virtue; for each will delight in the proper virtue of the other.... Unlike Plato, Aristotle was a married man, and apparently a devoted one" (172–73). Price adds in a footnote that Aristotle "commonsensibly, recognizes the value of children in cementing a marriage" (*Love and Friendship in Plato and Aristotle*, 172n8). See also Dobbs, "Family Matters."

35. Ross sums up: "Aristotle's argument is that intensity of affection can only be had by a sacrifice of extension. Plato's introduction of the crèche and the orphan-school, not to replace parents when they are dead or unfit for their responsibilities, but to replace them in all cases, is not likely to produce the affection he desires" (Ross, *Aristotle*, 253).

36. Aristotle, *Politics*, 1262a, p. 84.

37. Aristotle, *Politics*, 1262a, p. 85.

then I have no special friend. If everyone is my sexual partner, then no one is united particularly to me as my own sexual partner. Aristotle here returns to the point that we care about those with whom we have a specially intimate relationship. Lacking any such intimate relationships—if all children are the "sons" of all men and women, and if all women are the lovers of all men—"there is no reason why the so-called father should care about the son, or the son about the father."[38] Aristotle reiterates his point about the way in which we care for what is ours but do not care as much about what is common to everyone: "Of the two qualities which chiefly inspire regard and affection—that a thing is your own and that it is your only one—neither can exist in such a state as this."[39] Without marriage, a man will not have special "regard and affection" for any particular woman (and vice versa), with the result that far from acting as though he were married to all the women of the community, he will act as though he were married to none and will care little about any.

For Aristotle, then, another purpose that marriage serves is to promote "regard and affection" between a man and a woman. In *Nicomachean Ethics*, Aristotle describes "[t]he friendship between husband and wife" as in a certain sense "a natural instinct; since man is by nature a pairing creature."[40] Marriage fits with what most men and women want to do, namely, pair up in order to have companionship and a family. In this sense, Aristotle points out that "the family is an earlier and more fundamental institution than the state."[41] This point in itself sharply differentiates Aristotle's perspective on marriage from Plato's. Not only is marriage irreplaceable in fostering certain goods pertaining to the friendship of man and woman and to the raising of children, but also marriage is a natural instinct for most humans. To deprive humans of the fullness of marriage and the family is to inflict a wound on human nature.

Describing the distinctive friendship between a man and a woman enabled by marriage, Aristotle observes that it is a friendship based at the same time upon division of labor and upon pleasure. He states that "whereas with the other animals the association of the sexes aims only at continuing the species, human beings cohabit not only for the sake of begetting children but

---

38. Aristotle, *Politics*, 1262b, p. 86.

39. Aristotle, *Politics,*, 1262b, p. 86.

40. Aristotle, *The Nicomachean Ethics*, VIII.xii.7, p. 503. For a critique of Aristotle on marriage, arguing (at least partly rightly) that his account of the husband's prerogatives is inconsistent and unjust, see Pangle, *Aristotle and the Philosophy of Friendship*.

41. Aristotle, *The Nicomachean Ethics*, VIII.xii.7, p. 503. See Vodraska, *Philosophical Essays concerning Human Families*, chapter 4.

also to provide the needs of life."[42] In a stable marriage bond, the man and the woman help each other to survive and flourish. Aristotle adds that the friendship between a husband and a wife can also be grounded in virtue, in addition to utility and pleasure. Insofar as it is a virtuous friendship, it is real friendship. This requires that "the partners be of high moral character."[43]

In addition to fostering the friendship of the husband and wife, marriage assists the cultivation of love between parents and children. Aristotle comments that "parents love their children as part of themselves, whereas children love their parents as the source of their being."[44] He recognizes that parents generally love their children more than children love their parents, since a "progenitor is more attached to progeny than progeny to progenitor" and since "parents love their children as soon as they are born" (prior to when children consciously know their parents).[45] These goods of love are preserved by marriage, since marriage, broadly speaking, ensures that a father can love his children as his own.

Of course, Aristotle does not consider marriage to be necessary for friendship. A person can have a very satisfying friendship without having a marriage. For Aristotle, "one should love one's best friend most" and "the best friend is he that, when he wishes a person's good, wishes it for that person's own sake."[46] One's best friend can be one's wife, but for Aristotle, who unfortunately holds that women are lesser than men, one's best friend is more likely to be a male who is one's equal in virtue and dignity. In Aristotle's view, therefore, marriage can serve to foster a virtuous friendship between the husband and wife (assuming they are both virtuous), but what marriage accomplishes more efficaciously is securing the relationship between parents and children, largely for the sake of the flourishing of the

---

42. Aristotle, *The Nicomachean Ethics*, VIII.xii.7, p. 503.

43. Aristotle, *The Nicomachean Ethics*, VIII.xii.7, p. 503.

44. Aristotle, *The Nicomachean Ethics*, VIII.xii.2, p. 499. See the discussion of children as "part" of the parents (according to Aristotle and Thomas Aquinas) in Melissa Moschella, *To Whom Do Children Belong?*, 25–28; as well as her conclusions on 179–80.

45. Aristotle, *The Nicomachean Ethics*, VIII.xii.2, p. 499.

46. Aristotle, *The Nicomachean Ethics*, IX.viii.2, p. 549. For discussion, see Pangle, *Aristotle and the Philosophy of Friendship*, especially chapter 10. Pangle comments on Aristotle's placement of friends among "external goods": "Ordinary people who are not so crude as to think of friends as tools may still consider them as possessions. They imagine a happy man to be one blessed by fortune with money, good looks, a splendid sports car, beautiful women, a stable full of polo ponies, and rich, famous, glamorous friends. But a true friend, if he is another self, would seem not to be simply external to oneself but, in a deep sense, intertwined with one's own soul; a true friend is far more secure than goods that depend chiefly on fortune or public opinion; and most importantly, having a friend means at bottom not having a possession but engaging in an activity of the soul" (*Aristotle and the Philosophy of Friendship*, 184).

children. For Aristotle, marriage also has utility, in that a man and a woman bring different talents to a marriage and thereby build a thriving family together.

In sum, for Aristotle, Plato's idea of preventing the guardian class from marrying is disastrous, but not because it destroys the possibility of friendship, sexual intercourse, cohabitation, or economic welfare. All of these goods can be pursued and obtained without marriage. Instead, where Plato's idea of getting rid of marriage has an especially noxious effect is upon the well-being of children and the friendship of the father and mother. Children need to know their father and mother; children need to receive the special love and care of their father and mother. If marriage is taken away and men and women do not know who their children are, men and women will tend to care much less for either children or specific sexual partners. Marriage, as an institution, is centrally related to caring for and raising children by their father and mother, a great human interpersonal good that is deeply wounded by the absence of marriage.

II. Peter Lombard, Augustine, and John Chrysostom

Peter Lombard

Plato and Aristotle's debate makes clear that without the procreative end, marriage is dispensable, because the other goods associated with marriage can be attained in other ways—even if the special friendship between father and mother requires marriage. In this light, I now turn to examining patristic and medieval Christian theologies of marriage.[47] Rather than proceeding in chronological order, I begin with a brief look at Peter Lombard. Lombard's work is important because he wrote in the twelfth century, when marriage's status as one of the seven sacraments was being ratified and explained. Perry Cahall remarks, "Some of the great developments in sacramental theology and the theology of marriage can be attributed to Peter Lombard."[48] My purpose here is to indicate why Lombard so strongly associated marriage with the procreative end.

Lombard argues that the "final cause" or ultimate goal of marriage—the ultimate reason for which persons reasonably enter into marriage—must be the raising of children. This is so even if the marriage proves infertile, since that fact that marriage has an intrinsic goal does not mean that the goal

---

47. Because I discuss Thomas Aquinas's theology of marriage at length in chapter 4 of my *The Indissolubility of Marriage*, I leave Aquinas out of the present chapter.
48. Cahall, *The Mystery of Marriage*, 221.

need be met in all cases. Lombard states that "the principal final cause for the contracting of marriage is the procreation of offspring."[49] He cites not Aristotle, but Genesis 1. As already noted, when God creates human beings "male and female," God blesses them and instructs them, "Be fruitful and multiply, and fill the earth and subdue it" (Gen 1:27-28). Given that God's first command to the man and woman is to "be fruitful and multiply," Lombard assumes that not only are the man and woman a married couple, but also that the goal for which marriage (as a created reality) is instituted must be the begetting and raising of children.

Lombard recognizes that things other than the desire for children may lead a man and a woman toward marriage. For instance, a man and a woman may seek out marriage in order to satisfy the desire to have sexual intercourse in an orderly way, rather than having sex with diverse people randomly.[50] In this regard Lombard quotes 1 Corinthians 7:2, where Paul

---

49. Lombard, *The Sentences*, Book IV: *On the Doctrine of Signs*, Distinction XXX, ch. 3, p. 177. Cahall comments that for Lombard "marriage was instituted by the Lord before sin to serve the function of procreation, but . . . after sin it exists also as a remedy for concupiscence. Thus Lombard specified procreation and the avoidance of fornication respectively as the primary and secondary ends of marriage" (*The Mystery of Marriage*, 221). For further background to and discussion of Lombard's view of marriage, see Reynolds, *How Marriage Became One of the Sacraments*, 317-436. Reynolds provides valuable analysis of the understanding of marriage in the early twelfth century, pre-Lombard, anonymous sentential literature; and Reynolds also delves deeply into Lombard's contemporaries Hugh of Saint-Victor and Walter of Mortagne. For Lombard, as Reynolds says, "The chief reasons for marriage are the 'procreation of offspring' and the 'avoidance of fornication,' which correspond respectively to two of the three [Augustinian] goods of marriage: offspring and faith" (*How Marriage Became One of the Sacraments*, 429). Edward Schillebeeckx, O.P. points out that the early medieval theologians and canonists debated the question of what precisely constitutes a canonically valid marriage, not least given the fact that Mary and Joseph had a valid marriage without engaging in sexual intercourse. Schillebeeckx states that "the early schoolmen [such as Lombard] were very much concerned with the meaning of marriage as a human reality. And in this connection, too, there were the three distinct schools of thought . . . : the view that regarded marriage as a primarily sexual community; the second view that situated the essence of marriage in the interpersonal relationship of the partners of the marital community, which could be extended to sexual intercourse, but which nonetheless remained a full marriage—and indeed marriage in a very special and even sublime sense—even when sexuality played no part in it; and finally the third view, according to which marriage is regarded socially as the foundation of a human environment in which children could grow up. These three trends of thought certainly impinged upon each other at several points, but no synthesis was reached in the early period of scholasticism" (Schillebeeckx, *Marriage*, 293; see also Reynolds, *How Marriage Became One of the Sacraments*, 426-29). Schillebeeckx notes that Lombard placed the emphasis upon the man and woman's mutual consent as establishing a valid sacramental marriage.

50. See also Browning, *Marriage and Modernization*, 88.

teaches that "because of the temptation to immorality, each man should have his own wife and each woman her own husband." Among other relatively commonplace purposes for marriage his day, Lombard mentions the "reconciliation of enemies" (presumably feuding families or feuding royal houses) and "the beauty of the man or the woman, which often impels spirits enflamed with love to enter into marriage so that they may fulfil their desire."[51] Here he gives two biblical examples, Jacob's love for Rachel (which seemingly came about due to the fact that "Rachel was beautiful and lovely" [Gen 29:17]) and the permission given by Moses to the Israelites to the effect that if one of them sees "among the captives a beautiful woman" and has "desire for her," then he can take the woman as his wife (Deut 21:11). These secondary purposes involve reasons such as desire for sexual union, political peace, and love of physical beauty. All of these purposes, however—as Plato argues—can be accomplished in other ways than by marriage. It is procreation and the raising of children that *requires* the framework of marriage, as enabling the father to know who his children are and therefore be interested in caring for them.

Of course, Lombard does not limit the goal of marriage to procreation and the raising of children. As noted above, Aristotle recognizes that marriage helps to ensure a stable relationship between one man and one woman, by building up a thriving home; and Aristotle recognizes that marriage involves (or should involve) a friendship between the husband and the wife. Lombard describes a "threefold good of marriage, namely faith, offspring, and sacrament."[52] Since he draws this threefold good (as distinct from his theology of marriage as one of the seven sacraments) largely from Augustine, let me now move backward in time to describe briefly Augustine's theology of the threefold good of marriage.[53]

---

51. Lombard, *The Sentences*, Book IV, Distinction XXX, ch. 3, p. 17.

52. Lombard, *The Sentences*, Book IV, Distinction XXX, ch. 2, p. 176. Michael G. Lawler points out that with regard to "sacrament" (the third good of marriage), Lombard extends its meaning "beyond what Augustine intended. . . . For Augustine *sacramentum* was the commitment of the spouses to one another never to separate. For Lombard, it is a characteristic of the marriage, a characteristic that makes it an image of the union of Christ and the Church. A marriage between Christians, Lombard argues, can exist without the fidelity of the spouses; it can exist without offspring. But it cannot exist without the *sacramentum*, reflecting the union between Christ and the Church" (Lawler, *Marriage and Sacrament*, 91).

53. For a historical examination of the period between Augustine and Lombard—and thus of the mediation of Augustine's ideas to Lombard—see the lengthy treatment (noted above) in Reynolds's *How Marriage Became One of the Sacraments*.

Augustine

In his discussion of the development of Augustine's thought on marriage, Philip Reynolds observes: "Marriage is good, Augustine argues, because of its three benefits: faith, offspring, and sacrament. Augustine discovers the threefold structure of the goodness of marriage in the *De bono coniugali* [written c. 404 AD] and adheres to it thereafter."[54] Augustine holds that after the coming of Christ, procreation is not a duty for everyone, by contrast to what was the case prior to Christ's coming (see Genesis 1:28).[55] For a married couple, however, procreation (or openness to procreation) remains not only a duty but also a good.[56] Although Augustine is suspicious of fallen sexual desire, he thinks that marriage offers a salutary path for channeling such sexual desire, in accord with Paul's teaching in 1 Corinthians 7.[57] Reynolds concludes that for Augustine "the reason (*causa*) for marriage is the good of procreation: the begetting and rearing of children as members of the church, the body of Christ. In another sense, however, the proper reason for Christians to marry is not procreation but the remedy against

---

54. Reynolds, *How Marriage Became One of the Sacraments*, 108.

55. Carol Harrison argues that "though the celibate life will always be given a higher place by Augustine, the contrast with the married life will become less antithetic, to the point where the two can be seen as two different social identities which are yet characterized by the same ideals, the same goals, and the same temporal ambiguities" (Harrison, *Augustine*, 159). Harrison grants nonetheless that "patristic reflection on marriage tends to lurk in the dark shadows cast by the glorious ideal of virginity" (*Augustine*, 159).

56. See Reynolds, *How Marriage Became One of the Sacraments*, 108.

57. See Reynolds, *How Marriage Became One of the Sacraments*, 109. Augustine considers that marriage's role as a remedy for concupiscence is what generally prompts Christians to marry. For further discussion see Burke, "The 'Good' and the 'Bad' in Marriage" and "An R.I.P. for the *Remedium Concupiscentiae*." Burke's main point, with which Augustine would agree, is that if we are in a condition of real lust, we lack both the virtue of chastity and the virtue of charity. See also the superb discussion of Augustine on sex and marriage as well as the reception of Augustine's teachings on these topics over the centuries, in Dupont et al., "Sex." For clarifications regarding the "*remedium concupiscentiae*," see Vijgen, "The Intelligibility of Aquinas' Account"; and Crawford, *Marriage and the* Sequela Christi. Both Vijgen and Crawford note that the *remedium concupiscentiae* may be misunderstood to mean that "marriage is a kind of licit outlet for the proclivities resulting from concupiscence," whereas in fact the true meaning of the *remedium concupiscentiae* is that "marriage is a vocation to struggle with and defeat the effects of concupiscence" (*Marriage and the* Sequela Christi, 266). For an Eastern Orthodox perspective on marital sexuality that fits with the emphases of Vijgen and Crawford, see Muse, "Transfiguring 'Voluptuous Choice.'" For criticism of Augustine, see Brown, "Sexuality and Society."

lust.... But that does not imply that marriage has lost its essential relational to procreation."[58]

Regarding marriage's threefold good, Augustine's most influential work is his short anti-Pelagian treatise *On Marriage and Concupiscence* (*De nuptiis et concupiscentia*, written during 419-420).[59] In *On Marriage and Concupiscence*, Augustine identifies the "natural good of marriage" as "[t]he union ... of male and female for the purpose of procreation," inclusive of the raising of the child.[60] This is what distinguishes marriage from other forms of friendship and also from other frameworks in which the desire for sexual intercourse is satisfied. Augustine refers to the pairing of male and female birds and to their cooperation in building the nest, sitting on the eggs, and feeding the chicks. Humans who enter into marriage do so rationally, unlike birds, but the married couple, too, collaborates to raise the children in a shared home.

Augustine argues that procreation is the first good of marriage; this is the good of "fecundity" or "offspring."[61] He then describes fidelity (*fides*),

---

58. Reynolds, *How Marriage Became One of the Sacraments*, 120. It is noteworthy in this regard that, as Harrison points out, Augustine disputes Jerome's view that "a first marriage is a regrettable weakness"; for Augustine "marriage is good but virginity is better" (Harrison, *Augustine*, 160-61).

59. In this work, Augustine is defending his doctrine of the transmission of original sin (via sexual intercourse) against Julian of Eclanum's charge that Augustine's doctrine impugns marriage. See Reynolds, *How Marriage Became One of the Sacraments*, 113. For further background to and discussion of Augustine's theology of marriage, see Schmitt, *Le mariage Chrétien*; Hunter, *Marriage in the Early Church*; and Reynolds, *Marriage in the Western Church*—which offers valuable historical information despite Reynolds's polemicizing against indissolubility.

60. Augustine, *On Marriage and Concupiscence*, Book I, ch. 5, p. 265.

61. Augustine, *On Marriage and Concupiscence*, Book I, ch. 11, p. 268. For discussion of the interrelation of the three goods of marriage named by Augustine, see Cahill, "The Trinitarian Structure." Importantly, Augustine's interpretation of Genesis 1:28, and specifically of whether unfallen humans would have had sexual intercourse, changed early in the fifth century. Reynolds remarks, "In his *De Genesi contra Manichaeos* (388/389), Augustine defended the text [Gen 1:28] from Manichee criticism by applying the methods of spiritual interpretation that he had learned from Ambrose. The words that God spoke do not necessarily imply, he argues, that God commanded our first parents in Paradise to procreate sexually although they would take on that meaning after the fall, for one may interpret them spiritually as well as carnally.... Augustine's approach to the story of Adam and Eve changed radically during the first decade of the fifth century. Later, in the *Retractiones* (426/27), he would recall his interpretation of 'increase and multiply' in the *De Genesi contra Manichaeos* and categorically withdraw it" (*How Marriage Became One of the Sacraments*, 104-5). On Augustine's view of sex and the three goods of marriage, see also the brief sketch in Cahill, *Sex, Gender, and Christian Ethics*, 177-78, 187-88, in the context of her criticisms of the understanding of marriage doctrinally developed by the Catholic Church.

which he identifies as the second good of marriage. David Hunter points out the close link between Augustine's understanding of fidelity and marital chastity: "For Augustine fidelity is the commitment to engage in sexual relations only with one's spouse, and, therefore, to avoid adultery. But fidelity also involves the mutual responsibility of married persons to engage in sex with each other in order to relieve the pressure of sexual desire."[62] In Augustine's view, true fidelity or chastity can only arise from a living faith in the true God, since otherwise what one possesses is only the appearance of chastity due to fear of the temporal consequences of unchastity. This position fits with Augustine's general view that, given original sin, the seeming virtues of the pagans have good elements but cannot rise to the level of true virtue.[63] When the married couple possesses the good of fidelity, Augustine thinks, the married couple will live in harmonious unity. In light of the good of fidelity, he understands the marital relationship as "above all one of reciprocal friendship, fellowship, and love."[64]

The goods of procreation and fidelity are connected. As John Rist sums up Augustine's view, marriage is "a variety of friendship in which the sexual element is to the fore and is directly connected with children: babies are born in marriage 'from the parents' friendship' (*Sermon* 9.6.7)."[65]

For analyses that better assesses Augustine's context and task, see Waters, *The Family*, 18–23; Witte, *From Sacrament to Contract*, 65–75.

62. Hunter, "Marriage," 536.

63. See for example Wetzel, *Augustine and the Limits of Virtue*, 98–111. See also, with a broader perspective, Herdt, *Putting on Virtue*; Osborne, "The Augustinianism of Thomas Aquinas's Moral Theory"; Decosimo, *Ethics as a Work of Charity*.

64. Harrison, *Augustine*, 161. Arguing that Augustine is here christianizing the thought of Cicero, Harrison explains that "for Roman citizens, the ideal of *concordia* represented the highest expectation and greatest achievement of marriage—that the partners should live in harmony and unity, holding all things in common. *Concordia* in the family constituted the basis for harmony and unity in the city and in the State. As Cicero writes, 'The origin of society is in the joining (*coniugium*) of man and woman, next in children, then in the household (*una domus*), all things held in common; this is the foundation (*principium*) of the city and, so to speak, the seed-bed of the State (*seminarium rei publicae*)' [*De Officiis* 1.17.54]. In *On the Good of Marriage* Augustine takes over, and christianizes these ideas, describing a *concordia religiosa* (13.15). Referring to Acts 4:32—a text which will also be determinative of his description of the common monastic life—he suggests that the union of man and wife in marriage, with one heart and one mind towards God, signifies the unity of the heavenly city (18.21)" (Harrison, *Augustine*, 161). John M. Rist similarly affirms that for Augustine "marriage as a whole is a kind of friendship, and thus calls for affection and mutual companionship. Sexual behaviour has to be subordinated to that friendship" (Rist, *Augustine*, 197).

65. Rist, *Augustine*, 247.

Augustine identifies the third good of marriage as "a certain sacramental bond."[66] This good is described in Ephesians 5, which instructs husbands to love their wives as Christ loved the Church. For Augustine, the key aspect here is the indissolubility of the marriage bond.[67] The "sacrament" or "mystery" described in Ephesians 5:32 finds its proper meaning, according to Augustine, in Jesus' insistence in Matthew 19:8 (speaking to the Pharisees) that "[f]or your hardness of heart Moses allowed you to divorce your wives, but from the beginning it was not so." The "sacrament" is the Christological renewal of the meaning of marriage as it was intended to be "from the beginning."[68] Just as Christ will never dissolve his marriage with the Church, so also marriage, as it was intended to be from the beginning, cannot be dissolved. By his grace, Christ has ensured that this third good of marriage is now present once more, in addition to children and fidelity. Augustine explains that among Christians, therefore, "although women marry, and men take wives, for the purpose of procreating children, it is never permitted one to put away even an unfruitful wife for the sake of having another to bear children."[69]

In Augustine's day, of course, Roman law permitted easy divorce.[70] Against this, Augustine urges that for Christians even divorced and civilly remarried persons are looked upon as still married, in truth, to their living first partners. Such civilly re-married persons, Augustine says, are committing adultery. He draws this position from Jesus Christ's teachings in

66. Augustine, *On Marriage and Concupiscence*, Book I, ch. 11, p. 268.

67. Discussing Augustine on the three goods of marriage, Peter J. Elliott rightly clarifies: "We must be careful . . . not to equate it [the good of "sacrament"] with the second of the goods of Marriage, *fides*, as may happen if we apply our modern subjective understanding of 'commitment' to 'sacrament'" (Elliott, *What God Has Joined*, 79). Elliott is here criticizing Schillebeeckx's *Marriage*, 284.

68. See also La Bonnardière, "L'Interprétation augustinienne."

69. Augustine, *On Marriage and Concupiscence*, Book I, ch. 11, p. 268. Witte argues intriguingly that "Augustine's integrated understanding of the three goods of children, fidelity, and sacrament also highlighted three dimensions of marriage: the natural, the contractual, and the spiritual. For him, marriage is a natural institution, rooted in the created order and designed for the procreation of children. Marriage is a contractual institution, designed with a formal set of rights and duties that the couple needs to discharge faithfully. And marriage is a spiritual institution, modeled on the enduring mysterious covenant between Yahweh and Israel, Christ and his church. It was left to the medieval theologians and canonists, notably Thomas Aquinas, to bring these various goods and dimensions of marriage together into a more elaborate integration centered on marriage as a sacrament" (Witte, *From Sacrament to Contract*, 74-75).

70. For discussion of marriage and divorce in Greco-Roman thought and practice, see Treggiari, *Roman Marriage*. Both men and women had the right to divorce in the classical period of Rome, whereas in early Roman history divorce was more strictly limited and could only be initiated by the husband.

Matthew 19 (and parallels) and also from the teachings of Paul in 1 Corinthians 7.[71] With regard to marriage's good of "sacrament," Augustine holds that there is always (in Harrison's words) "an enduring marital 'thing' which survives the breakdown of marital relations, just as the 'sacramentum fidei' of baptism survives apostasy."[72]

John Chrysostom

In a homily on marriage, Chrysostom reflects upon Genesis 2:24, "Therefore a man leaves his father and his mother and cleaves to his wife, and they become one flesh." He asks how it is that a man and woman become "one body" or "one flesh," and he answers that it happens through procreation.[73] He explains that God, having divided human nature into male and female, "made it impossible for either half to procreate without the other" and thereby ensured that "children would be produced from a single source," namely the (married) couple.[74] No matter whether or not a child is conceived, the man and woman's sexual "intercourse effects the joining of their bodies, and they are made one."[75] Chrysostom stands amazed at what this unity can accomplish. He depicts the procreative process in poetic terms: "As if she were gold receiving the purest of gold, the woman receives the man's seed with rich pleasure, and within her it is nourished, cherished, and refined. It is mingled with her own substance and she then returns it as a child!"[76]

Achieving such a great thing as the production of a human child is indeed a work of true unity, a work that unites the couple in an extraordinary

---

71. For the development of Augustine's position in this regard, and for examination of other patristic views (as well as historical-critical exegesis of the relevant biblical texts), see my *The Indissolubility of Marriage*. See also, on Jesus' absolute rejection of divorce and remarriage, Collins, *What Are Biblical Values?*, 98–99.

72. Harrison, *Augustine*, 166, citing *On Marriage and Concupiscence*, Book I, ch. 10.

73. For contemporary inquiry into the same question, see Pruss, *One Body*; Girgis, Anderson, and George, *What Is Marriage?*, chapter 2. See also, for a specific focus on Pope John Paul II's theology of the body, Perez-Lopez, *Procreation*.

74. Chrysostom, "Homily 12: On Colossians 4:18," 75. In her Introduction to this volume, Catherine P. Roth compares Chrysostom's *On Virginity* with his homilies on Ephesians: "St. John seems to have changed the views which he expressed in his early treatise 'On Virginity.' There he said that God did not create man for marriage before the fall, whereas here he emphasizes the unity of Adam and Eve" (Roth, "Introduction" to *On Marriage and Family Life*, 7–24, at 17). Occasionally, Roth and Anderson have abridged the original sermons.

75. Chrysostom, "Homily 12," 76.

76. Chrysostom, "Homily 12," 76.

task. In sexual intercourse, the man and woman's bodies are intimately united (in accord with the relational fit of male penis and female vagina) whether or not a child is conceived, but the conception of a child displays the unity even more strongly. As Chrysostom says, "[t]he child is a bridge connecting mother and father" by uniting, in his or her person, the mother and father as permanently "one flesh."[77] The child contains the flesh of the father and the flesh of the mother, now joined inseparably. No wonder, then, that procreation is a great good of marriage.

Chrysostom also presents fidelity (or chastity) as a good of marriage, although he does not explicitly set forth three "goods" in the way that Augustine does. Chrysostom complains that at wedding celebrations, drunkenness and immodesty often take over, complete with "dancing girls" and such-like.[78] He bemoans the singing of songs devoted to "adultery, corruption of marriages, illicit loves, unlawful unions, and many other impious and shameful themes."[79] The problem is not that marriage involves sexual intercourse, which he has already praised in eloquent terms. The problem is that sexual intercourse will lead to division if chastity is not also valued. Chrysostom comments, "Marriage was not instituted for wantonness or fornication, but for chastity. Listen to what Paul says: 'Because of the temptation to immorality, each man should have his own wife and each woman her own husband.'"[80]

It is in this context that Chrysostom identifies two ends or purposes of marriage. He states that "[t]hese are the two purposes for which marriage was instituted: to make us chaste, and to make us parents."[81] He focuses on the way that marriage limits the bounds within which we pursue the fulfillment of sexual desire; marriage "sets a limit to desire by teaching us to keep to one wife [or one husband]."[82] For Chrysostom, "chastity takes precedence" among the two purposes, at least after Christ has come.[83] He gives two explanations for why the good of chastity or fidelity now takes precedence over the actual procreation of children. First, thanks to human obedience to the commandment to "be fruitful and multiply," there are today many humans in the world. There is thus no reason for taking another wife

77. Chrysostom, "Homily 12," 76.
78. Chrysostom, "Homily 12," 78.
79. Chrysostom, "Sermon on Marriage," 82.
80. Chrysostom, "Sermon on Marriage," 85.
81. Chrysostom, "Sermon on Marriage," 85.
82. Chrysostom, "Sermon on Marriage," 85.
83. Chrysostom, "Sermon on Marriage," 85. See Reynolds, *How Marriage Became One of the Sacraments*, 129.

(or having sexual intercourse with a servant, as Abraham did with Sarah's encouragement—an act whose virtuousness is defended by Chrysostom[84]) when one's wife is infertile. The same point holds for a woman who might otherwise seek another man if her husband were unable to beget children. To be married but childless is no longer a disgrace, because the most important thing is chastity or fidelity, rather than actually conceiving children. Second, prior to the coming of Christ and hope for bodily resurrection, men and women longed for children as a way of perpetuating their own lives and families upon the earth. Since Jesus has risen from the dead, there is no longer the urgent need to ensure that we have descendents in order for us to have a future. Marriage, however, helps to ensure that the act of sexual intercourse takes place in a well-ordered way, for the good of the man and woman and their children. On this basis, Chrysostom argues that today the fundamental reason for marrying is "to avoid fornication."[85]

With regard to the second purpose—the procreation and raising of children—Chrysostom recognizes that marriage is "a mystery of the Church" and "an image of the presence of Christ."[86] Chrysostom places mutual love at the center of this mystery, and he shows how this relates to the good of children. He states, "The love of husband and wife is the force that welds society together. . . . [W]hen harmony prevails, the children are raised well, the household is kept in order, and neighbors, friends and relatives praise the result. Great benefits, both for families and states, are thus produced."[87] In his homilies on Ephesians 5 and 6, Chrysostom instructs married couples about how to bear witness to the love of Christ. He urges husbands to call their wives not only by their names alone but also "with terms of endearment, honor, and love."[88] While accepting Paul's insistence that "the husband is the head of the wife as Christ is the head of the church" (Eph 5:23)—and thus accepting that husbands and wives are unequal in authority—Chrysostom underlines the point that no good Christian marriage can be a power struggle. On the contrary, he urges the husband to humble himself radically, and to tell his wife sincerely, "I have nothing of my own," that is to say nothing that does not belong to the wife.[89] The husband must sincerely say to his wife: "I am yours!"[90]

---

84. See Chrysostom, "Homily 20," 57, 59.
85. Chrysostom, "Sermon on Marriage," 86.
86. Chrysostom, "Sermon on Marriage," 77.
87. Chrysostom, "Homily 20," 44.
88. Chrysostom, "Homily 20," 63.
89. Chrysostom, "Homily 20," 63.
90. Chrysostom, "Homily 20," 63.

Indeed, for Chrysostom, marriage should be the greatest friendship. He affirms, "There is no relationship between human beings so close as that of husband and wife, if they are united as they ought to be."[91] Because this is so, he exhorts husbands, "Let us therefore painstakingly care for our wives and children."[92]

III. Pope Pius XI, Dietrich von Hildebrand, and Cormac Burke on Marriage's Ends

The above patristic and medieval background has exhibited the main lines of the Church's theological tradition regarding the ends and goods of marriage. However, by the early twentieth century, Catholic discussions of marriage sometimes focused simply on marriage's status as a permanent society contracted by the partners for the procreation of children and as a remedy for concupiscence, to the seeming neglect of the mutual love about which Chrysostom spoke eloquently and which Augustine identified especially with "sacrament."[93]

To solve this problem, in the 1920s Dietrich von Hildebrand argued for mutual love as marriage's primary "meaning," distinct from procreation as marriage's primary "purpose." Von Hildebrand's position became known as the "personalist" view of marriage. His work had an impact upon the encyclical on marriage published by Pope Pius XI in 1930, *Casti Connubii*. Although the encyclical was precipitated by the Anglican Church's decision to permit contraception, the encyclical sought to offer a full theology of marriage. *Casti Connubii* therefore deserves brief attention before I discuss von Hildebrand's work.

Pope Pius XI's Casti Connubii

In *Casti Connubii*, Pope Pius XI proclaims: "From God comes the very institution of marriage, the ends for which it was instituted, the laws that govern it, the blessings that flow from it; while man, through generous surrender of his own person made to another for the whole span of life, becomes with the help and cooperation of God, the author of each particular marriage."[94]

---

91. Chrysostom, "Homily 20," 43.
92. Chrysostom, "Homily 20," 58.
93. For background see Cahall, *The Mystery of Marriage*, 253–57; Shivanandan, *Crossing the Threshold of Love*, 199.
94. Pius XI, *Casti Connubii*, p. 7. For background, see Handren, *No Longer Two*;

He appreciates the self-surrender that grounds marriage and makes it an act of love toward the other person. He observes that in marriage "the souls of the contracting parties are joined and knit together more directly and more intimately than are their bodies."[95] They are knit together not by the emotion of love, but by love as an act of the rational will, permanently establishing a "union of souls" through the free surrendering of each person to the other.[96]

Citing Augustine, Pius XI then examines the three goods of Christian marriage: children, conjugal fidelity, and the sacrament. He first treats children, and here he points out that begetting children is inextricably linked with raising and educating the children. Second, he treats conjugal fidelity, by which he has in view both marital chastity (preeminently the avoidance of adultery and the giving of the marital debt) and "the love of husband and wife."[97] It is here that he celebrates Christ's selfless and "boundless love" for the Church.[98] With the love of husband and wife in view, he remarks that their mutual "effort to perfect each other, can in a very real sense, as the Roman Catechism teaches, be said to be the chief reason and purpose of matrimony, provided matrimony be looked at not in the restricted sense as instituted for the proper conception and education of the child, but more widely as the blending of life as a whole."[99]

After describing the first two goods—children and conjugal fidelity (inclusive of chastity and love)—he presents the third good, namely the sacrament. In fact, he indicates that the sacrament in a certain sense has the highest place. He states that "this accumulation of benefits [through conjugal fidelity] is completed and, as it were, crowned by that blessing of

---

Petri, *Aquinas and the Theology of the Body*, 46–51. Petri notes that "Pius XI's attempt to articulate the importance of the spouses' life of love, even as he was committed to the terminology of primary and secondary ends, was just the beginning of a shift to an emphasis on the personalist value of marriage" (*Aquinas and the Theology of the Body*, 51).

95. Pius XI, *Casti Connubii*, p. 6.
96. Pius XI, *Casti Connubii*, p. 6.
97. Pius XI, *Casti Connubii*, p. 13.
98. Pius XI, *Casti Connubii*, p. 13.
99. Pius XI, *Casti Connubii*, p. 14. Arguably, the distinction that von Hildebrand makes between "end" and "meaning" is paralleled by Pius XI through his distinction between marriage in the "restricted sense" and marriage viewed "more widely" (in light of the teaching of Ephesians 5). I note also that Pius XI has in view a Catholic couple in which both spouses have living faith and charity. On the topic of whether "a conscious, deliberate assent to the truths of faith in one or more of the spouses-to-be [is] a requirement for a valid celebration of the sacrament of marriage," see especially Schindler et al., "Faith and the Sacrament of Marriage," 309; Welch and Cahall, "An Examination of the Role of Faith."

Christian marriage which in the words of St. Augustine we have called the sacrament."[100] He explains that what he means by "the sacrament" is the indissolubility restored to marriage by Christ. This indissolubility makes of marriage "an efficacious sign of grace," because the sacrament enables the married couple to manifest the utterly indissoluble bond between Christ and his Church, as indicated in Ephesians 5.[101]

Certainly, Pius XI thinks that natural marriage should generally be indissoluble. He remarks, "in matrimony provision has been made in the best possible way" for the raising and education of children, "for, since the parents are bound together by an indissoluble bond, the care and mutual help of each is always at hand."[102] Even as a "natural" institution, marriage always involves in itself an indissoluble bond, even if the bond of "natural marriages between unbelievers" can in certain instances be set aside due to the baptism of one of the spouses (the Pauline Privilege).[103] With regard to the indissolubility of marriages between Christians, Pope Pius reaffirms the solemn teaching of the Church that, because it is God who has joined these marriages, not even a determination of the Church "can ever affect for any cause whatsoever a Christian marriage which is valid and has been consummated."[104] The key point is that this is not merely an external command; rather, the sacramental grace of marriage enables the couple to live out their indissoluble marriage in a sanctifying manner.[105]

In Pius XI's enumeration of the three goods of marriage, each of these goods can be described, from a certain angle, as the crown of marriage. Yet,

---

100. Pius XI, *Casti Connubi*, p. 17.
101. Pius XI, *Casti Connubi*, p. 17.
102. Pius XI, *Casti Connubi*, p. 11.
103. Pius XI, *Casti Connubi*, p. 19.
104. Pius XI, *Casti Connubi*, p. 19.

105. See Pius XI, *Casti Connubi*, p. 21. Citing canon law, Pius XI adds that "the sacramental nature is so intimately bound up with Christian wedlock that there can be no true marriage between baptized persons 'without it being by that very fact a sacrament.' By the very fact, therefore, that the faithful with sincere mind give such consent, they open up for themselves a treasure of sacramental grace from which they draw supernatural power for the fulfilling of their rights and duties faithfully, holily, perseveringly even unto death.... Nevertheless, since it is a law of divine Providence in the supernatural order that men do not reap the full fruit of the sacraments which they receive after acquiring the use of reason unless they cooperate with grace, the grace of matrimony will remain for the most part an unused talent hidden in the field unless the parties exercise these supernatural powers and cultivate and develop the seeds of grace they have received. If, however, doing all that lies within their power, they cooperate diligently, they will be able with ease to bear the burdens of their state and to fulfill their duties" (Pius XI, *Casti Connubi*, pp. 22–23).

he also points out that the first-named good—procreation and the raising of children—constitutes the primary end of marriage.

Dietrich von Hildebrand

Why, however, should marriage's primary end or purpose (or "ordering") be the procreation and raising of children? Why cannot a man and a woman (or, for that matter, two people) join together in marriage primarily for the purpose of cultivating their mutual love?

Some nineteenth- and early twentieth-century Catholic scholars insisted upon the centrality of love for defining the nature of marriage.[106] For example, in 1850 Ferdinand Probst published a multi-volume *Katholische Moraltheologie*, in which he includes the procreative end within the primary purpose of marriage, which he identifies as the communion in love (or shared life) of the married couple.[107] Similarly, Franz Xaver von Linsenmann's 1878 *Lehrbuch der Moraltheologie* emphasized the spiritual and moral purpose of marriage, giving this purpose priority over the procreative end.[108] Many German Catholic theologians adopted this approach in the 1930s, among them Fidelis Schwendinger, Norbert Rochell, Ernst Michel, Hermann Muchermann, Bernadin Krempel, and Herbert Doms.

When Herbert Doms's *Vom Sinn und Zweck der Ehe* (On the Meaning and End of Marriage) appeared in 1935, it ignited a controversy that eventually resulted in Pope Pius XII's 1944 reaffirmation (through a decree and a *responsio ad dubium* issued by the Roman Rota[109]) of the traditional view

---

106. See Glombik, *"Zweieinigkeit."* John T. Noonan has argued that in von Hildebrand's work, one finds that "for the first time, a Catholic writer taught that love was a requirement for lawful, marital coition. He tied this novel demand to an ancient term—*fides*, fidelity. Fidelity required that person meet person in a giving of self" (Noonan, *Contraception*, 495). This exaggerates the novelty of von Hildebrand's approach, not only with regard to his predecessors in the century before him, but also with regard to the patristic-medieval insistence upon charity (or at least natural love) as necessary for good interpersonal actions.

107. See Probst, *Katholische Moraltheologie*, vol. 2, 180; see Glombik, *"Zweieinigkeit,"* 81.

108. See Mackin, *What Is Marriage?*, 226. Mackin also draws attention to Koch's 1905 *Lehrbuch der Moraltheologie*, which prioritizes the married couple's communion of life (in mutual love, moral purity, and sacramental or spiritual growth). See Koch, *Lehrbuch der Moraltheologie*.

109. See the January 22, 1944 decree in *Acta Apostolicae Sedis* 36 (1944): 179–200, the relevant portions of which are translated into English in Liebard, ed., *Love and Sexuality*, 71–83; and the April 1, 1944 *responsio ad dubium* in *Acta Apostolicae Sedis* 36 (1944): 103. Petri summarizes: "The document clarifies the meaning of the word 'end' (*finis*) in the church's language about marriage. When the word *finis* is used in

of "the procreation and education of children as the primary end" of marriage.[110] Doms credited von Hildebrand's 1929 book *Die Ehe* with inspiring his own. Yet for Doms, unlike von Hildebrand, "the one immediate goal of intercourse—its first value—is the union of the spouses with two ulterior goals, their fulfillment as persons and the conception of a child. Procreation is only the primary end of marriage from the point of view of society."[111]

Von Hildebrand's *Die Ehe* was translated into English in 1942, and for this new edition von Hildebrand provided a Preface. In the Preface, he emphasizes that the philosophical and cultural context in which he originally wrote *Die Ehe* was marked by an "anti-personalism" for which humans are primarily "biological" realities.[112] Specifically, he mentions the danger of

---

canon law, it 'is taken in a technical sense and means a benefit which is meant to be obtained both on the part of nature and by the deliberate intention of the agent.' Following traditional Thomistic language, the decree goes on to speak of both a *finis operis* and a *finis operantis* in marriage. The *finis operis* in marriage 'is that good (*bonum*) which matrimony tends of its very nature to obtain, and which God the Creator gave to the institution of matrimony.' The *finis operantis* is that which the person intends in any action. This is the subjective aspect of marriage, why people choose to marry, and can be as varied as the couples themselves: personal fulfillment, a desire for a family, economic advantage, etc. The secondary ends mentioned in the Code of Canon Law—mutual help and the remedy for concupiscence—are each also a *finis operis*, but they are secondary ends *contingent* upon the primary end of procreation and the education of children. The procreation and education of children cannot properly be carried out without the mutual life of the spouses and a remedy for concupiscence" (Petri, *Aquinas and the Theology of the Body*, 55–56).

110. Cahall, *The Mystery of Marriage*, 260. See Doms, *Von Sinn und Zweck der Ehe*. This book appeared in English as Doms, *The Meaning of Marriage*. For Doms's critique of von Hildebrand's position, see Grabowski, "Person or Nature?" For discussion of Doms's perspective, see also Petri, *Aquinas and the Theology of the Body*, 53–55.

111. Shivanandan, *Crossing the Threshold of Marriage*, 201. Shivanandan cites Doms, *The Meaning of Marriage*, 83–97, and Mackin, *What Is Marriage?*, 230–35.

112. Dietrich von Hildebrand, *Marriage*, xxv. See also von Hildebrand, *In Defense of Purity*, originally published in German in 1927. I focus here on *Marriage*, since its influence was greater. In *In Defense of Purity*, 12–13, von Hildebrand unites the physical and spiritual meanings of the sexual act in a passage with which I fully agree and which merits quotation here: "the act of marriage signifies the mysterious creation of a new human being. It is no chance that God has invested that act with this creative significance. As God's love is the creative principle in the universe, so love is everywhere creation, and there is a profound significance in the nexus—at once symbol and reality—whereby from the creative act—in which two become one flesh from love and in love—the new human being proceeds.... Here also we can do justice to the significance of this mysterious process only if we take the union of love into full account. It is possible to gauge in its fullness and depth the sublimity of the connection between sex and the origin of a new human being, or to recognize all that is implied by the fact that it is no mere living thing, but a man, who comes into existence, if only we already understand the peculiar relationship that subsists between physical sex and wedded love. Sex, however, is a mystery, even apart from the fact that it is the source from which a

biological materialism, which deprives humans of freedom and turns marriage into a mere means for biological survival and reproduction. Without referring explicitly to the theological manuals of the early twentieth century, but in language whose application was clear, von Hildebrand warns against a situation in which "[h]uman life is considered exclusively from a biological point of view and biological principles are the measure by which all human activities are judged."[113] To avoid this situation, he proposes that reflection upon marriage should distinguish between marriage's "primary end," namely procreation, and marriage's "primary meaning," namely "the intimate union of two persons in mutual love."[114]

What are the consequences of distinguishing the "primary end" from the "primary meaning" of marriage? How can "meaning" and "end" be distinguished so that both remain "primary," without inevitably placing one or the other in a secondary position? Various scholars, including Geoffrey Grubb, Rolando Arjonillo, and Kevin Schemenauer, have emphasized that von Hildebrand's approach does not unseat the traditional order of the ends of marriage.[115] Indeed, Schemenauer holds that "von Hildebrand's treatment of conjugal love clarifies and enhances procreation's role in marriage."[116] Yet, he grants that "von Hildebrand does not offer a developed notion of the God-entrusted spousal mission to have and raise children," and he also finds that for von Hildebrand "conjugal love is the authentic motivation for and vitality of marriage."[117]

In his 1942 Preface, von Hildebrand contends that an understanding of the greatness of married love "is beginning to grow in different countries, and moral theologians are emphasizing the role of love in marriage, a role which was previously underestimated by some."[118] Previously, he thinks, the emphasis on the procreative end for defining marriage led to a

---

new human being proceeds. In its purely qualitative aspect also a mysterious character attaches ... to sex. That is sufficiently proved by its depth, centrality, and intimacy. In this domain man is faced at every turn by mystery. He surrenders himself after a unique fashion—encounters either the mystery of wedded love or the mystery of a terrible sin. Either the mysterious union of two human beings takes place in the sight of God (*in conspectu Dei*) or man flings himself away, surrenders his secret, delivers himself over to the flesh, desecrates and violates the secret of another, severs himself in a mysterious fashion from God."

113. Von Hildebrand, *Marriage*, xxv.

114. Von Hildebrand, *Marriage*, xxv.

115. See Grubb, *The Anthropology of Marriage*; Arjonillo, *Conjugal Love*; Schemenauer, *Conjugal Love and Procreation*.

116. Schemenauer, *Conjugal Love and Procreation*, xv.

117. Schemenauer, *Conjugal Love and Procreation*, xv–xvi.

118. Von Hildebrand, *Marriage*, xxvi.

theological inability to see the centrality of love for the actual meaning of a real marriage. He credits *Casti Connubii* for referencing (as noted above) "a passage of the Roman Catechism in which conjugal love is considered as the ultimate meaning of marriage."[119]

Investigating what makes marriage so great in the order of salvation, von Hildebrand suggests that God singles out marriage because of the role of mutual love in marriage.[120] Again, however, if love is marriage's reason for being, then how can the procreative end of marriage be the primary end? This question is intensified when von Hildebrand argues that marriage is not distinguished from other friendships specifically by its ordering to sexual intercourse and children. He considers that "quite independent of sensuality, conjugal love in itself constitutes a completely new kind of love. It involves a unique mutual giving of one's self, which is the outstanding characteristic of this type of love."[121] He seeks to define a unique "conjugal love," *unavailable* to other forms of friendship or human communion, without reference to sexual intercourse that possesses a procreative end. Yet, how could there be a "completely new kind of love" that involves "a unique mutual giving of one's self" and that is available *only* to the male-female married couple, unless we make reference to procreation?

Without raising such questions explicitly, von Hildebrand argues that marriage is unique, distinguished from all other possible human bonds of love, because in marriage alone "[n]ot only the heart but the entire personality is given up to the other."[122] By the "entire personality," he means the fact that a married couple consents to belong to each other "in an entirely exclusive manner."[123] As he sees it, no other human bond of love can rightly involve such self-surrender. In marrying, one consents to belong to one's spouse; one surrenders to one's spouse everything that one has. It is not simply a matter of walking "side by side" with shared interests or common decision-making.[124] Rather, it is a face-to-face immersion of one person in another. More profoundly than any other I-thou relationship between creatures, this mutually exclusive immersion in each other constitutes a total self-dispossession. Von Hildebrand states that "in the realm of created goods, conjugal love means living *for* one another," making the spouse "the

119. Von Hildebrand *Marriage*, xxvi.

120. Von Hildebrand calls love "the center and core" of marriage (*Marriage*, 5).

121. Von Hildebrand, *Marriage*, 7. I note that von Hildebrand's philosophy often parts ways rather decisively with Aristotle and Thomas Aquinas; see Waldstein's "Dietrich von Hildebrand and St. Thomas."

122. Von Hildebrand, *Marriage*, 8.

123. Von Hildebrand, *Marriage*, 8.

124. Von Hildebrand, *Marriage*, 9.

center of our life (as far as created goods are concerned)."[125] A particular man chooses this particular woman (and vice versa), and henceforth his (or her) interests and concerns are bound up in the particular one he (or she) has chosen, with an exclusive love. The spouses see into each other's very core, with an intimacy that no other human love possesses. Von Hildebrand states that "in natural conjugal love the real individuality of the partner is mysteriously revealed. The deep, secret meaning which permeates all his gifts and talents, the whole rhythm of his being, is disclosed at one glance through all his imperfections."[126]

Why, however, cannot two men who love each other not achieve the same kind of utterly exclusive and intimate love? Von Hildebrand is aware of this issue. He insists that the unique conjugal love that he has described, distinct though it is from "sexual relations," can in fact "only come into being between men and women and not between persons of the same sex."[127] He rejects reducing "conjugal love" to "friendship plus sexual relations, presupposing a difference of sex."[128] In such a case, he thinks, the character of the marital friendship would be equated with other friendships, and the real differentiation would consist in the male-female sexual relations within the friendship. This would mean that the differentiating character of the *love* is not appreciated. Von Hildebrand urges in this regard, "It would be incredibly superficial to consider as a mere biological difference the distinction between man and woman."[129] Instead, what we need to see is that man and woman are "two complementary types of the spiritual person of the human species."[130]

To my mind, two problems with von Hildebrand's argument arise here. First, it is difficult to demonstrate (to those who already doubt one's premises) that the "male" type of "spiritual person" is always a biological man. If it is simply a matter of differentiating "spiritual persons," then perhaps there could be a possibility of finding a man and a man, or a woman and a woman, who are sufficiently differentiated "spiritual persons." At least, by abstracting from male-female sexual relations, von Hildebrand has made it more difficult to argue against this possibility.

Second, when he criticizes the view that "conjugal love is just friendship plus sexual relations," von Hildebrand's phrase "friendship plus" is

125. Von Hildebrand, *Marriage*, 10.
126. Von Hildebrand, *Marriage*, 12.
127. Von Hildebrand, *Marriage*, 13.
128. Von Hildebrand, *Marriage*, 13.
129. Von Hildebrand, *Marriage*, 13.
130. Von Hildebrand, *Marriage*, 13.

questionable. In a marriage, are not the male-female sexual relations in some way intrinsic to the friendship? Given the goodness of sexual intercourse, we might suppose that it elevates the intimacy of the friendship and thereby in certain ways distinguishes and transforms the friendship, rather than supposing that it is a mere add-on to the friendship ("friendship plus sexual relations").

In short, I see no need to ground the distinctiveness of the marital friendship in the spiritual complementarity of the man and the woman as *spiritual persons*. The man and woman's biological sexual desire and intercourse also characterize the intimacy of their uniquely marital form of friendship. If so, then the procreative *end*, found in the act of sexual intercourse, is intrinsic to the constitutive *meaning* of marriage.

In my view, von Hildebrand unconsciously opens himself up to the later misuse of his thought by Todd Salzmann and Michael Lawler, who cite him approvingly in order to deny the teleological significance of "the *biological* structure of men and women" for identifying "the primary end of *human* marriage," and who also drive a sharp wedge between "one's body" and "one's very self."[131] The key is that von Hildebrand minimizes the "sexual sphere" and "sexual relations" by locating "[t]he special character of conjugal love" in the mutual dispossession of complementary spiritual persons, abstracted from the bodily act of sexual intercourse. The result is that sexual intercourse, with its bodily (and thus biological) procreative end, is no longer seen as constitutive to the "meaning" of marital love. The "end" and "meaning" are here marked off from each other in a mistaken manner.

Von Hildebrand presses his point further by remarking that "man and woman represent two different types of mankind, both having their respective significance according to the divine plan, and their special value quite apart from their procreative function."[132] I grant that man and woman are "two different types of mankind"—even if this difference can be easily exaggerated (in this regard Plato was certainly correct!)—but why the emphasis on "quite apart from their procreative function"? Certainly, to be a man or a woman, one does not need to procreate. But why not admit that the "procreative function" in many ways shapes male and female bodies, informing maleness and femaleness at a fundamental level? In fact, "procreative function" is intrinsic to the meaning of "man" and "woman."

Von Hildebrand goes on to invoke the Virgin Mary as the highest woman, as though this meant that "woman" (and thus also "man") should be defined in a spiritual manner "quite apart from . . . procreative function." But

---

131. Salzman and Lawler, *Sexual Ethics*, 30–31.
132. Von Hildebrand, *Marriage*, 13–14.

I do not see why this should be the case. Why not recognize "woman" to be a bodily-spiritual reality, in which case the "procreative function," though not in the Virgin Mary's case the procreative *action*, will have bodily-spiritual effects? The key, in my view, is not to set aside the "procreative function" as a merely "biological" reality. The procreative function belongs to the bodily-spiritual unity of the person and therefore has a bodily-spiritual *meaning* rather than being simply a mechanism for a merely bodily *end*. The bodily end (procreation) is never solely bodily, but always bodily-spiritual.

Von Hildebrand considers it best to differentiate man and woman metaphysically rather than biologically. He states that "the difference between man and woman is a metaphysical one," and he speculates that it is possible to divide even the angels into male and female.[133] As spiritual "types," and so "purely as spiritual persons," man and woman complement each other in marital unity.[134] Again, I find doubtful this emphasis on "purely as spiritual persons." The line between the "spiritual" and the "biological" in human beings is being drawn too sharply. Continuing along the same lines, von Hildebrand holds that the marital union is completed by the "full spiritual grasping of the beloved person, in which the charm of the other being is completely unfolded, the full bliss of the *I-thou* community realized."[135] This does not mean that he supposes that marriage should have no sexual relations. But he contends that if marriage is not rooted first in the (asexual) relationship of the complementary spiritual persons, then the marriage relationship will be vulnerable to selfish "sensuality" when the married couple touches upon "the sphere of sexuality."[136]

On this basis, von Hildebrand describes marital love—the self-dispossession of the complementary spiritual persons—as "the bridge" to the sexual sphere.[137] Without this *asexual* bridge, the sexual sphere (which he also terms the "sensual sphere") would not be fitted for true friendship.[138] He argues that defining marriage in terms of complementary spiritual persons ensures that marriage is not tainted with self-interest by contact with the sexual sphere. Because of the mutual self-dispossession of the complementary spiritual persons, married love in itself is spiritual rather than being "a compound of friendship and sensuality," which would be "repugnant"

---

133. Von Hildebrand, *Marriage*, 14.
134. Von Hildebrand, *Marriage*, 15.
135. Von Hildebrand, *Marriage*, 15.
136. Von Hildebrand, *Marriage*, 19.
137. Von Hildebrand, *Marriage*, 19.
138. Von Hildebrand, *Marriage*, 19.

and "discordant" as "a juxtaposition of heterogeneous elements."[139] Here again I find a troubling disjunction between the spiritual and the bodily in marriage.

Von Hildebrand goes on to suggest that because married love in itself is not bound together with sexuality, married love is able to sanctify sexuality. He reiterates that married love means that the "man and woman . . . give themselves to one another in the deepest sense of the word and belong to each other in an intimate interpenetration of their souls."[140] Once this has happened on the spiritual level—once married love (the "meaning" of marriage) has been established—then sexuality too can be recognized as itself having "sublime meaning . . . in the union of two beings in a complete spiritual-sensual union according to the words of our Lord and Savior Jesus Christ: 'And they shall be two in one flesh.'"[141] Once married love has been defined as asexual self-dispossession of two complementary spiritual persons, then sexuality ("complete spiritual-sensual union") can be enacted by the married couple in a manner that is sanctifying, because it embodies their already existing spiritual union. The troubling disjunction is fully apparent here.

At the same time, von Hildebrand makes clear that marriage is not a subjective reality that dissolves whenever "conjugal love" is not subjectively present. As an objective state of life, marriage requires a solemn and formal "act of the will" by which "the two partners give themselves expressly to each other, fully sanctioning this surrender for their entire lifetime"; and as a state of life, marriage "is fully actualized" when the two spouses, having solemnized their spiritual self-dispossession by their formal act of will, proceed to "consummate this surrender in bodily union."[142] Von Hildebrand emphasizes that it is impossible that marriage, as a state of life, can dissolve due to some later deficiency in married love. Marriage is an "objective bond" that possesses "objective validity"; once it has been "established, it persists as such, regardless of the sentiments or attitudes of the partners."[143]

He goes on to make clear that it is the mutual voluntary self-surrender to the other person, solemnized and made permanent in the formal marriage vow, that constitutes the marriage. It is this (spiritual) marriage vow that ensures that "[t]he union desired in conjugal love"—which he defines as a spiritual reality that forms a bridge to the sexual sphere—"becomes . . .

139. Von Hildebrand, *Marriage*, 19.
140. Von Hildebrand, *Marriage*, 19.
141. Von Hildebrand, *Marriage*, 19.
142. Von Hildebrand, *Marriage*, 21–22.
143. Von Hildebrand, *Marriage*, 22–23.

objectively real in its fullest sense," with the meaning that the "partners now belong wholly to each other."[144] This radical spiritual change, brought about by the free spiritual act of self-surrender to one's complementary spiritual person, leads to a bodily expression. He explains that the "decisive character of marriage . . . has a qualitative analogy in bodily surrender."[145] Although the sexual/bodily aspect is not present in the definition of married love or in the free vow that constitutes the marriage, the later sexual/bodily aspect expresses, analogously, what has first taken place spiritually in the marital vows of mutual surrender. He states, "The physical union of husband and wife constitutes such an ultimate intimacy between them that of its essence it is a surrender valid once and for all."[146] He grants that just as the primary meaning of marriage is a communion of self-dispossessing love, so also the primary meaning of sexual intercourse within marriage is self-dispossessing love.

Von Hildebrand accepts that "the meaning of physical consummation is not restricted to its function as a means of procreation."[147] While the procreative end of sexual intercourse undeniably belongs within the meaning of sexual actions, "this primary *end* is not the only *meaning* of the physical act. Subjectively speaking, it is not even its primary meaning. Its *meaning* is primarily the realization of the sublime communion of love," in a one-flesh union.[148] Of course, the secondary place of procreation does not imply that it is nothing. On the contrary, von Hildebrand holds that mutual self-dispossession, precisely as a spiritual attitude, does not allow for frustrating the procreative mystery built into the act by God himself. The act of surrendering oneself to one's spouse cannot include negating part of the bodily gift that each spouse should give to the other. He adds that a marriage in which the couple are unable to have children, due to a physical impairment, retains its ability to express self-dispossessing marital love and certainly can continue to express this through the physical act of sexual intercourse.[149] In his view, this shows again that even if sexual intercourse's "primary *end*" is procreation, nonetheless "the primary *meaning* of bodily union lies in the fulfillment of conjugal love."[150] Not childlessness, therefore, but infidelity

144. Von Hildebrand, *Marriage*, 23.
145. Von Hildebrand, *Marriage*, 24.
146. Von Hildebrand, *Marriage*, 24.
147. Von Hildebrand, *Marriage*, 25.
148. Von Hildebrand, *Marriage*, 26. Von Hildebrand argues that to think otherwise would be a "Protestant and Puritan conception, which even subjectively considers procreation as the sole meaning of the physical union" (*Marriage*, 26).
149. See also Calef, "The Radicalism of Jesus," 63.
150. Von Hildebrand, *Marriage*, 31.

(bodily or spiritual) is the fundamental threat to marriage: "Each spouse has a right to the love of the other."[151] Marriage's meaning is found above all in uniting "two human beings in boundless love into a complete union."[152]

When he turns formally to sacramental marriage (which he envisions as entered into solemnly and with full awareness of acting "for Christ and in Christ"), von Hildebrand begins by praising married love—in its natural state—as "a measure of the depth and greatness of the whole man" and as offering "the highest and noblest earthly happiness."[153] In sacramental marriage, then, married love ascends to still greater heights in its "completely new seriousness, purity, and unselfishness," its full "authentic dignity and ultimate solemnity" vis-à-vis the beloved, and its focus on the sanctification of the beloved in Christ.[154] In sacramental marriage, married love is so profound that it operates in each spouse as "a movement of spiritual ascension" and it gives each spouse "an insatiable longing to see the beloved more and more transformed into Christ."[155] But even though marriage's primary meaning is love, people do not have to measure up to an exalted standard of love in order to get married. He remarks, "Many people . . . are too coarse, too blunt, too primitive to experience such an ultimate conjugal love."[156]

In my judgment, von Hildebrand's approach in *Marriage* suffers from an inadequate integration of the bodily and the spiritual. This does not mean that I find nothing of value in his approach; far from it, especially

151. Von Hildebrand, *Marriage*, 33. Von Hildebrand adds, "Because our laziness, our dullness, and our constant falling back into the periphery stultifies our vision, it is difficult always to keep before us in all its same clarity and splendor the image of the other person so wonderfully revealed by love. We should and must fight against this dullness, for it constitutes a sin against the temple which we erected in our marriage" (*Marriage*, 33). He is aware that many marriages are imperfect or troubled; in such cases the married couple must continue to live out the objective bond, acting insofar as possible for the good of the other and seeking to interpret the other in the best possible light. He speaks of "the heroic suffering of the cross of an unhappy marriage" (*Marriage*, 37).

152. Von Hildebrand, *Marriage*, 38.

153. Von Hildebrand, *Marriage*, 42–43.

154. Von Hildebrand, *Marriage*, 44–46.

155. Von Hildebrand, *Marriage*, 48. Indeed, von Hildebrand holds that for the married couple, fostering the love found in such a marriage consists in "a *divine service*," because such a marriage consecrates the spouses to Christ in a manner similar to the vow of consecrated religious, even if it still remains the case that "the religious state surpasses marriage by far in its sacred character" due to the fact that the religious state involves a direct "wedding with Christ" (*Marriage*, 50, 53, 76).

156. Von Hildebrand, *Marriage*, 66. Although sexual desire or desire for economic influence and worldly power are objectionable and unworthy motives, he does not deny that people who marry for such reasons can enter into an objectively irrevocable marriage.

given the connections that can be drawn to Karol Wojtyła/John Paul II's thought.[157] I admire his insistence upon the fact that "the sexual gift of one person to another signifies an incomparably close union with that other and a self-surrender to him or her."[158]

Cormac Burke

I consider von Hildebrand to be largely an ally or fellow-worker in the theology of marriage, although I have noted serious problems in his approach. In order to clarify my position further, let me turn to the contemporary theologian and canon lawyer Cormac Burke. Though I agree with great deal of what Burke has to say and with his general perspective, I will raise some concerns about Burke's approach as well. Arguably, Burke too does not sufficiently appreciate the procreative end's ability to distinguish what makes marriage unique among human relationships.

In his *The Theology of Marriage*, Burke insists upon "the personalist character of conjugal procreativity."[159] As he rightly emphasizes, the procreative end is not merely, for humans, a biological end that can be distinguished sharply from the personal end of mutual love. On the contrary, "To speak disparagingly about 'biologism,' whenever stress is laid on the procreative aspect of marriage, betrays a fundamental lack of understanding of married personalism."[160] In the act of marital intercourse, which is

---

157. See also von Hildebrand's "Marriage as a Way of Perfection." I affirm that, as John Paul II says, Christian marriage requires respecting "both the value of the true union of the spouses (namely, personal communion) and that of responsible fatherhood and motherhood (in the mature form that is worthy of man)" (John Paul II, *Man and Woman*, 642). With reference to both *Humanae Vitae* and *Gaudium et Spes*, John Paul II adds, "In this renewed orientation, the traditional teaching on the ends of marriage (and on their hierarchy) is confirmed and at the same time deepened from the point of view of the interior life of the spouses, of conjugal and familial spirituality" (*Man and Woman*, 643). See also the reflections of the philosopher and culture-critic David K. O'Connor in his *Plato's Bedroom*, 167–68. Note, too, that I am not saying that all true marriages must be sexually consummated (as Mary and Joseph's was not). Rather, I am saying that the sexual (embodied) dimension of a marriage is not added onto a primary and constitutive spiritual dimension, even in marriages where there is no sexual consummation. Sexuality cannot be divided from human personhood in that way. Human persons are intrinsically sexual creatures, and this aspect cannot be kept back until a spiritual union has been constituted. On Mary's perpetual virginity, see Cavadini, "The Sex Life of Mary and Joseph."

158. Von Hildebrand, *In Defense of Purity*, 5. See also von Hildebrand, *The Encyclical* Humanae Vitae.

159. Burke, *The Theology of Marriage*, 64.

160. Burke, *The Theology of Marriage*, 64.

intrinsically ordered to procreation (even if that end cannot be attained for whatever reason), the couple is intimately open to each other. Marital intercourse is experienced as "uniquely capable of expressing their desire for union," and—without exaggerating the necessity of sexual intercourse in marriage—this means that "[a] married couple uniquely express their love for one another and are uniquely united in intercourse," because it involves the intimate offering of the whole self to the other person, in a way that is open to the extraordinary "gift of procreativity" even if the couple knows that procreation is unlikely or unable (barring a miracle) to occur.[161] Burke underscores that so long as the marital act is not deliberately closed to procreativity, marital intercourse and the procreative end belong to the outworking of the mutual love or the good of the spouses. Marital intercourse is "uniquely capable of contributing to the *bonum* of each spouse, maturing and 'realizing' each one and linking them together."[162]

For Burke, therefore, theologians must strive to avoid pitting mutual love against the procreative end.[163] Theologians should recognize how deeply integrated the two are, so that mutual love and sexual intercourse (when open to procreation), far from marking off separate domains (a spiritual

---

161. Burke, *The Theology of Marriage*, 64–65. Differentiating between the "essence" of marriage and its "ends," Burke adds that while the essence of marriage "cannot be without an 'ordination to' its ends," nonetheless "the actual end itself remains extrinsic to the essence, for the end may fail ever to be achieved without the essence failing in existence" (*The Theology of Marriage*, 91). Put otherwise, a marriage does not dissolve if the couple is barren or if the couple fails in fidelity or mutual love.

162. Burke, *The Theology of Marriage*, 65. For a helpful emphasis on the pleasure of sex as part of the marital gift of self, see Rubio, "The Practice of Sex." The prevalence in our culture of premarital sex (with multiple partners over time) damages marital sex; on this point see Chapman, *Things I Wish I'd Known*, 97–98; Zimmerman, "In Control?"

163. See also Burke's *Covenanted Happiness*, where he cautions against the tendency of "modern man . . . to create a new priority in the ends or purposes of marriage; his tendency to make the enjoyment of mutual love the main purpose, or even the whole and all-sufficient purpose, of marriage, at the same time as he reduces the mere possibility of children . . . to a mere factor which most couples may well want as part of their self-fulfillment, though other couples, with equal legitimacy, will perhaps prefer one or two cars or one or two homes" (14). As Burke goes on to say in the same context, "love in marriage is not meant to remain (and is not likely to survive if it does remain) just the love of two people for each other. It is meant to broaden, to spread out, to include more. Married love is really designed to become family love. . . . Sexual love and procreation are joined in God's plans, to form a strong natural support for marriage and happiness" (*Covenanted Happiness*, 17, 19). Burke rightly considers it mistaken to hold that "the procreative and the unitive aspects of the marital act [sexual intercourse] are *separable*, i.e., that the procreative aspect can be nullified without this in any way vitiating the conjugal act or making it less a unique expression of true marital love and union" (*Covenanted Happiness*, 31).

domain and a physical domain) in a marriage, are integrally united. The procreative end is not a sub-personal end that a purely spiritual love must integrate and sanctify.[164] Burke remarks, "Conjugality and procreativity are thus seen to have a natural complementarity. Conjugality means that both the man and woman are destined to become *spouses*: to unite themselves to each other in an act that is unitive precisely because it is oriented to procreativity."[165] Rather than separating a "primary meaning" (spiritual love) from a "primary end" (physical, procreative sexuality), it is necessary to appreciate their integration in marriage from the very outset.

Burke adds a further point, and here I begin to part ways with him. He argues that while it is correct to envision marriage as ordered to ends, it is not correct to attempt to organize these ends hierarchically, as though one were more important (existentially or definitionally) than another. Avoiding hierarchical language, we can say that in marriage's natural ordering to ends, "*both* the good of the spouses *and* the procreation/education of children have *personalist* value" and "the ends are naturally (institutionally) inseparable" so that there is "an *inter*-ordering, rather than a sub-ordination, between the ends."[166]

Is Burke right that the form of human friendship that we name "marriage" should be specified, not primarily in terms of procreation (the procreative end) or primarily in terms of mutual love (the good of the spouses), but equally and non-hierarchically in terms of procreation and mutual love? Burke's argument is that we cannot really separate these two ends even if we wanted to do so. Each end is entailed in the other, and so it is pointless to drive a wedge between the two by insisting upon defining marriage *primarily* in terms of one or the other. He observes, "Marriage was instituted for the maturing of the spouses, particularly through having a family and dedicating themselves to the task of raising children, and it was instituted for the procreation/education of children, to be achieved through the passing physical union and through the abiding and growing existential and organic unity between husband and wife."[167] In these two clauses, we see how the ends of mutual love and procreation are intertwined with each other.

---

164. Melissa Moschella puts this well when she defends "a view of the human person in which the body is an intrinsic and essential aspect of personal identity, not a mere extrinsic instrument of an 'I' or 'self'" (Moschella, *To Whom Do Children Belong?*, 36).

165. Burke, *The Theology of Marriage*, 65. Burke is here critiquing Herbert Doms, rather than von Hildebrand. But, as noted above, von Hildebrand's language also falls into the problem, by insisting that there must be a *purely* spiritual love that only then integrates the physical dimension (in which the procreative end is included).

166. Burke, *The Theology of Marriage*, 67.

167. Burke, *The Theology of Marriage*, 67–68.

PROCREATION AND MUTUAL LOVE

The purpose of marriage is mutual love ("the maturing of the spouses"), but this purpose is meant to be attained through the procreation and raising of children. Likewise, the purpose of marriage is the procreation and education of children, but this properly takes place within the context of the ever-developing mutual love of the spouses. Neither an arrangement for procreation and education that lacks the mutual love of the spouses, nor an arrangement for mutual love that deliberately lacks the procreation and education of children, truly fits the proper definition of marriage.[168]

Burke emphasizes, therefore, that nothing is gained by placing the two ends in competition, wherein one end receives the "primary" place over the other. Placing the procreative end over the end of mutual love only serves as fodder for the complaint that Church simply sees marriage as a breeding ground for more Catholics, with the couple's role being to subordinate themselves entirely to the task of procreating and raising children, until, without any care for their own personal development, they (the couple) wear out and die. If the goal is to uphold the procreative end of marriage, then for Burke this goal is best served not by insisting on the primacy of procreation, but by helping married couples to "see that their own mutual love, their happiness together, and the personal growth of each, are furthered by the enterprise of building a family according to God's plans."[169] When procreation and mutual love are thus integrally joined, as two sides of the same coin, it becomes apparent that it is in the common striving that is the procreation and raising of children that the married couple deepens and nourishes the love proper to marriage. Marriage and family life, in other words, go together. As Burke argues, "Inseparability gives a better idea of the mutual relation between these ends. It passes over the question of hierarchy, and looks rather to the essential *inter*-ordering of the ends. Each relates vitally and existentially to the other. Each depends on the other; they stand or fall together."[170] He concludes by suggesting that what is really at stake is whether married couples are aware that, in loving each other and building a family, they are not merely pursuing an immanent good but in fact are being opened, through self-gift, to configuration by grace to the love of Christ and the Church—an everlasting vocation.

Again, Burke rightly contends that theologians must avoid "the misleading tendency to present procreation as the institutional end of marriage

---

168. Burke also argues that an act of sexual intercourse in which the couple is using contraception does not serve to consummate a marriage, a claim with which I disagree.

169. Burke, *The Theology of Marriage*, 68.

170. Burke, *The Theology of Marriage*, 69.

and ... *bonum coniugum* as the personal end."[171] According to Janet Smith in her Foreword to his book, "Burke navigates skillfully between the traditional understanding of marriage that emphasizes procreation as the primary end of marriage and the personalist understanding that strives to delve more deeply into the spouses' experience of loving union, both physical and spiritual."[172] Burke undertakes this task within a context that, as he says, has involved twentieth-century theologians (and canonists) in a struggle between "two radically opposed fields of thought: a 'personalist-spouse-centered' view of the ends of marriage and an 'institutional-procreative' view."[173] He argues that the 1983 Code of Canon Law helped the Church move beyond this struggle by avoiding any hierarchy of marital ends. As he says, the Code "was the first magisterial document to describe these ends in new terms, omitting the former hierarchical order of one 'primary' and two 'secondary' ends and presenting the 'good of the spouses' (the *bonum coniugum*) and the 'procreation-education of children' as, so it seems, co-equal ends."[174] The *Catechism of the Catholic Church* follows the same non-hierarchical approach to the two ends of the "good of the spouses" (mutual love) and procreation.

Does this approach work? I think that it has some significant weaknesses. When inquiring into why procreation has traditionally been given hierarchical primacy, we can begin with the fact that in sketching the fundamental difference between marriage and other intimate human friendships, one discovers that if one begins with the procreative end, one can move easily to mutual love (because the family is a communion of love and the couple's bond of love flows into and is typically enriched by the body-soul act of marital intercourse). By contrast, if one begins with mutual love, one

---

171. Burke, *The Theology of Marriage*, 71. Burke's comments regarding Thomas Aquinas are relevant in this regard. Asking whether Aquinas gave any consideration to "the mutually enriching role, outside the purely procreative sphere, of the complementary relationship between husband and wife, in the development of human maturity," Burke answers in the affirmative, noting that Aquinas "teaches that man and woman are naturally inclined to marriage not only because of offspring but also because of 'the mutual help given to each other by the spouses in the home'" and also that Aquinas praises the unique friendship, "mutual sharing," and "spiritual union" of the married couple (*The Theology of Marriage*, 79–80). But for Burke, Aquinas's "concept of the *mutuum adiutorium* moves on a basically natural and earthbound level, with little or no suggestion that the mutual help has a supernatural purpose as its ultimate goal" (*The Theology of Marriage*, 81). I think that this conclusion is too harsh; how could a true "friendship" and "spiritual union" of two Christians, united in their "mutual sharing," not have an ultimate supernatural goal, even if also a this-worldly purpose?

172. Smith, "Foreword," in Burke, *The Theology of Marriage*, vii–xvii, at xi.

173. Burke, *The Theology of Marriage*, xxiv.

174. Burke, *The Theology of Marriage*, xxiv.

has relative difficulty in integrating, in a thoroughgoing way, the procreative end. For example, it can be tricky to articulate why mutual love, in marriage, must be between a man and a woman, rather than between persons of the same sex. Recall that von Hildebrand appeals to the spiritual complementarity of the sexes, but this notion is vague enough that it can be easily contested. Similarly, the *intrinsic* relation of male-female mutual love toward the end of procreation becomes somewhat difficult to defend. Although most couples who share mutual love do want children, some couples testify to having no desire whatsoever for children. One can respond that the latter couples are selfish and that their mutual love is in fact deficient, but this claim tends toward personal accusation and can be answered (whether adequately or not, it hardly matters) on equally charged personal grounds.

The fact that it is difficult, relatively speaking, to get to the "procreative end" when one begins with the end of "mutual love" should move us to think more concretely about what distinguishes marital friendships. Aristotle is a particular help here, because, as is his wont, he insists upon looking at concrete details. When we look at how marriage actually functions for most husbands and wives, we see that it establishes a basis for raising children and that it builds family structures (including, for infertile couples, by means of adoption or other hospitable practices). Practically speaking, everyone knows that it is generally easier to raise a child if one gets married beforehand. People generally get married with the intention, whether explicit or implicit, of having a family together. When one meets couples who have been married for ten years or more, most often one will meet their children. When the issue is raised in the concrete, the point is that marriage and family are well known to go together.

Concretely, too, the married people whom one meets are not likely to go on and on about their mutual love, though they do love each other. Rather than talking about their love for each other to the people they meet, married couples will tend to talk about their children. This does not mean, again, that infertile couples are excluded from this: on the contrary, infertile couples adopt children or reach out in other notable ways.

Of course, as I will discuss in chapter 7, procreation can and does proceed without marriage, and in some communities marriage seems to be nearly disappearing. Divorce and other grave marital problems deeply impact child-raising. But the deepest lived experience of most married couples—in terms of what they share together—has to do with the procreating and raising of children. It is noteworthy that the connection of marriage and childbearing is present throughout Scripture, whereas the connection of marriage with the development of the couple's mutual love is something that emerges over the course of scriptural history (with the gradual repudiation of polygamy) and is never dissociated from childbearing.

IV. Conclusion

In their *What Is Marriage?*, Sherif Girgis, Ryan T. Anderson, and Robert P. George recognize that child-raising is not "*necessary* for being spouses."[175] Of course this is true, or else couples who are unable to have children—whether because of age or a physical defect—could not marry. The procreative end that is found in marital sexual intercourse (and that is intrinsic to male-female sexual intercourse, even when the couple is infertile or employs contraception to ensure that actual procreation does not occur) does not mean, as I have noted above, that actual procreation has to take place in order for there to be a valid marriage. Likewise, a decision to have and raise children together does not mean that one has thereby *married* the other person.

Much like Aristotle and the tradition flowing from the Church Fathers, Girgis and his co-authors recognize that marriage and child-raising fit together like hand and glove. In human experience, it is incontestable that "family life specially *enriches* marriage" and "marriage is especially *apt* for family life."[176] The particular friendship called "marriage" is suited to the raising of children by their father and mother. No other human friendship is equally suited for this task, although children certainly *can* be raised within other human friendships, or, for that matter, communally. Girgis and his co-authors observe that as a concrete reality, "marriage is ordered to family life because the act by which spouses make love also makes new life [whether or not it does so in particular cases]; one and the same act both seals a marriage and brings forth children."[177] No doubt, there are other ways to produce and raise children, just as there are other human friendships. But as Girgis and his co-authors say, as a practical matter "marital cooperation in both sexual and domestic life is characteristically ordered to procreation and childrearing. Spouses develop and share their whole selves in the way best suited for honorably parenting—for example, with broad domestic sharing and permanent, exclusive commitment."[178]

This practical truth, namely the centrality of children for married life, does not mean that the procreative end is "primary" in the sense that the mutual love of the couple now becomes less important or less significant

---

175. Girgis, Anderson, and George, *What Is Marriage?*, 29.
176. Girgis, Anderson, and George, *What Is Marriage?*, 29.
177. Girgis, Anderson, and George, *What Is Marriage?*, 30.
178. Girgis, Anderson, and George, *What Is Marriage?*, 30–31.

for human flourishing. The primacy of the procreative end is not a primacy that belittles other ends of marriage. It is a primacy in defining what the specific nature of marriage is, but it is not a primacy in the sense that the couple should now regard their mutual love as of lesser importance—even for the raising of children. If the couple does not grow in mutual love, it is unlikely that they will be able to live well or to parent well, let alone live out their vocation in Christ. The title that José Granados gives to his book on marriage—*Una Sola Carne en un Solo Espíritu* (A Single Body in a Single Spirit)—is apropos, given the integral relationship between the two ends. Granados's book, which takes its bearings from the marital communion of the "body of the Church" with the "body of Christ" as "one single body,"[179] cuts against any body-spirit dualism that would distinguish in human life between a purely physical realm and a purely spiritual realm.

The primacy of the procreative end also fits with David Matzko McCarthy's insight, in his *Sex and Love in the Home*, that "love and affection attain their depth through common work and through a common vocation."[180] Criticizing von Hildebrand's perspective as overly romantic, McCarthy argues that von Hildebrand and others who focus on mutual love as the primary meaning provide an understanding of marriage that, when applied practically, "resonates more with private moments of passion than washing the dishes, dinner with the in-laws, cooperating with neighbors, and managing a home."[181] My own concern is largely that, by establishing mutual love on a basis that is utterly free of sexual attraction or desire, von

179. Granados, *Una Sola Carne*, 198–99; cf. 148–51 and elsewhere.

180. McCarthy, *Sex and Love*, 155.

181. McCarthy, *Sex and Love*, 64. McCarthy's approach receives criticism from Brent Waters: "For all his [McCarthy's] rich and informative description of daily life in a household and neighbourhood, what exactly constitutes a family remains vague. Is a family simply constituted by a group of adults and children who happen to spend more time with each other than with other adults and children in a neighbourhood, or is there some other biological, relational, or normative quality that McCarthy either refuses or is unable to name? At the end of the day what is portrayed is not so much a network of households within the social setting of the neighbourhood, but a loose confederation of parents and children who live in close proximity to each other. He wishes to affirm the open family, but for it to be genuinely open it must also be closed at some point" (Waters, *The Family*, 228; along the same lines, see Waters, "Marriage," 527). However, see McCarthy, "Cohabitation and Marriage," in which he astutely argues that "[o]ur current theology puts the weight of marriage on the interpersonal union and the strength of a 'relationship,' but this personalist fix is a fragile antidote to cohabitation and its logic of individualism" (120). He proposes instead to focus on "[t]he social and communal structure of marriage," i.e., marriage as an institution that has "procreative, public, and communal purposes" ("Cohabitation and Marriage," 120). To my mind, McCarthy has grasped a key point: marriage understood in light of the procreative end will be a public and communal reality and not simply a private affair.

Hildebrand then has difficulty integrating sexuality (including the procreative end) in an *intrinsic* way into the mutual love of the married couple. But McCarthy is right to add the point that marital mutual love should be understood in the concrete. As McCarthy says, "the priorities of personalism need to be reordered to reflect the actual nature of marriage.... [T]he institutional features of marriage make the relationship distinctive. It is not a value-added friendship. It is a marriage, not reducible to the general idea of an 'intimate relationship' that endures. The public structure of fidelity, permanence, and openness to children gives shape to the relationship."[182]

Here we may return to Augustine's three goods of marriage. As Beth Felker Jones says, "sex should embody three 'goods.'"[183] Sex, in order to be morally right, must be marital—it must be an expression of fruitfulness, fidelity, and indissolubility in configuration to and as a sign of the mutual love of Christ and the Church. All these are needed in marriage. The role of the hierarchical ordering of the ends of marriage is not to suggest that any of these goods is less necessary or less valuable. Rather, the primacy of procreation overcomes both Plato's assumption that marriage is unnecessary and the modern romantic assumption that all that the couple really need is each other.

The *Catechism* is right to speak of "the twofold end of marriage: the good of the spouses themselves and the transmission of life."[184] But the procreative end provides the context for the mutual-love end. It does so not least because it confirms that in marriage, "It is the vocation to lifelong fidelity and generation and generativity that sustains the changing relationship, not the relationship itself that sustains the vocation."[185] Burke agrees with this, and von Hildebrand, who was motivated by a concern to reinvigorate the end of mutual love at a time when the procreative end had been perhaps overly singled out, would surely also agree.

I hope that this chapter has helped to show why the procreative end was singled out so strongly in the earlier theological tradition, as well as by Aristotle and, for that matter, by Scripture in its manifold descriptions of marital relationships. Those who start with the procreative end—present even when the man and woman cannot conceive children—can easily integrate mutual love and can do so in a manner that makes clear why this mode of human friendship between a man and a woman receives so much attention and honor in society and in the Church.

182. McCarthy, "Cohabitation and Marriage," 136.
183. Jones, *Faithful*, 42.
184. *Catechism*, §2363.
185. McCarthy, "Cohabitation and Marriage," 139.

Chapter 6

Sacrament

The above chapters have proceeded on the assumption that marriage is a sacrament, and it is now time to defend this assumption. Let me first define what I mean by a "sacrament": it is "a sign efficaciously instituted by Christ, through which is conferred to a human person, in virtue of the redemption of humankind won by Christ on the Cross, the grace of salvation and sanctification."[1] Among the seven sacraments of the Church, the sacrament of marriage bestows upon the spouses a graced participation in the union of Christ and his Church.

Although medieval theologians developed the Church's doctrine of the seven sacraments, the patristics scholar John Cavadini has pointed out that "Scholastic sacramental theology does not come out of nowhere."[2] Medieval theology built upon Augustine's affirmation that marriage incorporates believers into "the transformative and healing love of Christ for the church."[3] Specially, the sacrament of Christian marriage configures the man and woman, as a married couple, to the eschatological union of Christ and the Church, established by Christ through his Cross and Resurrection.[4]

Admittedly, the present chapter will speak most directly to Catholics and Eastern Orthodox, since Protestants do not hold marriage to be a sacrament. But I also intend to be speaking to and learning from Protestants, who generally have a very high view of Christian marriage. Even while

---

1. Nicolas, *Synthèse dogmatique*, 1138. Nicolas provides an excellent account of why the "matter" of the sacrament of marriage must be a biological man and woman: see *Synthèse dogmatique*, 1141–44.
2. Cavadini, "The Sacramentality of Marriage," 167.
3. Cavadini, "The Sacramentality of Marriage," 168.
4. See Cavadini, "The Sacramentality of Marriage," 172.

denying that marriage is a sacrament, for example, John Calvin affirms that the Lord has both instituted marriage and (with respect to Christian marriage) "sanctified [it] with his blessing."[5] Brent Waters remarks with respect to present-day practice: "Although Protestant churches . . . do not regard marriage as a sacrament, many retain what may be characterized as an implicit sacramentality. Marriage is something more than a contract or special friendship."[6] The Reformed pastor John Piper likewise goes quite far when he proclaims, "Marriage is more wonderful than anyone on earth knows. The reasons it is wonderful can be learned only from God's special revelation and can be cherished only by the work of the Holy Spirit to enable us to behold and embrace the wonder."[7] Moreover, some Anglicans, including most recently Andrew Davison, have held marriage to be a sacrament.[8] The Lutheran theologian Robert Jenson, too, gets to the core of

---

5. Calvin, *Institutes*, Book II, ch. 8, p. 348. For Martin Luther's perspective, see his "Pagan Servitude of the Church," 326–40. Luther, of course, has a distinctive understanding of a "sacrament." Luther argues that "nowhere in Scripture do we read that anyone would receive the grace of God by getting married; nor does the rite of matrimony contain any hint that that ceremony is of divine institution. Nowhere do we read that it was instituted by God in order to symbolize something, although we grant that all things done in the sight of men can be understood as metaphors and allegories of things invisible. . . . There has been such a thing as marriage itself ever since the beginning of the world, and it also exists among unbelievers to the present day. Therefore no grounds exist on which the Romanists can validly call it a sacrament of the new law, and a function solely of the church. The marriages of our ancestors were no less sacred than our own, nor less real among unbelievers than believers. Yet no one calls marriage of unbelievers a sacrament. Also, there are irreligious marriages even amongst believers, worse than among any pagans. Why then should it be called a sacrament in such a case, and yet not among pagans?" ("Pagan Servitude of the Church," 326). For Luther, the meaning of Ephesians 5:32 is that "the sacrament is not in the marriage but in Christ and the Church," although at the same time Luther fully grants that "matrimony is a figure for Christ and the church" ("The Pagan Servitude of the Church," 329). Luther deeply appreciated marriage and himself enjoyed a very happy and rewarding marriage, rooted and grounded in faith in Christ. For further discussion, see Witte, *From Sacrament to Contract*; Harrington, *Reordering Marriage*.

6. Waters, "Marriage," in *Oxford Handbook of Sacramental Theology*, 517–30, at 522.

7. Piper, *This Momentary Marriage*, 29. Scott Hahn rightly says, "To the extent certain Protestant denominations recognize the true nature of marriage, they too participate in the sacrament and can therefore participate in the reinvigoration of the public understanding of that sacramentality" (Hahn, *The First Society*, 127).

8. See Davison, *Why Sacraments?*, 71. Davison, however, favors same-sex marriage by suggesting (even if tentatively) that the goods of marriage do not require a man and a woman, which strikes me as an error on many levels. For a similar favoring of same-sex marriage (on the grounds that this is a practical matter that allows for diversity in ecclesiastical laws and that is a case of the Church adjusting to civil law in an appropriate manner, given that specifications of the "matter" of sacraments are

the matter when he remarks, "In Israel and the church, marriage comes to mean participation in the Lord's own union with his people."[9] This chapter, therefore, should have ecumenical resonance, although its central task is to argue, in light of the concern that the medieval Catholic Church invented marriage as a "sacrament," that marriage is indeed properly understood as one of the seven sacraments.

Let me note at the outset that Catholic and (to a certain extent) Orthodox theologians recognize the intrinsic plausibility of concerns regarding the sacramental status of marriage. It is one thing to say, as John Meyendorff rightly does, that "marriage is a sacrament because in it and through it the Kingdom of God becomes a living experience," and to insist that "the Church, since its very early days, considered the legal or social institution of marriage as being transformed into a reality of the Kingdom ... if it was concluded between two members of the Body of Christ."[10] But it is another thing to admit the actual extent of the doctrinal development that in fact occurred. In a 1962 lecture, Joseph Ratzinger remarks that the Church's "explicit specification" of the sacraments "as only seven" took place in the twelfth century, which can seem rather shockingly late in the game.[11] Ratz-

---

determined by the Church rather than by divine law), see Tanner, "Hooker and the New Puritans." In the same volume, see also Rogers, "Trinity, Marriage, and Homosexuality," restating the arguments of his *Sexuality and the Christian Body*.

9. Jenson, *The Triune Story*, 43–44.

10. Meyendorff, *Marriage*, 73. Meyendorff contrasts this sharply with what he deems to be the Western perspective: "Broken by death, assimilated with a human agreement, marriage, in the prevailing Western view, is only an earthly affair, concerned with the 'body,' unworthy of entering the Kingdom of God. One can even wonder whether marriage, so understood, can still be called a sacrament. But, by affirming that the priest is the minister of the marriage, as he is also the minister of the Eucharist, the Orthodox Church implicitly integrates marriage in the *eternal* Mystery, where the boundaries between heaven and earth are broken and where human decision and action acquire an eternal dimension" (*Marriage*, 23). For Meyendorff, all depends upon whether the priest is the minister of the marriage (as distinct from the couple giving themselves to each other). It is mistaken to suggest that marriage, in the Catholic perspective, is not a mystery of the kingdom. It is indeed an eschatological sign and a participation by grace in the union of Christ and the Church. The fact that it comes to an end in the eschaton means that it is fulfilled (by being taken up into the perfect, consummated marriage of Christ and his Bride, in which God will be all in all and our union with each other will be perfect) rather than negated.

11. Ratzinger, "Sources of Revelation," 274. Raymond E. Brown, S.S. rightly warns against the view that "all the Christian dogmas from the divinity of Christ to the Assumption of Mary were known in apostolic times, and thus the development of doctrine consists merely in drawing forth from the deposit of faith (conceived in the manner of a bank deposit) the already formulated answers to problems that should never have arisen. For the historically conscious scholar, however, the problems that arose are precisely what brought really new insights and caused the Church to formulate her thought

inger explains, "It is not that earlier the corresponding seven realities were not present, but rather their order and the insight into them as belonging to the classification 'sacrament', in a word, the structuring of the sacramental cosmos" was "a process that involved a historical labor in the Holy Spirit."[12] But is this explanation true?

In his *How Marriage Became One of the Sacraments*, the Catholic historian Philip Reynolds has argued that the Church's arrival at the doctrine of the seven sacraments—and specifically at the doctrine of marriage as a sacrament—was indeed "a historical labor," but not a labor that is likely to have been guided by the Spirit in any particularly significant sense. In Reynolds's view, the Church's twelfth-century affirmation of marriage as a sacrament simply increased priestly power and chained believers to loveless marriages due to the doctrine of marital indissolubility. He suggests that Catholic priests took advantage of the near-ubiquity of marriage to create a sacrament over which they would have control.

Given the question of whether marriage really is a sacrament in the sense that the Church intends, the present chapter will unfold in three steps. First, I survey Reynolds's position as sketched in his book's summative first chapter. Second, in accord with Ratzinger's emphasis on the necessity of "a process of spiritual appropriation and of elaboration of the mystery of Christ,"[13] I explore the biblical testimony to the Christian community's Spirit-guided doctrinal development. In this section, I draw upon the work of the evangelical biblical scholar Craig Keener in his commentary on the Gospel of John. My emphasis in this second section is that "the actual being of the church and of her life in the Holy Spirit" between Christ's Ascension and his coming in glory has a purpose: during this time, as part of its evangelizing mission and liturgical communion with Christ the Head, the Church as the body of Christ deepens its understanding and reception of the gifts that Christ has given.[14]

Third and lastly, I appreciatively examine two expositions of the development of the Church's doctrine of marriage as a "sacrament": Edward Schillebeeckx's 1961 *Marriage: Human Reality and Saving Mystery* and Peter Elliott's 1987 *What God Has Joined . . .: The Sacramentality of Marriage*.

---

in a way not hitherto done" (*Jesus God and Man*, xi). He adds the crucial clarification that "a new formulation need not reflect the grasp of an entirely new truth; often a new formulation is an almost instinctive reaction in order to defend a truth that was previously accepted in a general and undifferentiated way but is now imperiled" (*Jesus God and Man*, xi–xii).

12. Ratzinger, "Sources of Revelation," 274.
13. Ratzinger, "Sources of Revelation," 274.
14. Ratzinger, "Sources of Revelation," 274.

Schillebeeckx is particularly strong in detailing the biblical foundations and the twelfth- and thirteenth-century developments, while Elliott traces an understanding of "sacramentality" as it fuels the development of sacramental doctrine. In coming to understand marriage as a sacrament, the Church arrived at the full implications of a reality that was already present in Jesus' eschatological healing and elevation of marriage.[15]

I. Philip Reynolds on the Church's Invention of Marriage as a Sacrament

In his massive and erudite historical study *How Marriage Became One of the Sacraments*, Philip Reynolds begins by observing that the doctrine that marriage is a sacrament "was one of the medieval church's contributions to western culture" and became a Catholic dogma at the Council of Trent in 1563.[16] Specifically, the doctrine that marriage is a sacrament arose in the twelfth century. It arose through a creative appropriation of Augustinian writings on marriage, in the context of "an effort on the part of bishops and clerics to take control over how people married" and to enforce the Church's rules for marriage, including what counts as valid "consent and consummation."[17] Reynolds aims to return to this period and to figure out what the arguments of the major innovators were, what their motivations were, and precisely what was new in their positions. He takes it as evident that "marriage did not fit the sacramental paradigm easily," so that in certain notable respects "marriage did not *look* like a sacrament."[18]

Reynolds grants that "belief that marriage was a holy estate, a Christian vocation, and a way of participating in the life of the church was ancient."[19] The new element, which began to develop around 1100, was the

---

15. See also de La Soujeole, "Development of Doctrine." Indebted to Schillebeeckx (and to the development of the notion of Christ and the Church as "sacraments" of salvation), de La Soujeole identifies the existence of a "sacramental 'chain,' which is founded in the very mystery of Christ and is completed in the 'concrete' act that touches man today. . . . What took place once for all through the mystery of the Incarnation—that covenant between the Word of God and a human nature like our own—spreads to others beyond the Incarnate Word so that the perfect economy of salvation as found in Christ reaches out to all people of all times and places" ("Development of Doctrine," 599). For further discussion see de La Soujeole, "The Economy of Salvation"; Schillebeeckx, *De sacramentele heilseconomie*.

16. Reynolds, *How Marriage Became One of the Sacraments*, xxv.

17. Reynolds, *How Marriage Became One of the Sacraments*, xxvi–xxvii.

18. Reynolds, *How Marriage Became One of the Sacraments*, xxvi.

19. Reynolds, *How Marriage Became One of the Sacraments*, 1.

understanding of marriage as a sacrament. This led to a new interpretation of Ephesians 5:32, with its reference to a "great mystery [*sacramentum*]," as referring to the mundane institution of marriage, rather than to Christ and the Church or to Genesis 2:24 understood prophetically. A few patristic and early medieval texts had made a similar suggestion, but Reynolds observes that these texts were few in number despite being very influential after 1100.

Reynolds takes the Council of Trent as his standpoint for looking back upon the earlier developments. At Trent, the sacraments of the New Law were defined as seven in number, sharing a common essence and a shared definition of being "efficacious sacred signs."[20] According to Trent, Jesus Christ instituted them all, and they all contain and cause in the recipient the grace that they signify, assuming there is no impediment to their reception. Trent condemned the Reformers for rejecting the Church's supposedly constant teaching about marriage's sacramental status. Nonetheless, as Reynolds points out, the bishops gathered at Trent were generally aware, historically speaking, that things were not so simple. For example, they knew that Peter Lombard denied that marriage causes the grace it signifies, and they knew that if marriage did not cause grace, then it did not fit the strict definition of a sacrament of the New Law. The Fathers of Trent also knew that no earlier Council or pope had pronounced dogmatically regarding the number of sacraments or the status of marriage as a sacrament.

Reynolds argues that Lombard's *Sentences* was decisive for the later history of the sacraments. By choosing to list seven sacraments and to include marriage among them, Lombard set the course for future developments. Later twelfth-century theologians, building upon Lombard, addressed the issue of when marriage was instituted as a sacrament. They held that it was instituted at creation and confirmed by Christ. Beginning with Alexander of Hales, theologians began to argue that marriage caused grace. (In his commentary on the *Sentences*, Thomas Aquinas agreed with Lombard on this point, but Aquinas changed his mind by the time of the *Summa contra Gentiles*.) The late-thirteenth-century theologian Peter John Olivi questioned marriage's full sacramentality, though he still counted it among the seven sacraments. He renewed the argument that marriage does not cause grace. His judgment on this matter, however, was declared heretical by a committee of his fellow Franciscan theologians.

In the period between Augustine and the twelfth century, Reynolds notes, there are very few theological texts on marriage. In the late eighth-century *Gregorian Sacramentary*, he finds a reference to the marriage of Adam and Eve that teaches that the "sacramentum" or mystery of Christ

---

20. Reynolds, *How Marriage Became One of the Sacraments*, 3.

and the Church is prefigured by marriage (according to Ephesians 5), rather than teaching that the sacrament itself is the couple's marriage. Reynolds highlights the fact that even texts that cite Ephesians 5 do not describe a marriage between a man and woman as a "sacrament." During this period, theologians held to Augustine's definition of a sacrament as involving word and matter, within a ritual celebration. They identified baptism and the Eucharist as the two fundamental sacraments and allowed various other ancillary rites also to bear the name "sacrament."

In the twelfth century—prior to Lombard—Nicholas of Clairvaux wrote a treatise on sacraments that names twelve sacraments (not including the Eucharist, but including marriage, along with a number of rites regarding consecrated virgins). The early twelfth-century theologian Hugh of Saint-Victor treats a large variety of major sacraments, minor sacraments, and preparatory sacraments without listing a specific number of "sacraments." Hugh suggests that everything that signifies a holy thing in a particular respect is a "sacrament."

Asking why Lombard's list of seven sacraments of the New Law proved so successful and enduring, Reynolds speculates that the reason was that the seven sacraments named by Lombard amplified the clergy's mediation of the sanctifying and remedial power of Christ's Cross. This emphasis on priestly authority and function was stimulated, Reynolds thinks, by the eleventh-century Gregorian Reform. He contends that the Gregorian Reform separated the clergy into a separate (now celibate) "caste," essentially cut off from "their local communities" and functioning instead "as members of a universal, hierarchically organized corporation."[21] In addition, he maintains that the Gregorian Reform "depended on the widespread but theologically questionable conviction among the laity that the mediation of the priesthood (*sacerdotium*) was vital for salvation, and that priests needed to be both pure and manly to perform this vital work."[22] As a result, priestly pastoral ministry was significantly expanded and was now seen to be much more necessary for the attainment of salvation on the part of the laity. Prior to the Gregorian Reform, the main task of priests (and Religious) was to pray and do good works. After the Gregorian Reform, there was a new central focus on pastoral care, not least through the (new) sacraments. This led, by Lombard's time, to a greater interest in "what a sacrament is, why each was instituted, what its composition is, and what the difference is between the sacraments of the Old Law and those of the New Law."[23]

21. Reynolds, *How Marriage Became One of the Sacraments*, 25.
22. Reynolds, *How Marriage Became One of the Sacraments*, 25.
23. Reynolds, *How Marriage Became One of the Sacraments*, 26. In the East,

Reynolds points out that what made the twelfth-century innovation easier—with respect to marriage taking a place among the (now seven) sacraments—was the fact that Augustine had spoken about one of the three goods of marriage as the "sacrament," the *bonum sacramenti*. Augustine meant by this simply the indissolubility of the marital bond; this is what the mystery or "great sacrament" of Ephesians 5:32 meant to express. Twelfth-century theologians, however, overlooked the difference between the "good of the sacrament" and marriage itself as a "sacrament." As a sign of Christ's union with the Church, marriage could easily be a "sacrament" in the prior broad usage of the term, which included any "sign of a sacred thing."[24] In the economy of salvation, which meant the "sacramental" economy (prior to the specification of the meaning of the term "sacrament" to apply to seven "sacraments"), marriage had always played a role, from marriage in the pre-fall garden of Eden to the hoped-for eschatological marriage of God and humankind. Thus, as Reynolds says, "Theologians during the first quarter of the twelfth century were familiar with use of the word *sacramentum* in the context of marriage ... and they extended it by applying current notions of sacramentality to marriage."[25] He adds that in the first quarter of the twelfth century, prior to Lombard, they did so without intending to add it to a list of seven sacraments.

Regarding the medieval systematic treatises on the sacraments (post-Lombard), Reynolds identifies their pastoral contributions as threefold: they gave a basic (if idealized) framework of meaning to a wedding; they ensured that marriage (now as a sacrament) would be under the Church's jurisdiction; and they placed marriage within the broader context of salvation history, above all as a lens through which to interpret the Church in relation to Christ. This third contribution made marriage into an ecclesial vocation or "a mode of participating in the life of the church."[26] The married couple, no less than the celibate priest or the consecrated religious, was thereby tied into a life that had its meaning in its relation to Christ (and the Church). Reynolds considers this to be a positive fruit of identifying marriage as one of the seven "sacraments," even if the fruit could have been obtained in another way.

---

however (as Reynolds is aware), Emperor Leo in 893 mandated that a marriage must receive a priestly blessing in order for the marriage to be valid. This action, undertaken in the East well prior to the West's Gregorian Reform and without any connection to priestly celibacy, suggests that the sacramental development of marriage is more complicated than Reynolds holds.

24. Reynolds, *How Marriage Became One of the Sacraments*, 29.
25. Reynolds, *How Marriage Became One of the Sacraments*, 29.
26. Reynolds, *How Marriage Became One of the Sacraments*, 31.

SACRAMENT

Viewing marriage as a "sacrament" meant focusing on the ritual celebration, the wedding vows, rather than focusing on daily married life. By contrast, theologians who doubted or denied the sacramental status of marriage, such as Olivi and Martin Luther, tended to focus their writing instead upon marriage as an "estate" or state of life.[27] In interpreting marriage as a sacrament, theologians placed the focus on the wedding day. A marriage could be invalidated by wrong intentions on the wedding day, but not by wrong intentions later on during married life.

When Reynolds speaks of the Church taking jurisdiction over marriage by deeming it a sacrament, he clarifies that by "Church" the medieval theologians had in view not simply the ordained clergy, but the whole hierarchically organized Body of Christ. At the same time, many medieval clerics considered the Church largely as Christ's bride, and in this regard the clergy's pastoral role—spiritual counsel and sacramental remedies—was at the forefront of the medieval outlook, since the Church functioned as a mother caring for her children. In this respect Reynolds notes the growing twelfth-century presence of the clergy both in the actual rite of marriage (the wedding day, now with the priest questioning the couple about impediments and about the freedom of their consent, culminating in the celebration of a nuptial Mass) and in the supervision of legal rules about marriage. Regarding the latter, he emphasizes that the Church, by deeming marriage a sacrament, gained "exclusive legal competence" over the determination of what constituted a valid marriage, dissolution of an invalid marriage, and divorce without possibility of remarriage.[28] By contrast, in the patristic period the Church lacked such jurisdiction, meaning that civil remarriage after divorce was permitted (by Roman law) despite the Church's condemnation of it on the basis of divine law. Reynolds grants that even though deeming marriage to be a sacrament was a sufficient condition for ensuring Church jurisdiction, it was not a necessary condition. The nobility and middle class willingly went along with the extension of the Church's authority.

Reynolds also examines the sign-character of marriage according to the medieval theologians who deemed marriage to be a sacrament. If marriage is a "sacrament," then it must be a "sign" of some sacred reality. Basing himself on Ephesians 5:31–32, Lombard held that marriage is a "sign" of the union of Christ and the Church. The "*res*" or "reality" of the sacrament is therefore the union of Christ and the Church, although other "*res*" were identified as well, such as the union of God and the soul in charity. As noted,

---

27. For more on Luther's theology of marriage (and related legal issues), see Witte, *From Sacrament to Contract*, 113–58; Harrington, *Reordering Marriage*. Witte also provides a thorough survey of Calvin's approach.

28. Reynolds, *How Marriage Became One of the Sacraments*, 36.

Lombard thought that marriage is a sacramental "sign" but not an efficacious "cause" of the union of Christ and the Church, whereas later medieval theologians thought of marriage as both a sign and cause. Reynolds recognizes that marriage's sign character is attested in Scripture: as we have seen, the Church (or Israel) is repeatedly described as Christ's (or God's) "bride," and certainly marriage—such as the wedding at Cana—stands as a figure of the eschatological marriage of Christ and his Church. The question is whether God (in creation) or Christ (in his public ministry) instituted marriage as a sacramental sign of the union of Christ and the Church.

Reynolds notes, too, that medieval interpreters often posited "two unions in carnal marriage: the union of wills (*consensus animarum*) and the union of bodies (*commixtio corporum*)."[29] According to Innocent III, it is the latter—the union of bodies—that constitutes the sacrament of marriage described in Ephesians 5:32 (the sign of the union of Christ and the Church). This is because the latter is indissoluble, whereas the former—the union of wills—is soluble, just as the union between a justified soul and God is soluble until death. Here Reynolds takes up medieval marriage sermons and argues that the preachers focused on creatively expounding the spiritual senses of marriage rather than on engaging in depth the lived details of human marriage. Reynolds concludes, "The laity must have sensed intuitively that all these spiritual parallels dignified their own marriages and made them sacred, but the preachers rarely encouraged them to do so or showed them how to make the comparison or to draw its lessons."[30]

Reynolds offers his own interpretation of Ephesians 5. Uncontroversially, he proposes that this passage "presents Christ's union with the church as the exemplar that Christian spouses should emulate in their own marriages."[31] Paul considers Christ's union with the Church to be a "marriage" in some more-than-metaphorical sense. It is not a mere metaphor to say that the Church is Christ's "bride"; the Church actually is, ontologically, the bride of Christ. This means that the marriage of Christ and the Church is in some sense a real "marriage." As a real exemplar of what *marriage* is, the marriage of Christ and his bride the Church stands as a model for human marriage.

In Reynolds's view, however, Augustine tragically misinterpreted both Ephesians 5 and Matthew 19:9. Regarding Matthew 19:9 (read in light of 1 Corinthians 7), Reynolds considers Augustine's critic Pollentius to be correct; and, indeed, much of Reynolds's work involves a polemic against the

---

29. Reynolds, *How Marriage Became One of the Sacraments*, 60.
30. Reynolds, *How Marriage Became One of the Sacraments*, 62.
31. Reynolds, *How Marriage Became One of the Sacraments*, 64.

doctrine of marital indissolubility. According to Pollentius, "adultery was a kind of spiritual death, which left the wronged partner free to remarry"; and Matthew 19:9's exception means that "a man who has divorced his wife because of her adultery is free to remarry."[32] Regarding Ephesians 5, Reynolds first points out that neither Augustine nor other patristic theologians equated "the great sacrament (*sacramentum magnum*) of Ephesians 5:32 with Christian marriage, as western theologians will do after 1100."[33] Instead, Augustine taught that the *sacramentum magnum* of Ephesians 5:32 either is Adam's statement in Genesis 2:24—interpreted as a prophecy of the union of Christ and his Church—or is the union of Christ and his Church. The "*sacramentum*" of marriage, then, consists its indissolubility, which in Christ's "city" ensures that husbands love their wives as Christ unbreakably loves the Church. Despite the emphasis on love, Reynolds notes that for Augustine a lack of love cannot dissolve a Christian marriage. Reynolds finds, therefore, that "Augustine's use of the analogy . . . is more legalistic than Paul's."[34] The medieval theologians kept the legalism but misunderstood Augustine's theology of the *sacramentum magnum*: "Augustine's sacrament *in* (i.e., between) Christ and the church became the medieval sacrament *of* (i.e., signifying) Christ and the church."[35]

Reynolds recognizes, however, that the doctrine that marriage is a sacrament (among the seven sacraments) did not emerge simply from the medieval reading of Ephesians 5:32; on the contrary, "the doctrine preceded and resulted in the interpretation [of Ephesians 5:32]," and the medieval "theologians did not base their defense of the doctrine on this verse," even though they cited it in discussing marriage as a sacrament.[36] The medieval theologians drew upon the whole of Ephesians 5 (and other texts) to arrive at the doctrine that marriage is a sacrament. But Reynolds holds that "whereas Paul had invoked the union of two in one flesh [Gen 2:24; Eph 5:31] to explain how the husband should cherish his wife, medieval theologians identified the union narrowly with sexual consummation, construed as the means of clinching the indissoluble contract."[37] Reynolds concludes that the medieval theologians were legalistic and blind to the constitutive

---

32. Reynolds, *How Marriage Became One of the Sacraments*, 112–13, with reference to Augustine's *De adulterinis coniugiis*.
33. Reynolds, *How Marriage Became One of the Sacraments*, 66.
34. Reynolds, *How Marriage Became One of the Sacraments*, 66.
35. Reynolds, *How Marriage Became One of the Sacraments*, 68.
36. Reynolds, *How Marriage Became One of the Sacraments*, 68.
37. Reynolds, *How Marriage Became One of the Sacraments*, 68.

power of mutual love in marriage, despite the evident fact that Paul held mutual love to be the very key to marriage in Christ.

For the medievals, Reynolds observes, marriage had dignity and holiness because it signified a holy thing. This was even the case for early medievals such as Bruno the Carthusian, who, while not counting marriage as a "sacrament" (in the sense of the seven sacraments), held that the two becoming one flesh in Genesis 2:24 signified the Son leaving his Father and his mother (the Synagogue) to cleave to the Church, and thereby signified the holy union of Christ and his Church. The point that Reynolds underlines here is that marriage's dignity and holiness, in the medieval view, derived not from human marriage itself, but from Christ's union with the Church,[38] despite the latter being much less knowable than the former. Reynolds also focuses on the way in which sexual intercourse functioned in medieval theology of marriage not as something dignified as such, but instead legalistically, as the mark of consummation. He shows that for Hugh of Saint-Victor, for example, "[t]he sexual dimension of marriage was a secondary, optional matter" and "the non-carnal union of affection between man and wife was intrinsically far greater and more valuable than sexual union."[39] The perfect marriage was the sexless marriage of Mary and Joseph.[40]

In addition, Reynolds addresses the diverse ways in which twelfth- and thirteenth-century theologians attempted to solve the problem of how the consent and consummation that establish a human marriage could cause what it signified, namely the union of Christ and the Church. Albert the Great's solution proved popular in the thirteenth and fourteenth centuries: the sacrament of marriage did not cause everything contained in the *res* of the union of Christ and the Church, but rather only caused an element of what is contained in this *res*, namely, the element of "conjugal grace."[41] Aquinas strengthens the solution by proposing that the grace received is the grace needed for the married couple to participate in the union of Christ and the Church. This solution, Reynolds thinks, has the problem of being only weakly distinguished from the grace of the other sacraments. Catholic

---

38. Of course, this is a significant part of the thesis of my own book, though I am aware that had not human marriage had its own profound created dignity, then the plan of salvation would not have included eschatological marriage conferring even greater dignity (in the order of grace) upon human marriage.

39. Reynolds, *How Marriage Became One of the Sacraments*, 74–75.

40. For theological reasons for this, without negating the relationship of sexuality and marriage, see the reflections of Cavadini, "The Sex Life of Mary and Joseph." For exegetical discussion of Mary's virginity and the status of Jesus' "brothers," see Prothro, "Semper Virgo?" Reynolds treats the matter as a myth.

41. Reynolds, *How Marriage Became One of the Sacraments*, 77.

theologians in the sixteenth century went further by holding that the grace of marriage was specifically conjugal love, strengthening and elevating the bond of the couple. Aware that the *magnum sacramentum* of Ephesians 5:32 did not mean one of the "sacraments," these theologians retrieved Ephesians 5:25 to argue that unless marriage in fact bestows sacramental grace, marriage could not live up to what Paul describes. Reynolds grants that "[t]his theology recovered something of the normative dimension of Paul's discourse on marriage in Ephesians 5:22–33."[42]

For Reynolds, nonetheless, the main medieval and Tridentine theologians of marriage failed in two primary ways. Historically speaking, they never adequately explained how marriage was a sacrament. Theologically speaking, they never adequately explained how marriage was a causal sign of the union of Christ and the Church. He notes that while the act of marrying could signify the spiritual *res* (union of Christ and the Church), "medieval theologians rarely construed real marriages—the mundane unions of Christian couples—as material signs revealing spiritual truths."[43] Rather than marriage being a "sign" of the union of Christ and the Church, Reynolds considers that medieval theology thought of things the other way round: the union of Christ and the Church is the "sign" to which real marriages need to be conformed.[44] On this view, he thinks, the best way to defend what the medievals were trying to do is to hold that "they conflated the relation of *res* and *signum* with that of exemplar and *exemplatum*."[45] Because marriage (the sign) was supposed to emulate or represent the exemplary signified (the union of Christ and the Church), marriage was holy.

Reynolds's fundamental claim is a theological one, rooted in his understanding of the relevant history. He implies that prior to the 1100s, marriage not only was not known as a "sacrament," but also it *was not* a sacrament. The sacramental status of marriage was invented by clergy who in the 1100s were seeking to emphasize and expand their role in mediating to laity the power of Christ's saving work, and who misunderstood (consciously or, more likely, unconsciously) Augustine's texts and biblical texts about marriage.

---

42. Reynolds, *How Marriage Became One of the Sacraments*, 79.

43. Reynolds, *How Marriage Became One of the Sacraments*, 82.

44. Surely both can be true. From the above chapters, it should be clear that I agree with the medieval theologians (and with Augustine) that the prime analogate of marriage, for Christians (in the inaugurated kingdom), is the eschatological marriage of God and his people. But this does not mean that human marriage is not a "sign" of the eschatological marriage.

45. Reynolds, *How Marriage Became One of the Sacraments*, 82.

II. The Inaugurated Kingdom as the Context for Doctrinal Development

Are Reynolds's claims correct? It is clear that Jesus did not reveal the realities of salvation in a manner that intended to do without the interpretive role of the ongoing community of his followers. He acted and taught in a way that was revelatory but that did not require him to spend years doctrinally catechizing. Put simply, he preached and acted with the purpose of accomplishing the inauguration of the kingdom of God. As Dale Allison comments after surveying a number of central passages of the Gospels: "our choice is not between an apocalyptic Jesus and some other Jesus; it is between an apocalyptic Jesus and no Jesus at all."[46] But numerous historical-critical biblical scholars have supposed that, after all, Jesus failed because the consummated kingdom has not arrived.

As Brant Pitre and others have shown, it is more reasonable to hold that Jesus intended to inaugurate the kingdom of God and did not presume that the consummation would come immediately. In his teachings and at his Last Supper, Jesus shows that he expects his followers to undertake a "New Exodus," nourished by the Eucharist as the "New Passover lamb" and configured to Christ in self-sacrificial love and endurance of tribulation.[47] For medieval theologians, as Reynolds recognizes, the Church is "the bride of Christ rather than his wife, for the union" of Christ and the Church is "still emerging" and will "not be fully realized until the *eschaton*."[48] The Church is the inaugurated kingdom of God, moving by faith toward the consummation that only Christ can bring about.[49] This is what Jesus envisioned at the Sermon on the Mount and the Last Supper.

The passage of time has a purpose in the journey of Christ's followers as the inaugurated kingdom. Time enables the Church to receive and appropriate Christ's revelatory words and deeds through faith, prayer, liturgical worship, contemplation, and the actions of the saints who are configured to Jesus' wisdom and charity. The Church exists not only in order to gather additional souls in every generation into God's kingdom, but also in order to grow into, by a process of development rather than rupture, the fullness

---

46. Allison, *Constructing Jesus*, 46–47.
47. See Pitre, *Jesus and the Last Supper*.
48. Reynolds, *How Marriage Became One of the Sacraments*, 76.
49. Scot McKnight rightly observes, "When comparing kingdom to church, most people make fundamental logical errors. The most common is to compare future kingdom and present church. Kingdom is a both-and, a now and a not yet. The church also is a both-and, a now and not yet. The church, then, is an eschatological reality" (McKnight, *Kingdom Conspiracy*, 206).

of divine revelation that has been given in and by Jesus Christ.⁵⁰ Christ's inaugurated kingdom is not merely a lifeless channel through which the deposit of faith happens to pass. The Church, as the inaugurated kingdom, is living and growing into the fullness of Christ.

In the Gospel of John, therefore, Jesus tells his disciples at his farewell discourse: "These things I have spoken to you, while I am still with you. But the Counselor, the Holy Spirit, whom the Father will send in my name, he will teach you all things, and bring to your remembrance all that I have said to you" (John 14:25-26). In a similar vein, Jesus goes on to teach: "I have yet many things to say to you, but you cannot bear them now. When the Spirit of truth comes, he will guide you into all the truth; for he will not speak on his own authority, but whatever he hears he will speak, and he will declare to you the things that are to come. He will glorify me, for he will take what is mine and declare it to you" (John 15:12-14). These statements fit with similar points made elsewhere in the New Testament. For example, in the Gospel of Luke, the risen Jesus comes to two of his disciples on the Emmaus Road, and "he interpreted to them in all the scriptures the things concerning himself" (Luke 24:27). The risen Jesus remains active in teaching the Church through the Spirit.

Paul makes clear that there will still be "prophets" and "teachers" in the Church (1 Cor 12:28)—an indication of ongoing growth in knowledge of divine revelation. Until the eschatological consummation, Paul says, "our knowledge is imperfect and our prophecy is imperfect" (1 Cor 13:9). Similarly, Ephesians 4 paints a portrait of the Church's ongoing growth into the fullness of Christ by means of the gifts that Christ sends in the Spirit. Paul explains that the Spirit's "gifts were that some should be apostles, some prophets, some evangelists, some pastors and teachers, for the equipment of the saints, for the work of ministry, for building up of the body of Christ, until we all attain to the unity of the faith and of the knowledge of the Son of God" (Eph 4:11-13).

More such texts could be cited, but let me attend here briefly to the Johannine passages, with the help of the historical-critical exegesis of the evangelical scholar Craig Keener. Commenting on John 14:26, Keener remarks that in the Dead Sea Scrolls too, the Holy Spirit appears "as a teacher," both with regard to inspiring specific prophets and with regard to providing wisdom or insights.⁵¹ With this background, Keener then interprets the significance of John 14:26. He observes, "The Paraclete had been sent not

---

50. See Newman, *Development of Christian Doctrine*. See also, for a contemporary retrieval and constructive proposal, Meszaros's *The Prophetic Church*.

51. Keener, *Gospel of John*, 977.

only to continue Jesus' presence in the experience of the community but also to expound the teachings of Jesus within the proper confines set by those teachings."[52]

For Keener, the "proper confines" are the Church itself. Jesus established his Church by reconfiguring the twelve tribes of Israel around himself, through his twelve disciples. The Holy Spirit will "expound" Jesus' teachings, that is to say, will enable the Church to interpret them and will guide the Church in that ongoing interpretation over time. Keener explains what he takes this to mean: "Such teaching, like haggadic midrash, could no doubt be expansive; but it would have to remain faithful to the Johannine Jesus tradition held by the community."[53] It cannot contradict the "Johannine Jesus tradition," even while it can draw out this tradition in an "expansive" manner. In Keener's view, the Gospel of John itself is likely such an expansion, under the Spirit's guidance, of the community's Jesus tradition. Keener underscores that "the Spirit's teaching is neither wholly innovative nor simply repetitive (for the latter, 'bring to remembrance' would have sufficed) but explanatory and applicational, like the exposition of Jewish sages."[54]

Keener adds that given the use of the word "Paraclete" (or "Advocate"), John "14:26 probably means that the Spirit will give wisdom in the hour of testing before the court of 'the world,' bringing to remembrance the polemic of the Fourth Gospel for use in debates with the hostile synagogue leaders and those influenced by them."[55] This may be so, but it is too narrow. In God's providence, a wider scope is envisioned than simply debates with Jewish opponents. Indeed, toward the end of his reflections on John 14:26, Keener affirms that the pedagogical and interpretive "ministry of the Spirit," vis-à-vis the words and deeds of Jesus, "cannot be limited to the apostolic witness nor to the Fourth Gospel itself. . . . The presence of the Spirit with them 'forever' indicates that this exposition is expected to continue in the community, not to end with the death of the apostles; the Paraclete would equip the community to confront ever new situations posed by the world's hostile charges."[56] The Spirit will continually equip the Church to proclaim Jesus' words and deeds and to interpret them in a way that attains to further

---

52. Keener, *Gospel of John*, 977.
53. Keener, *Gospel of John*, 977–78.
54. Keener, *Gospel of John*, 978.
55. Keener, *Gospel of John*, 979.
56. Keener, *Gospel of John*, 979. Keener insists, however, that this does not mean that "any given community would perpetually remain the normative arbiter" of the apostolic tradition (*Gospel of John*, 981n430).

depths of insight. The Gospel of John anticipates that "the Spirit's application of truth" will "remain faithful to the apostolic tradition."[57]

Commenting on John 16:13, where Jesus reiterates his promises about the Spirit whom he (and the Father) will send, Keener holds that Jesus' words apply "to the community, which probably identified more with the beloved disciple than with the apostles led by Peter."[58] Of course, the beloved disciple himself (or the evangelist) recognizes Peter as in a special way singled out by Jesus (see John 21). In the Gospel, the community of the beloved disciple is not cut off from the wider community of "the apostles led by Peter." In his discussion of John 16:13, Keener underscores that the mission of the Spirit/Paraclete is to guide or lead "the community with regard to the truth."[59] He considers it possible that the eschatological New Exodus "may be in the background" in John 16:13, but he places the emphasis on the Spirit's guiding the community to know "truth."[60] He concludes that what the Spirit will guide the community into is "more 'the whole truth,' the full revelation of God's character in Christ (14:6), than 'all possible knowledge on any subject.'"[61] This seems right, although I would speak of a deeper knowledge of what God has revealed in Christ, rather than simply "God's character in Christ." Keener goes on to say that John 16:13 views the Spirit "as the agent of Jesus active in and through the community."[62] The community is the inaugurated kingdom of the Messiah which, due to the Spirit, will not fail in the truth of its reception and proclamation of the fullness of Jesus' words and deeds.

Keener is aware of "the Roman Catholic position" that the reference to Spirit's future declaration to the community of "the things that are to

---

57. Keener, *Gospel of John*, 981n430. From a Catholic perspective, it is not that the "church of Rome" is the sole "normative arbiter"—as Keener fears—but that Jesus Christ promises that the Church around the world, led by the successors of the apostles (including, preeminently but not solely, the successor of Peter), will receive the guidance of the Spirit in remaining "faithful to apostolic tradition" while handing it on and interpreting its depths. Much depends on whether one thinks that the (Spirit-guided) Church was correct in affirming the existence of an ongoing Petrine ministry in the Church.

58. Keener, *Gospel of John*, 1036.

59. Keener, *Gospel of John*, 1036. He notes that some scholars have found eschatological significance in the verb "ὁδηγήσει" employed in this verse. Given that the Septuagint uses the same verb to describe God or Moses leading the Israelites on the Exodus, the verb here may alert us to a New Exodus. Keener recognizes that in Paul's letters, the Spirit's guidance pertains to the people of God on the New Exodus.

60. Keener, *Gospel of John*, 1037.

61. Keener, *Gospel of John*, 1038.

62. Keener, *Gospel of John*, 1039.

come" (John 16:13) should be understood "as a promise that the Spirit will superintend doctrinal developments in the later community."[63] I hold that this must be *one* of the things that the Spirit does, not least because John is fully aware that doctrinal controversies and divisions will arise, and that the Spirit-guided Church's unity in Christ will be (and in John's day already is being) sorely tested. Keener argues that it is more probable that John 16:13 is speaking about future trials that the community will have to undergo. But these two options are not mutually exclusive, because some of the trials will be doctrinal divisions. In terms of what the Spirit will reveal with respect to Christ, Keener maintains that "[f]or John, not all the Spirit's words will have been reported in the Fourth Gospel, but all of them will be consistent with it (cf. 1 John 4:1–3), just as all Jesus' words in the Fourth Gospel are consistent with the Jesus of history known to the witness behind the Johannine tradition."[64] This accords with the nature of proper doctrinal development. Development is not a distancing from Jesus, but rather the reverse: in a real sense, as Keener comments, "the prophetic Spirit enables the Johannine community to continue the first disciples' experience with Jesus."[65]

After Jesus' inauguration of the kingdom, therefore, much work remains to be done, even after the writing and canonizing of the books of New Testament,[66] with regard to the articulation of the inexhaustibly rich reality that Jesus has inaugurated by his gathering of the Twelve, teaching, miracles, Passion, Resurrection, Ascension, and sending of the eschatological Spirit upon his Body and bride. During the time in which the kingdom

63. Keener, *Gospel of John*, 1040.

64. Keener, *Gospel of John*, 1041.

65. Keener, *Gospel of John*, 1042. Here Keener notes the "Johannine polemic" against those who oppose John's understanding of Jesus (*Gospel of John*, 1042).

66. For background to the canon of Christian Scripture, see most recently Lim, *The Formation of the Jewish Canon*; Satlow, *How the Bible Became Holy*. Lim responds persuasively to Roger Beckwith, who argues on the basis of Matthew 23:34–36 that Jesus knew and implicitly affirmed a tripartite canon: see Beckwith, *The Old Testament Canon*; and Lim, *The Formation of the Jewish Canon*, 157–62. Lim grants that Luke 24:44 indicates a tripartite canon, though it does not identify which books belong to it. See also Evans, "The Scriptures of Jesus"; Hengel, *The Septuagint as Christian Scripture*. In his reconstruction of the late-Second Temple emergence of authoritative scriptural scrolls, Satlow shows that during Jesus' time "the limits of scripture—both *what* 'counts' and *how* it counts—were still fuzzy" (*How the Bible Became Holy*, 209). See also Joseph Ratzinger's remark that "[t]he Church possessed no formulated communication left as its own legacy by the last living Apostle concerning which books should go together to make up Scripture. Instead the Church had to ponder the effects in herself of the work of the Holy Spirit amid arduous historical questioning, before she separated from each other the books in which she did and did not recognize this Spirit and so separated normative expressions of its nature from books not containing this" (Ratzinger, "Sources of Revelation," 274).

has been inaugurated but not consummated, the Church learns what divine revelation is in its fullness, by growing (often due to controversies, but also due to evangelization, prayer, worship, and so on) in appreciation for the riches that have been given once and for all by the Lord Jesus. On the New Exodus, relying upon Christ's guidance through the Spirit, believers must seek the truth of Christ in response to the difficulties of each epoch.

What I am advocating here is essentially the position put forward by Yves Congar in his studies of Tradition and of the Holy Spirit (and thus of the Church as an eschatological reality, the inaugurated kingdom of Christ). In *The Prophetic Church*, Andrew Meszaros notes that for Congar, "developments in the tradition are ultimately rooted in the one deposit of faith delivered once and for all."[67] In part due to historical crises—whether caused by "heresies, discoveries, or political developments"—"there is indeed a growth, an accumulation, or a progress being made in the Church's understanding" of the deposit of faith.[68] Christ's inauguration of the eschatological kingdom means that the "time of the Church" (the period prior to the consummation) has profound significance, not only because it brings people into the mysteries accomplished by Christ, but also because it makes possible "humanity's contribution to, and participation in, the *fullness* of Christ which is to come at the consummation of a pilgrimage of struggle."[69]

III. Schillebeeckx and Elliott: Marriage and Doctrinal Development

Edward Schillebeeckx

In his *Marriage: Human Reality and Saving Mystery*, published in French in 1961, Edward Schillebeeckx devotes almost two hundred pages to marriage as a reality in the Old and New Testaments.[70] When he treats marriage in biblical Israel, he notes that especially in the Wisdom literature "the Genesis account of the creation and the prophetic message of God's covenant of grace as a marriage come together."[71] He observes that marriage, when used as an image of God's covenant with Israel, is associated with the Hebrew words for love, goodness, mercy, faithfulness, constancy, preference,

---

67. Meszaros, *The Prophetic Church*, 195. See also Müller, "Development or Corruption?"

68. Meszaros, *The Prophetic Church*, 196–97.

69. Meszaros, *The Prophetic Church*, 147.

70. Schillebeeckx, *Marriage*.

71. Schillebeeckx, *Marriage*, 62.

jealousy, and exclusivity. At both the human level (marriage between a man and woman) and the divine level (marriage between God and Israel), marriage involved a covenantal oath marking permanence. Marriage involved a one-flesh union, indeed even a becoming "one life," and included "mutual help, support, and solicitude."[72] He draws attention to the prophet Malachi's statements about marriage,[73] as well, of course, to the prophet Hosea's. From the very outset of creation (Genesis 1–2), furthermore, "[t]he community of marriage, as a gift of creation from the God of the covenant, was a first draft of the finished picture of grace, God's covenant with men."[74] Schillebeeckx argues that marriage in biblical Israel possessed a "prophetic form," because male-female marriage was seen to symbolize something extraordinarily profound on the level of divine election and covenant.[75]

Describing the "ethos" of Old Testament marriage, he notes the primacy of family and childbearing, often in the context of God's intervention on behalf of the childless, which he sees as prefiguring Christ's subordination of marriage and family to the kingdom of God. In treating polygamy, concubinage, and divorce, he suggests that Israel's movement was consistently toward monogamy and eventually also toward a critique of divorce (see Malachi 2:16), at least when the new partner was a non-Israelite.

Turning to the New Testament, he remarks that Christ insists upon indissoluble marriage in accord with God's plan from creation. In addition, Christ opens up the path of celibacy for the kingdom. The New Testament highlights the marriage of God and his people, in the "eschatological or heavenly glorification in which Christians, together with Christ, are to celebrate the eternal wedding-feast with God."[76] The Church is the bride of Christ. He examines what the New Testament says about marriage between Christians, arguing that the "household codes" are "inwardly transformed by being 'in Christ'" in accord with mutual self-subjection and *agape*.[77] With regard to the subordination of women (the headship of husbands) taught by Paul, he asks whether "the affirmations which the Bible makes about woman and marriage really [are] 'biblical' (that is, are they really divine declarations with the force of commandments), or are they merely structures set in an ancient historical and social framework, which Christians of that period

---

72. Schillebeeckx, *Marriage*, 67.

73. For historical-critical analysis showing that "Malachi identifies marriage as a covenant and . . . grounds this identification in his interpretation of the Adam and Eve narrative," see Hugenberger, *Marriage as a Covenant*; the quotation is from 280.

74. Schillebeeckx, *Marriage*, 70.

75. Schillebeeckx, *Marriage*, 81.

76. Schillebeeckx, *Marriage*, 108.

77. Schillebeeckx, *Marriage*, 137.

experienced 'in the Lord'?"[78] He answers that there are some culturally conditioned and changeable elements, but he finds that Scripture itself ensures that "the relative value of these elements is recognised."[79]

On this basis, Schillebeeckx turns to the development of the sacrament of marriage within Catholic theological and dogmatic understanding. He lays emphasis on the parallel between marriage's "definitive surrender to another person, without any foreknowledge of what may happen in the future," and Christianity's call for "definitive surrender" to God.[80] From this perspective, one can see why marriage is a "sacrament," in which "a secular reality, with its distinctive historical significance, is inwardly transformed into a religious reality."[81]

Schillebeeckx begins by outlining marriage in the Greco-Roman culture that Christianity entered. He then observes that "there was during the first three centuries a growing realisation in the church that marriage between two baptized persons, although a secular affair, had a special Christian and ecclesiastical significance."[82] Beginning in the fourth century, marriage came to involve a priestly blessing and "liturgical framework" of some kind, which served to affirm both God's place in the marriage and the sanctity of the marriage.[83] The first recorded nuptial mass, taking place in a church, comes from the early fifth century. The Church also identified impediments to a valid marriage, such as incest, abduction of the woman, and the king's giving a woman as a gift to a particular man.

In ninth-century France, "The strictly ecclesiastical legal form of the marriage contract came about mainly as a result of the misleading Pseudo-Isidorian writings," namely, decretals that sought to reform the French church by insisting upon indissolubility and upon respect for the

78. Schillebeeckx, *Marriage*, 175.
79. Schillebeeckx, *Marriage*, 187; cf. 193.
80. Schillebeeckx, *Marriage*, 207.
81. Schillebeeckx, *Marriage*, 207. In my view, the element of indissolubility—at the core of the sacrament—makes marriage an "eschatological" reality along lines that Brent Waters, from a Protestant perspective that denies that marriage is a sacrament in this sense, does not perceive. In his generally helpful book, Waters rightly insists upon differentiating the Church from the family, but he insists that the Christian family is not "an eschatological community" (Waters, *The Family*, 231). (Waters helpfully criticizes Maurice, an advocate of Christian socialism, for arguing that the Church should here and now displace the family: see Maurice, *Social Morality*, as discussed in *The Family*, 240.) The problem comes when Waters argues that "creation's destiny is not an eternal church" (*The Family*, 255)—a claim that depends for its intelligibility upon a reductive notion of "church," as though "church" meant bishops, pastors, councils, and buildings.
82. Schillebeeckx, *Marriage*, 260.
83. Schillebeeckx, *Marriage*, 251.

impediments to a valid marriage.[84] Throughout this section, however, Schillebeeckx emphasizes that Christian marriage remained grounded in the mutual consent of the baptized partners, rather than in any Church action. Even so, by around the year 1000, the Church had taken over jurisdictional power over marriage. In the ensuing centuries, too, the liturgical "part played by the priest gained immensely in significance. It was usually the priest who gave the bride to the bridegroom."[85] The practice of a nuptial mass became common. This fueled the movement toward understanding marriage as a sacrament.[86]

Schillebeeckx goes on to explore the scholastic debates and diverse early-medieval practices regarding the consummation of marriage: is marriage consummated by the spouses' mutual consent or by marital intercourse? The issue was complicated by the need to affirm the full validity of the marriage of Mary and Joseph. At some length, he traces the positions of various theologians, canonists, and popes. He examines liturgical developments as well. In light of the liturgical practice of the fifth through tenth centuries, he emphasizes that well before the twelfth century, the prevailing view of marriage was that it "is a secular reality, already meaningful in itself, but raised by the church's blessing of the bride or of the marriage itself to the level of a supernaturally meaningful reality."[87]

Also significant was the Church's reaction to the twelfth-century spread of Catharist and Albigensian rejection of the goodness of marriage. Taking note of sermons by Bernard of Clairvaux, Roger of Caen, and others, he suggests that "the concrete setting for the increasingly explicit awareness of the sacramental nature of marriage was provided by the situation of emergency which prevailed at this time, which forced the church to become aware of the need to think at a deeper level about the goodness and holiness of marriage."[88] He also notes that the priestly blessing in the marriage ceremony also began to be seen as indicative of a "sacrament." In this respect he compares Western understanding with that of the East: "Marriage was regarded in the Eastern Church primarily as an act of the priest, a liturgical

---

84. Schillebeeckx, *Marriage*, 268.

85. Schillebeeckx, *Marriage*, 277.

86. Schillebeeckx argues, "The patristic view that marriage was a moral obligation and indissoluble on a basis of the *Sacramentum*, and the scholastic view of marriage as an objective and indissoluble bond on the basis of a certain efficacy of the sacrament, are . . . complementary" (Schillebeeckx, *Marriage*, 284).

87. Schillebeeckx, *Marriage*, 311.

88. Schillebeeckx, *Marriage*, 313.

service or *akolouthia*, in which the faithful—and in particular the bride and bridegroom themselves—were actively involved."[89]

At this stage, Schillebeeckx brings up a point that carries much weight for Reynolds, namely, the Reformers' argument that the Church made marriage a "sacrament" in order to enhance the power of the priests.[90] Schillebeeckx argues that the connection of the "sacrament" with the liturgy of marriage, rather than with "marriage itself," opened the door to the problem later identified by the Reformers.[91] For Schillebeeckx, however, the Reformers' concern is historically unfounded. The Church gained jurisdictional authority not because of greed for priestly power, but in accord with the need to assert the public nature of marriage, its indissolubility, and the impediments to a valid marriage.

Addressing the specific question of the rise of the "seven sacraments," Schillebeeckx points out that the eleventh-century retrieval of the Augustinian *sacramentum* led to discussions about whether some "sacred signs," in addition to baptism and the Eucharist, had a special status and conferred grace.[92] Peter Lombard took up the view of "seven sacraments" and solidified it; but its popularity immediately after Lombard (prior to the spread of Lombard's authority in theology) shows that the view of "seven sacraments" would have won the day anyway. Notably, Schillebeeckx concludes that "Jesus' *logion* about the indissolubility of marriage was, from the point of view of the history of dogma, the basis of the scholastic assertion of the truly sacramental nature of marriage."[93]

He goes on to examine why theologians delayed in attributing to marriage a gift of grace or sanctifying power. Hugh of Saint-Victor did so, but without influence upon his immediate successors, in part because Hugh spoke of "two sacraments" (the spiritual consent and the physical consummation). In the early thirteenth century, William of Auxerre argued that marriage, as a remedy, preserves the spouses in grace. Alexander of Hales, influenced by Hugh, responded to William and proposed that Christian marriage disposes the couple to a spiritual communion of love, beyond

---

89. Schillebeeckx, *Marriage*, 315–16.

90. For a contemporary popular version of this argument, see also Wills, *Why Priests?*. For Wills, who writes as a Catholic, the only two real sacraments—and even then not quite in the sense taught by the Catholic Church—are baptism and the Eucharist.

91. Schillebeeckx, *Marriage*, 316.

92. For further background, see Bourgeois, *Être et signifier*.

93. Schillebeeckx, *Marriage*, 331. Sadly, less than a decade after the original publication of his book, Schillebeeckx himself rejected marriage's indissolubility in an essay published in 1970. See his "Christian Marriage."

what is possible for natural marriage. Schillebeeckx shows that Aquinas completes the movement toward a full understanding of the sanctifying grace bestowed by marriage. For Aquinas, "if God gave an ability to bring something about—in this case, the *bona matrimonii*—then he also gave the grace without which it was not possible to use this ability in a suitable way."[94]

For Schillebeeckx, the bottom line is that in Jesus' teachings about marriage, it is already clear that Jesus is elevating the created reality of human marriage into a sacred and sanctifying reality of the inaugurated kingdom of God—and the teaching of Ephesians 5 makes this even clearer. Schillebeeckx is able to perceive this in part because he devotes so much space to studying the Old Testament on marriage, both as a human institution and as representative of God's covenantal relationship with his people Israel. In inaugurating the kingdom and preparing for the wedding feast of God and his people, the eschatological bridegroom Jesus Christ also restores and elevates human marriage.

Peter J. Elliott

In his chapter "The Quest for the Sign" in *What God Has Joined . . .: The Sacramentality of Marriage*, Peter Elliott sketches the history of Christian marriage. He, too, argues that already in the New Testament, Paul (in Ephesians) understands that Jesus Christ's powerful teaching on marriage has elevated marriage "to the supernatural order."[95] It is this "supernatural order"—as distinct from the order of creation to which marriage also belongs—that Elliott has in mind when speaking about "sacramentality." He admits, of course, that Christ instituted no "new sign" for marriage.[96] Yet, because Christian marriage signifies the eschatological marriage of Christ and the Church, Christian marriage belongs to the supernatural order from the outset. In other words, it always was a sign that causes participation in the supernatural order, and so it always was a "sacrament."

Elliott first notes that Ignatius of Antioch and Tertullian, among the Fathers, speak of Christian marriage as being constituted in some way ecclesiastically. Clement of Alexandria and Origen affirm Christian marriage as a graced condition in which Christ is present. Ambrose suggests that marriage is sanctified by the blessing of a priest, and he states that Christ sanctifies marriage. Ambrosiaster draws an explicit connection between marriage and Ephesians 5, by remarking that marriage signifies the mystery

---

94. Schillebeeckx, *Marriage*, 337.
95. Elliott, *What God Has Joined*, 74.
96. Elliott, *What God Has Joined*, 74.

(*sacramentum*) of the unity of Christ and the Church. The Greek Fathers highlight Christ's presence and miracle at the wedding at Cana, by which Christ elevates and sanctifies marriage.

Elliott grants that the "mystery" or "*sacramentum*" of Ephesians 5 does not, for the Fathers, have the "meaning later developed by theologians as they sought to discern the exact number of the sacraments."[97] Yet, the Fathers always thought of marriage as a sacred sign, elevated to this status by Christ. Augustine highlights indissolubility as the meaning of the "*sacramentum*" referred to in Ephesians 5, and Elliot points out that indissolubility makes marriage a sacred state, comparable in its permanence to ordination and baptism. In its sign character, Christian marriage causes a change in what otherwise would be a merely natural reality. Specifically, Christian marriage—precisely as a sign of the union of Christ and the Church—causes marriage to be absolutely indissoluble. Elliott emphasizes that in *On Marriage and Concupiscence*, Augustine "points to the causality of the 'great mystery'" by citing Ephesians 5:25 and then affirming "that the 'effect of this sacred symbol (*sacramenti res*)' is indissolubility."[98] Christian marriage possesses a significatory (or "sacramental") participation in the saving mystery of Christ, given that it is Christ's saving work that grounds the indissolubility of Christ's union with the Church and so also the indissolubility of Christian marriage.[99]

For Elliott, the heart of the matter consists in tracing how Christ's healing and elevation of marriage into the supernatural order plays out in theological reflection over the centuries. In the centuries that followed Augustine, the main task in the West was that of Christianizing pagan practices and of ensuring that the nobility did not undermine Christian practice. In this regard, as Elliott shows, it became important to reflect upon consent and consummation, because this mattered when the nobility—for both political and personal reasons—wanted to renounce one partner and take another. Elliott's treatment of the medieval context and the reasons why the early scholastics sought to codify and develop the Church's sacramental doctrine (including determining the unique set of "seven sacraments") is less detailed than Schillebeeckx's, though he treats Lombard, Abelard, and others. Prior to Albert and Aquinas, Elliott finds three thirteenth-century thinkers who affirm that the sacrament of marriage involves the giving of grace (whether the grace of spiritual growth in mutual love, or remedial grace): Gandulf of Bologna, Alexander of Hales, and Bonaventure.

---

97. Elliott, *What God Has Joined*, 77.
98. Elliott, *What God Has Joined*, 82.
99. Elliott, *What God Has Joined*, 84.

Elliott gives Aquinas special attention, on the grounds that Aquinas is fully "able to include sexual love within sacramentality, because marriage as a 'natural state' already anticipates sacramentality."[100] In the Christian dispensation, marriage signifies Christ's union with his Church, even though of course marriage does not contain the full reality of this union. As a natural reality, marriage's intimate union manifests itself in three ways: by mutual love, by shared life together (including child-raising), and by one-flesh sexual union. The natural bond of marriage is thus capable of being elevated by Christ to signify the intimate and indissoluble union of Christ and the Church. For Aquinas, as Elliott says, "The [marital] bond disposes for a special, close, married participation in the unity of the Mystical Body."[101] Aquinas thus has an important role in helping the Church to understand the specific "sacramentality" of marriage, that is, the way in which marriage, having been elevated into the supernatural order by Christ, enables the spouses to live marriage in a new and elevated way of love, inclusive of the new absolute indissolubility of the marital bond.

Elliott is aware that Aquinas's position was not unanimously adopted by his fellow theologians; for example, in the early fourteenth century Durandus of Saint-Pourçain (Aquinas's fellow Dominican) denied that marriage was a sacrament, though under pressure he later reverted to Peter Lombard's view that marriage was a sacrament but not one that caused grace. In his early-fourteenth century conflict with spiritual Franciscans who sought a radical imitation of the life of Christ, Pope John XXII felt compelled to insist that marriage was a sacrament. The Council of Florence included marriage among the seven sacraments. Elliott summarizes the Council of Trent's position on the grace of the sacrament of marriage: "This Grace perfects the natural love of Marriage and strengthens the indissoluble unity of the couple. Thus Christ himself sanctifies the spouses."[102]

Elliott continues his exposition of the development of the understanding of marriage as a sacrament into the post-Tridentine period, with special attention to Robert Bellarmine's emphasis on the way in which the grace of the sacrament of marriage shapes the "lived union" of the couple (thereby

---

100. Elliott, *What God Has Joined*, 91. For more detailed studies of Aquinas on the sacrament of marriage and on marriage as a natural (created) reality, see my discussion of Aquinas and the secondary literature that I cite in chapter 4 of *The Indissolubility of Marriage*.

101. Elliott, *What God Has Joined*, 97.

102. Elliott, *What God Has Joined*, 74. 104. Reynolds, Schillebeeckx, and (to a lesser extent) Elliott all give significant attention to Trent's decree *Tametsi*, which ruled out "clandestine" marriages and brought marriage more firmly within the domain of the priest.

ensuring that the sacrament is not imagined to disappear in its power of grace after the consent and consummation).[103] He also gives particular attention to Matthias Joseph Scheeben's approach to the sacrament of marriage, in which Scheeben lays emphasis upon Ephesians 5:25-32. Elliott holds with Scheeben that this biblical passage is fundamental for showing the sacramentality of marriage—the power of the sacrament of marriage to cause grace, as a deepened participation in the salvific mystery of Christ. When he arrives at the twentieth century, Elliott attends appreciatively to Pius XI's *Casti Connubii*, Dietrich von Hildebrand, and the Second Vatican Council, among other sources.

At the end of his exposition, Elliott tests his argument regarding doctrinal development by applying John Henry Newman's seven notes, namely, "(1) preservation of type, (2) continuity of principles, (3) assimilative power, (4) logical sequence, (5) anticipation of its future, (6) conservative action on its past, and (7) chronic vigor."[104] Much depends upon the first "note," preservation of type. If in the apostolic witness there is no indication that Christ instituted marriage as a sacramental reality—a sacred sign that causes grace, a reality of the supernatural order that heals and elevates nature—then marriage surely cannot be a sacrament and the medieval determination that there are seven "sacraments" would be in error. But in fact, as Elliott says, "Jesus Christ raised the created reality of Marriage to a new dignity by requiring indissolubility and mutual fidelity."[105] Christ not only requires this, but also he gives the grace of the Holy Spirit to make it possible.

IV. Conclusion

Reynolds himself recognizes that marriage did not spring forth around 1100 as a new Christian reality. The development of sacramental doctrine about marriage had a rich foundation in biblical revelation. Rescinding the Mosaic permission of divorce, Jesus taught that "from the beginning" (Matt 19:4) marriage was a permanent one-flesh union between a man and woman who are joined by God and who therefore cannot be divided by any human power. His inauguration of the kingdom includes the restoration of marriage, made possible by the outpouring of the Spirit. The biblical scholar John Meier affirms that we can know with certainty that Jesus "forbade divorce and remarriage."[106] Jesus felt able to separate himself in this sharp way

---

103. Elliott, *What God Has Joined*, 106.
104. Elliott, *What God Has Joined*, 115.
105. Elliott, *What God Has Joined*, 115.
106. Meier, *A Marginal Jew*, 126.

from the Mosaic law because, Meier says, "[f]ar from seeing himself as just another teacher, Jesus consciously presented himself to his fellow Jews as the eschatological prophet."[107] Paul echoes Jesus' teaching about marriage; if a divorce has taken place, "Paul insists that there is to be no second marriage (thus echoing the clause 'and marries another' in Luke 16:18 and Mark 10:11), thus implying that the bond of the first marriage remains."[108]

The alarmed protest of Jesus' disciples against his strict doctrine (Matt 19:10) shows that a special grace is needed for people to live out the truth of Christian marriage. This special grace, Jesus implies, will come to those who have married each other as Christians, that is, within the context of the inaugurated kingdom, the Church. Since people will need a special grace to live out marriage the way that Jesus intends it to be, Christians who marry will receive this grace. It is no wonder, then, that when sacramental doctrine became widely debated—which, as we have seen, happened in the early Middle Ages—Catholic theologians and the Catholic Church determined that Jesus instituted Christian marriage as a "sacrament."

Reynolds is aware that according to Ephesians 5 (and indeed according to the Old Testament), a marriage between a man and a woman *signifies* something: namely, the marriage of God and humankind or the union of Christ and his Church. Furthermore, the fact that Paul exhorts Christian couples to live a married life that models Christ's love for the Church implies that grace must be present in their union in order for them to fulfill this exhortation. As Reynolds says, marriage signifies the union of Christ and his Church most perfectly when the man and woman love each other with self-sacrificial love. At the same time, the ongoing existence of the sacrament in the married couple does not depend upon whether the couple retains their love, because otherwise marriage could not be indissoluble in the way that Jesus says it is.

Benoît-Dominique de La Soujeole remarks that according to Christian faith, "the divine reality touches and saves us in and through the mediation of human realities, the first of which and the source of all the others is the humanity assumed by the Word."[109] Historical research provides insight into the concrete paths taken by the Church's doctrinal development with respect to marriage. Scripture, too, leads us to expect the ongoing unfolding of Christ's teaching in the Church through the Holy Spirit. But in the end, marriage's place among the seven sacraments flows from the incarnate Lord who, with divine authority, rescinded the Mosaic permission of divorce and

---

107. Meier, *A Marginal Jew*, 127.
108. Meier, *A Marginal Jew*, 126.
109. De La Soujeole, *Mystery of the Church*, 308. See also Torrell, *A Priestly People*.

made marriage into a restored reality of his inaugurated kingdom. Christian marriage, as a sacred sign of Christ's union with the Church, gives the spouses the grace of the Holy Spirit to enable them to live out their indissoluble marriage in the self-sacrificial love of Christ (Matt 19:3–9; Eph 5:25–33).

Chapter 7

SOCIAL JUSTICE

God created the entire cosmos for the marriage of God and his people, an eschatological marriage in which the entire renewed cosmos, translucent to divine charity, will everlastingly participate. As God's images, we are made for marital union with the holy Trinity in fruitful self-surrendering love. Given the fall of the first human couple, we relearn how to be married (to God and to our human spouse, unless we are single) by cleaving to the mercy and self-sacrificial love of Christ's Cross. This task is more than we can accomplish by our human resources, and so the sacrament of marriage gives spouses the grace of the Holy Spirit needed to live out the ends of their marriage, precisely by sharing more deeply in the eschatological marriage of Christ and the Church.[1]

In this final chapter, however, I ask whether the Christian doctrine of marriage actually serves human flourishing. Today, many people reject the Christian doctrine of marriage as opposed to societal progress.[2] Does

---

1. See Hahn, *The First Society*, 128–29: "The promotion of a secularized vision of natural marriage is often a good-faith attempt to make the truth of marriage accessible and acceptable to a secular liberal society. The unfortunate irony is that it is precisely that which makes it acceptable—its removal of anything supernatural—that makes it unsustainable. . . . Sacramentality isn't a bonus feature that we layer on top of natural marriage; rather, it's essential to *what marriage is* under the New Covenant."

2. See for example Lewis, *Full Surrogacy Now*. Although Lewis seeks to be shocking, her arguments are essentially those of Plato, enhanced by technology. I grant, of course, that historically (and even today) some Christian marriages have been unjust due to patriarchy, machismo, and so on. Browning cautions rightly, "Promoting marriage without effecting marriage reform can be highly disadvantageous to women in some parts of the world" (Browning, *Marriage and Modernization*, 219; though Browning goes on to advocate contraception and abortion). For a Muslim perspective that undercuts the equal dignity of women, see Hartford, *Upholding an Islamic Marriage*,

marriage as understood by Christians serve social justice? Answering in the affirmative, Perry Cahall has argued that the family, rooted in marriage, "is not just a recipient of the pastoral activity of the Church, but . . . also an active agent that contributes to accomplishing the Church's mission of bringing the love of Christ to all."[3] Brent Waters makes a similar point. He states that "there are theological reasons why Christians may affirm a particular, normative account of the family. As the most basic form of human association, the family is part of a vindicated creation being drawn towards its destiny in Christ."[4] In the inaugurated kingdom, the family plays a crucial role in social justice understood as the spread of self-giving love and care for others. Families ordered to (and by) Christ "do not turn in upon themselves, but evoke an unfolding love that is drawn towards more expansive spheres of association," that is to say, toward care of neighbor in various concrete ways.[5] Here it is also important to recognize that marriage, as a created reality, has accomplished great good in all cultures, Christian or not. For example, Jonathan Sacks points out that Jewish experience shows

---

84: "If she [the wife] goes out with her husband's permission, she must go out in proper hijab (covering) without make-up or perfume. She should not raise her voice or speak with men in the street unnecessarily, even if they are her husband's friends." See also the excerpts from sacred texts and classical theological and legal texts in Browning, Green, and Witte, eds., *Sex, Marriage, and Family*.

3. Cahall, *The Mystery of Marriage*, 323. For some Catholic theologians, however, marriage as the Church understands it is not a pressing topic of social ethics: see Astorga, *Catholic Moral Theology*. By contrast, see the links between the family and social justice drawn by Vodraska, *Philosophical Essays*, especially chapters 1, 2, and 5.

4. Waters, *The Family*, x.

5. Waters, *The Family*, x. Waters is aware of the criticisms of traditional marriage and family. He warns against responding to such charges solely in terms of the individual flourishing of members of the family, through "pragmatic appeals in behalf of the benefits families offer to its members, especially children" (*The Family*, x). Such benefits are important and will be part of the present chapter. But as Waters says, the goodness of the family is not solely about its goodness for its members, but also its goodness for others outside its bounds. For reflection on the Christian meaning of "justice," rooted in Greek sources and in Scripture (which itself incorporates both ancient Jewish and Hellenistic-Jewish understandings), see Phillips, *Mary, Star of Evangelization*, 52–58. In the course of evaluating Pedro Arrupe, S.J.'s understanding of *Gaudium et Spes* and the mission of the Church, Phillips points out the danger of a reductive sociological vision of the Church's mission: "If Christ is already present latently in a host culture and brought to fruition by the cultivation of value, then the Church's mission stands in real danger of being mistakenly appropriated as a mission to civilize: a mission to cultivate values as an end in itself. Moreover, if Christ is latent within culture and brought to birth by the cultivation of value, then cultivating value is in real danger of being understood as something that can bring not just a better world, but the genuinely *novum* world redeemed by Christ [i.e. the consummated kingdom]" (*Mary, Star of Evangelization*, 55).

how important stable and strong marriages are for breaking "the circle of deprivation."[6]

In what follows, I examine the relationship of marriage and social justice by means of three steps. I begin by examining the contrasting perspectives of two African American scholars, Christopher Brooks and (more briefly) Ta-Nehisi Coates. I find Brooks's insistence upon the societal importance of Christian marriage to be compelling, especially in light of the crisis of violence depicted by Coates. Second, I turn to marriage's numerous critics, who in recent scholarly or popular writings have sought either to reject or radically to reconceive marriage, and who find marriage unnecessary for having and raising children.[7] I examine the viewpoints of Clare Chambers, Mary Lyndon Shanley, and Rosanna Hertz, among others.

Third, I make a case for a strong connection between marriage and social justice. Here I rely upon the theological, sociological, and political insights found in the Catholic Church's *Compendium of the Social Doctrine of the Church*, the work of David Popenoe, and the recent analysis of governmental policy by the family-law scholar Helen Alvaré. Theologically and philosophically, the *Compendium* argues that marriage is prior to the state and therefore is at the root of social justice. Sociologically, Popenoe shows that marriage anchors the combination of father and mother in the raising of children. Politically, Alvaré makes clear that marriage, much more than any other arrangement, serves children's interests, whereas the liberal state has focused on adult sexual liberation.

A just society requires husbands and wives who are "living faithfully as one flesh according to God's design for sexuality, and fulfilling their vocations as parents."[8] Of course, Christians also have to be careful not to make the temporal reality of marriage into an ultimate good, as though grace were simply a matter of bringing into existence a really good human marriage.[9]

---

6. Sacks, "Jewish-Christian Dialogue," 170.

7. Although I do not discuss their works, I am aware that contemporary attempts to reconceive marriage often derive from the approaches of modern philosophers such as Karl Marx, Frederick Engels, John Stuart Mill, Sigmund Freud, and Bertrand Russell. For helpful discussion of this background, see Yenor, *Family Politics*. See Mill, *The Subjection of Women*; Engels, *The Origin of the Family*; Freud, *Civilization and Its Discontents*; Russell, *Marriage and Morals*. See also Urbinati, "Mill on Androgyny"; and Annas, "Mill and the Subjection of Women"; as well as Wilson, ed., *Reconceiving the Family*. See also Krouse's helpful "Patriarchal Liberalism and Beyond."

8. Cahall, *The Mystery of Marriage*, 326. See also Esolen, *Reclaiming Catholic Social Teaching*, 72. It should go without saying that, however beneficial, marriage or family cannot "redeem or carry the moral weight of the world" (McCarthy, *Sex and Love*, 110).

9. Jana Marguerite Bennett raises the concern that the emphasis on social justice, while good and even necessary in itself, often either imagines the Church as a private

SOCIAL JUSTICE

Jesus warns against such an attitude: "He who loves father or mother more than me is not worthy of me; and he who loves son or daughter more than me is not worthy of me" (Matt 10:37). In what follows, then, I do not intend to depict marriage merely as instrument for temporal flourishing.[10] But the justice of a society matters for the life of charity.

I. Urban Apologetics: Christopher W. Brooks and Ta-Nehisi Coates

In *Urban Apologetics: Why the Gospel Is Good News for the City*, Christopher Brooks comments, "No issue is more critical to the success and mission of the urban church than that of rebuilding the broken family."[11] In referring to the "urban church," Brooks—Senior Pastor at Evangel Ministries Church in Detroit—has in view the local churches comprised of "men and women who live, minister, and are called to reach the residents of our inner cities throughout America."[12] Brooks warns against the temptation to ignore the ills that plague urban areas, a temptation that arises because of the difficult nature of the crisis. Not only are there "now more young African-American

---

realm of religious faith that is connected to political life by families committed to social justice, or else presents the very purpose of the Christian family to be the building up temporal communities. In this regard, she criticizes aspects of J. McGinnis and K. McGinnis, "Family as Domestic Church"; Cahill, *Family*; Browning, *Marriage and Modernization*. See Bennett, *Water Is Thicker Than Blood*, 11–15. See also another book cited by Bennett: Post, *More Lasting Unions*. Although I agree with Bennett's fundamental concern, I would want to be careful in developing her contention (which is certainly true from one angle) that "the church is the place where all creation experiences disrupted fellowship with others, and interrupted family ties, in favor of a primary relationship with Jesus Christ" (*Water Is Thicker Than Blood*, 189). While the inbreaking of Jesus Christ requires this radical "primary relationship," family ties (husband and wife, father and mother and child, and so on) remain approved by Jesus and highly important for human flourishing of every kind. See also Bennett's "Singular Christianity"; Clapp, *Families at the Crossroads*. For a response to Clapp, see Waters, *The Family*, 249–50.

10. For a position that moves in this direction due to its conflation of nature and grace, see Rahner, "Marriage as a Sacrament." Although I do not discuss polygamy in this chapter, studies show that it fosters social injustice: see for example Barash, *Out of Eden*; Brooks, "The Problem with Polygamy," responding to Martha Nussbaum's May 2008 defense, on the University of Chicago Law School Faculty Blog, of nineteenth-century Mormon polygamy; and Henrich, Boyd, and Richerson, "The Puzzle of Monogamous Marriage." See also the defense of polygamy, arguing largely on the basis of the male's higher sexual drive, in Philips and Jones, *Polygamy in Islam*; as well as, more broadly, al-Kawthari, *Al-Arba'īn*. For a critical Catholic analysis of polygamy in Africa, see Ganye, "Monogamy and Polygamy."

11. Brooks, *Urban Apologetics*, 97.

12. Brooks, *Urban Apologetics*, 16.

men behind bars, on parole, or on probation than were enslaved in the 1850s," but also (and partly as a result) "over 70 percent of the babies born in my [Brooks's] community don't have a father in the home."[13]

Brooks has no doubt about the gospel's power "to transform every sector of our world for the good of men and to the glory of God."[14] The Bible shows that many of the same issues that plague urban communities today were problems for the biblical communities as well. One problem is that many people who live in urban areas no longer believe in God. Many people in urban areas also no longer believe in "the viability and workability of Christian ethics," which seem to have done little good in their community's experience.[15] The problem is that many Christians have not practiced what they preach.

Brooks urges: "The gospel should meet people at the point of their deepest confusion and at the height of their loftiest ideals."[16] Here is where Ta-Nehisi Coates's *Between the World and Me* comes in, although it was written after Brooks's book was published. The lofty ideal set forth by Coates is justice, specifically retributive justice that rectifies the relationship between victims and perpetrators. Having survived into middle age, unlike many young African American men, Coates comments: "I felt myself to be among the survivors of some great natural disaster, some plague, some avalanche or earthquake."[17] In the sixth grade, an enraged boy drew a gun and threatened to shoot him in the playground. He recalls hearing constantly about murders that were taking place locally. Thanks to television, he knew that "somewhere out there beyond the firmament, past the asteroid belt, there were other worlds where children did not regularly fear for their bodies," but he himself experienced relentless fear of violent death.[18] He describes the daily effort and alertness required simply to survive, including the survival rules of watching out for gangs and even of challenging them through one's own gang. As a child, there was no way to escape this fear: "Not being violent enough could cost me my body. Being too violent could cost me my body. We could not get out. . . . Fear ruled everything around me."[19]

---

13. Brooks, *Urban Apologetics*, 18. He cites Michelle Alexander, "More Black Men Are in Prison."

14. Brooks, *Urban Apologetics*, 20.

15. Brooks, *Urban Apologetics*, 20.

16. Brooks, *Urban Apologetics*, 30.

17. Coates, *Between the World and Me*, 129.

18. Coates, *Between the World and Me*, 20.

19. Coates, *Between the World and Me*, 28–29. Coates cannot avoid fearing for his son's life and remembering that America is literally built upon the enslavement and destruction of "black" bodies, which continues in "the killing fields of Chicago,

Coates is aware that if there is no God, it follows that no justice will ever be possible for the victimized, especially for the countless victims who are now dead. Sadly, he tells his son that "I have no God to hold me up," no God to give a meaning to someone's senseless death.[20] He assumes that "when they shatter the body they shatter everything."[21] Although he knows that everyone must die, he focuses upon African Americans who are at great risk of being killed randomly by police or by their fellows. He appreciates the awe-inspiring "fact of being human," the amazing fact of being a conscious creature among "all the matter floating through the cosmos," but from this vantage point he mourns the injustice of things all the more.[22]

Coates himself was raised by his mother and father. Along with other factors, this contributed to him attending Howard University, becoming a successful journalist, and becoming a bestselling author and cultural critic. His parents acted with justice toward him in this regard. He and his wife, as his book makes clear, have likewise acted with justice toward their son. Brooks's argument is that this primal enactment of justice—the father and mother raising their children—contributes greatly to building up just communities.

Brooks does not moralistically blame people living in urban areas. On the contrary, he rightly notes that "the urban family is beleaguered by the mistreatment done to it at the hands of poor public policy makers."[23] But he grants that there are also "self-inflicted wounds resulting from harmful personal lifestyle choices."[24] He is well aware that in difficult situations, with limited options and under great stress (and bearing burdens from one's own childhood), it is often much harder to choose the path that leads

---

of Baltimore, of Detroit," ghettos that were "created by the policy of the [American] Dreamers" (Coates, *Between the World and Me*, 79, 111). Coates admits to feeling rage, grounded in fear that America will destroy his son because his son has a "black" body.

20. Coates, *Between the World and Me*, 113.
21. Coates, *Between the World and Me*, 113.
22. Coates, *Between the World and Me*, 115. Despite the greatness and power of African American Christianity over the decades, neither "Christianity" nor "religion" is discussed in the essays in Crenshaw et al., eds., *Seeing Race Again*. See for example the solutions offered by Lipsitz, "The Sounds of Silence," 47–48. See also Carter's *Race*, although in my view (apart from problems with Carter's metanarrative about the Christian origins of racism) this book too needs a richer account of the gospel. See also Copeland, *Enfleshing Freedom*, 6, 122–24, drawing upon Douglas, *What's Faith Got to Do with It?*. Copeland argues at length that "Catholic church teaching on sex and sexuality manifests ambivalence and disquiet toward the body—female and homosexual bodies, in particular" (*Enfleshing Freedom*, 74).
23. Brooks, *Urban Apologetics*, 97.
24. Brooks, *Urban Apologetics*, 97.

to personal and communal flourishing. He warns, "The current condition of urban marriages and parenting has made effective discipleship nearly unachievable."[25] In his view, therefore, fixing marriage must become an absolute priority. He states, "Christianity must recognize the importance of a family structure that is stable and capable of living out the commandments of Christ for our homes."[26]

Brooks's goal in this part of his book is not to offer sociological analyses or solutions. Rather, based on his own experience, he argues that improving the condition of the Church in urban areas requires facing the truth that fatherless homes—homes without the stability of marriage, homes in which the children do not receive what they are owed in justice by their parents—cause deep harm to communities. He therefore wishes to bring forward the gospel's message for marriage. As he says, "while rejecting oversimplified answers, our focus is on the impact that the gospel can have upon urban marriages and parenting."[27]

The key, he argues, is for Christians to live out the following five scriptural pillars about marriage and the family:

- Marriage is honorable and for a lifetime (Heb 13:4).
- Children are a blessing from the Lord (Ps 127:3).
- Marriage is a covenant between one man and one woman (Matt 19:4–6).
- The purpose of the family is to reflect God's glory and to produce faithful followers of Christ (Deut 6:4–9; Eph 5:31–32).
- Each member of the family is expected to play a specific role: Men must lead; women must help; children must obey (1 Cor 11:3; Gen 2:18; Eph 6:1–3).[28]

For my purposes, attempts to define male headship need not come into play; the important thing instead is to insist upon the necessary place of men and fathers in the raising of children, and to do so in ways that affirm the distinctive strengths of men.[29] Paul's language of "headship" has

---

25. Brooks, *Urban Apologetics*, 97.
26. Brooks, *Urban Apologetics*, 97.
27. Brooks, *Urban Apologetics*, 98.
28. Brooks, *Urban Apologetics*, 99.

29. Anthony Esolen makes a case for the authority of the husband/father in the family, on the grounds that the reduction of the father's authority tends toward, and indeed is engineered to accomplish, the enhancement of the state's authority. In my view, this may indeed be the case, but we have to be careful not to define the father's authority over against the mother's. With great cogency, the concern about statism is

the purpose of affirming such strengths, but the problem—as Paul himself makes clear—is that "leading" and "helping" are insufficient categories for depicting the radical marital practice of mutual self-surrendering service.[30]

In drawing the connection between marriage and urban apologetics, Brooks cites the evangelical theologian Voddie Baucham's *Family Driven Faith*.[31] Baucham holds that a major reason for the loss of faith among young people is that Christian families have too often not lived up to their calling. When families are functioning healthily and with justice, young people can much more easily perceive the truth of the gospel. Brooks also quotes Sylvia Ann Hewlett and Cornel West's *The War Against Parents*. He affirms their contention that American "laws and policies" tend "to debilitate moms and dads and undermine their ability to weave the web of care that is so

---

articulated by Farrow, *Nation of Bastards*. See also Waters, "Marriage," 528–29.

30. See T. Keller and K. Keller, *The Meaning of Marriage*. Kathy Keller writes the chapter on headship. She centers her discussion upon Jesus Christ, who is the model for both what it means to be "head" and what it means to "be subject." This means, at the very least, that to be "head" does not involve wielding power over another person, because Jesus chose to exercise his headship over his Body the Church through love rather than through power. Keller underscores that "in the dance of the Trinity, the greatest [see Mark 10:32–45] is the one who is most self-effacing, most sacrificial, most devoted to the good of the Other" (*The Meaning of Marriage*, 199). Keller affirms that we cannot place people into airtight gender categories, and she notes that we must never "make light of the horrible record of abuse suffered by women at the hands of men who wielded twisted and unbiblical definitions of 'headship' and 'submission' as their primary weapon" (*The Meaning of Marriage*, 209). But she holds that, on the grounds that the Son obeys the Father as his head, the woman should ultimately obey the husband as her head when it comes down to decisions in which there is a disagreement that cannot be negotiated. She describes the husband as "leader" and the wife as "helper." See also her "Appendix: Decision Making and Gender Roles," 277–81. In my view, it is inevitably misleading to present the husband as "leader" over the wife or to put things in terms of "who gets to make the final decision." On the other side of the spectrum, Lisa Sowle Cahill argues, "Today it can no longer be taken for granted that there are clear differences between men and women, in terms of behavior and personality. Both sexes exhibit a spectrum of traits, and personality differences within each sex are often much greater than the differences between any particular man and woman" (Cahill, "Equality in Marriage," 68). I agree regarding the "spectrum of traits" and the need not to over-generalize, and Cahill does concede that "[i]t may be true that male and female humans, resembling other species of mammals, have some sex-based tendencies, related to reproductive behavior and reflecting differences in the brain, hormones, or prenatal environmental" (Cahill, "Equality in Marriage," 68). But her approach is not sufficient for addressing gender differences that affect what men and women (in general) look for in marital relationships. See also such works—whose science seems accurate though it has been contested—as Brizendine, *The Male Brain*; and Barash and Lipton, *Gender Gap*.

31. See Baucham, *Family Driven Faith*.

vitally important to our nation."³² In addition, Brooks credits Daniel Patrick Moynihan for having prophetically recognized "the triangular pathology of out-of-wedlock children, fatherlessness, and the decline in marriage as the formula for urban disaster."³³ In response to this "triangular pathology," Brooks emphasizes the need for apologetics: persuading young people of the truth of the gospel so that they can believe in it, be transformed by it, and transform their families and communities by its light.

Brooks puts the matter in strong terms: in impoverished urban areas, "the concept of marriage among minorities is on life support."³⁴ The problem is that even if fathers may feel some responsibility toward their children, they do not feel responsibility toward the mother(s) of their children, which results almost inevitably in frayed bonds with their children. But Brooks does not cast blame. Instead, he calls upon Christians to demonstrate the power of the gospel by living faithful, non-promiscuous, enduring marriages.

Yet, when men cannot find or keep jobs, women do not look upon them as good marriage partners. Men also have difficulty helping to raise children, if they are unable to find paying work. Likewise, women who lose custody of their children because of their own poverty may be unlikely to find solace in the gospel. Thus, Brooks connects his gospel message about marriage with an insistence upon economic outreach as well. The Church must be committed to helping out people when they cannot find work or are unable to pay for necessities. Brooks strongly affirms the need for the Church and society to provide "support in the areas of utilities, housing, employment, and child care."³⁵

II. Justice Through Rejecting or Reconceiving Marriage

Many scholars who specialize in the field of marriage and family would disagree with Brooks that the gospel's teachings on marriage are good news

---

32. See Hewlett and West, *The War Against Parents*, 124. Brooks registers disagreement with "several of their core premises," but he agrees with their point about the importance of mothers and fathers (Brooks, *Urban Apologetics*, 101).

33. Brooks, *Urban Apologetics*, 102.

34. Brooks, *Urban Apologetics*, 103. In support of this thesis, he cites the experience-based books of Daniels, *Ghettonation*; and Goodwin, *The Death of Hip Hop*.

35. Brooks, *Urban Apologetics*, 108. With regard to the broader economic impact of marriage (and divorce), as well as the impact of public policy (as of the early 2000s) upon marital status, see the essays in Grossbard-Shechtman, ed., *Marriage and the Economy*.

for the poor or good news for those who care about social justice. In this section, I attempt to set forth a representative selection of their views.[36]

In *Against Marriage*, Clare Chambers argues that marriage is essentially unjust.[37] She holds that marriage is unjust because it offends against both human equality and human liberty. State-regulated marriage offends against the state's duty to be neutral vis-à-vis all citizens, whatever their marital status. When there is oppression or injustice, the state should step in, but not otherwise. Thus, the state should not be involved in sanctioning marriage but rather should regulate various "relationship practices" to ensure that each of them has separate and appropriate regulations that ensure equality, liberty, and neutrality. Property, finances, child custody, and parenting should be regulated to ensure that "what justice requires" is secured "for everyone."[38]

Chambers proposes that "in the marriage-free state, a club or society that performed private marriages would *not* be able to deny marriage to lesbians and gays, for example, unless they were also not allowed to join the club."[39] Since "lesbians and gays" can join the Church by receiving baptism, it follows that if the Church wants to continue to perform the sacrament of marriage, the Church will have to affirm and practice marriage between persons of the same sex. Chambers thinks that the state should forbid the Church from engaging in discriminatory practices as defined by the state.[40]

---

36. See also, more broadly, the cultural critique offered by the feminist scholar Angela McRobbie: "Luminosity falls upon the girl who adopts the habits of masculinity including heavy drinking, swearing, smoking, getting into fights, having casual sex, flashing her breasts in public, getting arrested by the police, consumption of pornography, enjoyment of lap-dancing clubs and so on, but without relinquishing her own desirability to men, indeed for whom such seeming masculinity enhances her desirability since she shows herself to have a similar sexual appetite to her male counterparts" (McRobbie, *The Aftermath of Feminism*, 83). McRobbie sees all this as a hidden reassertion of patriarchy and its values, against feminism and its values. But for McRobbie, among the latter are the value of single motherhood and the rejection of privileging marriages in which the man and woman raise their children.

37. Chambers, *Against Marriage*. See also Metz, *Untying the Knot*.

38. Chambers, *Against Marriage*, 147. Here she praises the Law Commission of Canada's report *Beyond Conjugality*. Her faith in the ability of the state's regulatory system to secure justice is unquestioned.

39. Chambers, *Against Marriage*, 182.

40. See the instructive essay by Anderson, "How to Think About Sexual Orientation"; as well as Anderson's *Truth Overruled*. See also, from a perspective opposed to Anderson's, some of the essays in *Reasonable Accommodation*, discussed in Benson, "Contextual Analysis for Equality."

She rightly recognizes that "we cannot debate marriage without making value judgements about what marriage really is and why it is valuable."[41] In her view, "what marriage really is" includes its intrinsic patriarchal symbolism. The primary value judgment that we need to make about marriage, therefore, is that it is unjust because of its millennia-long association with patriarchal oppression. The institution of marriage has traditionally stigmatized other relationship-forms and other ways of raising children.[42] Marriage is a discriminatory institution in which the state, aided by cultural pressure and unequal economic practices, ensures that women "are better off married than unmarried."[43]

What about the argument that marriage has, over centuries, proven its value in successfully raising children, ensuring that the elderly have an adequate support system, and fostering profound interpersonal communion between the sexes? Chambers responds by pointing out that individuals have diverse needs. Many of these needs, she reasons, are not well served by marriage's tendency to be non-egalitarian and financially punitive (for the woman) in the distribution of work. She argues that "[i]t would be possible ... to introduce radically egalitarian legislation, or protection for vulnerable care-givers, that did not apply only to married couples, and this marriage-blind option is vastly superior."[44] Or as she puts it a bit earlier, "The right

---

41. Chambers, *Against Marriage*, 34.

42. On this view, simply adding persons with homosexual inclinations to the list of people who can marry each other would perpetuate these unjust stigmas against other forms of relationships and child-raising. For concerns along these lines, see also Card, "Against Marriage and Motherhood"; Butler, "Is Kinship Always Already Heterosexual?"; Franke, *Wedlocked*. She also criticizes Macedo, *Just Married*; Macedo, "Sexuality and Liberty." See also Halberstam, *Gaga Feminism*; as well as, from a different perspective, Raymond, *Women as Wombs*.

43. Chambers, *Against Marriage*, 38. I suppose that this is how Chambers would explain the fact that more women than men desire to be married.

44. Chambers, *Against Marriage*, 89. See also Fineman, *The Neutered Mother*, 165: "The egalitarian family as an articulated ideal is premised on the couple-based family unit. As such, it generates tension insofar as one of the goals to be attained by the partners is equal career or market proficiency. Equality in ambition in nonfamily members leaves the two-parent family an institution with potentially NO available caretakers." Fineman offers solutions quite similar to those of Chambers: "family policy is a form of state regulation. We must therefore be explicit about the norms and values motivating public and legal decisions about what should be protected or encouraged through social and economic subsidies. Furthermore, family policy must be secular, not based on a religious model. It should reference the functional aspirations we have for families in our society and be supportive of those aspirations. I therefore propose two recommendations for legal reform: the abolition of the legal supports for the sexual family [i.e. father-mother-child] and the construction of protections for the nurturing unit of caretaker and dependant exemplified by the Mother/Child dyad" (*The Neutered*

thing to do . . . is to level *up*: to ensure that those protections that currently exist for married women and men are extended to *all* women and men who are left vulnerable by relationships."[45] With regard to the raising of children, with its heavy cost financially and in terms of time, Chambers agrees that being raised by loving caregivers is better than being raised impersonally in an orphanage. She denies, however, that marriage is needed to secure loving caregiving.[46] She dismisses the value of stable marriages as distinct from stable relationships. Indeed, she maintains that "increased *divorce*" is "of considerable benefit to women," who would otherwise be stuck in unhappy marriages.[47]

Mother, 228). She goes on to explain the role that men would have here: "I believe that men can and should be Mothers. In fact, if men are interested in acquiring legal rights of access to children (or other dependents), I argue they *must* be Mothers in the stereotypical nurturing sense of that term—that is, engaged in caretaking. Second, the Child in my dyad stands for all forms of inevitable dependency—the dependency of the ill, the elderly, the disabled, as well as actual children" (*The Neutered Mother*, 234–35). See also Fineman, *The Autonomy Myth*.

45. Chambers, *Against Marriage*, 88.

46. Here she is arguing primarily against the idea of "minimal marriage" advanced by Elizabeth Brake, *Minimizing Marriage*. Notably, Brake herself argues that society should separate the "legal framework designating and supporting adult caring relationships from one regulating and supporting parenting" and, likewise, that "a just society should have an institution ensuring the welfare and development of children and protecting their relationships with their parents, but this should not be marriage" (*Minimizing Marriage*, 149, 151). Where Brake differs from Chambers is that Brake supports "minimal marriage," which she defines as a legal contract, or contractual institution, ensuring that "individuals can have legal marital relationships with more than one person, reciprocally or asymmetrically, themselves determining the sex and number of parties, the type of relationship involved, and which rights and responsibilities to exchange with each" (*Minimizing Marriage*, 157). For pro-marriage views that Chambers opposes, see Galston, *Liberal Purposes*; Galston, "The Reinstitutionalization of Marriage"; Galston, "Causes of Declining Well-Being." For arguments similar to Galston's, focusing on the importance of the family (as distinct from the state, but supported by the state), see McClain, *The Place of Families*.

47. Chambers, *Against Marriage*, 99. In praise of the benefits for women allegedly brought by increased divorce, see also Bernard, *The Future of Marriage*; as well as the overall perspective of such books as Perutz, *Marriage Is Hell* and Stacey, *In the Name of the Family*. For the actual impact of divorce upon children and for various methods of ameliorating this impact, see Pedro-Carroll, *Putting Children First*. Pedro-Carroll grants that for children, "divorce is second only to death in the degree of stress it creates and in the amount of time required to adjust to it" (*Putting Children First*, 9). She goes on to comment that according to sociological studies, "Adults whose parents divorced also experience diminished quality and stability of their own intimate relationships, and they are twice as likely to have their own marriages end in divorce" (*Putting Children First*, 51). See also Bonnell and Little, *The Co-Parenting Handbook*.

Another scholar of marriage, Mary Lyndon Shanley, insists that promoting marriage is dangerous for poor women, unless such efforts are made secondary to ensuring that poor women have access to a living wage and to jobs that accommodate "caregiving, through a shorter workweek and more flexible scheduling" as well as through the provision of "high-quality, affordable child care."[48] For Shanley, the key is first to put in place legal and economic standards that ensure "spousal equality" and that make it easy for both women and men "to shoulder the responsibilities of workers outside the home as well as family caregivers."[49] The gospel does not advocate the household reforms that Shanley considers to be necessary before marriage can be good news for women. She points out, "Addressing women's poverty by attaching them to men who can support them reinforces inequality and vulnerability within marriages. Inducing women to marry men may expose them and their children to domestic violence while failing to provide them with either the personal or community resources to extricate themselves from intolerable living conditions."[50] She therefore rejects the notion that marriage is an "effective antipoverty program," although she favors state support of marriage within a context that first promotes other reforms.[51] At the same time, she affirms that "marriage," when properly contextualized, can be a way of identifying and solidifying "the social and relational sides of our lives."[52]

Anca Gheaus argues in favor of legally establishing a temporary form of marriage, at least for couples who agree that they will not have children. In her view, "the erosion of the extreme, blind kind of commitment required by marriage without divorce is good news."[53] She notes with approval that it is no-fault divorce that has eroded "the robust kind of marital commitment that was made by future spouses entering a traditional marriage."[54]

48. Shanley, "Just Marriage," 25.
49. Shanley, "Just Marriage," 25.
50. Shanley, "Just Marriage," 24.
51. Shanley, "Just Marriage," 24.
52. Shanley, "Just Marriage," 28.
53. Gheaus, "The (Dis)value of Commitment," 220.
54. Gheaus, "The (Dis)value of Commitment," 220. From a quite different perspective, Scott Hahn helps us to perceive why views such as Gheaus's no longer seem as extreme as they once would have: see Hahn, *The First Society*, 123–24. Advocating for same-sex marriage, Mark D. Jordan argues that "[t]he staunchest advocates of 'traditional' marriage in America typically defend a notion of marriage that is not more than decades old. The notion resulted from extraordinary reversals in American gender relations, family structures, and household economy during the last century and a half" (Jordan, "Arguing Liturgical Genealogies," 115). In my view, however, generally what is meant by "traditional marriage" is simply the solemn union of a man and a woman

She proposes that the solution is to separate romantic or sexual love from commitment.

Along broadly similar lines, but with their own twist, Samantha Brennan and Bill Cameron urge that the state should "begin thinking about parenting contracts as separate from marriage contracts."[55] Here, the needed reform is the establishment of parenting contracts that would serve to raise the children born within the community. The breakdown of romantic relationships would then not be so devastating to families and communities, since the parenting of children would not be set within romantic relationships. Brennan and Cameron insist that "[w]hat is bad for children . . . is assuming that the commitment in marriage is or at least ought to be strong enough to bear the weight of their care."[56] Rejecting prior "traditional" understandings of marriage, above all the Christian one, they urge that the path forward is to focus on parenthood—on the parent-child relationship—rather than on marriage. They argue that emphasizing the parent-child relationship, disconnected from its traditional link with marriage, would likely "lead to a plethora of new ideas about how to raise children, all guided by a concern for their well-being and unshackled from the restrictions of marriage and other romantic relationships."[57]

Brennan and Cameron envision "a more specialized kind of parenting" that will make room "for people who might make extraordinary parents but are not particularly interested in a romantic relationship."[58] The co-parents may be friends or even may hardly know each other. What is important is that they desire to be parents and that they have identifiable parenting talents that will make their co-parenting a success. On this view, the co-parents do not need actually to be the mother and father of the child. Their "parenting contract" would "professionalize" the task of parenting and ensure that its obligations are met better than they are under the current system in which divorce often has disastrous effects on parenting.[59] Along similar lines, though without offering evidence, Jonathan Herring claims: "Children are, in fact, surprisingly flexible about parenthood and are happy

---

that is open to childbearing and that is intended to be enduring while both spouses live.

55. Brennan and Cameron, "Is Marriage Bad for Children?," 96.
56. Brennan and Cameron, "Is Marriage Bad for Children?," 96.
57. Brennan and Cameron, "Is Marriage Bad for Children?," 95.
58. Brennan and Cameron, "Is Marriage Bad for Children?," 93.
59. Brennan and Cameron, "Is Marriage Bad for Children?," 92. For practical suggestions rooted in a wide knowledge of actual co-parenting in situations of separation or divorce, along lines quite different from those of Brennan and Cameron, see Bonnell and Little, *The Co-Parenting Handbook*.

to accept, for example, that they have two mothers or two fathers. It is society which has more difficulty accepting this than children themselves."[60]

Brian Willoughby and Spencer James's sociological study *The Marriage Paradox* primarily examines the views about marriage held by "white and middle-class emerging adults [i.e. people in their early twenties] living in the heart of the United States."[61] These young people expect to get married eventually and they consider marriage to be important, but they do not associate marriage with self-sacrifice. They recognize that sacrifice is necessary to have a good career, and they willingly put in such sacrifice. But they do not associate their work—in which they give up certain goods for the sake of larger career goals—with what is necessary for having a good marriage. Their ideal marriage would reduce the stress in their lives, would be more romantically compelling than their current relationships, and "would provide a respite from the anxieties of educational and career pressures."[62]

At the same time, the young adults studied by Willoughby and James do associate marriage strongly with commitment, indeed with lifelong commitment. The tension identified by Willoughby and James consists in how marriage can be conceived of as a lifelong commitment while, at the same time, marriage is also imagined to consist fundamentally in a romantic union that involves no sacrifice of any personal or professional goals. In addition, Willoughby and James find another tension. The young adults they studied affirm that marriage is the best context for raising children, and they also generally express a desire eventually to get married. But they deny that marriage is "needed for society" in the sense of being a "need" for male-female coupling and for the raising of children in a just manner.[63]

---

60. Herring, *Family Law*, 55. Herring adds, "Traditionalists see it as beneficial for a child to have a contribution of a male and a female adult at the heart of their lives. To others, that demonstrates the greatest weakness of the genetic approach: it fails to acknowledge the diversity in family life. It means a same-sex couple will not be able to be parents together of a child. Further, it means a child cannot have more than two parents; even though many children will in fact have several adults who fulfil the role of parents" (*Family Law*, 54). At the same time, Herring grants that "there is a special bond between biological parents and their children. Most parents feel an incredibly strong bond with their children from the moment of birth" (*Family Law*, 56). It is true, of course, that a child cannot have more than two biological parents, and that (except in the case of cloning) these parents will be one man and one woman, to both of whom the child will genetically owe a great deal.

61. Willoughby and James, *The Marriage Paradox*, 193.

62. Willoughby and James, *The Marriage Paradox*, 195.

63. Willoughby and James, *The Marriage Paradox*, 196–97. See also Waite et al., eds., *The Ties That Bind*; as well as Waite and Gallagher, *The Case for Marriage*. Drawing upon the work of the United States Conference of Catholic Bishops as well as upon Cherlin, *The Marriage Go-Round*, David Matzko McCarthy points out, "Cohabitation

More women than men want to marry, and more women than men want to have children.[64] The stories in Rosanna Hertz's *Single by Chance, Mothers by Choice: How Women Are Choosing Parenthood without Marriage and Creating the New American Family* are instructive in this regard. A typical story comes from a thirty-five-year-old woman who has a good career but no marriage prospects. She decides to become a mother via an anonymous sperm donor; when this works well, she has another child by a different anonymous sperm donor. Another typical story comes from a woman who, after a series of relationships with men, finds herself at age thirty-six in a difficult position. She remarks that "as I got older, the men already had children or clearly didn't want them."[65] Eventually, she decided to adopt, and she found a man who, though he does not live with her, nonetheless forms a part of her life and her son's.

Hertz concludes from such stories and from the relevant sociological data that "we can no longer deny that the core of family life is the mother and her children," rather than also the father.[66] Although a sperm is still necessary—and so in a biological sense a father is still necessary (although

---

makes women more vulnerable to abuse, and women who bear children in the context of cohabitation are more likely to raise these children alone" (McCarthy, "Cohabitation and Marriage," 121). See also Smock et al., "'Everything's There Except Money.'"

64. See for example Regnerus, *Cheap Sex*. See also, for the different things that women and men (speaking generally) seek in sexual intimacy, Lisa Cahill, *Sex, Gender, and Christian Ethics*; as well as the Rabbinic Jewish assumption that "a woman's desire to be married is greater than a man's" (Novak, "Jewish Marriage," 107).

65. Hertz, *Single by Chance*, xiii.

66. Hertz, *Single by Chance*, xviii. See also the perspective of Fineman, *The Neutered Mother*. Concerned that the central role of the mother in raising children is being compromised by law courts, Fineman complains that "[w]hile judicial resolutions thus far seem to be tempered by the continued primacy of maternal interest in regard to nonmarital children, the preference for mothers is eroding rapidly. . . . Proponents of unwed and other fathers' rights argue, however, that there are no relevant differences between mothers and fathers that should have legal significance and dismiss, out of hand, arguments based on statistically demonstrated disparities in investment in and commitment to children. Nor do these advocates find persuasive the vast differences in the nature of women's physical and psychological reproductive functions during pregnancy" (*The Neutered Mother*, 86–87). Fineman sees this situation as a new expression of patriarchy, denying in a new way the needs and reality of women. She notes that women suffer when, through "the de-gendered components of the neutered institution of 'parenthood,'" "caretaking is devalued and biological and economic connection are deemed of paramount importance" (*The Neutered Mother*, 70–71). Fineman strongly defends the value of single motherhood, warning against rhetoric that "constructs single motherhood as dangerous and even deadly, not only to the single mothers and their children but to society as a whole" (*The Neutered Mother*, 117). Her argument is that the "family" needs to be redefined so as not to center around "the notion of husband and wife as a couple forming the basic family core" (*The Neutered Mother*, 160).

advances in human genetic manipulation may change this)—it is no longer necessary for a child to have an *identifiable* father.

Hertz's focus is largely on middle-class women. She notes that much of what prevented her interviewees from getting married was their emphasis on their own careers during their twenties as well as their increased selectivity in approaching marriage. She notes that a quarter of her interviewees had cohabited with a partner at some point and that almost all of them had experienced long-term relationships. Especially with regard to cohabiting couples, final "breakups often occurred when talk of children became serious."[67] She details the women's struggles to find a man who desired commitment, or (for the lesbian women, comprising 17 percent of the study) to find a woman who would agree to a stable relationship with children. In the end, as she notes, her interviewees "shed the burden of marriage, determined to win the race to motherhood alone," through anonymous sperm donation, in vitro fertilization, and other arrangements.[68]

In the families crafted by these single women, it is still the case that "'father' occupies a lead role in the master narrative of family life," given societal expectations.[69] Women who conceive by known sperm donors seek to ensure "that the child will have at least a face for his or her father, even though this man is not expected to have a social relationship with the child."[70] By contrast, women who use an anonymous sperm donation must work harder to sketch the child's father solely on the basis of the personal details listed on the sperm donation form. Hertz states, "The mother and child together fashion a suitable father, bringing an anonymous donor to life from a list of details."[71] Hertz attributes all this to "the power of cultural

---

67. Hertz, *Single by Chance*, 10.

68. Hertz, *Single by Chance*, 11. See also Browning, *Marriage and Modernization*, 94. See also the reflections of Angelo Scola (though not directed specifically toward the practice of anonymous sperm donation): "The absence of paternity—understood here not only in the decisive sense of the male figure, but more globally as that function of generation which includes the mother—is simultaneously cause and effect of freedom's 'illness,' and therefore of the obscuring of the fundamental human experience of the relationship between the 'I' and reality. Before all else, it is clear that the lack of paternity is a symptom of the loss of a sense of origins. That which a child is, he receives from his parents.... But if the memory of origins is lost—and the story of a child's origins can be told him only by his parents!—then freedom can no longer receive even the energy of desire which reality awakens in the subject" (Scola, *The Nuptial Mystery*, 151–52). See also Scola's discussion of technology-aided "procreation that does not pass through the sexual act": *The Nuptial Mystery*, 135–37.

69. Hertz, *Single by Chance*, 55.

70. Hertz, *Single by Chance*, 55.

71. Hertz, *Single by Chance*, 55. In his *Do Fathers Matter?*, Paul Raeburn offers some anecdotal stories about adult children seeking their biological fathers. I suspect that

norms to define how families should be,"[72] but it seems to me that what we are dealing with here is the fact that the child intuitively knows that, in justice, he or she should be raised by a mother and father.[73] When one lacks a mother or a father, one knows that something has gone wrong, and one instinctively seeks to know the missing parent. The same instinct is found in the mothers: "I look at my baby's face and wonder about the sperm donor. Who does my son look like and who will he take after?"[74] Hertz adds that "the child must rely on the mother's imagination because the child cannot see herself or himself in the glass. Mother and child actively talk about the donor as together they imagine the donor as part of creating a sense of the child's identity.... [T]hrough such creation the mother and child take comfort in giving this role of a father meaning in their lives."[75]

---

many children of anonymous sperm donors would agree with the following: "Another woman, Alana, is the daughter of a sperm donor whose identity and whereabouts she tried to discover, only to find that her birth father was untraceable. When she told a friend that she hoped to someday meet a man with whom she could have kids, the friend replied, 'You don't have to have a man in your life to have children.' Alana was stung by the response. Her mother had decided to have a child without a man in her life, and that decision had devastated Alana. After giving the matter some thought, she wrote a response to her friend's remark: 'As a matter of fact, you *do* need a man to have a child—and a woman too! Kids (like me!) eventually grow brains and realize that they've been suckered out of a major, *major* requisite for happiness.' She refers to sperm donation as 'deliberate spiritual robbery.' Alana desperately wants to know something about her biological heritage. It's not just that she wishes she had known more about her father; it's that knowing him would be knowing more about who *she* is. A talented musician, Alana told me she hopes to become famous enough through her music that one day her father will spot her face on an album cover, see that she resembles him, and recognize that she must be his daughter. And that he will get in touch" (*Do Fathers Matter?*, 230–31).

72. Hertz, *Single by* Chance, 56.

73. The theologian Julie Hanlon Rubio argues that "[t]he claim that children will be harmed in same-sex families is difficult to maintain. If studies do not yet prove the goodness of same-sex parenting, they cannot prove its harm. It seems too early to conclude that two married parents of the same gender cannot offer the same love and stability as do two heterosexuals" (Rubio, *Hope for Common Ground*, 110). Even if there were not studies that show that lesbian couples are indeed less stable—and there are such studies—Rubio has missed the key point: a child does not simply have two "parents," rather each child in truth has a mother and a father, and a child is harmed when it is deprived of being raised by his or her mother and father.

74. Hertz, *Single by Chance*, 60.

75. Hertz, *Single by Chance*, 62–63. Hertz explains further, "In most of these women's narratives, anonymous donors have not rejected their offspring but have instead given the mothers the most awesome gift of their lives. The anonymous donor is not the 'bad dad' who walked out (e.g., divorced fathers or birth fathers), but a 'good man' who helped the mother and child become a family. These women recast the anonymous donor as doing something positive for them and hence for the child. The mother and

Other single mothers described by Hertz deliberately become pregnant during a relationship but give birth after the relationship has ended, generally due to the man being a "deadbeat," lacking responsibility and motivation. Such single mothers often find that the father, in the absence of romantic involvement with the mother, lacks interest in helping to raise the child. Hertz concludes that her "interviews . . . reveal an intense and deepening confusion about what exactly fathers bring to families."[76]

In the above, I have identified the contemporary call for the state to replace fathers with supposedly more secure and more feasible forms of state-backed contractual caregiving for children. Fathers especially are no longer seen as necessary; all that is needed is a donor sperm. These perspectives, in my view, are engines of social and familial injustice, in part because they reject the justice owed to children, who deserve to be raised by their mother and father.

---

child can fantasize together about the genetic father. In addition, the anonymous donor cannot disappoint the child in ways that dads often do. Creating a visual and idealized image has protective power until the child is an adolescent" (*Single by Chance*, 63). Something has clearly gone very wrong here; an injustice has been perpetrated, but Hertz is unable to name it. Without explicitly recognizing the intense pathos of what she is describing, Hertz notes, "Mothers report that their children's early questions are about kinship boundaries and formation: who's included, who's not, and who's missing. But the questions are not simply an exercise in taxonomy. They are about identity and place, that is, 'Who is my dad and where is he?'" (*Single by Chance*, 64). Yet, Hertz at least partly recognizes the fundamental problem: "the broader cultural values of privacy and anonymity of donors structure the psychological price the children may pay. The child is denied full knowledge of his or her genealogical heritage and the face of the father" (*Single by Chance*, 65). Hertz goes on to ask, "What is the psychological status of the father when the father is only a sperm?" (*Single by Chance*, 67), and she observes that "[m]others carefully store, as though they are cherished mementos, secondhand information and passing comments given to them by various medical personnel who actually met the anonymous donor. The mementos are eventually passed from mother to child. . . . Mother and child cannot help noticing that the genes of an anonymous man have left unanswered questions in their lives" (*Single by Chance*, 68–69). Additionally, Hertz (without commenting on the injustice of the situation) states that often the donors are chosen by more than one woman, meaning that the child often has numerous half-siblings. Hertz remarks that "nothing prevents donor-assisted families from locating other mothers and children who share the same donor's ID number. Some women in this study (as well as a large number who are presently listed on national internet registries) wanted to meet other children who shared the same donor father. They viewed meeting genetic half siblings and the other mothers as providing paternal kin ties and additional social identity" (*Single by Chance*, 71).

76. Hertz, *Single by Chance*, 177.

III. Marriage as Necessary for Social Justice

In this final section, I offer arguments regarding marriage's necessity for social justice. I advocate three basic ideas. First, the family, with its structure of husband, wife, and children, is an institution ordained by God in creation as part of human flourishing. Second, contemporary critiques of the family are largely (de facto) critiques of the necessity of fathers, and these critiques are based upon deeply flawed premises. Third, society's effort to make do without marriage as a stable institution arises from a focus upon the free expression of adult sexuality and inevitably leaves children to bear the severe emotional and economic penalties that result. Thus, in this section I will be arguing that Christopher Brooks is essentially correct. Recall that while Brooks is aware of the numerous factors (including economic ones) that contribute to the loss of marriage culture in large segments of contemporary society, his main call is for a renewal of Christian marriage rooted in the wisdom of the gospel. Here I will survey three works: the Catholic Church's *Compendium of the Social Doctrine of the Church*, David Popenoe's *Life Without Father*, and Helen Alvaré's *Putting Children's Interests First in U.S. Family Law and Policy*.

Compendium of the Social Doctrine of the Church

Marriage receives a prominent place in the Pontifical Council for Justice and Peace's 2004 *Compendium of the Social Doctrine of the Church*. The *Compendium* is intended to serve as a catechism for understanding how the realities professed by the Catholic Church ought to shape the social order in justice and peace. The key contribution of the *Compendium* for my purposes is its insistence upon the link between social justice and Christian marriage. It offers grounding in theological anthropology for why this is so, including focusing on the fact that human flourishing involves the mutual self-giving love (or gift of self) that is manifested in the permanent bond of the man and woman in sharing together the task of raising their children.

The *Compendium* teaches that the idea of the "family" is not a human construction but a divinely instituted reality that comprises the "first natural society."[77] As such, the family has priority over the state, which does not have authority to alter the family's nature. In the familial environment fostered by "the mutual giving of self on the part of man and woman united in marriage," children are born and raised in accord with their dignity.[78] The

---

77. Pontifical Council for Justice and Peace, *Compendium*, §211.
78. Pontifical Council for Justice and Peace, *Compendium*, §212.

Compendium suggests that justice within the family is founded upon the specific love and commitment of the man and the woman, which involves "a total and exclusive gift of person to person" and enables the children to be raised by the mother and father (including, in an extended sense, in the case of adoption).[79]

Only in marriage, which involves a man and a woman, do we find love "manifested as the total gift of two persons in their complementarities."[80] The complementarity of man and woman is, in the plan of creation, ordered to flourishing family life. A woman brings to a marriage and family things that a man does not bring, and vice versa—even allowing for the fact that men and women can do many of the same things. Obviously, two men cannot procreate a child together, and neither can two women. Thus, gender is not a dispensable factor in marriage, but rather belongs to the particular kind of bond that it is. Similarly, when a marriage is viewed as a temporary or merely contractual relationship, such a relationship is not yet a true marriage; it has not yet arrived at the love (or justice) that opens it outward.[81]

David Popenoe's Life Without Father

The significance of marriage for social justice, especially with respect to children, has been indicated by a number of sociological studies.[82] The

---

79. Pontifical Council for Justice and Peace, *Compendium*, §216. See Moore, *Adopted for Life*; Merida and Morton, *Orphanology*. Moore emphasizes the Church's identity as a family, leaving himself open to the critique of conflating the Church and the family. But Moore's valuation of adoption is sound. With regard to Merida and Morton's work, I note the evident point, which idealism can obscure, that parents should seek carefully to measure the impacts that adoption or foster-parenting will have upon their existing family before committing to take on (additional) adoptive or foster children.

80. Pontifical Council for Justice and Peace, *Compendium*, §223.

81. For sociological analysis of the transition of cohabiting couples to marriage, see Baker and Elizabeth, *Marriage in an Age of Cohabitation*. They comment that "many long-term cohabitants live in a similar manner to married couples, and most cohabitants who stay together eventually marry. . . . [M]any participants in our study reported that their partners were accorded a higher level of inclusion in their families following their marriage" (*Marriage in an Age of Cohabitation*, 176).

82. See for example Whitehead, *The Divorce Culture*; Wallerstein, Lewis, and Blakeslee, *The Unexpected Legacy of Divorce*. Jacqueline Rose complains that "lone mothers have been targeted for especially vindictive treatment. . . . In troubled times, the most vulnerable always tend to be the easiest targets of hatred. But might there also be a connection between the demand for singular devotion so regularly directed at mothers and the hostility that single mothers . . . have historically provoked?" (Rose, *Mothers*, 28). Rose does not here seem to take seriously the real need for children to have a father, a need that is the likeliest cause for the rising level of concern about single mothers as their number has increased. Rose adds that "[i]t is, of course, a

sociologist David Popenoe's *Life Without Father: Compelling New Evidence That Fatherhood and Marriage Are Indispensable for the Good of Children and Society* appeared in 1996 and was republished with some new material in 2009.[83] In his introduction to the new edition, Popenoe presents marriage in terms of justice toward children. He describes marriage as an institution currently in decline but one whose main purpose is crucial: bonding "fathers to their children, and to the mothers of those children."[84] He grants that the physical survival of the mother and her children no longer depends upon the presence of the father. He affirms, too, that both fathers and mothers often have a desire to care for and raise their children. But in light of sociological data, he notes that this desire, in general, "is far stronger in women than in men, making the mother-child bond so prominent in human affairs."[85] In his view, this should not mean returning to traditional gender roles within marriage. Instead, we must find new ways to ensure that men marry and that marriages endure, so that children will not be harmed.

For Popenoe, it is evident that there are important differences between men and women, generally speaking, in terms of how they relate to their children. In the book's opening pages, he argues that by and large, "Men are not biologically as attuned to being committed fathers as women are to being committed mothers."[86] Single women often choose to become mothers, exhibiting a strong desire to have children. It is far rarer to find a single man who is willing to procure and raise a child by himself.

At the same time, Popenoe finds that the committed presence of fathers is generally needed for the flourishing of children.[87] This finding is, Popenoe

---

predominantly white, middle-class domestic ideal that is being promoted" (*Mothers*, 32), but I would respond that what is generally sought is that children would be raised by their mother and father, living together as a household.

83. Popenoe, *Life Without Father*; Popenoe, *Families Without Fathers*. I will quote from the more recent edition. For appreciative discussion of Popenoe's project, see Browning, "Modernization," 252–54. Browning differentiates his position from Popenoe's in that the renewal of the institution of marriage that Popenoe envisions "gives little attention to the role of religious institutions in this cultural work" ("Modernization," 254). Here Browning has in view a number of Popenoe's writings, but especially Popenoe's *Disturbing the Nest*.

84. Popenoe, *Families Without Fathers*, viii.

85. Popenoe, *Families Without Fathers*, ix.

86. Popenoe, *Families Without Fathers*, 4.

87. See also Pruett, *Fatherneed*; Raeburn, *Do Fathers Matter?*; Lamb, ed., *The Role of the Father*; Snarey, *How Fathers Care for the Next Generation*; Parke, *Fatherhood*. For the contrary position, arguing that fathers (as such) really are not needed for child-raising, see the work of the influential judge Richard Posner, *Sex and Reason*. See also Brake, *Minimizing Marriage*, 147: "A typical case for monogamous different-sex marriage points out that single-parent families have higher rates of poverty, and that

recognizes, something that many people today wish were not true. In favor of the view that fathers are no longer particularly needed, Popenoe lists the following claims: now that women are integrated in the workforce, women no longer need men as providers; the stigma against single mothers is no longer operative; the husband-wife model is patriarchal and oppressive of women; men are prone to irresponsible and at times violent behavior; men cannot be counted upon by their dependents, and so it is a mistake for a woman to count upon a man; and mothers can do pretty much everything that fathers can do.

After admitting that each of these claims has at least "some truth,"[88] Popenoe cites a number of sociological studies indicating that, even when controlling for income, children who grow up with both their mother and their father have significantly better outcomes. He notes that the solution is not to encourage stepfamilies, stepfathers, or live-in boyfriends or partners who are not the biological father. Studies show that what is needed is the biological father. He explains that the biological father "can be replaced adequately here and there, and obviously not all biological fathers are good fathers, but in general males biologically unrelated to their children cannot be expected to have the same motivation and dedication to raising those children as males raising their own biological offspring."[89] He grants, of course, that there are many exceptions, just as there are many cigarette smokers who live to a very old age and do not die of smoking-related diseases. There are bad biological fathers, and there are good stepfathers or partners. But the overall findings paint a picture that is what common sense would suggest: for men, being the biological father of the children generally results in much better parenting, and this has a generally positive impact upon the children. Moreover, the mother and the father together are better than a single mother in terms of outcome for the child. In saying this, he recognizes that "social science evidence is never conclusive."[90] But in

---

children do best in low-conflict marriages with both marriages with both biological parents. However, empirical findings of the benefits of marriage are mixed: While low-conflict marriage appears to benefit children, the presence of step-parents does not, and children appear to benefit from divorce in high-conflict families. . . . Marriage can benefit, but it can also harm. Moreover, we should approach correlations between marriage and child welfare with caution. Some apparent benefits can be explained by 'selection bias'—the more educated and wealthier are likelier to have children within marriage." These points are well known to Popenoe (and Helen Alvaré, whose work I discuss below).

88. Popenoe, *Families Without Fathers*, 7.

89. Popenoe, *Families Without Fathers*, 9–10.

90. Popenoe, *Families Without Fathers*, 229, endnote 4. Among the works that he cites are McLanahan and Sandefur, *Growing Up with a Single Parent*; Kamark and

reporting the current research, he observes that the evidence seems clear at the moment.

The first response to the hope that (biological) fathers are no longer needed in the home, then, is to observe that sociological data indicates that in fact they are needed. The second response inquires into the importance of fathers from another angle. Popenoe employs contemporary scientific research into male-female differences to explain why "virtually all children clearly distinguish a mother role from a father role, even if some contemporary adults do not seem to be able to."[91] Generally speaking, he reports that four areas of significant biological difference between men and woman have been found by scientists. These areas are the following: "aggression and general activity level; cognitive skills; sensory sensitivity; and sexual and reproductive behavior."[92] Boys are more aggressive; females have greater verbal ability and males greater visual-spatial and mathematical ability; females are more sensitive to sensory information, more interested in faces and people, and more proficient in personal relationships.[93] All these claims are generalizations that, in individual cases, may not apply, but overall they provide some guidance.

Popenoe observes that in handling infants, mothers have a head start because they have given birth and can breastfeed. Mothers are also "more able to read an infant's facial expressions, handle with tactile gentleness, and soothe with the use of voice."[94] Drawing upon the research of Alice Rossi, Popenoe adds that in handling toddlers, men and women often act differently: "while women provide comfort and emotional acceptance, men typically are more active and arousing in their nurturing activities, fostering certain physical skills and emphasizing autonomy."[95] Similar differences appear in how men and women (fathers and mothers) engage with teenagers. Men focus more on physical play; men are generally more firm in their attitude toward their teenagers' behavior; men encourage risk-taking and competitiveness; men seek to make their children independent. Women focus more on caretaking; women adopt a more responsive attitude toward

---

Galston, *Putting Children First*; Biller, *Fathers and Families*.

91. Popenoe, *Families Without Fathers*, 10.
92. Popenoe, *Families Without Fathers*, 10.
93. See Archer and Lloyd, *Sex and Gender*; Pool, *Eve's Rib*.
94. Popenoe, *Families Without Fathers*, 11.
95. Popenoe, *Families Without Fathers*, 11. See Rossi, "Parenthood in Transition." See also Don Browning's important analysis of "the 'male problematic'—the growing worldwide trend for males to drift away from families" (Browning, *Marriage and Modernization*, 88). These elements, in my view, are behind the biblical teaching about "headship."

their teenagers' behavior; women encourage emotional security and relationships; women seek to ensure their children's immediate well-being.

The third reason that Popenoe gives for the importance of biological fathers being in the home and assisting with child-raising is that being "unattached" results in worse behavior and shorter life for men. In order to raise their children, men are more willing to commit themselves to self-sacrificial work habits. This results in men taking better care of themselves, and in their being taken better care of.

Unfortunately, as of 1996, "Close to 40 percent of all children do not live with their biological fathers"—a percentage that is now significantly higher.[96] This situation is a bad thing. It is an injustice, and due to its impact upon unattached men and upon women raising children in financial difficulty, it has caused and is causing further societal injustices. Popenoe emphasizes that while women can dissociate marriage and child-raising more easily—they are inclined to raise the children whom they bear, whether or not they are married—men tend not to raise their children unless they are committed in marriage to the mother. In contemporary culture, however, this important connection between marriage and child-raising is not appreciated. Popenoe comments, "In place of commitment and obligation to others, especially children, marriage has become mainly a vehicle for the emotional fulfillment of the adult partners."[97] This situation undermines the likelihood that men will participate fully in the raising of their children. Popenoe contends that "the larger truth is that most divorced fathers in America ... lose almost all contact with their children over time. They withdraw from their children's lives."[98] Even if this claim sounds exaggerated, divorce undoubtedly tends in this direction. As Popenoe says, "Childrearing is one of the most time-intensive of all human activities, and it is very difficult to perform it well in absentia."[99] This is especially the case, as he

---

96. Popenoe, *Families Without Fathers*, 19.

97. Popenoe, *Families Without Fathers*, 24. He also points out that "divorce surely is taking place at ever lower levels of marital stress. Divorce was once limited to those marriages which had broken down irreparably, often because one spouse was seriously pathological, irresponsible, or incompetent. Today divorce may occur simply because a better partner has been located.... In many ways marriage has become one of the least binding of legal contracts, a kind of temporary business partnership with an illusory contract in which neither party involved will be held liable for breaking any promises that are made" (*Families Without Fathers*, 29–30).

98. Popenoe, *Families Without Fathers*, 27. See also Martha Fineman's sociological observation that "[f]athers, as a group, do not have an impressive record when it comes to continuing relationships with, or meeting responsibilities for, their children postdivorce" (Fineman, *The Neutered Mother*, 119).

99. Popenoe, *Families Without Fathers*, 27. In this discussion, he cites Seltzer,

says, when one or both spouses remarry. He cites sociological studies that indicate that children, after a divorce, tend not to see their fathers regularly. This is the conclusion of Frank Furstenberg and Andrew Cherlin's *Divided Families: What Happens to Children When Parents Part*.[100]

Generally speaking, then, "when men are active parents, it is only to the children who live with them."[101] But Popenoe goes on to show that as stepfathers, men are much less active than are biological fathers (living in the home) toward their own children. In addition, stepfamilies have a higher break-up rate than do two-biological-parent families. This relative lack of attention and higher instability has a negative effect upon children.

Given that many children never experience a father in the home, Kathryn Edin and Maria Kefalas's *Promises I Can Keep: Why Poor Women Put Motherhood Before Marriage* is also noteworthy. They observe that "American children suffer from more family disruption than children anywhere else in the industrialized world."[102] In their view, marriage-promoting programs are not the answer, because the women in their study do not marry in large part because of their men's "chronic infidelity, physical abuse, alcoholism and drug addiction, criminal activity, and incarceration."[103] Yet, Edin and Kefalas arrive at the same conclusion as does Popenoe. Edin and Kefalas place this conclusion in italics: "*The point is that living apart from either biological parent at any point during childhood is what seems to hurt children.*"[104]

"Consequences of Marital Dissolution." He also engages such works as C. Everett and S. Everett, *Healthy Divorce*; Waite and Lillard, "Children and Marital Disruption"; Seltzer, "Fathers and Children Who Live Apart"; Furstenberg, Nord, Peterson, and Zill, "The Life Course of Children of Divorce"; Seltzer and Bianchi, "Children's Contact with Absent Parents"; Mott, "When Is a Father Really Gone?"

100. See Furstenberg and Cherlin, *Divided Families*.

101. Popenoe, *Families Without Fathers*, 32. He notes that polling data confirms the effects: "only 31 percent of adult children of divorced parents felt close to their fathers, compared to 77 percent of those whose parents are still married and live together" (Popenoe, *Families Without Fathers*, 32).

102. Edin and Kefalas, *Promises I Can Keep*, 213. They explain, "Though some European countries have similarly high rates of nonmarital childbearing, unmarried European parents usually cohabit and tend to stay together for decades [thus treating cohabitation as a form of marriage], whereas their U.S. counterparts typically break up within a couple of years. U.S. divorce rates among couples with children, while lower than for couples without, are also much higher than those of other Western industrialized countries. The fragility of both marriage and cohabitation means that by age fifteen, only half of American children live with both biological parents, whereas roughly two-thirds of Swedish, Austrian, German, and French children do so, as do nearly nine in ten children in Spain and Italy" (*Promises I Can Keep*, 213).

103. Edin and Kefalas, *Promises I Can Keep*, 214.

104. Edin and Kefalas, *Promises I Can Keep*, 215. See also McLanahan, "Parent Absent or Poverty."

Edin and Kefalas nonetheless assume that the present situation, in which so many children are not raised by their biological father and mother, is here to stay and cannot be changed.[105]

I accept their important point that poor women "are often reluctant to marry because of the dangerously low quality of the relationships they are in," and I agree with them that "it is not enough to focus solely on male employment," necessary as jobs are.[106] In my view, however, this is where the gospel comes in—and the transformative power of the Holy Spirit, which men, whether poor or middle-class or wealthy, need for the accomplishment of good marriages. Through faith in Christ, a person receives what Edin and Kefalas identify as necessary for human flourishing, namely, "the opportunity to give of oneself, and the chance to feel useful to others."[107] Edin and Kefalas also comment upon the need for positive role models of marriage in economically poor communities.[108] The Church should be the

---

105. This is also the position of Goode, *World Changes in Divorce Patterns*. For discussion of Goode's position, see Browning, *Marriage and Modernization*, 8–14. Browning discusses Popenoe's more optimistic position at *Marriage and Modernization*, 14–20. Browning sides with Popenoe, but notes that Popenoe generally neglects the important role of religion in any renewal of marriage practices. He states, "Popenoe hopes that religion can help stabilize the postmodern family, but makes little effort to develop a theory of how religious institutions can reconstruct cultural values pertinent to marriage and family. . . . If the family issue is first of all a cultural issue, as Popenoe and his colleagues believe, then religion, as it did in the past, must play a decisive role today in the reconstruction of marriage and family ideals" (*Marriage and Modernization*, 20). See also, for conclusions similar to those of Popenoe, Wolfe, *Whose Keeper?*

106. Edin and Kefalas, *Promises I Can Keep*, 216. They observe that "poor women insist that their poverty is part of what makes marriage so difficult to sustain. Their keen observations of middle-class behavior tell them that given all the expectations Americans now place on it, modern-day marriage is hard enough without the added burden of financial worries. How, they ask, can an economically strained marriage hope to survive?" (*Promises I Can Keep*, 218). Edin and Kefalas also address the economic situation of poor young women, on the grounds that their poverty and lack of opportunity lead poor young women to have a child as a way of establishing "a sense of self-worth and meaning" (*Promises I Can Keep*, 219). They also point out that of children living only with their mothers, half live in a condition of poverty.

107. *Promises I Can Keep*, 217.

108. Julie Hanlon Rubio agrees that "Christians cannot blame poor families for poverty" and that "[t]he strength, love, and hope of poor mothers who continue to bear and raise children in imperfect circumstances must be recognized" (*Hope for Common Ground*, 111). Because she is "promarriage" (*Hope for Common Ground*, 113), however, she gently disagrees with some aspects of Keri Day's view that (in Rubio's words) "if churches go along with the government's efforts to control women's sexuality and childbearing by encouraging marriage and discouraging divorce, they implicitly affirm the narrative of the 'immoral poor' who need only embrace personal responsibility to escape poverty" (*Hope for Common Ground*, 111). See Day, "Saving Black America."

place where such role models are found. As Brooks realizes, this is a crucial mission for a Church committed to social justice.

Popenoe concludes that our contemporary culture is almost what one would invent if one wished to undercut "fatherhood and men's contribution to family life."[109] He lists the following elements that contribute to this undercutting: marriage as based upon happiness rather than upon lifelong commitment; the ease of divorce; an emphasis that other family forms are just as good as being raised by one's biological mother and father; the glorification of sex and the easy availability of sexual substitutes to marriage; an educational system that never praises or prepares for family life but instead focuses solely on preparing for outside jobs; an emphasis on individual fulfillment; a downplaying of the value of children and child-raising; a failure to teach about how male gender roles include fathering; and the notion that to be a father is the same as to be a mother and that fathers are replaceable by women. All these things feed into the current situation of widespread father-absence.

Popenoe identifies "the most deleterious effects of fatherlessness" as "juvenile delinquency, teenage childbearing, child abuse, and violence against women."[110] He recognizes that such things exist even in some homes where fathers are present. His point is simply that, if sociological studies are to be believed, their frequency is significantly increased by the absence of a father in the home.[111] Girls are seven times more likely to be sexually abused in their home by stepfathers (by comparison to the rate of abuse of girls in their home by biological fathers). Single mothers commit significantly more abuse than do mothers married to the biological father, and the same is true for single fathers by comparison to fathers married to the biological mother. In addition, "Mothers' boyfriends are overwhelmingly represented in physical-abuse statistics, especially for serious abuse."[112]

---

109. Popenoe, *Families Without Fathers*, 48.

110. Popenoe, *Families Without Fathers*, 59.

111. Popenoe points out that in the early 1970s, many scholars still believed that conflict between parents has a worse impact upon children than does divorce and the absence of a father (or mother) in the home. Such a view is still held in 1994, though in a chastened form, in Burns and Scott, *Mother-Headed Families*.

112. Popenoe, *Families Without Fathers*, 70.

Helen M. Alvaré's Putting Children's Interests First in US Family Law and Policy

Popenoe employs sociological and scientific research to document the importance for social justice of retaining fatherhood through encouraging male-female marriage. Along complementary lines, Helen Alvaré makes the case that the public-policy priorities of government must be shifted toward the needs of children if the economically impoverished in our society are going to be given a fair chance to flourish.

Alvaré begins with the government's extensive promotion of birth control.[113] Although the function of birth control is to prevent births and thereby to give adults the freedom to express themselves sexually, nonetheless as governmental spending on birth control has skyrocketed, so has the number of children born into nonmarital contexts. Alvaré notes with significant understatement, "New patterns of nonmarital sexual activity did not promote couple stability."[114]

As Alvaré emphasizes, the United States government "explicitly links consensual adult sexual expression with profound human goods, while regularly remaining agnostic to the parents' marital status."[115] It is this agnosticism that she challenges: being raised by one's married (biological) mother and father is significantly better for the wellbeing of children than any other alternative.[116] Alvaré cites studies on child development during the first 1,000 days, showing that both prenatally and after birth, young children of single mothers fall behind in cognitive and developmental ways.[117] She adds

---

113. See also Rhoades and Stanley, *Before "I Do"*; McIlhaney and Bush, *Hooked*; Busby et al., "Sowing Wild Oats." See also Giddens, *The Transformation of Intimacy*.

114. Alvaré, *Putting Children's Interests First*, 3.

115. Alvaré, *Putting Children's Interests First*, 13. One exception that Alvaré identifies is the Supreme Court's valuation of a stable, marital family as part of the Supreme Court's decision in favor of same-sex marriage. But as she points out, in same-sex marriage, "the children involved will be separated from their biological mother or father or both, in every case" (*Putting Children's Interests First*, 13). Another exception has to do with teen pregnancy, where the government at times has warned that "teen parents' non-marital children may suffer" (*Putting Children's Interests First*, 13).

116. See for example Daly and Wilson, "The 'Cinderella Effect'"; Wilcox, "#Yes-WomenAndChildren." Note that the data regarding children raised by same-sex couples is indeterminate for various reasons, and ideology means that research in this field is professionally dangerous unless one's conclusions match the cultural norms assumed by academia. See Marks, "Same-Sex Parenting"; Schumm, "A Review and Critique." See also Cherlin, "American Marriage"; Akerlof, Yellen, and Katz, "Out-of-Wedlock Childbearing in the United States." In my footnotes, I will regularly cite the studies upon which Alvaré's conclusions rest.

117. See Thurow, *The First 1000 Days*; First 1001 Days All Party Parliamentary

that biological parents in a cohabiting relationship do not invest in their children in these years as much as married parents. This is in part because "mothers' parenting is influenced by partner support, and fathers' parenting is influenced by his attachment to the mother."[118] Non-married (cohabiting) households are also generally less stable than married households. Regarding children born to cohabiting but not married parents, Alvaré notes that a large percentage will not be living with both parents by age three.[119] Furthermore, when a single parent gets a new partner or remarries, this is not associated with better outcomes for children.

Alvaré recognizes the impact of factors such as poverty, lack of education, bad neighborhoods, and association with crime and drugs. Nonmarital parenting involves a vicious circle, since its prevalence is increased by these factors and also leads to the perpetuation of such factors in the next generation. Single parenting in itself tends to increase poverty since one parent has to bear the burden alone. But "even *after* controlling for income," nonmarital parenting generally has worse outcomes than marital parenting.[120] Even for very poor children, being raised by their married biological parents generally offers a better outcome than any alternative. Furthermore, as noted above, being married seems to influence male actions and to lead men to work harder and to be more stable.[121] Likewise, being married generally reduces the stress and burden upon the mother, due to more support from the father and from extended family.[122]

Group, *Building Great Britons*; Hart and Risley, *Meaningful Differences*; Heckman, "Economics of Investing in Disadvantaged Children."

118. Alvaré, *Putting Children's Interests First*, 60. See Manning, "Cohabitation and Child Wellbeing"; Yogman and Garfield, "Fathers' Roles"; Ribar, "Why Marriage Matters"; Amato, "More than Money?"; Amato, Meyers, and Emery, "Changes in Nonresident Father-Child Contact."

119. By contrast, for enthusiastic theological approval of pre-marital cohabitation—arguing that it is possible to distinguish "between prenuptial and non-nuptial cohabitation" (167)—see Risch, "Cohabitation." Risch is indebted to Michael G. Lawler and Adrian Thatcher, who take the same position as she does: see Lawler, *Marriage and the Catholic Church*, 162–92; Thatcher, "Living Together before Marriage." See also the chapter on "Cohabitation and the Process of Marrying" in Salzman and Lawler, *Sexual Ethics*, 123–54. For her part, Alvaré cites McLanahan, "Diverging Destinies"; Lee and McLanahan, "Family Structure and Child Development"; Evans and Wachs, eds., *Chaos and Its Influence*.

120. Alvaré, *Putting Children's Interests First*, 62. See Child Trends, "Family Structure: Indicators on Children and Youth"; Mayer, *What Money Can't Buy*; McLanahan and Percheski, "Family Structure and Reproduction of Inequalities."

121. See Lerman and Wilcox, *For Richer, For Poorer*.

122. See McLanahan, "Fragile Families." See also Schneider, "Lessons Learned from Non-Marriage Experiments."

Alvaré finds that nonmarital parenting has a significant link with the growing gap between the rich and poor in the United States. She cites such works as Ralph Banks's *Is Marriage for White People? How the African American Marriage Decline Affects Everyone*.[123] In such studies, one finds strong connections between nonmarital parenting and the children's lack of economic mobility. Although various factors cause this, one of the important factors is lack of marriage. Recent studies also show that there is a gender gap: compared with girls raised without their fathers, boys raised without their fathers do worse over the long run, both economically and educationally.[124]

The United States government pretends that there is no intrinsic "link between sex and procreation," and the government firmly refuses to find "anything of special value in a married couple's ability to procreate children."[125] But it is not that the United States government lacks evidence that being raised by one's married biological parents is beneficial for children. Possessed of this evidence, the government has responded in two main ways. First, it has sought to make up for the lack of two parents by means of large spending on poverty programs.[126] For married families, the poverty rate is 6 percent, while for children in single-mother households (which comprise 84 percent of single-parent households), the poverty rate is 31 percent. Thus, a great deal of the poverty funding goes to single-mother households.[127]

The second way that the government has responded is by trying to limit births to single mothers by promoting and funding birth control and abortion. Single women living in poverty, often African American and Hispanic in background, receive free contraception under Title X and other programs. Hormonal contraceptives have been linked to increased risk for stroke, blood clots, bone loss, breast and cervical cancer, and depression, in addition to the fact that research indicates that contraceptive hormones "affect both brain structure and function" and "may alter women's partner preferences in a way disadvantageous to the stability of a relationship after

---

123. Banks, *Is Marriage for White People?* See also Chetty et al., "Where Is the Land of Opportunity?"; Högnäs and Carlson, "Like Parent, Like Child?"; Guzzo, "New Partners, More Kids."

124. See Bertrand and Pan, "The Trouble with Boys."

125. Alvaré, *Putting Children's Interests First*, 52, 55. See also Alstott, *No Exit*; Weissbourd, *The Vulnerable Child*.

126. See Eberstadt, "The Vindication of *The Manhattan Declaration*," 86.

127. See also Alvaré, *Putting Children's Interests First*, 79, citing Lesaux and Jones, *Early Childhood Education*; Bradbury et al., *Too Many Children Left Behind*.

the woman ceases using the pill."[128] Furthermore, contraception results in an increased willingness to have sex outside marriage, with the result (given contraceptive failure) of more children conceived outside marriage.[129] Another result has been more exposure to sexually transmitted diseases such as syphilis, gonorrhea, and chlamydia.[130]

Government has valorized "individualism in the sexual arena" and has targeted poor women, especially, for this message.[131] Alvaré therefore proposes a formal governmental affirmation of "a child's right to know and be cared for by both of his or her parents."[132] She quotes a dissenting opinion written by Supreme Court Justice Sonia Sotomayor that insists upon a child's right to know his or her biological father and that describes a child's inability to know both biological parents as an immeasurable loss.[133] Given the needs of children and the reality of "familial interdependency,"[134] the procreation of children should be socially encouraged to take place within a marriage. This is actually what most people desire for themselves: not individual sexual gratification, but "a 'couple orientation' and a desire for commitment."[135]

---

128. Alvaré, *Putting Children's Interests First*, 92–93. On the link between hormonal birth control and an increased risk of breast cancer and cervical cancer, see Miller, "Birth Control and Cancer." See also Little, "Oral Contraceptive Use"; Pletzer and Kerschbaum, "Fifty Years of Hormonal Contraception"; Skovlund et al., "Association of Hormonal Contraception with Depression." Despite widespread use of birth control, the rate of unintended pregnancy was 49 percent in 2013. See U.S. Department of Health and Human Services, *Female Contraceptive Development Program*.

129. See Akerlof, Yellen, and Katz, "Out-of-Wedlock Childbearing in the United States"; Finer, "Trends in Premarital Sex." Some scholars—such as Isabel Sawhill—celebrate the shift to nonfertile sexuality made possible by long-lasting hormonal contraceptives: see Sawhill, *Generation Unbound*.

130. See Alvaré, *Putting Children's Interests First*, 99.

131. Alvaré, *Putting Children's Interests First*, 142. At the same time, government has argued that "when children are born, we must turn on a dime and embrace an ethic of solidarity, generosity, and even altruism toward our own children, and toward others'" (*Putting Children's Interests First*, 142). See also Lareau, *Unequal Childhoods*. See also Moran, *Teaching Sex*.

132. Alvaré, *Putting Children's Interests First*, 114. She directs attention to Blauwhoff, *Foundational Facts, Relative Truths*; Scheib, Ruby, and Benward, "Who Requests Their Sperm Donor's Identity?"; Marquardt, *My Daddy's Name Is Donor*.

133. See Adoptive Couple v. Baby Girl, 133 S. Ct. 2552, 2574.

134. Alvaré, *Putting Children's Interests First*, 116. For emphasis on the need for society to value the tasks undertaken by caretakers, she directs attention to Martha Fineman's work (while recognizing that Fineman's perspective differs from her own in various ways), as well as to Kittay, *Love's Labor*, and Glendon, *The Transformation of Family Law*.

135. Alvaré, *Putting Children's Interests First*, 117. She adds, "The best accepted measure of human sexual practice in the United States, *The Social Organization of*

IV. Conclusion

As Brent Waters says, for many contemporary scholars "there is no inherent nature of the familial association that should be honoured and supported, both in respect to its internal ordering and its ordering to broader associations."[136] In this vein, the political theorist Susan Moller Okin argues that the accomplishment of full gender equality means that the state must take over the task of childcare, by providing and regulating it so as to ensure that traditional family structures no longer constrain and burden women and no longer distort children's understanding of justice.[137] I began this chapter with the polar opposite viewpoint, Brooks's *Urban Apologetics*, which urges that social justice in urban communities requires proclaiming and living the gospel's teachings on marriage. Likewise, Popenoe and Alvaré also make a persuasive case regarding the need to reinvigorate marriage.

Is this feasible in modern society? Stephanie Coontz has argued that while a bad marriage is bad for both the man and the woman, it is worse for the woman, "because even a miserable wife tends to feed her husband more vegetables, schedule his medical checkups, and shoulder much of the housework and the emotional work that make life function smoothly."[138] Coontz therefore favors what she calls the "marriage revolution," in which marriage is seen as primarily being about self-fulfillment.[139]

Sexuality: Sexual Practices in the United States, indicates that Americans are happiest with their sex lives on average, when they are highly committed to another person, and oriented to the other's happiness as well as their own" (*Putting Children's Interests First*, 117). See also Waite and Joyner, "Emotional and Physical Satisfaction with Sex." For further social-scientific data, showing the same results, see Muise et al., "Keeping the Spark Alive." See also the important results of Oliver and Hyde, "Gender Differences in Sexuality"; Schmitt et al., "Universal Sex Differences." Alvaré goes on to say that studies of young-adult "hook-up" culture show differences between men and women, with women being "regularly less satisfied than men with casual sex" and with women being subjugated to unwarranted sex (Alvaré, *Putting Children's Interests First*, 122). Among the multiple books cited by Alvaré on hook-up culture is Freitas, *The End of Sex*. For a broadly compelling account of marriage that is both explicitly Christian and geared toward appreciating the structures of created flourishing, see Morse, "Why Marriage Belongs to God."

136. Waters, *The Family*, 267.

137. See Okin, *Justice, Gender, and the Family*. See also the discussion in Waters, *The Family*, 74–82, with reference to Okin as well as to Rawls, *A Theory of Justice*; and Rawls, *Political Liberalism*. Waters traces this perspective to Immanuel Kant, to whom he attributes the view that "social and political construction is an act of free human will" (Waters, *The Family*, 69). He cites Kant, *Political Writings*; and Kant, *The Metaphysics of Morals*.

138. Coontz, *Marriage, a History*, 310.

139. Coontz, *Marriage, a History*, 308.

The problem is that the focus on individual self-fulfillment has not proven adequate to caring for the needs of children, and, besides, self-fulfillment is generally found in enduring relationships of interdependence with others. This is the message that the *Compendium of the Social Doctrine of the Church* inculcates in its anthropology of self-gift, which undergirds its account of Christian marriage as a pillar of social justice. Rather than a "marriage revolution" of self-fulfillment—which has not worked for children—what people truly need is a gospel-based "marriage revolution" rooted in fruitful self-surrendering love, imaging the triune God. Although the teachings of the New Testament condemn abuse, adultery, and un-Christ-like power-plays, there is no doubt that in past cultures, despite the nominal prevalence of Christianity, men were allowed to act in these ways. The true Christian revolution in marriage is founded upon Christ's love for us on the Cross, and this revolution is made possible by the outpouring of the Holy Spirit that fuels repentance, faith, and transformation of heart.[140] Such a revolution in marriage would bring with it other goods of a just society, such as increased almsgiving and volunteer work, fewer acts of criminality, and better outcomes for children.[141]

Due to the ever-new beauty of the gospel, I believe that there is a marriage revolution waiting to happen even now. Awaiting Christ's consummation of the marriage of God and creation, believers do not need to marry: consecrated celibacy and singleness also bear a distinctive eschatological witness that fosters social justice. But, through the grace of the sacrament of marriage, believers in every generation have discovered not only what the sociologist Mary Eberstadt calls "the inextricable way in which Christianity and the family depend for their support on one another,"[142] but also the freedom for self-surrendering love that fosters a just society. Such love anticipates the coming fullness of the eschatological marriage of God and his people, for which "the whole creation has been groaning with labor pains together until now" (Rom 8:22).

---

140. Waters warns against the notion that "the family and the church are both redemptive institutions, and thereby correlative agencies rather than the former being subordinate to the latter" (Waters, *The Family*, 38). I agree that it is the Church that is the redemptive institution, and the family is subordinate to the Church. Because of his view that marriage is not a sacrament, Waters misses the way in which Christ draws marriage (and the family) into the dynamism of the inaugurated kingdom.

141. See Eberstadt, *How the West Really Lost God*; Brooks, *Who Really Cares*; Johnson, *More God, Less Crime*; Davies, *The Strange Death of Moral Britain*.

142. Eberstadt, *How the West Really Lost God*, 201.

Conclusion

In his *History of the Arians*, Athanasius writes that "our Savior is so gentle that He teaches thus, 'If any man wills to come after me,' and 'Whoever wills to be my disciple' [Mt 16:24]; and coming to each He does not force them, but knocks at the door and says, 'Open unto me, my sister, my spouse' [Song 5:2; cf. 5:1]; and if they open to Him, He enters in, but if they delay and will not, He departs from them."[1] For Athanasius, as for other Christian readers of the Song of Songs, the "beloved" is the bridegroom God/Christ and the bride Israel/Church. Yet viewed from another angle, the Song of Songs is an erotic poem about a male-female human relationship. Both angles are important; the eschatological marriage and earthly marriage must be held tightly together.[2]

This has been the premise of the present book, which began with a chapter exploring the eschatological marriage of God and his people.[3] Nicholas Healy has remarked that "God seeks a covenant or a communion with his creation—a relationship of reciprocal love. The privileged image for this covenant in both the Old and the New Testament is spousal or nuptial love."[4] As the Bridegroom who has inaugurated the eschatological wedding, Jesus Christ has superabundantly fulfilled the covenant. Yet, does this fulfillment in Christ overshadow the value of human marriage? I have suggested in this book that the answer is no. Human marriage is a sacramental

---

1. Athanasius, *History of the Arians*, §33, 281.

2. No doubt, this can be difficult to do, especially for theologians who refuse to romanticize marriage (and sexuality) after the fall. For a helpful discussion of how to hold the two together, focusing on Bernard of Clairvaux's commentary on the Song of Songs, see Roberts, *Creation and Covenant*, 79-97.

3. Waters argues that Christian marriage witnesses to God's providence and has a "teleological and eschatological orientation toward larger spheres of affinity," but that in fact there is a (constructive) "tension between the church as eschatological witness and the family as providential witness" (Waters, *The Family*, xiii).

4. Healy, "Marriage, Priesthood, and the Sincere Gift," 322.

sign of the self-surrendering love and justice of the eschatological marriage for which God created us. As Thomas Knieps-Port le Roi puts it, "between the unity of marriage and the unity of Christ and the church there is the same relationship as the one that exists between the order of creation and the order of redemption. The covenant is the reason for creation."[5]

In this light, the Song of Songs takes on special significance. Paul Griffiths states that between the fifth and the sixteenth centuries, the Song of Songs "attracted more commentary [among Christians] than any other scriptural book."[6] Griffiths is aware that the Song of Songs does not explicitly discuss anything but human erotic yearning. He points out, "The Lord is not named in the Song; neither is Jesus, neither is Mary, and neither is the church. Even the people of Israel are scarcely there, making an explicit entry only because of the naming of places in which they live."[7] Although the Song of Songs has long been interpreted as being about the nuptial relationship of God and his people, its plain sense portrays human lovers. Indeed, J. Cheryl Exum, joined by the majority of modern exegetes, thinks "the Song is not an allegory" but rather is solely "a great love poem," even if one easily susceptible to allegorical interpretation.[8] For Exum, the Song of Songs describes the erotic "love between a woman and a man"; this is how "the poet represents it" and therefore what the poem intends.[9]

---

5. Knieps-Port le Roi, "Sacramental Marriage and Holy Orders," 141. I critique some aspects of Knieps-Port le Roi's later work on marriage in my *Indissolubility of Marriage*.

6. Griffiths, *Song of Songs*, xxxii. See Arminjon, *The Cantata of Love*; Astell, *The Song of Songs*; Turner, *Eros and Allegory*; Norris, ed., *The Song of Songs*. Griffiths's *Christian Flesh* construes the human body as something that the human person uses for diverse ends, as distinct from teleological accounts. By contrast, as will be clear, I agree with Gerald Gleeson that the fundamental issue is "how we are to understand the psycho-physical-spiritual unity of the human person. Are we persons who *use their bodies* in the service of psychological experiences [love and/or pleasure], or are we body-soul unities—persons who are *living, sexually differentiated bodies*?" (Gleeson, "Should the Church Change Its Teaching?," 42).

7. Griffiths, *Song of Songs*, xxxviii. Note that Griffiths distinguishes between allegory and figural-typological readings; the latter do not dismiss the plain sense of the text. The Song of Songs thus can figurally represent Christ and the Church without ceasing to be also about two human lovers. As Griffiths points out, Rabbi Joseph B. Soloveitchik also insists upon retaining both the literal and the figural senses of the Song of Songs: see Soloveitchik, *And from There You Shall Seek*, 151–53.

8. Exum, *Song of Songs*, 77.

9. Exum, *Song of Songs*, 84. Exum's main argument is this: "When biblical writers used symbolic language to make a point, they were not usually subtle about it" (Exum, *Song of Songs*, 76). She also records recent efforts to fight "heteronormative" or "heterosexist" readings of the Song of Songs: see Burrus and Moore, "Unsafe Sex"; Ostriker, "A Holy of Holies."

Yet, although the Song of Songs contains "not a single overt reference to God, to prayer, or to any aspect of Israel's religious practice or tradition," nonetheless, as Ellen Davis says, "the Song is thick with words and images drawn from earlier books" of the Hebrew Scriptures.[10] Davis therefore advocates retaining both the human relationship between the man and the woman and God's relationship with Israel-Church. The marriage of God and humankind has been inaugurated in Christ, but it is yet to be fully consummated; in the present world Christ's followers undergo tribulation in configuration to his Cross, so that by the grace of his Holy Spirit we may move from selfish self-love to cruciform self-giving love of God and neighbor, and thereby enter fully into communion with Triune Love.[11]

Given that the eschatological marriage has been promised and inaugurated but we are still living in the fallen world, the Church yearns "for fuller union with Christ and fuller understanding of the gift given."[12] This fruitful yearning is the Bride's calling out for the consummated marriage that the Bridegroom, too, desires. Along these lines, Origen conceives of the Song of

---

10. Davis, *Proverbs, Ecclesiastes, and the Song of Songs*, 231. Davis goes on to say, "I hope to show that the sexual and the religious understandings of the Song are mutually informative, and that each is incomplete without the other. For a holistic understanding of our own humanity suggests that our religious capacity is linked with an awareness of our own sexuality. Fundamental to both is a desire to transcend the confines of the self for the sake of intimacy with the other. Sexual love provides many people with their first experience of ecstasy, which literally means 'standing outside oneself.' Therefore the experience of healthy sexual desire can help us imagine what it might mean to love God truly—a less 'natural' feeling for many of us, especially in our secular society. On the other hand, from what the Bible tells us about God's love we can come to recognize sexual love as an arena for the formation of the soul. Like the love of God, profound love of another person entails devotion of the whole self and steady practice of repentance and forgiveness; it inevitably requires suffering and sacrifice. A full reading of the Song of Songs stretches our minds to span categories of experience that our modern intellects too neatly separate" (*Proverbs, Ecclesiastes, and the Song of Songs*, 233). See also Exum, *Song of Songs*, 64, citing Fox, *Song of Songs*, 239–43 and Pope, *Song of Songs*, 145–53.

11. As Servais Pinckaers, O.P. describes the sufferings praised by the Beatitudes (in Jesus' Sermon on the Mount), "We can compare the work of the beatitudes to that of a plow in the fields. Drawn along with determination, it drives the sharp edge of the plowshare into the earth and carves out, as the poets say, a deep wound, a broad furrow. ... In the same way the word of the beatitudes penetrates us with the power of the Holy Spirit in order to break up our interior soil. It cuts through us with the sharp edge of trials and with the struggles it provokes. It overturns our ideas and projects, reverses the obvious, thwarts our desires, and bewilders us, leaving us poor and naked before God. All this, in order to prepare a place within us for the seed of new life" (Pinckaers, *The Pursuit of Happiness*, 154).

12. Griffiths, *Song of Songs*, xli. For helpful Thomistic insights into the theology of gift, see Rineau, *"Celui qui donne."*

Songs as "the bridegroom's perfect marriage-song" and as the expression of "the mind and voice of the Bridegroom—in short, the perfect textual manifestation of the 'perfect mystery' into which all Scripture ultimately aims to initiate the soul."[13]

Having accepted that we have no access to the intention of the poet who wrote the Song of Songs, the Lutheran theologian Robert Jenson aptly observes that "[o]f the intent of whoever definitively made Scripture of the Song, we can be more certain: they intended the Song to be about Israel and the Lord."[14] For this reason, Jenson feels quite comfortable perceiving theological allegory in the Song of Songs. Crucially, however, he adds that "the Song's canonical plain sense *rightly* takes human sexual love as an analogue of love between the Lord and Israel."[15] This means that human love—and human marriage—is capable of functioning as an analogue, even if not the prime analogate. We can truly say that "if human sexuality"—and, I would add, human marriage—"can be an analogue of divine-human love, it must somehow be correlate to, or able to be correlate to, that love."[16]

Admittedly, when the Church Fathers read the Song of Songs, they generally thought not about human marriage but rather about mystical embrace of God. Yet Augustine (representing the West) and John Chrysostom (representing the East), as I have argued in this book, had a rich and profound understanding of human marriage, which they did not attempt to spiritualize away. The Church Fathers recognized that Jesus Christ has healed and elevated human marriage by pouring out his Spirit, and they understood why one might think of the married couple as imaging God. They saw the importance of the fact that the first sin arose from within a marriage and distorted not just our individual relationship with God, but our primal human communion. They appreciated the need for the married couple to flourish by cleaving to Christ's self-surrendering Cross.

As understood through divine revelation, then, marriage surely serves as a fitting "analogue of divine-human love."[17] Jenson goes on to make a crucial clarification: "this does not mean that our eroticism is the original

---

13. King, *Origen on the Song of Songs*, 265; I am quoting also the subtitle of the book. Although for Origen the pneumatization or spiritualization is all-embracing (and thus the ongoing role of the body becomes difficult to discern), I agree with him that the Song of Songs presents and even, in the Spirit-filled reader, in a certain sense enacts "the 'perfect mystery' of the supercelestial bridal-chamber" (*Origen on the Song of Songs*, 270).

14. Jenson, *Song of Songs*, 11.

15. Jenson, *Song of Songs*, 13.

16. Jenson, *Song of Songs*, 13.

17. Jenson, *Song of Songs*, 13.

and that we construe God's relation to his people by projecting it."[18] In fact, the truth is "[j]ust the other way around."[19] God's eternal plan to accomplish the marriage of God and creation is what that justifies Christian theology in spending so much effort in the analysis of human marriage.[20]

More than once in this book, I have drawn attention to Matthias Joseph Scheeben. Let me do so once more. Scheeben urges Christians "to glory in the exalted mysteries" that we possess "by the grace of God," and to praise "the incredible magnificence of the mysteries."[21] Emphasizing that God created the world for the purpose of the nuptial union of Christ and the Church, he recognizes that "Christian marriage . . . has a real, essential, and intrinsic reference to the mystery of Christ's union with His Church. It is rooted in this mystery and is organically connected with it, and so partakes of its nature and mysterious character."[22] Since this is so, the failure to contemplate Christian marriage theologically would be tragic.

Books on Christian marriage, then, cannot be merely how-to manuals, counter-cultural guides to the joys of traditional family life, or even (solely) erudite descriptions of the moral requisites of marriage. As I have sought to show, Christian marriage is ultimately intelligible only within its theological context. The evangelical pastor Ray Ortlund proclaims: "The whole of cosmic reality exists as the venue for the eternal honeymoon of the perfect husband with his perfect bride in marital bliss forever and ever."[23] This language may sound saccharine and lacking in analogical caution. The cosmos is not merely a "venue." But, properly understood (insofar as the great mystery can be understood!), the marriage of Christ and his bride is indeed the goal of the entire creation. Christian understanding of marriage must continually have this goal in view.

In this light, the chapters of the present book fit together. First, I examined Scripture's teachings about the marriage of God and his people in light of contemporary challenges to those teachings (chapter 1). Given the nuptial goal of creation, human marriage's theological place is rightly expansive, as I sought to show in the next three chapters. Chapter 2 inquired into what marriage can teach us by analogously imaging the Trinity's self-surrendering fruitfulness. Chapter 3 probed the implications of the fact

18. Jenson, *Song of Songs*, 14.

19. Jenson, *Song of Songs*, 14.

20. For a theological response to changes in marriage law (especially same-sex marriage), see Farrow, *Nation of Bastards*.

21. Scheeben, *The Mysteries of Christianity*, 7.

22. Scheeben, *The Mysteries of Christianity*, 601.

23. Ortlund, *Marriage and the Mystery*, 111.

that original sin distorted the primordial marriage. Chapter 4 explored how the Cross of Christ pertains to the healing and elevating of marriage. On the basis of these chapters, I took up three "practical" questions regarding Christian marriage. Chapter 5 defended the prioritization of the procreation and raising of children as the primary end of marriage, in accord with the fruitfulness of marital love. Chapter 6 argued that a biblical understanding of doctrinal development indicates that marriage's inclusion among the seven sacraments was not a mere invention of the Church, but rather flows from Christ's eschatological promise to renew and elevate marriage among his followers. Chapter 7 proposed that Christian marriage belongs centrally to social justice and thereby to building up the kingdom of God in love.

Commenting on *Gaudium et Spes*, Bernard Häring remarks that this Pastoral Constitution of the Second Vatican Council places marriage "first among the burning questions of our time."[24] Häring's moral theology, with its neo-probabilist emphasis on conscience and its breathless sense of "a new age and its new difficulties," has serious deficiencies.[25] But he is right about marriage's importance in our day. This is so not only because of the challenges faced by marriage as a human reality, but also because of the neglect, perhaps especially among Catholics, of marriage's eschatological signification. Andrew Davison puts it well: marriage "is not only blessed by Christ [at Cana]," but also "it is a symbol of the relation of God to his people in Christ," given that Christ is the "bridegroom" and "the life of the world to come is described as a wedding feast (Matt. 22.1–14; 25.1–13; Rev. 19.6–8)."[26]

At the same time, we cannot romanticize marriage.[27] Fallen human nature—including marriage—is healed and elevated in the sacrament by the

24. Häring, "Part II, Chapter I," 229.

25. Häring, "Part II, Chapter I," 229. For further discussion see my "Pinckaers and Häring on Conscience."

26. Davison, *Why Sacraments?*, 71.

27. See Cloutier, "Marriage and Sexuality," 316–17: "Sacramentality is not centrally about the love of the couple, but about the couple's placement within the salvation history that is the life of the Church and of their individual baptismal identities as disciples of Christ." Cloutier earlier states with regard to *Gaudium et Spes*: "A central problem arises when the pronouncements of *Gaudium et Spes* are taken out of the context of the original intent of the constitution, a document wherein the Church seeks to enter into dialogue with the modern world. . . . Read outside this context, the constitution's treatment is often taken to be a redefining of Church teaching on marriage, one which de-emphasizes procreation in light of a newfound respect for the natural and supernatural power and promise of interpersonal love. The loss of *Gaudium et Spes*' context is particularly awkward when the document is used as the basis for developing novel understandings of the sacramentality of marriage, rather than as a way to dialogue with those outside the Church" ("Marriage and Sexuality," 313). See also Cloutier, *Love*,

crucified Christ who has been raised and exalted. This means that marriage cannot be approached simply as the cozy life together of the spouses, but must be seen in light of the radical mission of the Church, above all its orientation in cruciform self-surrendering love to eschatological consummation.

Because God created humans for the eschatological marriage, we need to learn afresh how to sing the Song of self-surrendering love. Human marriage is not required for singing this Song; consecrated virgins and single people sing it as well, with their own eschatological inflection. But if human marriage is the central analogue for the purpose of all creation, then it is especially important that we get this Song right when it comes to human marriage. Resisting the temptation to address the practical questions and controversies first, our primary task must be to attune human marriage to the Trinity, as well as to our fallenness and to Christ's Paschal mystery. We are then prepared to offer a theological account of marriage vis-à-vis the raising of children, the love of the spouses, the grace of the sacrament, and the justice of our families and communities.

Christians are called to think boldly about marriage, more boldly than the utopian imaginings of either the romantic right or the neo-Marxist left that dominate the cultural scene today. To say this is not to offer a triumphalist portrait of a vigorous Christianity fighting off "modernity." The contrary is true of our churches today. Theological thinking must face the terrible mess that Christians have made over the centuries by accommodating to destructive cultural norms, such as the abusive patriarchy that allowed husbands such as Niccolò Machiavelli, in supposedly Catholic fifteenth-century Italy, to keep his wife under lock and key while himself engaging in adultery.[28] Though history should have made us repentant, Gabriele Kuby has shown how eager we Catholics today are to embrace present-day destructive cultural norms.[29]

With faith and repentance, dependent upon Christ and his Spirit, let us praise God for his eternal purpose to unite creation intimately to his own unfathomably wondrous triune life of love. Attending to the love and responsibilities of Christian marriage—and instructed by the witness of consecrated virginity and singleness—let us look forward to "the holy city, New Jerusalem, coming down out of heaven from God, prepared as a bride adorned for her husband" (Rev 21:2). Striving to practice Christian marriage in contemporary culture, let us "sing the Lord's song in a foreign land"

Reason, and God's Story, chapter 7.

28. See King, *Machiavelli*.

29. Kuby, *The Global Sexual Revolution*. See also Siggelkow and Büscher, *Deutschlands sexuelle Tragödie*.

(Ps 137:4), trusting anew in the promise: "Blessed are those who are invited to the marriage supper of the Lamb" (Rev 19:9).

Bibliography

Abma, Richtsje. *Bonds of Love: Methodic Studies of Prophetic Texts with Marriage Imagery (Isaiah 50:1–3 and 54:1–10, Hosea 1–3, Jeremiah 2–3)*. Assen, The Netherlands: Van Gorcum, 1999.
Adoptive Couple v. Baby Girl, 133 S. Ct. 2552, 2574 (2013) (Sotomayor, J. dissenting).
Akerlof, George, Janet L. Yellen, and Michael L. Katz. "An Analysis of Out-of-Wedlock Childbearing in the United States." *The Quarterly Journal of Economics* 111 (1996) 277–317.
Alexander, Michelle. "More Black Men Are in Prison Today Than Were Enslaved in 1850." *Huffington Post*. October 12, 2011. http://www.huffingtonpost.com/2011/10/12/michelle-alexander-more-black-men-in-prison-slaves-1850_n_1007368.html.
Alison, James. "Following the Still Small Voice: Experience, Truth, and Argument as Lived by Catholics around the Gay Issue." In *Sexuality and the U.S. Catholic Church: Crisis and Renewal*, edited by Lisa Sowle Cahill, John Garvey, and T. Frank Kennedy, S.J., 163–82. New York: Crossroad, 2006.
al-Kawthari, Muhammad Ibn Adam. *Al-Arba'īn: Elucidation of Forty Ḥadīths on Marriage*. London: Turath, 2013.
Allison, Dale C., Jr. *Constructing Jesus: Memory, Imagination, and History*. Grand Rapids: Baker Academic, 2010.
Alstott, Anne L. *No Exit: What Parents Owe Their Children and What Societies Owe Parents*. Oxford: Oxford University Press, 2004.
Alvaré, Helen M. *Putting Children's Interests First in U.S. Family Law and Policy: With Power Comes Responsibility*. Cambridge: Cambridge University Press, 2018.
Amato, Paul R. "More than Money? Men's Contributions to Their Children's Lives." In *Men in Families: When Do They Get Involved? What Difference Does It Make?*, edited by Alan Booth and Ann C. Crouter, 241–78. New York: Psychology, 1998.
Amato, Paul R., Catherine E. Meyers, and Robert E. Emery. "Changes in Nonresident Father-Child Contact from 1976 to 2002." *Family Relations* 58 (2009) 41–53.
Andersen, Francis I., and David Noel Freedman. *Hosea*. Garden City, NY: Doubleday, 1980.
Anderson, Gary A. *The Genesis of Perfection: Adam and Eve in Jewish and Christian Imagination*. Louisville: Westminster John Knox, 2001.
Anderson, Ryan T. "How to Think About Sexual Orientation and Gender Identity (SOGI) Policies and Religious Freedom." In *Equality and Non-discrimination: Catholic Roots, Current Challenges*, edited by Jane F. Adolphe, Robert L. Fastiggi, and Michael A. Vacca, 42–62. Eugene, OR: Pickwick, 2019.

———. *Truth Overruled: The Future of Marriage and Religious Freedom*. Washington, DC: Regnery, 2015.

Annas, Julia. "Mill and the Subjection of Women." *Philosophy* 52 (1977) 179-94.

Aquinas, Thomas. *Summa contra gentiles*. Book Three: *Providence*. Translated by Vernon J. Bourke. Notre Dame: University of Notre Dame Press, 1975.

———. *Summa contra gentiles*. Book Four: *Salvation*. Translated by Charles J. O'Neil. Notre Dame: University of Notre Dame Press, 1975.

———. *Summa theologiae*. Translated by Fathers of the English Dominican Province. Westminster, MD: Christian Classics, 1981.

Archer, J., and B. Lloyd. *Sex and Gender*. Cambridge: Cambridge University Press, 1985.

Aristotle. *The Nicomachean Ethics*. Rev. ed. Translated by H. Rackham. Cambridge, MA: Harvard University Press, 1934.

———. *Politics*. Translated by Benjamin Jowett. New York: Random House, 1943.

Arjonillo, Rolando B. *Conjugal Love of the Ends of Marriage: A Study of Dietrich von Hildebrand and Herbert Doms in the Light of the Pastoral Constitution 'Gaudium et Spes'*. Bern: Peter Lang, 1998.

Arminjon, Blaise. *The Cantata of Love: A Verse-by-Verse Reading of the Song of Songs*. Translated by Nelly Marans. San Francisco: Ignatius, 1988.

Arnold, Bill T. *Genesis*. Cambridge: Cambridge University Press, 2009.

Astell, Ann W. *The Song of Songs in the Middle Ages*. Ithaca, NY: Cornell University Press, 1990.

Astorga, Christina A. *Catholic Moral Theology and Social Ethics: A New Method*. Maryknoll, NY: Orbis, 2014.

Athanasius. *History of the Arians*. In *Athanasius: Select Works and Letters*, edited by Archibald Robertson, translated by M. Atkinson. Vol. 4 of *Nicene and Post-Nicene Fathers, Second Series*, edited by Philip Schaff and Henry Wace, 266-302. Peabody, MA: Hendrickson, 1995.

Augustine. *City of God*. Translated by Henry Bettenson. New York: Penguin, 1984.

———. *Confessions*. Translated by Henry Chadwick. Oxford: Oxford University Press, 1991.

———. *On Marriage and Concupiscence*. Translated by Peter Holmes. In Augustine, *Anti-Pelagian Writings*. Vol. 5 of the *Nicene and Post-Nicene Fathers, First Series*, edited by Philip Schaff, 263-308. Peabody, MA: Hendrickson, 1995.

———. *The Trinity*. Translated by Edmund Hill, O.P. Brooklyn, NY: New City, 1991.

Austriaco, Nicanor Pier Giorgio, O.P. "Understanding Sexual Orientation as a *Habitus*: Reasoning from the Natural Law, Appeals to Human Experience, and the Data of Science." In *Leaving and Coming Home: New Wineskins for Catholic Sexual Ethics*, edited by David Cloutier, 101-18. Eugene, OR: Cascade, 2010.

Ayres, Lewis. *Augustine and the Trinity*. Cambridge: Cambridge University Press, 2010.

Baker, Maureen, and Vivienne Elizabeth. *Marriage in an Age of Cohabitation: How and When People Tie the Knot in the Twenty-First Century*. Oxford: Oxford University Press, 2014.

Bal, Mieke. *Lethal Love: Feminist Literary Readings of Biblical Love Stories*. Bloomington, IN: Indiana University Press, 1987.

———. "Metaphors He Lives By." *Semeia* 61 (1993) 185-207.

Balthasar, Hans Urs von. *The Christian State of Life*. Translated by Mary Frances McCarthy. San Francisco: Ignatius, 1983.

———. *The Glory of the Lord: A Theological Aesthetics*. Vol. 1, *Seeing the Form*, translated by Erasmo Leiva-Merikakis, edited by Joseph Fessio, S.J. and John Riches. San Francisco: Ignatius, 1982.

———. "The Marian Mold of the Church." In *Mary: The Church at the Source*, translated by Adrian Walker, 125–44. San Francisco: Ignatius, 2005.

———. *Martin Buber and Christianity: A Dialogue between Israel and the Church*. Translated by Alexander Dru. London: Harvill, 1961.

———. *New Elucidations*. Translated by Mary Theresilde Skerry. San Francisco: Ignatius, 1986.

———. *Theo-Drama: Theological Dramatic Theory*. Vol. 2, *The Dramatis Personae: Man in God*. Translated by Graham Harrison. San Francisco: Ignatius, 1990.

———. *Theo-Logic: Theological Logical Theory*. Vol. 2, *Truth of God*. Translated by Adrian J. Walker. San Francisco: Ignatius, 2004.

———. *Theo-Logic: Theological Logical Theory*. Vol. 3, *The Spirit of Truth*. Translated by Graham Harrison. San Francisco: Ignatius, 2005.

———. *The Theology of Karl Barth: Exposition and Interpretation*. Translated by Edward T. Oakes, S.J. San Francisco: Ignatius, 1992.

Banks, Ralph Richard. *Is Marriage for White People? How the African American Marriage Decline Affects Everyone*. New York: Penguin, 2011.

Barash, David P. *Out of Eden: The Surprising Consequences of Polygamy*. Oxford: Oxford University Press, 2016.

Barash, David P., and Judith Eve Lipton. *Gender Gap: The Biology of Male-Female Differences*. New Brunswick, NJ: Transaction, 2001.

Barber, Michael. "The New Temple, the New Priesthood, and the New Cult in Luke-Acts." *Letter and Spirit* 8 (2013) 101–24.

Baril, Gilberte. *The Feminine Face of the People of God: Biblical Symbols of the Church as Bride and Mother*. Translated by Florestine Audette. Collegeville, MN: Liturgical, 1990.

Barth, Karl. *Church Dogmatics*. Vol. 3, *The Doctrine of Creation*, Part 1, edited by G. W. Bromiley and T. F. Torrance. Translated by J. W. Edwards, O. Bussey, and H. Knight. Edinburgh: T. & T. Clark, 1958.

———. *Church Dogmatics*. Vol. 3, *The Doctrine of Creation*, Part 2, edited by G. W. Bromiley and T. F. Torrance. Translated by H. Knight, G. W. Bromiley, J. K. S. Reid, and R. H. Fuller. Edinburgh: T. & T. Clark, 1960.

———. *Church Dogmatics*. Vol. 3, *The Doctrine of Creation*, Part 4, edited by G. W. Bromiley and T. F. Torrance. Translated by A. T. Mackay, T. H. L. Parker, H. Knight, H. A. Kennedy, and J. Marks. Edinburgh: T. & T. Clark, 1961.

Barton, John. *Ethics in Ancient Israel*. Oxford: Oxford University Press, 2014.

Baucham, Voddie, Jr. *Family Driven Faith*. Wheaton, IL: Crossway, 2007.

Bauer, Angela. *Gender in the Book of Jeremiah: A Feminist-Literary Reading*. New York: Peter Lang, 1999.

Baumann, Gerlinde. *Love and Violence: Marriage as Metaphor for the Relationship between YHWH and Israel in the Prophetic Books*. Translated by Linda M. Maloney. Collegeville, MN: Liturgical, 2003.

Beaman, Lori G., ed. *Reasonable Accommodation: Managing Religious Diversity*. Vancouver: University of British Colombia Press, 2012.

Beckwith, Roger. *The Old Testament Canon of the New Testament Church and Its Background in Early Judaism*. London: SPCK, 1985.

Benardete, Seth. *Socrates' Second Sailing: On Plato's Republic*. Chicago: University of Chicago Press, 1989.
Benedict XVI. *Deus Caritas Est*. Vatican translation. Boston: Pauline, 2006.
———. *Jesus of Nazareth*. Vol. 1, *From the Baptism in the Jordan to the Transfiguration*, translated by Adrian J. Walker. New York: Doubleday, 2007.
———. [Joseph Ratzinger.] "On the schema On the Sources of Revelation: address to the German-speaking bishops, October 10, 1962." In "Six Texts by Prof. Joseph Ratzinger as Peritus before and during Vatican Council II," edited and translated with introduction and commentary by Jared Wicks, S.J., *Gregorianum* 89 (2008) 269–85 [233–311].
———. [Joseph Ratzinger.] "The Sign of the Woman: An Introductory Essay on the Encyclical *Redemptoris Mater*." In *Mary: The Church at the Source*, translated by Adrian Walker, 37–95. San Francisco: Ignatius, 2005.
———. *Verbum Domini*. Vatican translation. Boston: Pauline, 2010.
Bennett, Jana Marguerite. "Singular Christianity: Marriage and Singleness as Discipleship." In *Leaving and Coming Home: New Wineskins for Catholic Sexual Ethics*, edited by David Cloutier, 85–100. Eugene, OR: Cascade, 2010.
———. *Water Is Thicker Than Blood: An Augustinian Theology of Marriage and Singleness*. Oxford: Oxford University Press, 2008.
Benson, Iain T. "The Necessity for a Contextual Analysis for Equality and Non-Discrimination." In *Equality and Non-discrimination: Catholic Roots, Current Challenges*, edited by Jane F. Adolphe, Robert L. Fastiggi, and Michael A. Vacca, 63–75. Eugene, OR: Pickwick, 2019.
Berger, Brigitte, and Peter L. Berger. *The War over the Family: Capturing the Middle Ground*. Garden City, NY: Anchor, 1983.
Bernard, Jessie. *The Future of Marriage*. New York: World, 1972.
Berry, Wendell. "Sex, Economy, Freedom, and Community." In *Sex, Economy, Freedom, and Community: Eight Essays*, 117–73. New York: Pantheon, 1993.
Bertrand, Marianne, and Jessica Pan. "The Trouble with Boys: Social Influences and the Gender Gap in Disruptive Behavior." *American Economic Journal of Applied Economics* 5 (2013) 1–35.
Biale, David. *Eros and the Jews: From Biblical Israel to Contemporary America*. New York: Basic, 1992.
Biller, Henry B. *Fathers and Families: Paternal Factors in Child Development*. Westport, CT: Auburn House, 1993.
Bird, Phyllis. "'To Play the Harlot': An Inquiry into an Old Testament Metaphor." In *Gender and Difference in Ancient Israel*, edited by Peggy L. Day, 75–94. Minneapolis: Fortress, 1989.
Birot, Antoine. *La dramatique trinitaire de l'amour: Pour une introduction à la théologie trinitaire de Hans Urs von Balthasar et Adrienne von Speyr*. Paris: Parole et Silence, 2009.
———. "Le fondement christologique et trinitaire de la différence sexuelle chez Adrienne von Speyr." *Revue Catholique Internationale: Communio* 31 (2006): 123–35.
Blankenhorn, Bernhard, O.P., et al. "Aquinas and Homosexuality: Five Dominicans Respond to Adriano Oliva." *Angelicum* 92 (2015) 297–302.
Blauwhoff, Richard J. *Foundational Facts, Relative Truths: A Comparative Law Study on Children's Right to Know Their Genetic Origins*. Cambridge: Intersentia, 2009.

BIBLIOGRAPHY

Bloom, Allan. "Interpretive Essay." In *The Republic of Plato*. Translated and with an Interpretive Essay by Allan Bloom. New York: Basic, 1968.
Bluestone, Natalie Harris. *Women and the Ideal Society: Plato's Republic and Modern Myths of Gender*. Amherst, MA: University of Massachusetts Press, 1987.
Blumenthal, David R. *Facing the Abusing God: A Theology of Protest*. Louisville, KY: Westminster John Knox, 1993.
Bobonich, Christopher. "Plato's Politics." In *The Oxford Handbook of Plato*, edited by Gail Fine, 311–35. Oxford: Oxford University Press, 2008.
Boda, Mark J. *The Heartbeat of Old Testament Theology: Three Creedal Expressions*. Grand Rapids: Baker Academic, 2017.
Bonaventure. *On the Reduction of the Arts to Theology*. Translated by Zachary Hayes, O.F.M. St. Bonaventure, NY: Franciscan Institute, 1996.
———. *The Triple Way*. Translated by Peter Damian M. Fehlner, F.I. New Bedford, MA: Academy of the Immaculate, 2012.
Bonhoeffer, Dietrich. *Creation and Fall*. Translated by John C. Fletcher. In *Creation and Fall and Temptation: Two Biblical Studies*. New York: Simon & Schuster, 1997.
Bonnell, Karen, with Kristin Little. *The Co-Parenting Handbook: Raising Well-Adjusted and Resilient Kids from Little Ones to Young Adults Through Divorce or Separation*. Seattle, WA: Sasquatch, 2017.
Bott, Travis J. "Praise and Metonymy in the Psalms." In *The Oxford Handbook of the Psalms*, edited by William P. Brown, 131–46. Oxford: Oxford University Press, 2014.
Bourg, Florence Caffrey. "Multi-Dimensional Marriage Vocations and Responsible Parenthood." In *Leaving and Coming Home: New Wineskins for Catholic Sexual Ethics*, edited by David Cloutier, 147–72. Eugene, OR: Cascade, 2010.
Bourgeois, Daniel. *Être et signifier. Structure de la sacramentalité comme signification chez saint Augustin et saint Thomas d'Aquin*. Paris: J. Vrin, 2016.
Bouyer, Louis. *The Meaning of Sacred Scripture*. Translated by Mary Perkins Ryan. Notre Dame, IN: University of Notre Dame Press, 1958.
———. *The Seat of Wisdom: An Essay on the Place of the Virgin Mary in Christian Theology*. Translated by A. V. Littledale. New York: Random House, 1962.
Bradbury, Bruce, Miles Corak, Jane Waldfogel, and Bott Elizabeth Washbrook. *Too Many Children Left Behind: The U. S. Achievement Gap in Comparative Perspective*. New York: Russell Sage Foundation, 2015.
Brake, Elizabeth. *Minimizing Marriage: Marriage, Morality, and the Law*. Oxford: Oxford University Press, 2012.
Brechtel, Lyn. "What If Dinah Is Not Raped?" *Journal for the Study of the Old Testament* 62 (1994) 19–36.
Brennan, Samantha, and Bill Cameron. "Is Marriage Bad for Children?: Rethinking the Connection Between Having Children, Romantic Love, and Marriage." In *After Marriage: Rethinking Marital Relationships*, edited by Elizabeth Brake, 84–99. Oxford: Oxford University Press, 2016.
Brenner, Athalya. "Pornoprophetics Revisited: Some Additional Reflections." *Journal for the Study of the Old Testament* 70 (1996) 63–86.
———. "Women's Traditions Problematized: Some Reflections." In *On Reading Prophetic Texts: Gender-Specific and Related Studies in Memory of Fokkelien van Dijk-Hemmes*, edited by Bob Becking and Meindert Dijkstra, 53–66. Leiden: E. J. Brill, 1996.

BIBLIOGRAPHY

Brenner, Athalya, and Fokkelien van Dijk-Hemmes. *On Gendering Texts: Female and Male Voices in the Hebrew Bible*. Leiden: Brill, 1993.
Brizendine, Louann. *The Male Brain: A Breakthrough Understanding of How Men and Boys Think*. New York: Random House, 2010.
Bromiley, Geoffrey W. *God and Marriage*. Grand Rapids: Eerdmans, 1980.
Brooke, Christopher N. L. *The Medieval Idea of Marriage*. Oxford: Oxford University Press, 1989.
Brooks, Arthur. *Who Really Cares: The Surprising Truth about Compassionate Conservatism*. New York: Basic, 2002.
Brooks, Christopher W. *Urban Apologetics: Why the Gospel Is Good News for the City*. Grand Rapids: Kregel, 2014.
Brooks, Thom. "The Problem with Polygamy." *Philosophical Topics* 37 (2009) 109–22.
Brown, Peter. *The Body and Society: Men, Women and Sexual Renunciation in Early Christianity*. London: Faber & Faber, 1989.
———. "Sexuality and Society in the Fifth Century A.D.: Augustine and Julian of Eclanum." In *Tria Corda: Scritti in onore di Arnaldo Momigliano*, edited by E. Gabba, 49–70. Como: New Press, 1983.
Brown, Raymond E., S.S. *The Gospel According to John (xiii–xxi)*. Garden City, NY: Doubleday, 1970.
———. *Jesus God and Man: Modern Biblical Reflections*. New York: Macmillan, 1967.
Browning, Don S. "Can Marriage Be Defined?" In *Equality and the Family: A Fundamental, Practical Theology of Children, Mothers, and Fathers in Modern Societies*, 207–19. Grand Rapids: Eerdmans, 2007.
———. *Marriage and Modernization: How Globalization Threatens Marriage and What to Do about It*. Grand Rapids: Eerdmans, 2003.
———. "Modernization: Critical Familism and the Reconstruction of Marriage." In *Equality and the Family: A Fundamental, Practical Theology of Children, Mothers, and Fathers in Modern Societies*, 244–62. Grand Rapids: Eerdmans, 2007.
———. "The Relation of Practical Theology to Theological Ethics." In *Equality and the Family: A Fundamental, Practical Theology of Children, Mothers, and Fathers in Modern Societies*, 391–408. Grand Rapids: Eerdmans, 2007.
Browning, Don, Bonnie Miller-McLemore, Pamela Couture, Bernie Lyon, and Robert Franklin. *From Culture Wars to Common Ground*. Louisville, KY: Westminster John Knox, 1997.
Browning, Don S., and Gloria Rodriguez. *Reweaving the Social Tapestry: Towards a Public Philosophy and Policy for Families*. New York: W. W. Norton, 2001.
Browning, Don S., M. Christian Green, and John Witte Jr., eds. *Sex, Marriage, and Family in World Religions*. New York: Columbia University Press, 2006.
Brownson, James V. *Bible, Gender, Sexuality: Reframing the Church's Debate on Same-Sex Relationships*. Grand Rapids: Eerdmans, 2013.
Brueggemann, Walter. *Genesis*. Louisville, KY: Westminster John Knox, 2010.
———. "A Response by Walter Brueggemann." In *Prophecy and Power: Jeremiah in Feminist and Postcolonial Perspective*, edited by Christl M. Maier and Carolyn J. Sharp, 224–33. London: Bloomsbury, 2013.
Brugger, Christian. "Reason's 'Wax Nose': Moral Disagreement, Self-Determination, and the Epistemic Death of Natural Law." In *Living the Catholic Tradition: Philosophical and Theological Considerations*, edited by Renée Köhler-Ryan, 142–61. Steubenville, OH: Franciscan University Press, 2019.

Brunner, Emil. *Das Gebot und die Ordnungen: Entwurf einer protestantisch-theologischen Ethik.* Tübingen: Mohr, 1932.

Burke, Cormac. *Covenanted Happiness: Love and Commitment in Marriage.* San Francisco: Ignatius, 1990.

———. "The 'Good' and the 'Bad' in Marriage according to St. Augustine." In *The Theology of Marriage: Personalism, Doctrine, and Canon Law*, 125–63. Washington, DC: Catholic University of America Press, 2015.

———. "An R.I.P. for the *Remedium Concupiscentiae*." In *The Theology of Marriage: Personalism, Doctrine, and Canon Law*, 181–242. Washington, DC: Catholic University of America Press, 2015.

———. *The Theology of Marriage: Personalism, Doctrine, and Canon Law.* Washington, DC: Catholic University of America Press, 2015.

Burns, Alisa, and Cath Scott. *Mother-Headed Families and Why They Have Increased.* Hillsdale, NJ: Lawrence Erlbaum Associates, 1994.

Burrus, Virginia, and Stephen D. Moore. "Unsafe Sex: Feminism, Pornography, and the Song of Songs." *Biblical Interpretation* 11 (2003) 24–52.

Busby, Dean M., Brian J. Willoughby, and Jason S. Carroll. "Sowing Wild Oats: Valuable Experience or a Field Full of Weeds?" *Personal Relations* 20 (2013) 706–18.

Butler, Judith. "Is Kinship Always Already Heterosexual?" *differences: A Journal of Feminist Cultural Studies* 13 (2002) 14–44.

Cahall, Perry J. *The Mystery of Marriage: A Theology of the Body and the Sacrament.* Chicago: Hillenbrand, 2016.

———. "The Trinitarian Structure of St. Augustine's Good of Marriage." *Augustinian Studies* 34 (2003) 223–32.

Cahill, Lisa Sowle. "Equality in Marriage: The Biblical Challenge." In *Marriage in the Catholic Tradition: Scripture, Tradition, and Experience*, edited by Todd A. Salzman, Thomas M. Kelly, and John J. O'Keefe, 66–75. New York: Crossroad, 2004.

———. *Family: A Christian Social Perspective.* Minneapolis: Fortress, 2000.

———. "Same-Sex Marriage and Catholicism: Dialogue, Learning, and Change." In *More than a Monologue: Sexual Diversity and the Catholic Church.* Vol. 2, *Inquiry, Thought, and Expression*, edited by J. Patrick Hornbeck II and Michael A. Norko, 141–55. New York: Fordham University Press, 2014.

———. *Sex, Gender, and Christian Ethics.* Cambridge: Cambridge University Press, 1996.

Calame, Claude. *The Poetics of Eros in Ancient Greece.* Translated by Janet Lloyd. Princeton, NJ: Princeton University Press, 1999.

Calef, Susan A. "The Radicalism of Jesus the Prophet: Implications for Christian Family." In *Marriage in the Catholic Tradition: Scripture, Tradition, and Experience*, edited by Todd A. Salzman, Thomas M. Kelly, and John J. O'Keefe, 53–64. New York: Crossroad, 2004.

Calvin, John. *Institutes of the Christian Religion.* Translated by Henry Beveridge. Grand Rapids: Eerdmans, 1989.

Cambe, Michel. "L'influence du Cantique des Cantiques sur le Nouveau Testament." *Revue Thomiste* 62 (1962) 5–26.

Cantalamessa, Raniero, O.F.M. Cap. *The Gaze of Mercy: A Commentary on Divine and Human Mercy.* Translated by Marsha Daigle-Williamson. Frederick, MD: The Word Among Us, 2015.

Card, Claudia. "Against Marriage and Motherhood." *Hypatia* 11 (1996) 1–23.
Carmichael, Calum. *Sex and Religion in the Bible*. New Haven, CT: Yale University Press, 2010.
Carroll, Robert P. "Desire Under the Terebinths: On Pornographic Representation in the Prophets—A Response." In *The Latter Prophets: A Feminist Companion to the Bible (First Series)*, edited by Athalya Brenner, 275–307. Sheffield: Sheffield Academic, 1995.
Carter, J. Kameron. *Race: A Theological Account*. Oxford: Oxford University Press, 2008.
Casanova, Carlos A., and Ignacio Serrano del Pozo. "An Assessment of the Being and Operation of Mary's Marriage." *The Thomist* 83 (2019) 31–55.
Catechism of the Catholic Church. 2d ed. Vatican City: Libreria Editrice Vaticana, 1997.
Catherine of Siena. *The Letters of Catherine of Siena*. Vol. III, edited and translated by Suzanne Noffke, O.P. Tempe, AZ: Arizona Center for Medieval and Renaissance Studies, 2007.
Catholic Theological Society of America. *Human Sexuality: New Directions in American Catholic Thought*. New York: Paulist, 1977.
Cavadini, John C. "Feeling Right: Augustine on the Passions and Sexual Desire." In *Visioning Augustine*, 110–37. Oxford: Wiley-Blackwell, 2019.
———. "Ideology and Solidarity in Augustine's City of God." In *Augustine's City of God: A Critical Guide*, edited by James Wetzel, 93–110. Cambridge: Cambridge University Press, 2012.
———. "Reconsidering Augustine on Marriage and Concupiscence." *Augustinian Studies* 48 (2017) 183–99.
———. "The Sacramentality of Marriage in the Fathers." In *Visioning Augustine*, 156–83. Oxford: Wiley-Blackwell, 2019.
———. "The Sex Life of Mary and Joseph." *Nova et Vetera* 13 (2015) 365–77.
———. "Spousal Vision: A Study of Text and History in the Theology of Saint Augustine." In *Visioning Augustine*, 211–38. Oxford: Wiley Blackwell, 2019.
Chambers, Clare. *Against Marriage: An Egalitarian Defence of the Marriage-Free State*. Oxford: Oxford University Press, 2017.
Chapman, Cynthia R. *The Gendered Language of Warfare in the Israelite-Assyrian Encounter*. Winona Lake, IN: Eisenbrauns, 2004.
Chapman, Gary D. *Things I Wish I'd Known Before We Got Married*. Chicago: Northfield, 2010.
Chavasse, Claude. *The Bride of Christ: An Enquiry into the Nuptial Element in Early Christianity*. London: Religious Book Club, 1939.
Cherlin, Andrew J. "American Marriage in the Early Twenty-First Century." *The Future of Children* 15 (2005) 33–55.
———. *The Marriage Go-Round*. New York: Knopf, 2009.
Chetty, Raj, Nathaniel Hendren, Patrick Kline, and Emmanuel Saez. "Where Is the Land of Opportunity? The Geography of Intergenerational Mobility in the United States." *The Quarterly Journal of Economics* 129 (2014) 1553–1623.
Child Trends. "Family Structure: Indicators on Children and Youth." www.childtrends. org/wp-content/uploads/2015/03/59_Family_Structure.pdf.
Chrysostom, John. *Homilies on Genesis 1–17*. Translated by Robert C. Hill. Washington, DC: Catholic University of America Press, 1986.

———. "Homily 12: On Colossians 4:18." In *On Marriage and Family Life*, translated by Catherine P. Roth and David Anderson, 73–80. Crestwood, NY: St. Vladimir's Seminary Press, 1986.

———. "Homily 20: On Ephesians 5:22–33." In *On Marriage and Family Life*, translated by Catherine P. Roth and David Anderson, 43–64. Crestwood, NY: St. Vladimir's Seminary Press, 1986.

———. "Homily 21: On Ephesians 6:1–4." In *On Marriage and Family Life*, translated by Catherine P. Roth and David Anderson, 65–72. Crestwood, NY: St. Vladimir's Seminary Press, 1986.

———. *On Marriage and Family Life*. Translated by Catherine P. Roth and David Anderson, 73–80. Crestwood, NY: St. Vladimir's Seminary Press, 1986.

———. "Sermon on Marriage." In *On Marriage and Family Life*, translated by Catherine P. Roth and David Anderson, 81–88. Crestwood, NY: St. Vladimir's Seminary Press, 1986.

———. *On Virginity; Against Remarriage*. Translated by Sally Rieger Shore. Lewiston, NY: Edwin Mellen, 1983.

Clapp, Rodney. *Families at the Crossroads: Beyond Traditional and Modern Options*. Downers Grove, IL: InterVarsity, 1993.

Cloutier, David. "Composing Love Songs for the Kingdom of God? Creation and Eschatology in Catholic Sexual Ethics." *Journal of the Society of Christian Ethics* 24 (2004) 71–88.

———. *Love, Reason, and God's Story: An Introduction to Catholic Sexual Ethics*. Winona, MN: Anselm Academic, 2008.

———. "Marriage and Sexuality." In *The Oxford Handbook of Catholic Theology*, edited by Lewis Ayres and Medi Ann Volpe, 310–28. Oxford: Oxford University Press, 2019.

Coates, Ta-Nehisi. *Between the World and Me*. New York: Random House, 2015.

Code of Canon Law: Latin-English Edition: New English Translation (Codex Iuris Canonici). Washington, DC: Canon Law Society of America, 1998.

Collin, Thibaud. *Le mariage Chrétien a-t-il encore un avenir? Pour en finir avec les malentendus*. Paris: Artège, 2018.

Collins, Adela Yarbro. *Mark: A Commentary*. Minneapolis: Fortress, 2007.

Collins, John J. *What Are Biblical Values? What the Bible Says on Key Ethical Issues*. New Haven, CT: Yale University Press, 2019.

Coontz, Stephanie. *Marriage, a History: How Love Conquered Marriage*. New York: Penguin, 2005.

Copeland, M. Shawn. *Enfleshing Freedom: Body, Race, and Being*. Minneapolis: Fortress, 2010.

Cornwall, Susanna. *Controversies in Queer Theology*. London: SCM, 2011.

Corvino, John, and Maggie Gallagher. *Debating Same-Sex Marriage*. Oxford: Oxford University Press, 2012.

Cotter, David W., O.S.B. *Genesis*. Collegeville, MN: Liturgical, 2003.

Crawford, David S. "Christian Community and the States of Life: A Reflection on the Anthropological Significance of Virginity and Marriage." *Communio* 29 (2002) 337–65.

———. *Marriage and the* Sequela Christi: *A Study of Marriage as a "State of Perfection" in the Light of Henri de Lubac's Theology of Nature and Grace*. Rome: Lateran University Press, 2003.

Crenshaw, Kimberlé Williams, Luke Charles Harris, Daniel Martinez HoSang, and George Lipsitz, eds. *Seeing Race Again: Countering Colorblindness across the Disciplines.* Oakland, CA: University of California Press, 2019.

Crombie, I. M. *An Examination of Plato's Doctrine.* Vol. 1. London: Routledge & Kegan Paul, 1962.

Cross, Frank Moore. "Kinship and Covenant in Ancient Israel." In *From Epic to Canon: History and Literature in Ancient Israel*, 3–21. Baltimore: Johns Hopkins University Press, 1998.

d'Avray, David L. *Medieval Marriage Sermons: Mass Communication in a Culture without Print.* Oxford: Oxford University Press, 2001.

———. *Medieval Marriage: Symbolism and Society.* Oxford: Oxford University Press, 2005.

———. *Papacy, Monarchy and Marriage, 860–1600.* Cambridge: Cambridge University Press, 2015.

Daly, Martin, and Margo Wilson. "The 'Cinderella Effect': Elevated Mistreatment of Stepchildren in Comparison to Those Living with Genetic Parents." www.cep.ucsb.edu/buller/cinderella%20effect%20facts.pdf.

Daniels, Cora. *Ghettonation: Dispatches from America's Culture War.* New York: Doubleday, 2007.

Davies, Andrew. *Double Standards in Isaiah: Re-evaluating Prophetic Ethics and Divine Justice.* London: T. & T. Clark, 2000.

Davies, Christie. *The Strange Death of Moral Britain.* New Brunswick, NJ: Transaction, 2004.

Davis, Ellen F. *Getting Involved with God: Rediscovering the Old Testament.* Cambridge: Cowley, 2001.

———. *Proverbs, Ecclesiastes, and the Song of Songs.* Louisville, KY: Westminster John Knox, 2000.

———. *Wondrous Depth: Preaching the Old Testament.* Louisville, KY: Westminster John Knox, 2005.

Davison, Andrew. *Why Sacraments?* Eugene, OR: Cascade, 2013.

Day, Keri. "Saving Black America: A Womanist Analysis of Faith-Based Initiatives." *Journal of the Society of Christian Ethics* 33 (2013) 63–81.

Day, Peggy L. "Adulterous Jerusalem's Imagined Demise: Death of a Metaphor in Ezekiel XVI." *Vetus Testamentum* 50 (2000) 285–309.

———. "Metaphor and Social Reality: Isaiah 23.17–18, Ezekiel 16.35–37 and Hosea 2.4–5." In *Inspired Speech: Prophecy in the Ancient Near East. Essays in Honor of Herbert B. Huffmon*, edited by John Kaltner and Louis Stulman, 63–71. London: T. & T. Clark International, 2004.

de La Soujeole, Benoît-Dominique, O.P. "The Economy of Salvation: Entitative Sacramentality and Operative Sacramentality." *The Thomist* 75 (2011) 537–53.

———. *Introduction to the Mystery of the Church.* Translated by Michael J. Miller. Washington, DC: Catholic University of America Press, 2014.

———. "The Sacraments and the Development of Doctrine." In *The Oxford Handbook of Sacramental Theology*, translated by Dominic M. Langevin, O.P., edited by Hans Boersma and Matthew Levering, 590–602. Oxford: Oxford University Press, 2015.

de Lubac, Henri, S.J. *Catholicism: A Study of Dogma in Relation to the Corporate Destiny of Mankind.* London: Burns, Oates and Washbourne, 1950.

Decosimo, David. *Ethics as a Work of Charity: Thomas Aquinas and Pagan Virtue.* Stanford, CA: Stanford University Press, 2014.

Dempsey, Carol J. "The 'Whore' of Ezekiel 16: The Impact and Ramifications of Gender-Specific Metaphors in Light of Biblical Law and Divine Judgment." In *Gender and Law in the Hebrew Bible and the Ancient Near East*, edited by Victor H. Matthews, Bernard M. Levinson, and Tikva Frymer-Kensky, 57–78. Sheffield: Sheffield Academic, 1998.

den Bok, Nico. *Communicating the Most High: A Systematic Study of Person and Trinity in the Theology of Richard of St. Victor (†1173).* Paris: Brepols, 1996.

Dijk-Hemmes, Fokkelien van. "The Metaphorization of Woman in Prophetic Speech: An Analysis of Ezekiel 23." In *The Latter Prophets: A Feminist Companion to the Bible (First Series)*, edited by Athalya Brenner, 244–55. Sheffield: Sheffield Academic, 1995.

Diriart, Alexandra, C.S.J. "Un amour sauvé: la forme pascale de la vie conjugale." *Nova et Vetera* 92 (2017) 271–99.

Dobbs, Darrel. "Family Matters: Aristotle's Appreciation of Women and the Plural Structure of Society." *American Political Science Review* 90 (1996) 74–89.

Dolan, Timothy. "Why Marriage Matters Most: Sharing the Gospel in Matrimony." In *Life, Marriage, and Religious Liberty: What Belongs to God, What Belongs to Caesar: Essays for the Tenth Anniversary of* The Manhattan Declaration, edited by David S. Dockery and John Stonestreet, 63–83. New York: Post Hill, 2019.

Doms, Hebert. *The Meaning of Marriage.* Translated by George Sayer. London: Sheed & Ward, 1939.

———. *Von Sinn und Zweck der Ehe.* Breslau: Ostdeutsche Verlagsanstalt, 1935.

Donoghue, Denis. *Metaphor.* Cambridge, MA: Harvard University Press, 2014.

Douglas, Kelly Brown. *What's Faith Got to Do with It? Black Bodies/Christian Souls.* Maryknoll, NY: Orbis, 2005.

Dozeman, Thomas B. *Exodus.* Grand Rapids: Eerdmans, 2009.

Dupont, Anthony, Wim François, Paul van Geest, and Mathijs Lamberigts. "Sex." In *The Oxford Guide to the Historical Reception of Augustine*, vol. 3, edited by Karla Pollmann with Willemien Otten, 1726–37. Oxford: Oxford University Press, 2013.

Dupré, Louis, and Constance Dupré. "The Indissolubility of Marriage and the Common Good." In *The Bond of Marriage: An Ecumenical and Interdisciplinary Study*, edited by William W. Bassett, 181–99. Notre Dame, IN: University of Notre Dame Press, 1968.

Eberstadt, Mary. *How the West Really Lost God.* West Conshohocken, PA: Templeton, 2013.

———. "The Vindication of *The Manhattan Declaration*, Then and Now." In *Life, Marriage, and Religious Liberty: What Belongs to God, What Belongs to Caesar*, edited by David S. Dockery and John Stonestreet, 81–90. New York: Post Hill, 2019.

Edin, Kathryn, and Maria Kefalas. *Promises I Can Keep: Why Poor Women Put Motherhood Before Marriage.* 2d ed. Berkeley, CA: University of California Press, 2011.

Eilberg-Schwartz, Howard. *God's Phallus and Other Problems for Men and Monotheism.* Boston: Beacon, 1994.

———. *The Savage in Judaism: An Anthropology of Israelite Religion and Ancient Judaism.* Bloomington, IN: Indiana University Press, 1990.

Elliott, Peter J. *What God Has Joined . . . : The Sacramentality of Marriage*. New York: Alba House, 1990.
Ellwood, Gracia Fay. *Batter My Heart*. Wallingford, PA: Pendle Hill, 1988.
Elshtain, Jean Bethke. *Public Man, Private Woman*. Princeton, NJ: Princeton University Press, 1981.
Emery, Gilles, O.P. "Essentialism or Personalism in the Treatise on God in St. Thomas Aquinas?" Translated by Matthew Levering. In Emery, *Trinity in Aquinas*, 2d ed., 165–208. Naples, FL: Sapientia, 2006.
Engels, Frederick. *The Origin of the Family, Private Property and the State*. Translated by Ernest Untermann. Chicago: Charles H. Kerr & Co., 1908.
Ephrem the Syrian. *The Commentary on Genesis*, Section II. In St. Ephrem, *Hymns on Paradise*, translated by Sebastian Brock, 197–227. Crestwood, NY: St. Vladimir's Seminary Press, 1990.
———. *Hymns on Paradise*. Translated by Sebastian Brock. Crestwood, NY: St. Vladimir's Seminary Press, 1990.
Esolen, Anthony. *Defending Marriage: Twelve Arguments for Sanity*. Charlotte, NC: Saint Benedict, 2014.
———. *Reclaiming Catholic Social Teaching: A Defense of the Church's True Teachings on Marriage, Family, and the State*. Manchester, NH: Sophia Institute, 2014.
Evans, Craig. "The Scriptures of Jesus and His Earliest Followers." In *The Canon Debate*, edited by Lee Martin McDonald and James A. Sanders, 185–95. Peabody, MA: Hendrickson, 2002.
Evans, Gary W., and Theodore D. Wachs, eds. *Chaos and Its Influence on Children's Development: An Ecological Perspective*. Washington, DC: American Psychological Association, 2009.
Evdokimov, Paul. *Orthodoxy*. Translated by Jeremy Hummerstone with Callan Slipper. Hyde Park, NY: New City, 2011.
———. *The Sacrament of Love: The Nuptial Mystery in the Light of the Orthodox Tradition*. Translated by Anthony P. Gythiel and Victoria Steadman. Crestwood, NY: St. Vladimir's Seminary Press, 1985.
Everett, Craig A., and Sandra Volgy Everett. *Healthy Divorce*. San Francisco: Jossey-Bass, 1994.
Exum, J. Cheryl. *Plotted, Shot, and Painted: Cultural Representations of Biblical Women*. Sheffield: Sheffield Academic, 1996.
———. *Song of Songs: A Commentary*. Louisville, KY: Westminster John Knox, 2005.
Fagerberg, David W. *Consecrating the World: On Mundane Liturgical Theology*. Kettering, OH: Angelico, 2016.
Farley, Margaret A. "Celibacy under the Sign of the Cross." In *Sexuality and the U.S. Catholic Church: Crisis and Renewal*, edited by Lisa Sowle Cahill, John Garvey, and T. Frank Kennedy, S.J., 126–43. New York: Crossroad, 2006.
———. *Just Love: A Framework for Christian Sexual Ethics*. New York: Continuum, 2008.
Farrow, Douglas. *Nation of Bastards: Essays on the End of Marriage*. Toronto: BPS, 2007.
Fastiggi, Robert L. "Human Equality and Non-discrimination in Light of Catholic Theology and Magisterial Teachings." In *Equality and Non-discrimination: Catholic Roots, Current Challenges*, edited by Jane F. Adolphe, Robert L. Fastiggi, and Michael A. Vacca, 1–11. Eugene, OR: Pickwick, 2019.

Fehribach, Adeline, S.C.N. *The Women in the Life of the Bridegroom: A Feminist Historical-Literary Analysis of the Female Characters in the Fourth Gospel.* Collegeville, MN: Liturgical, 1998.

Feser, Edward. "In Defense of the Perverted Faculty Argument." In *Neo-Scholastic Essays*, 378–415. South Bend, IN: St. Augustine's, 2015.

Feuillet, André. *Le Mystère de l'amour divin dans la théologie johannique.* Paris: Gabalda, 1972.

Fine, Cordelia. *Delusions of Gender: How Our Minds, Society, and Neurosexism Create Difference.* New York: Norton, 2010.

Fineman, Martha Albertson. *The Autonomy Myth: A Theory of Dependency.* New York: The New Press, 2004.

———. *The Neutered Mother, the Sexual Family, and Other Twentieth Century Tragedies.* New York: Routledge, 1995.

Finer, Lawrence B. "Trends in Premarital Sex in the United States: 1954–2003." *Public Health Reports* 122 (2007) 73–78.

First 1001 Days All Party Parliamentary Group. *Building Great Britons: Conception to Age Two.* https://plct.files.wordpress.com/2012/11/building-great-britons-report-conception-to-age-2-feb-2015.pdf.

Fitzmyer, Joseph A., S.J. *The Gospel According to Luke (X–XXIV).* Garden City, NY: Doubleday, 1985.

Foreman, Benjamin A. *Animal Metaphors and the People of Israel in the Book of Jeremiah.* Göttingen: Vandenhoeck & Ruprecht, 2011.

Fox, Michael V. *The Song of Songs and the Ancient Egyptian Love Songs.* Madison, WI: University of Wisconsin Press, 1985.

Franke, Katherine. *Wedlocked: The Perils of Marriage Equality—How African Americans and Gays Mistakenly Thought the Right to Marry Would Set Them Free.* New York: New York University Press, 2015.

Franzmann, Majella. "The City as Woman: The Case of Babylon in Isaiah 47." *Australian Biblical Review* 43 (1995) 1–19.

Freitas, Donna. *The End of Sex.* New York: Basic, 2013.

Freud, Sigmund. *Civilization and Its Discontents.* New York: Norton, 2005.

Frishman, Judith. "Why Would a Man Want to Be Anyone's Wife? A Response to Satlow." In *Families and Family Relations: As Represented in Early Judaisms and Early Christianities: Texts and Fictions*, edited by Jan Willem van Henten and Athalya Brenner, 43–48. Leiden: Deo, 2000.

Frymer-Kensky, Tikva. *In the Wake of the Goddesses: Women, Culture, and the Biblical Transformation of Pagan Myth.* New York: Free, 1992.

Furstenberg, Frank, Jr., and Andrew J. Cherlin. *Divided Families: What Happens to Children When Parents Part.* Cambridge, MA: Harvard University Press, 1991.

Furstenberg, Frank, Jr., Christine W. Nord, James L. Peterson, and Nicholas Zill. "The Life Course of Children of Divorce: Marital Disruption and Parental Contact." *American Sociological Review* 48 (1983) 656–68.

Gagnon, Robert A. J. *The Bible and Homosexual Practice: Texts and Hermeneutics.* Nashville, TN: Abingdon, 2001.

Gaillardetz, Richard R. *A Daring Promise: A Spirituality of Christian Marriage.* 2d ed. Liguori, MO: Liguori, 2007.

Galambush, Julie. *Jerusalem in the Book of Ezekiel: The City as Yahweh's Wife.* Atlanta: Scholars, 1992.

Gallagher, Maggie. "The Case Against Same-Sex Marriage." In *Debating Same-Sex Marriage*, 91–178. Oxford: Oxford University Press, 2012.

Galston, William A. "Causes of Declining Well-Being among U.S. Children." In *Sex, Preference, and Family: Essays on Law and Nature*, edited by David M. Estlund and Martha C. Nussbaum, 290–305. Oxford: Oxford University Press, 1997.

———. *Liberal Purposes*. Cambridge: Cambridge University Press, 1991.

———. "The Reinstitutionalization of Marriage: Political Theory and Public Policy." In *Promises to Keep: Decline and Renewal of Marriage in America*, edited by David Popenoe, Jean Bethke Elshtain, and David Blankenhorn, 271–90. Lanham, MD: Rowman & Littlefield, 1996.

Ganye, Antoine. "Monogamy and Polygamy: Challenge and Concern for the Truth of Love in African Cultures." In *Christ's New Homeland—Africa: Contribution to the Synod on the Family by African Pastors*, translated by Michael J. Miller, 112–26. San Francisco: Ignatius, 2015.

Gathercole, Simon J. "Sin in God's Economy: Agencies in Romans 1 and 7." In *Divine and Human Agency in Paul and His Cultural Environment*, edited by John M. G. Barclay and Simon J. Gathercole, 158–72. London: T. & T. Clark, 2007.

Gendron, Lionel. *Mystère de la Trinité et Symbolique familiale: approche historique*. Rome: Pontifica Universitas Gregoriana, Facultas Theologiae, 1975.

Gheaus, Anca. "The (Dis)value of Commitment to One's Spouse." In *After Marriage: Rethinking Marital Relationships*, edited by Elizabeth Brake, 204–24. Oxford: Oxford University Press, 2016.

Giddens, Anthony. *The Transformation of Intimacy: Sexuality, Love, and Eroticism in Modern Societies*. Stanford, CA: Stanford University Press, 1993.

Girgis, Sherif, Ryan T. Anderson, and Robert George. *What Is Marriage? Man and Woman: A Defense*. New York: Encounter, 2012.

Gleeson, Gerald. "Should the Church Change Its Teaching on Sexual Morality?" In *Contemplating the Future of Moral Theology: Essays in Honor of Brian V. Johnstone, C.Ss.R.*, edited by Robert C. Koerpel and Vimal Tirimanna, C.Ss.R, 38–54. Eugene, OR: Pickwick, 2017.

Glendon, Mary Ann. *The Transformation of Family Law*. Chicago: University of Chicago Press, 1989.

Glombik, Konrad. *"Zweieinigkeit"—Herbert Doms (1890–1977) und sein Beitrag zum personalistischen Eheverständnis*. Berlin: LIT Verlag, 2016.

Goode, William. *World Changes in Divorce Patterns*. New Haven, CT: Yale University Press, 1994.

Goodwin, Brady "Phanatik," Jr. *The Death of Hip Hop, Marriage and Morals: Helping Youth Resurrect Culture, Family and Faith*. Philadelphia: Urban Remix Project, 2011.

Goody, Jack. *The Development of the Family and Marriage in Europe*. Cambridge: Cambridge University Press, 1994.

Gordon, Pamela, and Harold C. Washington. "Rape as a Military Metaphor in the Hebrew Bible." In *The Latter Prophets: A Feminist Companion to the Bible (First Series)*, edited by Athalya Brenner, 308–25. Sheffield: Sheffield Academic, 1995.

Gove, Walter. "Sex, Marital Status, and Mortality." *American Journal of Sociology* 79 (1973) 45–67.

Grabowski, John S. "Person or Nature? Rival Personalisms in Twentieth-Century Catholic Ethics." In *Transformed in Christ: Essays on the Renewal of Moral Theology*, 84–108. Ave Maria, FL: Sapientia, 2017.
Granados, José. *Una Sola Carne en un Solo Espíritu: Teología del Matrimonio*. Madrid: Ediciones Palabra, 2014.
Gregory of Nazianzus. "Oration 31: On the Holy Spirit." In *On God and Christ: The Five Theological Orations* and *Two Letters to Cledonius*, translated by Lionel Wickham, 117–47. Crestwood, NY: St. Vladimir's Seminary Press, 2002.
Griffiths, Paul J. *Christian Flesh*. Stanford, CA: Stanford University Press, 2018.
———. *Song of Songs*. Grand Rapids: Brazos, 2011.
Grossbard-Shechtman, Shoshana A., ed. *Marriage and the Economy: Theory and Evidence from Advanced Industrial Societies*. Cambridge: Cambridge University Press, 2003.
Grosz, Elizabeth. "Refiguring Lesbian Desire." In *Race, Class, Gender, Sexuality: The Big Questions*, edited by Naomi Zack, Laurie Shrage, and Crispin Sartwell, 268–81. Oxford: Blackwell, 1998.
Grubb, Geoffrey. *The Anthropology of Marriage in Significant Roman Catholic Documents from Casti Connubii to Gaudium et Spes (Doms, Hildebrand)*. PhD diss., Saint Louis University, 1986.
Gumbleton, Thomas. "A Call to Listen: The Church's Pastoral and Theological Response to Gays and Lesbians." In *More Than a Monologue: Sexual Diversity and the Catholic Church*, vol. 1, *Voices of Our Times*, edited by Christine Firer Hinze and J. Patrick Hornbeck II, 55–69. New York: Fordham University Press, 2014.
Guroian, Vigen. *The Orthodox Reality: Culture, Theology, and Ethics in the Modern World*. Grand Rapids: Baker Academic, 2018.
Guzzo, Karen Benjamin. "New Partners, More Kids: Multiple-Partner Fertility in the United States." *The American Academy of Political and Social Science* 654 (2014) 66–86.
Haag, Pamela. *Marriage Confidential: The Post-Romantic Age of Workhorse Wives, Royal Children, Undersexed Spouses, and Rebel Couples Who Are Re-Writing the Rules*. New York: HarperCollins, 2011.
Hadjadj, Fabrice. *Qu'est-ce qu'une famille? suivi de La Transcendance en culottes et autres propos ultra-sexistes*. Paris: Salvator, 2014.
Hahn, Scott W. *The First Society: The Sacrament of Matrimony and the Restoration of the Social Order*. Steubenville, OH: Emmaus Road, 2018.
———. *Kinship by Covenant: A Canonical Approach to the Fulfillment of God's Saving Promises*. New Haven, CT: Yale University Press, 2009.
Halberstam, J. Jack. *Gaga Feminism: Sex, Gender, and the End of Normal*. Boston: Beacon, 2012.
Handren, Walter J., S.J. *No Longer Two: A Commentary on the Encyclical* Casti Connubii *of Pius IX*. Westminster, MD: Newman, 1955.
Häring, Bernard, C.Ss.R. "Part II, Chapter 1: Fostering the Nobility of Marriage and the Family." In *Commentary on the Documents of Vatican II*, vol. 5, *Pastoral Constitution on the Church in the Modern World*, edited by Herbert Vorgrimler, translated by W. J. O'Hara, 225–45. New York: Herder and Herder, 1969.
Harrington, Daniel J., S.J., and James F. Keenan, S.J. *Paul and Virtue Ethics: Building Bridges between New Testament Studies and Moral Theology*. Lanham, MD: Rowman & Littlefield, 2010.

Harrington, Joel F. *Reordering Marriage and Society in Reformation Germany.* Cambridge: Cambridge University Press, 1995.
Harrison, Carol. *Augustine: Christian Truth and Fractured Humanity.* Oxford: Oxford University Press, 2000.
Hart, Betty, and Todd R. Risley. *Meaningful Differences in the Everyday Experience of Young American Children.* Baltimore: Paul H. Brookes, 1995.
Hartford, Hedaya. *Initiating and Upholding an Islamic Marriage.* 3rd ed. Amman, Jordan: Dar al-Fath Research & Publishing, 2007.
Hauerwas, Stanley. "Sex and Politics: Bertrand Russell and 'Human Sexuality.'" *Christian Century* (April 19, 1978) 417–22.
Healy, Nicholas J. *The Eschatology of Hans Urs von Balthasar: Being as Communion.* Oxford: Oxford University Press, 2004.
———. "Marriage, Priesthood, and the Sincere Gift of Self." *Communion* 45 (2018) 320–33.
Heckman, James C. "Skill Formation and the Economics of Investing in Disadvantaged Children." *Science* 312 (2006) 1900–1902.
Hegel, G. W. F. *Elements of the Philosophy of Right.* Edited by Allen W. Wood. Translated by H. B. Nisbet. Cambridge: Cambridge University Press, 1991.
Hemming, Laurence Paul. "Can I Really Count on You?" In *Authorizing Marriage? Canon, Tradition, and Critique in the Blessing of Same-Sex Unions*, edited by Mark D. Jordan, 68–80. Princeton, NJ: Princeton University Press, 2006.
Hendrix, Harville. *Getting the Love You Want.* New York: Henry Holt, 1988.
Hengel, Martin. "The Interpretation of the Wine Miracle at Cana: John 2:1–11." In *The Glory of Christ in the New Testament: Studies in Christology*, translated by Gerhard Schmidt, edited by L. D. Hurst and N. T. Wright, 83–112. Oxford: Clarendon, 1987.
———. *The Septuagint as Christian Scripture: Its Prehistory and the Problem of Its Canon.* London: Continuum, 2002.
Henrich, Joseph, Robert Boyd, and Peter J. Richerson. "The Puzzle of Monogamous Marriage." *Philosophical Transactions of the Royal Society B* 367 (2012) 657–69.
Herdt, Jennifer A. *Putting on Virtue: The Legacy of the Splendid Vices.* Chicago: University of Chicago Press, 2008.
Herlihy, David. *Medieval Households.* Cambridge, MA: Harvard University Press, 1985.
Herring, Jonathan. *Family Law: A Very Short Introduction.* Oxford: Oxford University Press, 2014.
Hertz, Rosanna. *Single by Chance, Mothers by Choice: How Women Are Choosing Parenthood Without Marriage and Creating the New American Family.* Oxford: Oxford University Press, 2006.
Heschel, Abraham Joshua. *The Prophets.* New York: Harper & Row, 1962.
Hewlett, Sylvia Ann, and Cornel West. *The War Against Parents: What We Can Do for America's Beleaguered Moms and Dads.* New York: Houghton Mifflin, 1998.
Hibbs, Thomas S. "Creation, Gratitude and Virtue." *Journal of Law, Philosophy and Culture* 3 (2009) 101–14.
Hildebrand, Dietrich von. *In Defense of Purity: An Analysis of Catholic Ideals of Purity and Virginity.* Steubenville, OH: Hildebrand, 2017.
———. *The Encyclical* Humanae Vitae: *A Sign of Contradiction. An Essay on Birth Control and Catholic Conscience.* Steubenville, OH: Hildebrand, 2018.

———. *Marriage: The Mystery of Faithful Love*. Translated by Dietrich von Hildebrand, Emmanuel Chapman, and Daniel Sullivan. Manchester, NH: Sophia Institute, 1991.

———. "Marriage as a Way of Perfection." In *Marriage in the Light of Vatican II*, edited by J. T. McHugh, 121–44. Washington, DC: Family Life Bureau of the United States Catholic Conference, 1968.

Hill, Wesley. "Gunning for Complementarity." Review of *Bible, Gender, Sexuality: Reframing the Church's Debate on Same-Sex Relationships*, by James V. Brownson. *The Living Church* (June 7, 2013). https://livingchurch.org/2013/06/07/gunning-complementarity/.

———. *Washed and Waiting: Reflections on Christian Faithfulness and Homosexuality*. Grand Rapids: Zondervan, 2010.

Hines, Melissa. *Brain Gender*. Oxford: Oxford University Press, 2005.

Hofer, Andrew, O.P., ed. *Divinization: Becoming Icons of Christ Through the Liturgy*. Chicago: Hillenbrand, 2015.

Hogan, Margaret Monahan. *Marriage as a Relationship: Real and Rational*. Milwaukee: Marquette University Press, 2002.

Hogan, Richard M., and John M. LeVoir. *Covenant of Love: Pope John Paul II on Sexuality, Marriage, and Family in the Modern World, with a Commentary on Familiaris Consortio*. 2d ed. San Francisco: Ignatius, 1992.

Högnäs, Robin S., and Marcia J. Carlson. "Like Parent, Like Child? The Intergenerational Transmission of Nonmarital Childbearing." *Social Science Research* 41 (2012) 1480–94.

Holt, Else K. "'The Stain of Your Guilt Is Still Before Me' (Jeremiah 2:22): (Feminist) Approaches to Jeremiah 2 and the Problem of Normativity." In *Prophecy and Power: Jeremiah in Feminist and Postcolonial Perspective*, edited by Christl M. Maier and Carolyn J. Sharp, 101–16. London: Bloomsbury, 2013.

Hooker, Morna D. *The Gospel According to Saint Mark*. Peabody, MA: Hendrickson, 1991.

Hsu, Albert Y. *Singles at the Crossroads: A Fresh Perspective on Christian Singleness*. Downers Grove, IL: InterVarsity, 1997.

Huehnergard, John. "Biblical Notes on Some New Akkadian Texts from Emar (Syria)." *Catholic Biblical Quarterly* 47 (1985) 428–34.

Hugenberger, Gordon Paul. *Marriage as a Covenant: A Study of Biblical Law and Ethics Governing Marriage Developed from the Perspective of Malachi*. Leiden: E. J. Brill, 1994.

Hunter, David G. "Marriage." In *Augustine through the Ages: An Encyclopedia*, edited by Allan D. Fitzgerald, O.S.A., 535–37. Grand Rapids: Eerdmans, 1999.

———. *Marriage in the Early Church*. Minneapolis: Fortress, 1992.

Jacobitz, Gerard. "Seminary, Priesthood, and the Vatican's Homosexual Dilemma." In *More than a Monologue: Sexual Diversity and the Catholic Church*. Vol. 2, *Inquiry, Thought, and Expression*, edited by J. Patrick Hornbeck II and Michael A. Norko, 86–105. New York: Fordham University Press, 2014.

Jenson, Robert W. *Song of Songs*. Louisville, KY: Westminster John Knox, 2005.

———. *The Triune Story: Collected Essays on Scripture*. Edited by Brad East. Oxford: Oxford University Press, 2019.

Jerome. *Commentary on Ezekiel*. Translated by Thomas P. Scheck. New York: Paulist, 2017.

BIBLIOGRAPHY

John Paul II. *Familiaris Consortio*. November 22, 1981. http://w2.vatican.va/content/john-paul-ii/en/apost_exhortations/documents/hf_jp-ii_exh_19811122_familiaris-consortio.html.

———. [Wojtyła, Karol.] *The Jeweler's Shop: A Meditation on the Sacrament of Matrimony, Passing on Occasion into a Drama*. Translated by Boleslaw Taborski. San Francisco: Ignatius, 1992.

———. "Letter to Families." Rome: Libreria Editrice Vaticana, 1994.

———. [Wojtyła, Karol.] *Love and Responsibility*. Translated by H. T. Willetts. New York: Farrar, Straus and Giroux, 1981.

———. *Man and Woman He Created Them: A Theology of the Body*. Translated by Michael Waldstein. Boston: Pauline, 2006.

———. *Mulieris Dignitatem*. August 15, 1988. http://w2.vatican.va/content/john-paul-ii/en/apost_letters/1988/documents/hf_jp-ii_apl_19880815_mulieris-dignitatem.html.

———. *Redemptoris Mater*. March 25, 1987. http://w2.vatican.va/content/john-paul-ii/en/encyclicals/documents/hf_jp-ii_enc_25031987_redemptoris-mater.html.

Johnson, Byron. *More God, Less Crime: Why Faith Matters and How It Could Matter More*. West Conshohocken, PA: Templeton, 2011.

Johnson, Luke Timothy. "Scripture and Experience." *Commonweal* 134:12 (June 15, 2007) 14–17.

———. *The Writings of the New Testament: An Interpretation*. Philadelphia: Fortress, 1986.

Jones, Beth Felker. *Faithful: A Theology of Sex*. Grand Rapids: Zondervan, 2015.

Jordan, Mark D. "Arguing Liturgical Genealogies, or, The Ghosts of Weddings Past." In *Authorizing Marriage? Canon, Tradition, and Critique in the Blessing of Same-Sex Unions*, 102–20. Princeton, NJ: Princeton University Press, 2006.

Juel, Donald. *Messianic Exegesis: Christological Interpretation of the Old Testament in Earliest Christianity*. Philadelphia: Fortress, 1988.

Kaczor, Christopher. "Being in Love and Begetting a Child: A Greek Myth of *Eros* and the Christian Mystery of Marriage." In *Sexuality and the U.S. Catholic Church: Crisis and Renewal*, edited by Lisa Sowle Cahill, John Garvey, and T. Frank Kennedy, S.J., 52–67. New York: Crossroad, 2006.

Kamark, Elaine Ciulla, and William A. Galston. *Putting Children First: A Progressive Family Policy for the 1990s*. Washington, DC: Progressive Policy Institute, 1990.

Kant, Immanuel. *The Metaphysics of Morals*. Translated by Mary Gregor. Cambridge: Cambridge University Press, 1996.

———. *Political Writings*. Edited by Hans Reiss, translated by H. B. Nisbet. Cambridge: Cambridge University Press, 1991.

Kasper, Walter. *Theology of Christian Marriage*. Translated by David Smith. New York: Seabury, 1980.

Keating, Daniel A. *Deification and Grace*. Naples, FL: Sapientia, 2007.

Keating, James. *Remain in Me: Holy Orders, Prayer, and Ministry*. New York: Paulist, 2019.

Keefe, Alice A. *Woman's Body and the Social Body in Hosea*. Sheffield: Sheffield Academic, 2001.

Keener, Craig S. *A Commentary on the Gospel of Matthew*. Grand Rapids: Eerdmans, 1999.

———. *The Gospel of John: A Commentary*. Vol. 2. Grand Rapids: Baker Academic, 2012.
Keller, Kathy. "Appendix: Decision Making and Gender Roles." In *The Meaning of Marriage: Facing the Complexities of Commitment with the Wisdom of God*, 277–81. New York: Riverhead, 2011.
Keller, Timothy, with Kathy Keller. *The Meaning of Marriage: Facing the Complexities of Commitment with the Wisdom of God*. New York: Riverhead, 2011.
Kereszty, Roch A., O.Cist. *The Church of God in Jesus Christ: A Catholic Ecclesiology*. Washington, DC: Catholic University of America Press, 2019.
Kerr, Fergus. *Immortal Longings: Versions of Transcending Humanity*. London: SPCK, 1997.
King, Heather. *Ravished: Notes on Womanhood*. N.p.: Holy Hell Books, 2019.
King, J. Christopher. *Origen on the Song of Songs as the Spirit of Scripture: The Bridegroom's Perfect Marriage-Song*. Oxford: Oxford University Press, 2005.
King, Ross. *Machiavelli: Philosopher of Power*. New York: HarperCollins, 2007.
Kipnis, Laura. *Against Love: A Polemic*. New York: Pantheon, 2003.
Kittay, Eva Feder. *Love's Labor: Essays on Women, Equality, and Dependency*. New York: Routledge, 1999.
———. *Metaphor: Its Cognitive Force and Linguistic Structure*. Oxford: Clarendon, 1987.
Knieps-Port le Roi, Thomas. "Sacramental Marriage and Holy Orders: Toward an Ecclesial Ministry for Married People." Translated by David Dawson Vasquez. In *Marriage in the Catholic Tradition: Scripture, Tradition, and Experience*, translated by David Dawson Vasquez, edited by Todd A. Salzman, Thomas M. Kelly, and John J. O'Keefe, 134–43. New York: Crossroad, 2004.
Koch, Anton. *Lehrbuch der Moraltheologie*. Freiburg im Breisgau: Herdersche-Verlagshandlung, 1905.
Krouse, Richard W. "Patriarchal Liberalism and Beyond: From John Stuart Mill to Harriet Taylor." In *The Family in Political Thought*, edited by Jean Bethke Elshtain, 145–72. Amherst, MA: University of Massachusetts Press, 1982.
Kuby, Gabriele. *The Global Sexual Revolution: Destruction of Freedom in the Name of Freedom*. Translated by James Patrick Kirchner, with a foreword by Robert Spaemann. Kettering, OH: Angelico, 2015.
Küng, Hans. *On Being a Christian*. Translated by Edward Quinn. New York: Doubleday, 1976.
Kupczak, Jarosław, O.P. *Destined for Liberty: The Human Person in the Philosophy of Karol Wojtyła/John Paul II*. Washington, DC: Catholic University of America Press, 2000.
———. *Gift and Communion: John Paul II's Theology of the Body*. Translated by Agata Rottkamp, Justyna Pawlak, and Orest Pawlak. Washington, DC: Catholic University of America Press, 2014.
La Bonnardière, A.-M. "L'Interprétation augustinienne du *magnum sacramentum* de Éphés. 5,32." *Recherches Augustiniennes* 12 (1977) 3–45.
Lamb, Michael E., ed. *The Role of the Father in Child Development*. 3rd ed. New York: Wiley, 1997.
Lang, U. M. *Turning Towards the Lord: Orientation in Liturgical Prayer*. San Francisco: Ignatius, 2004.

Lareau, Annette. *Unequal Childhoods: Class, Race and Family Life*. 2d ed. Berkeley, CA: University of California Press, 2011.

Lasch, Christopher. *Haven in a Heartless World: The Family Besieged*. New York: Basic, 1977.

Lasnoski, Kent J. *Vocation to Virtue: Christian Marriage as a Consecrated Life*. Washington, DC: Catholic University of America Press, 2014.

Law Commission of Canada. *Beyond Conjugality: Recognizing and Supporting Close Personal Adult Relationships*. Ottawa: Law Commission of Canada, 2001.

Lawler, Michael G. *Marriage and Sacrament: A Theology of Christian Marriage*. Collegeville, MN: Liturgical, 1993.

———. *Marriage and the Catholic Church: Disputed Questions*. Collegeville, MN: Liturgical, 2002.

Lee, Dohoon, and Sara McLanahan. "Family Structure and Child Development: Instability, Selection, and Population Heterogeneity." *American Sociological Review* 80 (2015) 738–63.

Leithart, Peter J. *Traces of the Trinity: Signs of God in Creation and Human Experience*. Grand Rapids: Brazos, 2015.

Lerman, Robert I., and W. Bradford Wilcox. *For Richer, For Poorer: How Family Structures Economic Success in America*. Washington, DC: American Enterprise Institute and Institute for Family Studies, 2014.

Lesaux, Nonie K., and Stephanie M. Jones. *The Leading Edge of Early Childhood Education: Linking Science to Policy for a New Education*. Cambridge, MA: Harvard Education, 2016.

Levenson, Jon D. *The Love of God: Divine Gift, Human Gratitude, and Mutual Faithfulness in Judaism*. Princeton, NJ: Princeton University Press, 2016.

Levering, Matthew. *The Achievement of Hans Urs von Balthasar*. Washington, DC: Catholic University of America Press, 2019.

———. *Aquinas's Eschatological Ethics and the Virtue of Temperance*. Notre Dame: University of Notre Dame Press, 2019.

———. *Dying and the Virtues*. Grand Rapids: Eerdmans, 2018.

———. *Engaging the Doctrine of Creation: Cosmos, Creatures, and the Wise and Good Creator*. Grand Rapids: Baker Academic, 2017.

———. *Engaging the Doctrine of Revelation: The Mediation of the Gospel through Church and Scripture*. Grand Rapids: Baker Academic, 2014.

———. *Engaging the Doctrine of the Holy Spirit: Love and Gift in the Trinity and the Church*. Grand Rapids: Baker Academic, 2016.

———. *The Indissolubility of Marriage: Amoris Laetitia in Context*. San Francisco: Ignatius, 2019.

———. *An Introduction to Vatican II as an Ongoing Theological Event*. Washington, DC: Catholic University of America Press, 2017.

———. *Jewish-Christian Dialogue and the Life of Wisdom: Engagements with the Theology of David Novak*. New York: Continuum, 2010.

———. "Pinckaers and Häring on Conscience." *Journal of Moral Theology* 8: Special Issue 2 (2019) 134–165.

———. "The Unbearability of Annihilation: Job's Challenge to His Creator." In *Christian Dying: Witnesses from the Tradition*, edited by George Kalantzis and Matthew Levering, 11–40. Eugene, OR: Cascade, 2018.

Lewis, Sophie. *Full Surrogacy Now: Feminism Against Family*. New York: Verso, 2019.

BIBLIOGRAPHY

Liebard, Odile M., ed. *Love and Sexuality: Official Catholic Teachings*. Wilmington, NC: Mcgrath, 1978.

Lim, Timothy H. *The Formation of the Jewish Canon*. New Haven, CT: Yale University Press, 2013.

Lindström, Fredrik. *God and the Origin of Evil: Contextual Analysis of Alleged Monistic Evidence in the Old Testament*. Lund: CWK Gleerup, 1983.

Lipsitz, George. "The Sounds of Silence: How Race Neutrality Preserves White Supremacy." In *Seeing Race Again: Countering Colorblindness across the Disciplines*, edited by Kimberlé Williams Crenshaw, Luke Charles Harris, Daniel Martinez HoSang, and George Lipsitz, 23–51. Oakland, CA: University of California Press, 2019.

Little, Anthony C. "Oral Contraceptive Use in Women Changes Preferences for Male Facial Masculinity and Is Associated with Partner Facial Masculinity." *Psychoneuroendocrinology* 38 (September 2013) 1777–85.

Lombard, Peter. *The Sentences*. Book IV, *On the Doctrine of Signs*. 4th ed. Translated by Giulio Silano. Toronto: Pontifical Institute of Mediaeval Studies, 2010.

Lombardo, Nicholas E., O.P. *The Father's Will: Christ's Crucifixion and the Goodness of God*. Oxford: Oxford University Press, 2013.

Lossky, Vladimir. *In the Image and Likeness of God*. Edited by John H. Erickson and Thomas E. Bird. Crestwood, NY: St. Vladimir's Seminary Press, 1974.

Liebard, Odile, ed. *Love and Sexuality*. Translated by Odile Liebard. Wilmington, NC: Mcgrath, 1978.

Lowery, Mark. "The Nature and Ends of Marriage: A New Proposal." *The Jurist* 65 (2005) 98–118.

Ludwig, Paul W. "Eros in the *Republic*." In *The Cambridge Companion to Plato's Republic*, edited by G. R. F. Ferrari, 202–31. Cambridge: Cambridge University Press, 2007.

Lumen Gentium. In *Vatican Council II*, vol. 1, *The Conciliar and Postconciliar Documents*. Rev. ed. Edited by Austin Flannery, O.P., 350–426. Northport, NY: Costello, 1996.

Luther, Martin. "The Pagan Servitude of the Church." Translated by Bertram Lee Woolf. In *Martin Luther: Selections from His Writings*, edited by John Dillenberger, 249–359. New York: Doubleday, 1962.

Macedo, Stephen. *Just Married: Same-Sex Couples, Monogamy, and the Future of Marriage*. Princeton, NJ: Princeton University Press, 2015.

———. "Sexuality and Liberty: Making Room for Nature and Tradition?" In *Sex, Preference, and Family: Essays on Law and Nature*, edited by David M. Estlund and Martha C. Nussbaum, 86–101. Oxford: Oxford University Press, 1997.

Mackin, Theodore, S.J. *What Is Marriage?* New York: Paulist, 1982.

Mangina, Joseph L. *Revelation*. Grand Rapids: Brazos, 2010.

Manning, Wendy D. "Cohabitation and Child Wellbeing." *The Future of Children* 25 (2015) 51–61.

Mansini, Guy, O.S.B. "Aristotle and Aquinas's Theology of Charity in the *Summa Theologiae*." In *Aristotle in Aquinas's Theology*, edited by Gilles Emery, O.P., and Matthew Levering, 121–38. Oxford: Oxford University Press, 2015.

Marks, Loren. "Same-Sex Parenting and Children's Outcomes: A Closer Examination of the American Psychological Association's Brief on Lesbian and Gay Parenting." *Social Science Research* 41 (2012) 735–51.

Marquardt, Elizabeth. *My Daddy's Name Is Donor*. New York: Institute for American Values, 2010.

Martin, Dale. "Familiar Idolatry and the Christian Case against Marriage." In *Authorizing Marriage? Canon, Tradition, and Critique in the Blessing of Same-Sex Unions*, edited by Mark D. Jordan, 17–40. Princeton, NJ: Princeton University Press, 2006.

———. *New Testament History and Literature*. New Haven, CT: Yale University Press, 2012.

———. "Paul Without Passion: On Paul's Rejection of Desire in Sex and Marriage." In *Constructing Early Christian Families: Family as Social Reality and Metaphor*, edited by Halvor Moxnes, 201–15. London: Routledge, 1997.

———. *Sex and the Single Savior: Gender and Sexuality in Biblical Interpretation*. Louisville, KY: Westminster John Knox, 2006.

Martin, Francis. "Male and Female He Created Them: A Summary of the Teaching of Genesis Chapter One." *Communio* 20 (1993) 240–65.

Martin, James, S.J. *Building a Bridge: How the Catholic Church and the LGBT Community Can Enter into a Relationship of Respect, Compassion, and Sensitivity*. 2d ed. New York: HarperCollins, 2018.

Maurice, F. D. *Social Morality: Twenty-One Lectures Delivered in the University of Cambridge*. London: Macmillan, 1869.

Mayer, Susan E. *What Money Can't Buy: Family Income and Children's Life Chances*. Cambridge, MA: Harvard University Press, 1998.

McAllister, Robert J. *Living the Vows: The Emotional Conflicts of Celibate Religious*. New York: Harper & Row, 1986.

McCarthy, David Matzko. "Cohabitation and Marriage." In *Leaving and Coming Home: New Wineskins for Catholic Sexual Ethics*, edited by David Cloutier, 119–43. Eugene, OR: Cascade, 2010.

———. *Sex and Love in the Home: A Theology of the Household*. 2d ed. London: SCM, 2004.

McCarthy, Dennis J. "Notes on the Love of God in Deuteronomy and the Father-Son Relationship Between Yahweh and Israel." *Catholic Biblical Quarterly* 27 (1965) 144–48.

———. *Treaty and Covenant*. 2d ed. Rome: Pontifical Biblical Institute, 1978.

McClain, Linda. *The Place of Families: Fostering Capacity, Equality, and Responsibility*. Cambridge, MA: Harvard University Press, 2006.

McGinnis, James B., and Kathleen McGinnis. "Family as Domestic Church." In *One Hundred Years of Catholic Social Thought*, edited by John A. Coleman, 120–34. Maryknoll, NY: Orbis, 1991.

McIlhaney, Joe S., Jr., and Freda McKissic Bush. *Hooked: New Science on How Casual Sex Is Affecting Our Children*. Chicago: Northfield, 2008.

McKnight, Scot. *The Heaven Promise: Engaging the Bible's Truth About Life to Come*. Colorado Springs, CO: WaterBrook, 2015.

———. *Kingdom Conspiracy: Returning to the Radical Mission of the Local Church*. Grand Rapids: Brazos, 2014.

McLanahan, Sara S. "Diverging Destinies: How Children Are Faring under the Second Demographic Transition." *Demography* 41 (2004) 607–27.

———. "Fragile Families and the Reproduction of Poverty." *Annals of the American Academy of Political and Social Science* 621 (2009) 111–31.

———. "Parent Absent or Poverty: Which Matters More?" In *Consequences of Growing Up Poor*, edited by Greg Duncan and Jeanne Brooks-Gunn, 35–44. New York: Russell Sage Foundation, 1997.

McLanahan, Sara, and Christine Percheski. "Family Structure and the Reproduction of Inequalities." *Annual Review of Sociology* 34 (2008) 257–76.

McLanahan, Sara, and Gary Sandefur. *Growing Up with a Single Parent*. Cambridge, MA: Cambridge University Press, 1994.

McRobbie, Angela. *The Aftermath of Feminism: Gender, Culture and Social Change*. London: SAGE, 2009.

McWhirter, Jocelyn. *The Bridegroom Messiah and the People of God: Marriage in the Fourth Gospel*. Cambridge: Cambridge University Press, 2006.

Meier, John P. *A Marginal Jew: Rethinking the Historical Jesus*. Vol. 4, *Law and Love*. New Haven, CT: Yale University Press, 2009.

Méndez-Montoya, Ángel F., O.P. "Eucharistic Imagination: A Queer Body-Politics." *Modern Theology* 30 (2014) 326–39.

Merida, Tony, and Rick Morton. *Orphanology: Awakening to Gospel-Centered Adoption and Orphan Care*. Birmingham, AL: New Hope, 2011.

Meszaros, Andrew. *The Prophetic Church: History and Doctrinal Development in John Henry Newman and Yves Congar*. Oxford: Oxford University Press, 2016.

Metz, Tamara. *Untying the Knot: Marriage, the State, and the Case for Their Divorce*. Princeton, NJ: Princeton University Press, 2010.

Meuffels, H. U. *Einbergung des Menschen in das Mysterium der dreieinigen Liebe. Ein trinitarische Anthropologie nach Hans Urs von Balthasar*. Würzburg: Echter, 1991.

Meyendorff, John. *Marriage: An Orthodox Perspective*. 3rd ed. Yonkers, NY: St. Vladimir's Seminary Press, 1975.

Meyers, Carol L. *Discovering Eve: Ancient Israelite Women in Context*. Oxford: Oxford University Press, 1988.

Middleton, J. Richard. *The Liberating Image: The Imago Dei in Genesis 1*. Grand Rapids: Brazos, 2005.

Mill, John Stuart. *The Subjection of Women*. London: Longmans, Green and Co., 1869.

Miller, Kelli. "Birth Control and Cancer: Which Methods Raise, Lower Risk." *The American Cancer Society*. January 21, 2016. www.cancer.org/cancer/news/features/birth-control-cancer-which-methods-raise-lower-risk.

Minz, K.-H. *Pleroma Trinitatis. Die Trinitätstheologie bei Matthias Joseph Scheeben*. Bern: Lang, 1982.

Moberly, R. W. L. *Prophecy and Discernment*. Cambridge: Cambridge University Press, 2006.

Moore, Russell. *Adopted for Life: The Priority of Adoption for Christian Families and Churches*. 2d ed. Wheaton, IL: Crossway, 2015.

Moran, Jeffrey. *Teaching Sex: The Shaping of Adolescence in the 20th Century*. Cambridge, MA: Harvard University Press, 2000.

Morrow, Maria C. "Pornography and Penance." In *Leaving and Coming Home: New Wineskins for Catholic Sexual Ethics*, edited by David Cloutier, 62–84. Eugene, OR: Cascade, 2010.

Morse, Jennifer Roback. "Why Marriage Belongs to God, Not to the State." In *Life, Marriage, and Religious Liberty: What Belongs to God, What Belongs to Caesar*, edited by David S. Dockery and John Stonestreet, 91–102. New York: Post Hill, 2019.

Moschella, Melissa. *To Whom Do Children Belong? Parental Rights, Civic Education, and Children's Autonomy*. Cambridge: Cambridge University Press, 2016.
Mott, Frank L. "When Is a Father Really Gone? Paternal-Child Contact in Father-Absent Homes." *Demography* 27 (1990) 499–517.
Moughtin-Mumby, Sharon. *Sexual and Marital Metaphors in Hosea, Jeremiah, Isaiah, and Ezekiel*. Oxford: Oxford University Press, 2008.
Muir, Steven C. "Accessing Divine Power and Status." In *Early Christian Ritual Life*, edited by Richard E. DeMaris, Jason T. Lamoreaux, and Steven C. Muir, 38–54. New York: Routledge, 2018.
Muise, Amy, Emily A. Impett, Aleksandr Kogan, and Serge Desmarais. "Keeping the Spark Alive: Being Motivated to Meet a Partner's Sexual Needs Sustains Sexual Desire in Long-Term Romantic Relationships." *Social Psychological and Personality Science* 4 (2013) 267–73.
Müller, Gerhard. "Development or Corruption? Can There Be 'Paradigm Shifts' in the Interpretation of the Deposit of Faith?" In *The Power of Truth: The Challenges of Catholic Morals and Doctrine Today*, 23–35. San Francisco: Ignatius, 2019.
Muse, Stephen. "Transfiguring 'Voluptuous Choice': Christian Marriage as a Spiritual Path." In *Glory and Honor: Orthodox Christian Resources on Marriage*, edited by David C. Ford, Mary S. Ford, and Alfred Kentigern Siewers, 117–28. Yonkers, NY: St. Vladimir's Seminary Press, 2016.
Nelson, James B. *Embodiment: An Approach to Sexuality and Christian Theology*. Minneapolis: Augsburg, 1978.
Neusner, Jacob. *Israel's Love Affair with God: Song of Songs*. Valley Forge, PA: Trinity International, 1993.
Newman, John Henry. *An Essay on the Development of Christian Doctrine*. Notre Dame, IN: University of Notre Dame Press, 1989.
Newsom, Carol A., and Sharon H. Ringe, eds. *The Women's Bible Commentary*. Louisville, KY: Westminster John Knox, 1992.
Nichols, Aidan, O.P. *Romance and System: The Theological Synthesis of Matthias Joseph Scheeben*. Denver: Augustine Institute, 2010.
Nicolas, Jean-Hervé, O.P. *Synthèse dogmatique: De la Trinité à la Trinité*. Paris: Beauchesne, 1985.
Noonan, John T. *Contraception: A History of Its Treatment by the Catholic Theologians and Canonists*. Cambridge, MA: Harvard University Press, 1986.
Noriega, José. *Eros e Agape nella vita coniugale*. Siena: Cantagalli, 2008.
Norris, Richard A., Jr., ed. *The Song of Songs Interpreted by Early Christian and Medieval Commentators*. Translated by Richard A. Norris, Jr. Grand Rapids: Eerdmans, 2003.
Novak, David. "Jewish Marriage: Nature, Covenant, and Contract." In *Jewish Justice: The Contested Limits of Nature, Law, and Covenant*, 101–23. Waco, TX: Baylor University Press, 2017.
Oakes, Kenneth. "Gathering Many Likenesses: Trinity and Kenosis." *Nova et Vetera* 17 (2019) 871–91.
O'Brien, Julia M. *Challenging Prophetic Metaphor: Theology and Ideology in the Prophets*. Louisville, KY: Westminster John Knox, 2008.
O'Connor, David K. *Plato's Bedroom: Ancient Wisdom and Modern Love*. South Bend, IN: St. Augustine's, 2015.
O'Connor, Kathleen M. *Jeremiah: Pain and Promise*. Minneapolis: Fortress, 2011.

———. *Lamentations and the Tears of the World*. Maryknoll, NY: Orbis, 2002.
O'Donovan, Oliver. *Resurrection and Moral Order: An Outline for Evangelical Ethics*. 2d ed. Grand Rapids: Eerdmans, 1994.
O'Gorman, Margaret, and Anne Peper Perkins. *Living True: Lesbian Women Share Stories of Faith*. Saint Louis, MO: PenUltimate, 2014.
Okin, Susan Moller. *Justice, Gender, and the Family*. New York: Basic, 1989.
Oliva, Adriano, O.P. *L'amicizia più grande: Un contributo teologico alle questioni sui divorziari risposati e sulle coppie omosessuali*. Florence: Nerbini, 2015.
Oliver, Mary Beth, and Janet Shibley Hyde. "Gender Differences in Sexuality: A Meta-Analysis." *Psychological Analysis* 114 (1993) 29–51.
O'Meara, Dominic J. *Platonopolis: Platonic Political Philosophy in Late Antiquity*. Oxford: Oxford University Press, 2003.
O'Regan, Cyril. *The Anatomy of Misremembering: Von Balthasar's Response to Philosophical Modernity*. Vol. 1, *Hegel*. New York: Crossroad, 2014.
Ortlund, Raymond C., Jr. *Marriage and the Mystery of the Gospel*. Wheaton, IL: Crossway, 2016.
———. *God's Unfaithful Wife: A Biblical Theology of Spiritual Adultery*. Downers Grove, IL: InterVarsity, 1996.
Osborne, Thomas M., Jr. "The Augustinianism of Thomas Aquinas's Moral Theory." *The Thomist* 67 (2003) 279–305.
Ostriker, Alicia. "A Holy of Holies: The Song of Songs as Countertext." In *The Song of Songs: A Feminist Companion to the Bible (Second Series)*, edited by Athalya Brenner and Carole R. Fontaine, 36–54. Sheffield: Sheffield Academic, 2000.
Otten, Willemien. "Augustine on Marriage, Monasticism, and the Community of the Church." *Theological Studies* 59 (1998) 385–405.
Ouellet, Marc Cardinal. *Divine Likeness: Toward a Trinitarian Anthropology of the Family*. Translated by Philip Milligan and Linda M. Cicone. Grand Rapids: Eerdmans, 2006.
Pangle, Lorraine Smith. *Aristotle and the Philosophy of Friendship*. Cambridge: Cambridge University Press, 2003.
Parke, R. D. *Fatherhood*. Cambridge, MA: Harvard University Press, 1993.
Parmisano, Stan, O.P. *The Craft of Love: Love and Indissolubility in Christian Marriage*. Antioch, CA: Solas, 2009.
Pastoral Constitution on the Church in the Modern World, *Gaudium et Spes*. In *Vatican Council II*, vol. 1, *The Conciliar and Postconciliar Documents*. Rev. ed. Edited by Austin Flannery, O.P., 903–1001. Northport, NY: Costello, 1996.
Pedro-Carroll, JoAnne. *Putting Children First: Proven Parental Strategies for Helping Children Thrive Through Divorce*. New York: Penguin, 2010.
Pennington, Jonathan T. *The Sermon on the Mount and Human Flourishing: A Theological Commentary*. Grand Rapids: Baker Academic, 2017.
Perel, Esther. *The State of Affairs: Rethinking Infidelity*. New York: HarperCollins, 2017.
Perez-Lopez, Angel. *Procreation and the Spousal Meaning of the Body: A Thomistic Argument Grounded in Vatican II*. Eugene, OR: Pickwick, 2017.
Perrin, Nicholas. *Jesus the Priest*. Grand Rapids: Baker Academic, 2018.
Perutz, Kathrin. *Marriage Is Hell*. New York: William Morrow, 1972.
Petri, Thomas, O.P. *Aquinas and the Theology of the Body: The Thomistic Foundations of John Paul II's Anthropology*. Washington, DC: Catholic University of America Press, 2016.

Pfnausch, E. G. "The Good of the Spouses in Rotal Jurisprudence: New Horizons." *The Jurist* 56 (1996) 527–56.

Philips, Abu Ameenah Bilal, and Jamila Jones. *Polygamy in Islam*. Riyadh: International Islamic, 2005.

Phillips, Jacob. *Mary, Star of Evangelization: Tilling the Soil and Sowing the Seed*. New York: Paulist, 2018.

Pinckaers, Servais, O.P. *The Pursuit of Happiness—God's Way: Living the Beatitudes*. Translated by Mary Thomas Noble, O.P. Eugene, OR: Wipf and Stock, 1998.

Piper, John. *This Momentary Marriage: A Parable of Permanence*. Wheaton, IL: Crossway, 2009.

Pitre, Brant. *Jesus the Bridegroom: The Greatest Love Story Ever Told*. New York: Random House, 2014.

———. *Jesus and the Last Supper*. Grand Rapids: Eerdmans, 2017.

Pitre, Brant, Michael P. Barber, and John A. Kincaid. *Paul, a New Covenant Jew: Rethinking Pauline Theology*. Grand Rapids: Eerdmans, 2019.

Pius XI. *Casti Connubii*. Boston: St. Paul Books & Media, n.d.

Pius XII. April 1, 1944 *responsio ad dubium* in *Acta Apostolicae Sedis* 36 (1944) 103.

Plato. *Republic*. Translated by Paul Shorey. In *The Collected Dialogues of Plato*, edited by Edith Hamilton and Huntington Cairns, 576–844. Princeton, NJ: Princeton University Press, 1961.

Pletzer, Elinda A., and Hubert H. Kerschbaum. "Fifty Years of Hormonal Contraception—Time to Find Out What It Does to Our Brain." *Frontiers in Neuroscience* 8 (August 2014) 1–6.

Podella, Thomas. *Das Lichtkleid JHWHs. Untersuchungen zur Gestalthaftigkeit Gottes im Alten Testament und seiner altorientalischen Umwelt*. Tübingen: J. C. B. Mohr, 1996.

Pontifical Council for Justice and Peace. *Compendium of the Social Doctrine of the Church*. Vatican City: Libreria Editrice Vaticana, 2004.

Pool, Robert. *Eve's Rib: Searching for the Biological Roots of Sex Differences*. New York: Crown, 1994.

Pope, Marvin H. *Song of Songs: A New Translation with Introduction and Commentary*. Garden City, NY: Doubleday, 1977.

Pope, Stephen J. "The Magisterium's Arguments against 'Same-Sex Marriage': An Ethical Analysis and Critique." *Theological Studies* 65 (2004) 530–65.

Popenoe, David. *Disturbing the Nest: Family Change and Decline in Modern Societies*. Piscataway, NJ: Transaction, 1988.

———. *Families Without Fathers: Fathers, Marriage and Children in American Society*. 2d ed. New Brunswick, NJ: Transaction, 2009.

———. *Life Without Father: Compelling New Evidence That Fatherhood and Marriage Are Indispensable for the Good of Children and Society*. New York: Simon & Schuster, 1996.

Porter, Jean. "Contraceptive Use and the Authority of the Church: A Case Study on Natural Law and Moral Discernment." In *A Just and True Love: Feminism at the Frontiers of Theological Ethics: Essays in Honor of Margaret A. Farley*, edited by Maura A. Ryan and Brian F. Linnane, S.J., 369–405. Notre Dame, IN: University of Notre Dame Press, 2007.

Posner, Richard. *Sex and Reason*. Cambridge, MA: Harvard University Press, 1992.

Post, Stephen G. *More Lasting Unions: Christianity, the Family and Society*. Grand Rapids: Eerdmans, 2000.

Price, A. W. *Love and Friendship in Plato and Aristotle*. 2d ed. Oxford: Oxford University Press, 1997.

Probst, Ferdinand. *Katholische Moraltheologie*. Vol. 2. Tübingen: H. Laupp, 1850.

Prothro, James. "Semper Virgo? A Biblical Review of a Debated Dogma." *Pro Ecclesia* 28 (2019) 78–97.

Pruett, Kyle D. *Fatherneed: Why Father Care Is as Essential as Mother Care for Your Child*. New York: Random House, 2000.

Pruss, Alexander. *One Body: An Essay in Christian Sexual Ethics*. Notre Dame, IN: University of Notre Dame Press, 2013.

Przywara, Erich, S.J. *Analogia Entis: Metaphysics: Original Structure and Universal Rhythm*. Translated by John R. Betz and David Bentley Hart. Grand Rapids: Eerdmans, 2014.

Raeburn, Paul. *Do Fathers Matter? What Science Is Telling Us About the Parent We've Overlooked*. New York: Farrar, Straus and Giroux, 2014.

Rahner, Karl, S.J. "Marriage as a Sacrament." In *Sexuality, Marriage, and Family: Readings in the Catholic Tradition*, edited by Paulinus Ikechukwu Odozor, C.S.Sp., 351–66. Notre Dame, IN: University of Notre Dame Press, 2001.

Ramage, Matthew J. *Dark Passages of the Bible: Engaging Scripture with Benedict XVI and Thomas Aquinas*. Washington, DC: Catholic University of America Press, 2013.

Rawls, John. *Political Liberalism*. New York: Columbia University Press, 1996.

———. *A Theory of Justice*. Oxford: Oxford University Press, 1972.

Raymond, Janice G. *Women as Wombs: Reproductive Technologies and the Battle Over Women's Freedom*. San Francisco: Harper, 1993.

Regnerus, Mark. *Cheap Sex: The Transformation of Men, Marriage, and Monogamy*. Oxford: Oxford University Press, 2017.

Reimers, Adrian J. *An Analysis of the Concepts of Self-Fulfillment and Self-Realization in the Thought of Karol Wojtyła, Pope John Paul II*. Lewiston, NY: Edwin Mellen, 2001.

Reno, R. R. *Genesis*. Grand Rapids: Brazos, 2010.

Reynolds, Philip L. *How Marriage Became One of the Sacraments: The Sacramental Theology of Marriage from Its Medieval Origins to the Council of Trent*. Cambridge: Cambridge University Press, 2016.

———. *Marriage in the Western Church: The Christianization of Marriage during the Patristic and Early Medieval Periods*. Leiden: Brill, 1994.

Rhoades, Galena K., and Scot M. Stanley. *Before "I Do": What Do Premarital Experiences Have to Do with Marital Quality Among Today's Young Adults?* The National Marriage Project, University of Virginia, 2014. www.nationalmarriageproject.org/wordpress/wp-content/uploads/2014/08/NMP-BeforeIDoReport-Final.pdf.

Ribar, David. "Why Marriage Matters for Child Wellbeing." *The Future of Children* 25 (2015) 11–27.

Rineau, Louis-Marie. "*Celui qui donne*." *Le don d'après saint Thomas d'Aquin*. Paris: Parole et Silence, 2016.

Risch, Gail. "Cohabitation: Integrating Ecclesial and Social Scientific Teaching." In *Marriage in the Catholic Tradition: Scripture, Tradition, and Experience*, edited by Todd A. Salzman, Thomas M. Kelly, and John J. O'Keefe, 156–68. New York: Crossroad, 2004.

Rist, John M. *Augustine: Ancient Thought Baptized*. Cambridge: Cambridge University Press, 1994.

Roberts, Christopher C. *Creation and Covenant: The Significance of Sexual Difference in the Moral Theology of Marriage*. New York: T. & T. Clark International, 2007.

Roberts, William P. "Christian Marriage: A Divine Calling." In *Marriage in the Catholic Tradition: Scripture, Tradition, and Experience*, edited by Todd A. Salzman, Thomas M. Kelly, and John J. O'Keefe, 98–108. New York: Crossroad, 2004.

Rogers, Eugene F., Jr. *Sexuality and the Christian Body: Their Way into the Triune God*. Oxford: Blackwell, 1999.

———. "Trinity, Marriage, and Homosexuality." In *Authorizing Marriage? Canon, Tradition, and Critique in the Blessing of Same-Sex Unions*, edited by Mark D. Jordan, 151–64. Princeton, NJ: Princeton University Press, 2006.

Rose, Jacqueline. *Mothers: An Essay on Love and Cruelty*. New York: Farrar, Straus and Giroux, 2018.

Ross, David. *Aristotle*. 6th ed. With an introduction by John L. Ackrill. London: Routledge, 1995.

Rossi, Alice. "Parenthood in Transition: From Lineage to Child to Self-Orientation." In *Parenting Across the Life Span*, edited by Jane B. Lancaster, Jeanne Altmann, Alice Rossi, and Lonnie R. Sherrod, 31–81. New York: Aldine de Gruyter, 1987.

Rubio, Julie Hanlon. *A Christian Theology of Marriage and Family*. New York: Paulist, 2003.

———. *Hope for Common Ground: Mediating the Personal and the Political in a Divided Church*. Washington, DC: Georgetown University Press, 2016.

———. "Living the Dual Vocation of Christian Parenthood." In *Marriage in the Catholic Tradition: Scripture, Tradition, and Experience*, edited by Todd A. Salzman, Thomas M. Kelly, and John J. O'Keefe, 193–200. New York: Crossroad, 2004.

———. "The Practice of Sex in Christian Marriage." In *Leaving and Coming Home: New Wineskins for Catholic Sexual Ethics*, edited by David Cloutier, 226–49. Eugene, OR: Cascade, 2010.

Russell, Bertrand. *Marriage and Morals*. London: Allen & Unwin, 1929.

Russell, Jeffrey Burton. *Paradise Mislaid: How We Lost Heaven—and How We Can Regain It*. Oxford: Oxford University Press, 2006.

Rutledge, Fleming. *The Crucifixion: Understanding the Death of Jesus Christ*. Grand Rapids: Eerdmans, 2015.

Sacks, Jonathan. *The Great Partnership: God, Science and the Search for Meaning*. London: Hodder & Stoughton, 2011.

———. "Jewish-Christian Dialogue: The Ethical Dimension." In *Tradition in an Untraditional Age: Essays on Modern Jewish Thought*, 161–81. London: Valentine, Mitchell, 1990.

Sacks, Sheldon, ed. *On Metaphor*. Chicago: University of Chicago Press, 1979.

Sacra Romana Rota. January 22, 1944 decree. *Acta Apostolicae Sedis* 36 (1944) 179–200.

Salzman, Todd A., and Michael G. Lawler. "Cohabitation and the Process of Marrying." In *Sexual Ethics: A Theological Introduction*, 123–54. Washington, DC: Georgetown University Press, 2012.

———. *Sexual Ethics: A Theological Introduction*. Washington, DC: Georgetown University Press, 2012.

———. *The Sexual Person: Toward a Renewed Catholic Anthropology.* Washington, DC: Georgetown University Press, 2008.

Sanderson, Judith E. "Nahum." In *The Women's Bible Commentary*, edited by Carol A. Newsom and Sharon H. Ringe, 217–21. Louisville, KY: Westminster John Knox, 1992.

Sarna, Nahum M. *Exploring Exodus: The Origins of Biblical Israel.* New York: Schocken, 1996.

Satlow, Michael L. *How the Bible Became Holy.* New Haven, CT: Yale University Press, 2014.

———. "The Metaphor of Marriage in Early Judaism." In *Families and Family Relations: As Represented in Early Judaisms and Early Christianities: Texts and Fictions*, edited by Jan Willem van Henten and Athalya Brenner, 13–42. Leiden: Deo, 2000.

Sawhill, Isabel. *Generation Unbound: Drifting into Sex and Parenthood without Marriage.* Washington, DC: Brookings Institution, 2014.

Scheeben, Matthias Joseph. *Handbook of Catholic Dogmatics*, Book One: *Theological Epistemology*, Part One: *The Objective Principles of Theological Knowledge.* Translated by Michael J. Miller. Steubenville, OH: Emmaus Academic, 2019.

———. *Handbuch der katholischen Dogmatik.* Freiburg: Herder, 1873–87.

———. *The Mysteries of Christianity.* Translated by Cyril Vollert, S.J. New York: Crossroad, 2006.

Scheib, Joanna E., Alice Ruby, and Jean Benward. "Who Requests Their Sperm Donor's Identity? The First Ten Years Information-Releases to Adults with Open-Identity Donors." *Mental Health, Sexuality and Ethics* 107 (2017) 483–93.

Schemenauer, Kevin. *Conjugal Love and Procreation: Dietrich von Hildebrand's Superabundant Integration.* Lanham, MD: Lexington, 2011.

Schillebeeckx, Edward, O.P. "Christian Marriage and the Reality of Complete Marital Breakdown." In *Catholic Divorce: The Deception of Annulments*, edited by Pierre Hegy and Joseph Martos, 82–107. New York: Continuum, 2000.

———. *Le mariage est un sacrement.* Paris: Office Général de Livre, 1961.

———. *Marriage: Human Reality and Saving Mystery.* Translated by N. D. Smith. London: Sheed and Ward, 1965.

———. *De sacramentele heilseconomie.* Antwerp: 't Groeit and H. Nelissen, 1952.

Schindler, D. C. "The Crisis of Marriage as a Crisis of Meaning: On the Sterility of the Modern Will." *Communio* 41 (2014) 331–71.

Schindler, David L. "Catholic Theology, Gender, and the Future of Western Civilization." *Communio* 20 (1993) 200–239.

———. "Liturgy and the Integrity of Cosmic Order: The Theology of Alexander Schmemann." In *Ordering Love: Liberal Societies and the Memory of God*, 288–309. Grand Rapids: Eerdmans, 2011.

Schindler, David L., et al. "Faith and the Sacrament of Marriage: A Response to the Proposal of a New '*Minimum Fidei*' Requirement." *Communio* 42 (2015) 309–30.

Schmemann, Alexander. *For the Life of the World: Sacraments and Orthodoxy.* 2d ed. Crestwood, NY: St. Vladimir's Seminary Press, 1973.

———. *Introduction to Liturgical Theology.* Translated by Asheleigh E. Moorehouse. Crestwood, NY: St. Vladimir's Seminary Press, 2003.

Schmitt, David et al. "Universal Sex Differences in the Desire for Sexual Variety: Tests from 52 Nations, 6 Continents and 13 Islands." *Journal of Personality and Social Psychology* 85 (2003) 85–103.

Schmitt, Émile. *Le mariage Chrétien dans l'oeuvre de saint Augustin*. Paris: Études Augustiniennes, 1983.
Schmitz, Kenneth L. *At the Center of the Human Drama: The Philosophy of Karol Wojtyła/Pope John Paul II*. Washington, DC: Catholic University of America Press, 1994.
Schnackenburg, Rudolf. *The Epistle to the Ephesians: A Commentary*. Translated by Helen Heron. Edinburgh: T. & T. Clark, 1991.
Schneider, Daniel. "Lessons Learned from Non-Marriage Experiments." *The Future of Children* 25 (2015) 155-78.
Schneiders, Sandra M. *Selling All: Commitment, Consecrated Celibacy, and Community in Catholic Religious Life*. New York: Paulist, 2002.
———. *Written That You May Believe: Encountering Jesus in the Fourth Gospel*. New York: Crossroad, 1999.
Schönborn, Christoph, O.P. *Loving the Church: Spiritual Exercises Preached in the Presence of Pope John Paul II*. Translated by John Saward. San Francisco: Ignatius, 1998.
Schumacher, Michele M. *A Trinitarian Anthropology: Adrienne von Speyr and Hans Urs von Balthasar in Dialogue with Thomas Aquinas*. Washington, DC: Catholic University of America Press, 2014.
Schumm, Walter R. "A Review and Critique of Research on Same-Sex Parenting and Adoption." *Psychological Reports* 119 (2016) 641-760.
Sciglitano, Anthony C., Jr. *Marcion and Prometheus: Balthasar against the Expulsion of Jewish Origins from Modern Religious Dialogue*. New York: Crossroad, 2014.
Scola, Angelo. *The Nuptial Mystery*. Translated by Michelle K. Borras. Grand Rapids: Eerdmans, 2005.
Seitz, Christopher R. *Prophecy and Hermeneutics: Toward a New Introduction to the Prophets*. Grand Rapids: Baker Academic, 2007.
Seltzer, Judith A. "Consequences of Marital Dissolution for Children." *Annual Review of Sociology* 20 (1994) 235-66.
———. "Relationships Between Fathers and Children Who Live Apart: The Father's Role after Separation." *Journal of Marriage and the Family* 53 (1991) 79-101.
Seltzer, Judith A., and Susan M. Bianchi. "Children's Contact with Absent Parents." *Journal of Marriage and the Family* 50 (1988) 663-77.
Setel, T. Drorah. "Prophets and Pornography: Female Sexual Imagery in Hosea." In *Feminist Interpretation of the Bible*, edited by Letty M. Russell, 86-95. Philadelphia: Westminster, 1985.
Shanley, Mary Lyndon. "Just Marriage: On the Public Importance of Private Unions." In *Just Marriage*, edited by Joshua Cohen and Deborah Chasman, 3-31. Oxford: Oxford University Press, 2004.
Shannon, William H. *The Lively Debate: Response to* Humanae Vitae. New York: Sheed & Ward, 1970.
Sheridan, Mark, O.S.B. *Language for God in Patristic Tradition: Wrestling with Biblical Anthropomorphism*. Downers Grove, IL: IVP Academic, 2015.
Sherwood, Yvonne. *The Prostitute and the Prophet: Reading Hosea in the Late Twentieth Century*. London: T. & T. Clark International, 2004.
Shields, Mary E. *Circumscribing the Prostitute: The Rhetorics of Intertextuality, Metaphor, and Gender in Jeremiah 3.1-4.4*. London: T. & T. Clark International, 2004.

———. "Gender and Violence in Ezekiel 23." *Society of Biblical Literature 1998 Seminar Papers* 37, Part 1 (1998) 86–105.
Shivanandan, Mary. *Crossing the Threshold of Love: A New Vision of Marriage*. Washington, DC: Catholic University of America Press, 1999.
Siggelkow, Bernd, and Wolfgang Büscher. *Deutschlands sexuelle Tragödie: Wenn Kinder nicht mehr lernen, was Liebe ist*. Asslar: Gerth Medien, 2008.
Skovlund, Charlotte Wessel, Lina Steinrud Mørch, Lars Vedel Kessing, Øjvind Lidegaard. "Association of Hormonal Contraception with Depression." *Journal of the American Medical Association, Psychiatry* 73 (2016) 1154–62.
Smith, Janet E. "Foreword." In *The Theology of Marriage: Personalism, Doctrine, and Canon Law*, by Cormac Burke, vii–xvii. Washington, DC: Catholic University of America Press, 2015.
———. *Self-Gift: Essays on* Humanae Vitae *and the Thought of John Paul II*. Steubenville, OH: Emmaus Academic, 2018.
Smith, Mark S. *The Early History of God: Yahweh and Other Deities in Ancient Israel*. 2d ed. Grand Rapids: Eerdmans, 2002.
———. *How Human Is God? Seven Questions about God and Humanity in the Bible*. Collegeville, MN: Liturgical, 2014.
———. *The Origins of Biblical Monotheism: Israel's Polytheistic Background and the Ugaritic Texts*. Oxford: Oxford University Press, 2001.
Smock, Pamela J., Wendy D. Manning, and Meredith Porter. "'Everything's There Except Money': How Money Shapes Decisions to Marry Among Cohabitors." *Journal of Marriage and Family* 67 (2005) 680–96.
Snarey, John. *How Fathers Care for the Next Generation: A Four-Decade Study*. Cambridge, MA: Harvard University Press, 1993.
Soloveitchik, Joseph B. *Abraham's Journey: Reflections on the Life of the Founding Patriarch*. Edited by David Shatz, Joel B. Wolowelsky, and Reuven Ziegler. New York: Toras HoRav Foundation, 2008.
———. *And from There You Shall Seek*. Translated by Naomi Goldblum. Jersey City, NJ: Ktav, 2008.
Speyr, Adrienne von. *Die Schöpfung*. Edited by Hans Urs von Balthasar. Einsiedeln: Johannes Verlag, 1972.
———. *Theologie der Geschlechter*. Edited by Hans Urs von Balthasar. Einsiedeln: Johannes Verlag, 1969.
Springborg, Patricia. *Royal Persons: Patriarchal Monarchy and the Feminine Principle*. London: Unwin Hyman, 1990.
Sri, Edward. *Men, Women, and the Mystery of Love: Practical Insights from John Paul II's* Love and Responsibility. Cincinnati: Servant, 2015.
Stacey, Judith. *In the Name of the Family: Rethinking Family Values in a Postmodern Age*. Boston: Beacon, 1996.
Staniloae, Dumitru. *The Experience of God: Orthodox Dogmatic Theology*. Vol. 2, *The World: Creation and Deification*. Translated and edited by Ioan Ionita and Robert Barringer. Brookline, MA: Holy Cross Orthodox, 2000.
———. *The Experience of God: Orthodox Dogmatic Theology*. Vol. 5, *The Sanctifying Mysteries*, translated and edited by Ioan Ionita and Robert Barringer. Brookline, MA: Holy Cross Orthodox, 2012.
Stoyanov, Yuri. *The Other God: Dualist Religions from Antiquity to the Cathar Heresy*. New Haven, CT: Yale University Press, 2000.

Strauss, Leo. *The City and the Man.* Chicago: Rand McNally, 1964.
Surmanski, Albert-Marie, O.P. Unpublished translation of Jerome's *Commentarium in Naum.*
Tanner, Kathryn. "Hooker and the New Puritans." In *Authorizing Marriage? Canon, Tradition, and Critique in the Blessing of Same-Sex Unions,* edited by Mark D. Jordan, 121–38. Princeton, NJ: Princeton University Press, 2006.
Tarwater, John K. *Marriage as Covenant: Considering God's Design at Creation and the Contemporary Moral Consequences.* Lanham, MD: University Press of America, 2006.
Thatcher, Adrian. "Living Together before Marriage: The Theological and Pastoral Opportunities." In *Celebrating Christian Marriage,* edited by Adrian Thatcher, 55–70. Edinburgh: T. & T. Clark, 2001.
———. *Marriage after Modernity: Christian Marriage in Postmodern Times.* Sheffield: Sheffield Academic, 1999.
Thérèse of Lisieux. *Story of a Soul: The Autobiography of St. Thérèse of Lisieux,* translated by John Clarke, O.C.D. Washington, DC: ICS, 1996.
Therrien, Michel. "The Practice of Responsible Parenthood, NFP, and the Covenantal Unity of Spouses." In *Leaving and Coming Home: New Wineskins for Catholic Sexual Ethics,* edited by David Cloutier, 173–205. Eugene, OR: Cascade, 2010.
Thistlethwaite, Susan Brooks. "Every Two Minutes: Battered Women and Feminist Interpretation." In *Feminist Interpretation of the Bible,* edited by Letty M. Russell, 96–107. Philadelphia: Westminster, 1985.
Thomas, Gary. *Sacred Marriage: What If God Designed Marriage to Make Us Holy More Than to Make Us Happy?* 2d ed. Grand Rapids: Zondervan, 2015.
Thurow, Roger. *The First 1000 Days: A Crucial Time for Mothers and Children—and the World.* Philadelphia: Public Affairs, 2016.
Torrell, Jean-Pierre, O.P. *A Priestly People: Baptismal Priesthood and Priestly Ministry.* New York: Paulist, 2013.
Treggiari, Susan. *Roman Marriage: Iusti Coniuges from the Time of Cicero to the Time of Ulpian.* Oxford: Oxford University Press, 1991.
Troeltsch, Ernst. "Historical and Dogmatic Method in Theology." In *Religion in History,* translated by James Luther Adams and Walter F. Bense, 11–32. Edinburgh: T. & T. Clark, 1991.
Turner, Denys. *Eros and Allegory: Medieval Exegesis of the Song of Songs.* Kalamazoo, MI: Cistercian, 1995.
Turner, Philip. *Sex, Money and Power: An Essay in Christian Social Ethics.* Cambridge, MA: Cowley, 1985.
Tushnet, Eve. "O Tell Me the Truth About Love." In *More Than a Monologue: Sexual Diversity and the Catholic Church,* vol. 1, *Voices of Our Times,* edited by Christine Firer Hinze and J. Patrick Hornbeck II, 26–31. New York: Fordham University Press, 2014.
United States Conference of Catholic Bishops. Pastoral Letter *Marriage: Love and Life in the Divine Plan.* Washington, DC: United States Conference of Catholic Bishops, 2009.
U.S. Department of Health and Human Services. *Female Contraceptive Development Program (U01).* November 5, 2013. www.grants.nih.gov/grants/guide/rfa-files/RFA-HD-14-024.html.

Urbinati, Nadia. "John Stuart Mill on Androgyny and Ideal Marriage." *Political Theory* 19 (1991) 626–48.
Vijgen, Jörgen. "The Intelligibility of Aquinas' Account of Marriage as *Remedium Concupiscentiae* in His Commentary on 1 Corinthians 7, 1–9." In *Towards a Biblical Thomism: Thomas Aquinas and the Renewal of Biblical Theology*, edited by Piotr Roszak and Jörgen Vijgen, 219–41. Pamplona: EUNSA, 2018.
Vodraska, Stanley. *Philosophical Essays concerning Human Families*. Lanham, MD: University Press of America, 2014.
Waite, Linda J., and Kara Joyner. "Emotional and Physical Satisfaction with Sex in Married, Cohabiting, and Dating Sexual Unions: Do Men and Women Differ?" In *Sex, Love, and Health in America: Private Choices and Public Policies*, edited by Edward O. Laumann and Robert T. Michael, 239–74. Chicago: University of Chicago Press, 2001.
Waite, Linda, and Lee A. Lillard. "Children and Marital Disruption." *American Journal of Sociology* 96 (1991) 930–53.
Waite, Linda, and Maggie Gallagher. *The Case for Marriage*. New York: Doubleday, 2000.
Waite, Linda J., Christine Bachrach, Michelle Hindin, Elizabeth Thompson, and Arland Thornton, eds. *The Ties That Bind: Perspectives on Marriage and Cohabitation*. New York: Aldine de Gruyter, 2000.
Waldstein, Michael. "Covenant and the Union of Love in M. J. Scheeben's Theology of Marriage." *Letter and Spirit* 3 (2007) 139–52.
———. "Dietrich von Hildebrand and St. Thomas Aquinas on Goodness and Happiness." *Nova et Vetera* 1 (2003) 403–63.
Walker, Adrian J., and Rachel M. Coleman. "The Saving Difference." *Communio* 42 (2015) 184–91.
Wallenfang, Donald. *Metaphysics: A Basic Introduction in a Christian Key*. Eugene, OR: Cascade, 2019.
Wallerstein, Judith, Julia Lewis, and Sandra Blakeslee. *The Unexpected Legacy of Divorce: A Twenty-Five Year Landmark Study*. New York: Hyperion, 2000.
Walton, John H. *The Lost World of Genesis One: Ancient Cosmology and the Origins Debate*. Downers Grove, IL: IVP Academic, 2009.
Waters, Brent. *The Family in Christian Social and Political Thought*. Oxford: Oxford University Press, 2007.
———. "Marriage." In *The Oxford Handbook of Sacramental Theology*, edited by Hans Boersma and Matthew Levering, 517–30. Oxford: Oxford University Press, 2015.
Weaver, Natalie Kertes. *Marriage and Family: A Christian Theological Foundation*. Winona, MN: Anselm Academic, 2009.
Weems, Renita J. *Battered Love: Marriage, Sex, and Violence in the Hebrew Prophets*. Minneapolis: Fortress, 1995.
———. "Gomer: Victim of Violence or Victim of Metaphor?" *Semeia* 47 (1989) 87–104.
Weinfeld, Moshe. "Sabbath, Temple and the Enthronement of the Lord—The Problem of the Sitz im Leben of Genesis 1.1—2.3." In *Mélanges bibliques et orientaux en l'honneur de M. Henri Cazelles*, edited by A. Caquot and M. Delcor, 502–12. Neukirchener-Vluyn: Neukirchener, 1981.
Weissbourd, Richard. *The Vulnerable Child: What Really Hurts America's Children and What We Can Do About It*. Reading, MA: Addison-Wesley, 1996.

Welch, Lawrence J., and Perry Cahall. "An Examination of the Role of Faith in Matrimonial Consent and the Consequences for the Sacrament of Marriage." *Nova et Vetera* 16 (2018) 311–42.
Wenham, Gordon J. *Genesis 1–15*. Nashville, TN: Thomas Nelson, 1987.
Wettstein, Howard. "God's Struggles." In *Divine Evil?: The Moral Character of the God of Abraham*, edited by M. A. Bergmann, M. J. Murray, and M. C. Rea, 321–34. Oxford: Oxford University Press, 2011.
Wetzel, James. *Augustine and the Limits of Virtue*. Cambridge: Cambridge University Press, 1992.
Wheeler-Reed, David. *Regulating Sex in the Roman Empire: Ideology, the Bible, and the Early Christians*. New Haven, CT: Yale University Press, 2017.
White, Thomas Joseph, O.P. *The Incarnate Lord: A Thomistic Study in Christology*. Washington, DC: Catholic University of America Press, 2015.
———. *The Light of Christ: An Introduction to Catholicism*. Washington, DC: Catholic University of America Press, 2017.
Whitehead, Barbara Dafoe. *The Divorce Culture: Rethinking Our Commitments to Marriage and Family*. New York: Random House, 1996.
Wilcox, W. Bradford. "#YesWomenAndChildren Are Safer Within Intact Marriages." *The Federalist*. January 56, 2015. www.thefederalist.com/2015/01/06/yesallwomenandchildren-are-safer-within-intact-marriages/.
Willoughby, Brian J., and Spencer L. James. *The Marriage Paradox: Why Emerging Adults Love Marriage Yet Push It Aside*. Oxford: Oxford University Press, 2017.
Wills, Garry. *Why Priests? A Failed Tradition*. New York: Penguin, 2013.
Wilson, Robin Fretwell, ed. *Reconceiving the Family*. Cambridge: Cambridge University Press, 2006.
Witte, John, Jr. *From Sacrament to Contract: Marriage, Religion, and Law in the Western Tradition*. 2d ed. Louisville, KY: Westminster John Knox, 2012.
Wolfe, Alan. *Whose Keeper? Social Science and Moral Obligation*. Berkeley, CA: University of California Press, 1989.
Wolfe, Christopher. "Homosexuality and the Church." In *Sexuality and the U.S. Catholic Church: Crisis and Renewal*, edited by Lisa Sowle Cahill, John Garvey, and T. Frank Kennedy, S.J., 144–62. New York: Crossroad, 2006.
Wolff, Hans Walter. *Hosea*. Translated by Gary Stansell. Philadelphia: Fortress, 1974.
Wrenn, Lawrence. "Refining the Essence of Marriage." *The Jurist* 46 (1986) 537–45.
Wright, N. T. *Paul and the Faithfulness of God*. Book II. Minneapolis: Fortress, 2013.
———. *Surprised by Hope: Rethinking Heaven, the Resurrection, and the Mission of the Church*. New York: HarperCollins, 2008.
Wright, Wendy M. "The Christian Spiritual Life and the Family." In *Marriage in the Catholic Tradition: Scripture, Tradition, and Experience*, edited by Todd A. Salzman, Thomas M. Kelly, and John J. O'Keefe, 185–92. New York: Crossroad, 2004.
Yarbro Collins, Adela. *Mark: A Commentary*. Minneapolis: Fortress, 2007.
Yenor, Scott. *Family Politics: The Idea of Marriage in Modern Political Thought*. Waco, TX: Baylor University Press, 2011.
Yogman, Michael, and Craig F. Garfield. "Fathers' Roles in the Care and Development of Their Children." *Pediatrics* 138 (2016) doi: 10.1542/peds.2016-1128.

Yunis, Harvey. "The Protreptic Rhetoric of the *Republic*." In *The Cambridge Companion to Plato's Republic*, edited by G. R. F. Ferrari, 1–26. Cambridge: Cambridge University Press, 2007.

Zimmerman, Kari-Shane Davis. "In Control? The Hookup Culture and the Practice of Relationships." In *Leaving and Coming Home: New Wineskins for Catholic Sexual Ethics*, edited by David Cloutier, 47–61. Eugene, OR: Cascade, 2010.

Zimmermann, Nigel. *Facing the Other: John Paul II, Levinas, and the Body*. Eugene, OR: Cascade, 2015.

Zolli, Eugenio. *Prima dell' alba. Autobiografia autorizzata*. San Paolo: Cinisello Balsamo, 2004.

Index

abduction, 205
Abelard, Peter, 209
Abma, Richtsje, 60–61
abortion, 214n2, 244
Abraham, 28n3, 58, 93, 141, 162
Acts of the Apostles, 158n64
Adam, 157n61, 204n73; and creation of Eve, 42–43, 63, 73–77, 85, 94–95, 100–104; marriage of to Eve, 25n83, 63, 89, 92–94, 101–3, 105, 108–9, 160n74, 190–95, 198, 212; priesthood of, 15–16; sex of prior to creation of Eve, 6n25; sin of, 8–9, 13n37, 28n3, 91–93, 96–99, 106–8; as type of Jesus, 82, 90–91
Africa, 150, 217n10
Akiba, Rabbi, 37
akolouthia, 207
Albert the Great, 196, 209
alcoholism, 142n9, 239
Alexander of Hales, 190, 207, 209
allegorical interpretation, 31, 48–49, 57–58, 249
Allison, Dale, 198
Alvaré, Helen, xiii–xiv, 12, 21, 216, 233, 236n87, 242–46
Amalek, 53
Ambrose, 58, 157n61, 208
Ambrosiaster, 208
Amoris Laetitia, 9–10
analogia relationis, 81
analogy of being (*analogia entis*), 3–4, 80
Anderson, Gary A., 108n88

Anderson, Ryan, 24n79, 160, 182, 223n40
Anglican Church, 163
annulment, 10n32, 24
Anselm, 119
Aquinas, Thomas. *See* Thomas Aquinas
Aristotle, 10, 112n6, 144–45, 147n22, 149–55, 169, 181–82, 184
Arjonillo, Rolando, 168
Arnold, Bill T., 93–95, 98, 108
Ascension of Christ, 188, 202
Athanasius, 248
Augustine, 8, 10, 18, 31, 53, 58–59, 64, 66–68, 70–71, 77, 84–85, 92–94, 105–9, 137n104, 144, 153, 155–61, 163–65, 184–85, 190–92, 194–95, 197, 209, 251
Austriaco, Nicanor, 141–42

Baal, 35, 46, 94
Balthasar, Hans Urs von, 3n11, 8, 21, 64–74, 76–87, 119n31
Banks, Ralph, 244
baptism, 18, 42–43, 121, 160, 165, 191, 207, 209, 223
Baril, Gilberte, 39
Barth, Karl, 65, 77–83, 85
Barton, John, 50–51
Baruch, books of, 89
Baucham, Voddie, 221
Baumann, Gerlinde, 7, 31, 47, 49–52, 54, 56–57
Beatitudes, 250n11
Beckwith, Roger, 202n66

INDEX

Bellarmine, Robert, 210
Benedict XVI, Pope, 21, 42, 59, 116, 187–88, 202n66
Bennett, Jana, 17–18, 114n13, 117–18, 217n9
Bernard of Clairvaux, 206, 248n2
biblical exegesis. *See* exegesis, biblical
birth control, 24, 163, 179, 182, 214, 242, 244–45
Blondel, Maurice, 65–66
Bonaventure, 2–4, 67, 75, 209
Bonhoeffer, Dietrich, 79
bonum coniugum (good of the spouses), 10, 142–43, 177–78, 180, 184
Bourg, Florence Caffrey, 140
Bouyer, Louis, 1–2, 26n84
Brake, Elizabeth, 225n46, 235n87
Brennan, Samantha, 227
Brooks, Christopher, 11, 216–22, 233, 241
Brown, Peter, 6n23, 156n57
Brown, Raymond, 43, 187n11
Browning, Don, 112n6, 114, 142n9, 145n16
Brownson, James V., 144–45
Brueggemann, Walter, 62
Brunner, Emil, 83
Bruno the Carthusian, 196
Buber, Martin, 64, 69, 71n47, 77
Burke, Cormac, 10, 143–44, 156n57, 163, 176–80

Cahall, Perry, xiii, 119–20, 133n87, 135n97, 142–43, 153–54, 157n61, 163–64, 167n110, 215–16
Cahill, Lisa Sowle, 12, 23n77, 139n2, 157n61, 217n9, 221n30, 229
Calvary, 9
Calvin, John, 186, 193n27
Cameron, Bill, 227
Cana, wedding at, 6, 39n39, 194, 209, 253
Carroll, Robert, 52–53
Casti Connubii, 144, 163–65, 169, 211

Catechism of the Catholic Church, the, 23, 44–45, 88n129, 113, 142n10, 164, 169, 180, 184, 233
Cathars, 5, 206
Catherine of Siena, 9, 120–25, 129, 136
Catholic Church, xiii, 10n32, 23–24, 55n96, 140, 157n61, 187, 207n90, 212, 216, 219n22, 233, 243n119
Catholic social teaching, 144n15, 216n8
Cavadini, John, xiv, 93, 105n73, 108, 137n104, 176n157, 185, 196n40
celibacy, 18, 24n80, 117–18, 124, 140n6, 156n55, 191–92, 204
Chambers, Clare, 216, 223–25
chastity, 11n34, 59n107, 23–24, 118n31, 134, 156n57, 158, 161–62, 164
Cherlin, Andrew, 228n63, 239, 242n116
chuppah, 38n37
Cicero, 58, 158n64
Claudel, Paul, 65–66
Clement of Alexandria, 208
Cloutier, David, 4n17, 24n81, 92, 116n23, 140–41, 253n27
Coates, Ta-Nehisi, 11, 216–19
Code of Canon Law, the, 142–43, 167n109, 180
cohabitation, 24, 114, 145–46, 151, 153, 183–84, 228–30, 234n81, 239n102, 243
Collins, Adela Yarbro, 41
Collins, John J., 5–6, 22n74, 29n7, 91n2, 160n71
commixtio corporum, 194
Compendium of the Social Doctrine of the Church, 12, 216, 233–34, 247
confirmation, sacrament of, 18
Congar, Yves, 203
consensus animarum, 194
contraception. *See* birth control
Coontz, Stephanie, 246
Corinthians, Epistles to the, 5, 15, 18, 59, 72, 82n105, 90–91, 127–28, 156, 160, 194, 199, 220

294

INDEX

Cotter, David W., 93, 98-99, 108
creation, xiiin1, 58, 75-76, 89n1, 215, 217n9, 231, 247; Apostle Paul on, 91-92; Barth on, 77-79, 81-83; and institution of marriage, 93-94, 98-100, 103, 106, 110, 138, 167n112, 190, 194, 203-4, 208, 233-34; purpose of, ix-xi, 1-4, 6-8, 11n34, 13-15, 17-18, 20-22, 25-27, 63-64, 138; transformation of, 31n14, 39, 117n27
Cross, Frank Moore, 33
Cross of Christ, xiii, 1, 191; as consummation of God's marriage to His people, 4, 41-44, 87, 185; as paradigm of marital love, 4, 9, 13, 22, 63, 76, 111-13, 115-29, 134-38, 214, 247, 250-51, 253

daughters of Zion, 45, 51
Davies, Andrew, 51
Davies, Christie, 247n141
Davis, Ellen, 38, 250
Davison, Andrew, 186, 253
Day, Keri, 240n108
Day, Peggy L., 30n11
Dead Sea Scrolls, 199
deification, 1, 31n15, 90, 109
Deus Caritas Est, 116
Deuteronomy, 33n25, 37, 57, 155, 220
devil, the. See Satan
Diriart, Alexandra, 116-18, 120, 136
diseases, sexually transmitted, 245
divorce, 5, 12, 24, 29n7, 54, 114, 140, 146n20, 159-60, 181, 195, 204, 211-12, 222n35, 225-27, 231n75, 234n82, 236n87, 238-41; in Roman law, 159, 193
doctrinal development, vii, ix, 11, 202, 254; and theology of marriage, 153, 156, 160n71, 187-90, 198-99, 202-3, 205-6, 210-12
dogmatic theology, method of, vii-viii, x-xi
Dolan, Timothy, 65
Doms, Herbert, 166-67, 178n165
Dozeman, Thomas, 34-35
Durandus of Saint-Pourçain, 210

Eberstadt, Mary, 12n35, 244n126, 247
Ebner, Ferdinand, 69, 71
Eden, garden of, 99, 106n80, 192, 217n10
Edin, Kathryn, 239-40
Elkanah, 141
Elliott, Peter, 11, 159n67, 188-89, 203, 208-11
environmental movement, xi
Ephesians, Epistle to the, x, 2, 5n21, 18, 43, 73, 82n105, 87, 92, 112-13, 115, 125-27, 134, 159-60, 162, 164-65, 186n5, 190-95, 197, 199, 208-9, 211-13, 220
Ephrem the Syrian, 8, 15-16, 92, 99-102, 109
eros, 55n95, 73, 87, 95-96, 105n73, 108, 116, 145-46
Esolen, Anthony, 139, 216n8, 220n29
Eucharist, 10n32, 18, 43, 73, 117n26, 121, 187n10, 191, 198, 207
eugenics, 148
Evdokimov, Paul, 1n1, 18-19, 65, 85-86
Eve, 6n25, 8, 13n37, 16, 25n83, 28n3, 42-43, 63-64, 82, 89-90, 94-95, 98, 157n61, 160n74, 190, 204n73; equality of with Adam, 100-104, 107-9; as gift, 99, 105; as image of trinitarian persons, 73-77, 85; sin of, 91-93, 96, 101, 106-7. *See also* Adam
exegesis, biblical, viii, 39n30; allegorical, 31, 58; of Genesis, 91n2; historical-critical, x, 160n71, 199
exile, Babylonian, 48, 53
Exum, Cheryl, 48-49, 52, 56-57, 249-50
Ezekiel, 29, 34-36, 41, 46-49, 53, 56-58
Ezra, books of, 89

fall, the, x-xi, 1, 8-9, 73, 78, 81n98, 89-90, 92-94, 103, 106-9, 138, 157n61, 160n74, 192, 214, 248n2. *See also* original sin
Familiaris Consortio, 117-18, 136
fatherlessness, 51, 220, 222, 241

Fehribach, Adeline, 44
feminism, 28, 44n55, 50, 55n94, 223–24
Fineman, Martha, 224n44, 225n44, 229n66, 238n98, 134
Fitzmyer, Joseph, 40
Florence, Council of, 210
fornication, 56n97, 154n49, 161–62
Freud, Anna, 148n31
Freud, Sigmund, 216n7
fruit, forbidden, 16, 91, 96, 101–2, 104, 107, 109
Furstenberg, Frank, 239

Gandulf of Bologna, 209
Gaudium et Spes, 9n32, 27n2, 81n99, 111–13, 142–44, 176, 215n5, 253
gender roles, 39, 50n74, 138, 221n30, 235, 241
Genesis, 6n25, 8, 11n34, 14–15, 43, 62–63, 73, 76, 78–80, 82, 91–105, 108–10, 126, 140, 145n15, 154, 156, 160, 190, 195–96, 203–4
genocide: as commanded by God, 51, 56
George, Robert P., 24n79, 160n73, 182
Gheaus, Anca, 226
Girgis, Sherif, 24n79, 160n73, 182
Gnostics, 5
God. *See* YHWH
Granados, José, 182
Greek Fathers, 209
Gregorian Reform, 191–92
Gregorian Sacramentary, 190
Griffiths, Paul, 249–50
Grubb, Geoffrey, 168
Guroian, Vigen, 25

Hahn, Scott, 31–33, 93n4, 139, 186n7, 214n1, 226n54
Hannah, 141
Häring, Bernard, 9n32, 253
Hauerwas, Stanley, 115
Healy, Nicholas, xiii, 68, 248
heaven, 6–7, 15, 19, 39, 47, 62n1, 72, 91, 143n11, 158n64, 187n10, 254
Hebrews, Epistle to the, 16, 30, 220

Hebrew Scriptures. *See* Old Testament
Hegel, Georg Friedrich, 64, 68–71, 77
Herring, Jonathan, 227–28
Hertz, Rosanna, 216, 229–32
Hewlett, Sylvia Ann, 221–22
hijab, 215n84
Hildebrand, Dietrich von, xiii, 10, 144, 163–64, 166–76, 178n165, 181, 183–84, 211
historical-critical research, 31, 58, 62, 160, 198–99. *See also* exegesis, biblical
Hooker, Morna, 41
Hosea, 28–30, 34–35, 45n65, 49–50, 54–56, 59, 61n112, 204
Howard University, 219
Hsu, Albert, 17
Huehnergard, John, 54
Hugh of Saint-Victor, 154n49, 191, 196, 207
Humanae Vitae, 83n123, 176
Hunter, David, 157–58

idolatry, 6, 29n8, 34–35, 46, 51, 58, 129
Ignatius of Antioch, 208
image of God (*imago Dei*), x–xi, xiii, 8, 13–15, 25n83, 29n7, 62–89, 92, 110, 116, 119, 138, 214, 252–53
incest, 147, 205
Innocent III, Pope, 194
intrinsically evil action, 54
in-vitro fertilization, 139n2, 230
Isaiah, 28, 30, 34–35, 45–47, 51, 55n94, 58, 60
Islam, 214–15, 217n10
Israel, 3, 4, 7, 13, 15, 28–42, 44–45, 50–61, 78–79, 86n120, 89–90, 93–94, 140, 159, 187, 194, 200–201, 203–4, 208, 248–51
I-Thou relation, 69–72, 77–78, 80, 169, 172

Jacob, 39n39, 141, 155
James, Spencer, 228
Jenson, Robert, 13, 141, 186–87, 251–52

Jeremiah, 29, 34–36, 39–40, 45, 50, 52–53, 57–58, 60–61
Jerome, 31, 47–49, 52, 57–60, 157n58
Jerusalem, 30n11, 38–39, 48–50, 53
John, Epistles of, 58, 202
John, Gospel of, 2, 6, 17, 38–39, 42–43, 188, 199–202
John Chrysostom, 8, 10, 49, 85, 92, 102–6, 109, 144, 153, 160–63, 251
John of the Cross, 4
John Paul II, 8, 9, 18n59, 65, 84–86, 116–18, 120, 129–37, 160n73, 174, 176
John the Baptist, 38–39
John XXII, Pope, 210
Jones, Beth Felker, 184
Jones, Jamila, 217n10
Jones, Stephanie, 244n127
Joshua, book of, 51, 53
Judah, region of, 39–40, 53
Judges, book of, 51
Julian of Eclanum, 157n59

Kant, Immanuel, 129, 246n137
Keefe, Alice, 50n72, 54–56, 58
Keenan, James, 22–23
Keener, Craig, 42n47, 188, 199–202
Kefala, Maria, 239–40
Keller, Kathy, 114–15, 221n30
Keller, Timothy, 113–16, 221n30
King, Heather, 2
kingdom of God, 4–7, 15, 18–22, 26–27, 113, 126, 138, 133n15, 187, 197–99, 201–4, 208, 211–13, 215, 247n140, 254
Kings, books of, 15, 56n97
Kittay, Eva, 53n86, 245n134
Knieps-Port le Roi, Thomas, 249
Krempel, Bernadin, 166
Kuby, Gabriele, 22n74, 254
Küng, Hans, 28

Lamb, marriage of the, 3, 16, 25–26, 39–40, 44–45, 88, 108, 254–55
Lamentations, 51n77, 53n88
Lang, Uwe Michael, 2
Lasnoski, Kent, 117n27, 143

La Soujeole, Benoît-Dominique de, 212
Last Supper, 40–41, 198
Lawler, Michael, 10n32, 24, 155n52, 171, 243n119
lesbians, 23n78, 230–31
Levenson, Jon D., 1, 4–5, 7n28, 28–29, 31–32, 36–38
liberal Catholic theology, xi
liberal historicism, 19n62
liberalism, 138–39, 147n23, 214n1, 216
Linsenmann, Franz Xaver von, 166
Lombard, Peter, 144, 153–55
Lossky, Vladimir, 14
Luke, Gospel of, 40–42, 199, 202n66, 212
Lumen Gentium, 118, 143n11
Luther, Martin, 112n6, 186n5, 193

Machiavelli, Niccolò, 254
Malachi, book of, 204
male headship, 101, 126–27, 162, 204, 220–21, 230, 237n95
Manichees, 5, 157n61
Mark, Gospel of, 5, 40–42, 212, 221n30
marriage, sacrament of, x, 4, 10–12, 19–22, 24–25, 45, 111, 117–18, 120n36, 126, 133n87, 175, 214, 217n10; grace of, 165, 186n5, 196–97, 209–14, 247, 254; historical development of, 140, 153–57, 159, 164–65, 185–98, 205–12
marriage of Christ and Church, 1–4, 7, 9, 13, 18–19, 25n83, 42, 59, 87, 109, 111, 113, 126–27, 129, 144–45, 159, 162, 164, 187n10, 198, 208, 214, 249–50, 253
marriage of God: and Church, 18–20; and creation 1–8, 13, 20, 22, 92, 110, 138, 247, 252; and humankind, x, 5–6, 16, 27, 31–32, 41–44, 59, 63, 73, 82, 86–87, 89, 93, 97, 101, 109–11, 137, 192, 197n44, 204, 212, 214, 248, 250, 252; and Israel, 13, 28–32, 34–44,

46, 48–49, 52–53, 58–61, 79, 140n6, 204, 208, 248
Martin, Dale, 5n21
Martin, Francis, 63
Martin, James, 23
martyria, 22
Marx, Karl, 216n7
Mary, 171–72, 215n5, 249; assumption of, 187n11; as image of the Trinity, 72, 75, 86; marriage of to Joseph, 25n82, 154n49, 176n157, 196, 206; as personification of the Church, 20–21, 55n96, 62n1, 72, 87
Mary Magdalene, 39n39
Mary of Bethany, 39n39
masturbation, 24
materialism, biological, 168
Matthew, Gospel of, 3, 5–6, 15, 19, 40–42, 107, 159–60, 194–95, 202n66, 211, 213, 217, 220, 253
McCarthy, David Matzko, 183–84, 216n8, 228–29
McCarthy, Dennis, 33
McRobbie, Angela, 223n36
McWhirter, Jocelyn, 39
Meier, John, 211–12
Meszaros, Andrew, 199n50, 203
Meyendorff, John, 187
Michel, Ernst, 166
Middleton, Richard, 14
midrash, 37n34, 200
Mill, John Stuart, 216n7
misogyny, 50n72, 52, 55–56
Mosaic Law, 211–12
Moses, 32–34, 37–38, 40, 57, 155, 159, 201n59
Moynihan, Daniel Patrick, 222
Muchermann, Hermann, 166
Mulieris Dignitatem, 86

Nahum, 46–47, 54
Neoplatonism, 146n18
Neusner, Jacob, 36–37
New Jerusalem, 16–17, 39, 44
Newman, John Henry, 199n50, 211
Nicholas of Clairvaux, 191

Nicomachean Ethics (Aristotle), 151–52
Novak, David, 63, 140n6, 229n64
nuptial mass, 193, 205–6
Nussbaum, Martha, 217n10

O'Connor, David, 176n157
O'Connor, Kathleen, 53
Okin, Susan Moller, 246
Old Testament, 2n7, 33, 202n66; marital motifs in, 1, 3, 7, 31, 36, 38, 45, 49, 51n77, 57–59, 140, 144n15, 204, 208, 212, 250; messianic prophecies of, 39, 41. *See also* individual Old Testament books
Olivi, Peter John, 190, 193
O'Meara, Dominic, 146n18
one-flesh unity, 5, 12–13, 25n82, 92–95, 98, 100–101, 109, 113, 126, 160–61, 167, 173, 195–96, 204, 206, 210–11
ordination, sacrament of, 209
Origen, 54, 62n1, 208, 250–51
original sin, x–xi, 1, 8–9, 89, 92, 99, 105, 109, 113, 157–59, 253. *See also* fall, the
Orthodox Church, ix, 11, 21, 57, 185, 187n10, 206
Ortlund, Ray, 252
Ouellet, Marc, 65, 75n66, 84–86
out-of-wedlock children, 222, 242n116, 245n129

Passover, 40, 198
patriarchy, 55n94, 214n2, 223n36, 229n66, 254
Paul, Apostle, 5–6, 18, 82n105, 89–92, 94, 119–21, 125–29, 144n15, 154, 156, 160–62, 194–95, 197, 199, 201n59, 204, 208, 212, 221
Pauline Privilege, 165
Peter, Apostle, 201
Peter, Epistles of, 16
Pharisees, sect, 12n34, 159
Pinckaers, Servais, 250n11, 253n25
Piper, John, 9, 186

Pitre, Brant, 7, 31–44, 59n108, 127n68, 198
Pius XI, Pope, 144, 163–65, 211
Pius XII, Pope, 166
Plato, 10, 144–51, 153, 155, 171, 176n157, 184, 214n2
Podella, Thomas, 54
Politics (Aristotle), 149–51
Pollentius, 194–95
polygamy, 139, 182, 204, 217n10
Pontifical Council for Justice and Peace, the, 233–34
Popenoe, David, 12, 216, 235–42, 246
pornography, 52, 134, 223n36
poverty, 118n31, 222, 226, 235n87, 239–40, 243–44
priesthood, xi, 14, 16–17, 22, 33, 191
Probst, Ferdinand, 166
Proclus, 146n18
procreation, 10, 12, 24n79, 55, 61n112, 81, 96, 106, 138–47, 149, 151, 153–63, 165–69, 171–84, 230n68, 234, 244–45, 253
prostitute: Israel as, 29–30, 35, 45–46, 48, 57, 59n107
Proverbs, book of, 28n37, 250n10
Przywara, Erich, 3–4
Psalms, xiii, 26, 37, 39n39, 42n46, 220, 255
Puritans, 174n148, 187

Qur'ān, 30n12

Rachel, 39n39, 141, 155
racism, 219n22
Rahner, Karl, 217n10
Ratzinger, Joseph. *See* Benedict XVI, Pope
Reformers, Protestant, 11, 190, 207
remarriage, 24, 160n71, 193, 211
remedium concupiscentiae (remedy for concupiscence), 143n11, 154n49, 156n57, 163, 167n109
Reno, R. R., 92–93, 95–99, 108
Republic (Plato), 10, 145–49
resurrection, 19–20; first, 16; general, 15, 128, 137, 162; of Jesus, 39n39, 44, 91, 112, 185, 202

Revelation, book of, 2–3, 16, 25n83, 39–40, 44–45, 88, 92, 108, 253–55
Reynolds, Philip, 140n6, 154n49, 156–57, 161n83, 188–98, 207, 210–12
Richard of St. Victor, 64, 66–67, 75, 77
Rist, John, 158
Roger of Caen, 206
Romans, Epistle to the, 82, 90–91, 97, 108, 117n27, 119, 121, 127, 247
Rose, Jacqueline, 234n82
Rosenzweig, Franz, 69, 71n47
Rossi, Alice, 237
Rota, Roman, 166
Rubio, Julie Hanlon, 7, 138, 177n162, 231n73, 240n108
Russell, Bertrand, 115n16, 216n7

sabbath, 15, 46
Sacks, Jonathan, 1, 215–16
sacramentum magnum (great sacrament), x, 126, 145, 190, 192, 195, 197, 209, 252
Salzman, Todd, 22–24, 171, 243n119
Samaritan woman, 39n39
same-sex marriage, 23–25, 139, 142n9, 144n15, 186n8, 223, 226n54, 242n115, 252n20
Samuel, books of, 53, 141
Sarna, Nahum, 32
Satan, 94, 97, 103, 107, 123
Saul, 53
Scheeben, Matthias Joseph, vii–viii, x, 8, 64, 72–77, 83–85, 211, 252
Schemenauer, Kevin, 168
Schillebeeckx, Edward, 11, 154n49, 159n67, 188–89, 203–10
Schindler, David L., 21, 164n99
Schmemann, Alexander, 20–22
scholasticism, 3, 154; and marriage 185, 206–7
Schumacher, Michele, 64
Schwendinger, Fidelis, 166
science, 221n30; social, 236
Second Vatican Council, xiii, 27n2, 111, 142n9, 211, 253

Sermon on the Mount, 6n24, 198, 250n11
serpent, the, 91, 94, 96–98, 100–103, 107. *See also* Satan
sexual intercourse, 5n21, 223n36, 229–30, 241, 245–46, 249n9; in biblical teaching, 6n25, 34–35, 50n72, 55n94, 129–30; and the fall, 103, 106, 109; homosexual, 22–25, 142n9, 144n15; obsolescence of in eschaton, 19; in Plato, 10, 147–49, 153; and procreation, 139–40, 154, 156–58, 160, 169–71, 174, 176–79, 182–84, 244; as theological analogy, 13n37, 77, 167–68, 250–51; as union, 93–95, 140, 155, 160–62, 195–96, 210
Shanley, Mary Lyndon, 216, 226
Sheridan, Mark, 49
Sinai, 28n3, 32–34, 40, 42, 140n6
singleness, 2, 6n23, 8, 11, 17–19, 21, 64, 69, 82, 85, 98, 117n27, 122, 138, 214, 247, 254
single parents, 11, 223n36, 229–32, 234–36, 241–44
situation ethics, 130
Smith, Janet, 180
Smith, Mark, 57–58
social justice, 11–12, 114n13, 139n3, 214–17, 219, 221, 223, 225, 227, 229, 231, 233–35, 237, 239, 241–43, 245–47, 253
Socrates, 10, 145–50
solidarity, 8–9, 59, 61, 93, 119, 245n131
Soloveitchik, Joseph B., 27–29, 249n7
Song of Songs, 1, 3–4, 36–39, 62, 78, 83n108, 144n15, 248–52
Sotomayor, Sonia, 245
sperm donation, 11, 148n31, 229–32, 245n132
Speyr, Adrienne von, 64
Staniloae, Dumitru, 17
step-parents, 236, 239, 241
Strauss, Leo, 145, 148n31
Supreme Court of the United States, the, 242n115, 245

surrogacy, 11, 139n2, 214n2
Synoptic Gospels, 40–41. *See also* individual synoptic gospels

Tabernacle, the, 15–16
Tametsi, 210n102
Tarwater, John K., 11–12
teen pregnancy, 241–42
Temple of Solomon, 16
Temple, 48, 89, 94
Tertullian, 208
Thatcher, Adrian, 139n2, 243n119
Theodore of Asine, 146n18
Thessalonians, Epistles to the, 5
Thomas, Gary, 118
Thomas Aquinas, 11n34, 19n61, 23n77, 25, 32n18, 53–54, 63n5, 66n17, 68, 70, 84, 88n129, 112n6, 116–17, 119n32, 152–53, 156n57, 158–59, 164n94, 167, 169n121, 179–80, 190, 196, 208–10
Timothy, Epistles to, 91, 97, 108n88
Tobit, book of, 42n46
Trent, Council of, 189–90, 210

United States Conference of Catholic Bishops, the, 87–88, 113, 228n63

Vatican II. *See* Second Vatican Council
Verbum Domini, 59
violence, domestic, 12, 29n7; God as perpetrator of, 31, 58–60
violence, sexual, 45, 54; God as perpetrator of, 47–50, 52, 57n98

Walker, Adrian J., 139n4
Walter of Mortagne, 154n49
Walton, John, 15,
Waters, Brent, 5–6, 114n13, 117–18, 136–39, 158n61, 183n181, 186, 205n81, 215, 217n9, 221n29, 246–48
Wenham, Gordon, 93
West, Cornel, 221–22
Wheeler-Reed, David, 5
White, Thomas Joseph, 30

Whitehead, Barbara Dafoe, 234n82
William of Auxerre, 207
Willoughby, Brian, 228
Wills, Gary, 119, 207n90
Wojtyła, Karol. *See* John Paul II

Wright, N. T., 14–15, 89–90

YHWH, 35, 79; as abusive male, 28, 30, 45, 47, 49–52, 60–61

www.ingramcontent.com/pod-product-compliance
Lightning Source LLC
Chambersburg PA
CBHW021650230426
43668CB00008B/581